5 | 1 | 70

THE TOMB OF THE VENERABLE BEDE
(from the engraving in Billings's *Durham Cathedral*)

B E D E

HIS LIFE, TIMES, AND WRITINGS

ESSAYS IN COMMEMORATION
OF THE TWELFTH CENTENARY
OF HIS DEATH

EDITED BY

A. HAMILTON THOMPSON

WITH AN INTRODUCTION BY
THE RIGHT REV.
THE LORD BISHOP OF DURHAM

OXFORD
AT THE CLARENDON PRESS

Oxford University Press, Ely House, London W. 1

GLASGOW NEW YORK TORONTO MELBOURNE WELLINGTON
CAPE TOWN SALISBURY IBADAN NAIROBI LUSAKA ADDIS ABABA
BOMBAY CALCUTTA MADRAS KARACHI LAHORE DACCA
KUALA LUMPUR SINGAPORE HONG KONG TOKYO

FIRST PUBLISHED 1935

REPRINTED LITHOGRAPHICALLY IN GREAT BRITAIN
AT THE UNIVERSITY PRESS, OXFORD
BY VIVIAN RIDLER
PRINTER TO THE UNIVERSITY
1969

PREFACE

THE inception of this book of Essays is due to the Bishop of Durham, whose zeal for the history and antiquities of his diocese would not suffer the twelve-hundredth anniversary of the death of Bede to pass by without some tribute by living scholars to the memory of the great saint and scholar who spent his whole life within the boundaries of that district and whose body was eventually laid to rest in the cathedral church of Durham. It was hoped at first that the volume might have appeared simultaneously with the commemoration festivals which were held in May of this year at Durham and Jarrow; but it was found necessary to postpone publication till later, and the book now sees the light at the close of a year memorable to all who took part in those concourses for the enthusiasm which the name of Bede still has power to awaken in his fellow countrymen.

The plan of the work owes much to Dr. Claude Jenkins, who made preliminary suggestions with regard to subjects and writers and has himself contributed a chapter distinguished by rare insight into the spirit of Bede's writings. The first four essays deal with the life of Bede and its historical setting, the remainder with his work and thought. No attempt has been made to reflect every aspect of the wide field which he covered. Historians of social order have already dug deeply in the rich mine of the *Historia Ecclesiastica*, and to their researches little remains to be added from this source. It was originally intended to include a separate chapter upon Bede as a man of science. This, however, was found impracticable. His most important work in this direction, his contribution to chronology, is treated by Dr. Levison in connexion with his work as an historian, while another side of it is discussed by Dr. Jenkins in a different context, and its sources form part of Professor Laistner's account of the library to which Bede had access.

The thanks of the editor are due to the Bishop of Durham for supplying the introduction, and to all the contributors for their ready response to his invitation and for their kindness and patience. The index is the work of Miss Beatrice Hamilton Thompson, M.A., B.Litt., librarian of St. Hugh's College, Oxford.

ADEL, LEEDS　　　　　　　　　　　　　　　　　　A. H. T.
October 1935.

CONTENTS

SELECT BIBLIOGRAPHY

IN this list of books those only are given which are referred to in footnotes by the names of their authors or editors or by abbreviated titles. In each case the full title of the work is preceded by the name or abbreviation used in the text. Where no place of publication is mentioned London is understood.

ADAMNAN. *Vita S. Columbae* [*P.L.* lxxxviii]. See FOWLER, REEVES.

Arch. *Archaeologia: or, Miscellaneous Tracts relating to Antiquity*, vol. i–. 1773, &c. [Soc. Antiq. London.]

Arch. Ael. *Archaeologia Aeliana: or, Miscellaneous Tracts relating to Antiquity*, vol. i–. [Soc. Antiq. Newcastle-upon-Tyne.]

BALDWIN BROWN, G. *The Arts in Early England*, vols. i–vi, pt. 1. 1903–30 (vol. ii, new ed. recast and enlarged, 1925).

BARING GOULD, S. *The Lives of the Saints.* 13 vols. in 15 parts, 1873–98.

BEDE. *Works.* See GILES, PLUMMER, SMITH, STEVENSON. For list *see* index.

BELLESHEIM, A. *Geschichte der Katholischen Kirche in Irland, von der Einführung des Christenthums bis auf die Gegenwart.* 3 vols. Mainz, 1890–1.

Bev. Chapter Act-Book. *Memorials of Beverley Minster: the Chapter Act-Book of the Collegiate Church of St. John of Beverley, A.D. 1286–1347,* with illustrative documents and introd. by A. F. Leach. 2 vols. Durham, 1897–1903. [Surtees Soc., vols. xcviii, cviii.]

BOUTFLOWER, D. S. *Life of Ceolfrid, Abbot of Wearmouth and Jarrow.* Sunderland, 1912.

BRIGHT, W. *Chapters of Early English Church History*, 3rd ed. Oxford, 1897.

BROWNE, G. F. *The Ancient Cross Shafts at Bewcastle and Ruthwell.* Cambridge, 1916.

—— *The Venerable Bede, his Life and Writings*, 1919.

—— *St. Aldhelm*, 1903.

BURY, J. B. *The Life of St. Patrick and his Place in History*, 1905.

Cath. Encycl. *The Catholic Encyclopaedia.* 15 vols., ind. and supp. New York [1913].

COLGRAVE. *The Life of Bishop Wilfrid by Eddius Stephanus*: text, translation and notes by B. Colgrave. Cambridge, 1927.

COLLINGWOOD, W. G. *Northumbrian Crosses of the pre-Norman Age*, 1927.

Corpus script. eccl. Lat. *Corpus scriptorum ecclesiasticorum Latinorum,* ed. consitio Academiae Litterarum Caesareae Vindobonensis, vol. i–. Vienna, 1866, &c.

CRAWFORD, S. J. *Anglo-Saxon Influence on Western Christendom, A.D. 600–800.* Oxford, 1933.

x   SELECT BIBLIOGRAPHY

D.C.B. Dictionary of Christian Biography. 4 vols., 1877–87.

D.N.B. Dictionary of National Biography, 1885, &c.

Dict. Eng. Ch. Hist. Ollard, S. L., and Crosse, G., *Dictionary of English Church History,* new ed. 1919.

EBERT, A. *Allgemeine Geschichte d. Literatur des Mittelalters im Abendlande.* 3 vols. Leipzig, 1874–87.

EDDIUS STEPHANUS. *Vita Wilfridi episcopi.* See COLGRAVE.

Eng. Hist. Rev. The English Historical Review, vol. i–. 1886, &c.

FOWLER. *Vita S. Columbae auctore Adamnano,* ed. J. T. Fowler, 2nd ed. Oxford, 1920.

FULLER, THOMAS. *Church History of Britain,* 1655.

GILES. *Opera Ven. Baedae quae supersunt,* ed. J. A. Giles. 12 vols. 1843–4.

H.A. Historia abbatum auctore Baeda.

H.A.An. Historia abbatum auctore anonymo.

H.E. Baedae Historia Ecclesiastica gentis Anglorum.

HADDAN, A. W., and STUBBS, W. (H. & S.). *Councils and Ecclesiastical Documents relating to Great Britain and Ireland.* 3 vols. (4 pts.). Oxford, 1869–78.

HAUCK, A. *Kirchengeschichte Deutschlands.* Pts. i–v. Leipzig, 1887–1911.

Hist. Ch. Ireland. History of the Church of Ireland from the Earliest Times to the Present Day, ed. W. A. Phillips. 3 vols. Oxford, 1933.

Hist. Ch. York. The Historians of the Church of York and its Archbishops, ed. J. Raine (Rolls Ser., no. 71). 3 vols., 1879–94.

HOWORTH, Sir H. H. *The Golden Days of the Early English Church from the Arrival of Theodore to the Death of Bede.* 3 vols., 1917.

HUGHES, H. D. *History of Durham Cathedral Library.* Durham, 1925.

HUNT, W. *The English Church from its Foundation to the Norman Conquest (597–1066)* [*A History of the English Church,* ed. Hunt and W. R. W. Stephens, vol. i], 1899 (repr. 1901).

HUTCHINSON, W. *History and Antiquities of Durham.* 3 vols. Newcastle and Carlisle, 1785–94.

JULIAN, J. *A Dictionary of Hymnology.* Rev. ed. with supp., 1915.

KER, W. P. *The Dark Ages.* Edinburgh, 1923.

Leg. Aur. Jacobus de Voragine, *Legenda Aurea.* Cologne, 1483.

M.G.H. Monumenta Germaniae historica, ed. Pertz, G. H., &c. 1826, &c.

MANITIUS, M. *Zu Aldhelm und Beda.* Vienna, 1886.

MAUNDE THOMPSON, SIR E. *An Introduction to Greek and Latin Palaeography.* Oxford, 1912.

Mem. Ripon. Memorials of the Church of SS. Peter and Wilfrid, Ripon [ed. J. T. Fowler]. 4 vols. Durham, 1882–1908. [Surtees Soc., vols. lxxiv, lxxviii, lxxxi, cxv.]

Mem. Southwell. *Visitations and Memorials of Southwell Minster*, ed. A. F. Leach. Camden Soc., N.S., vol. xlviii. 1891.

Mon. Alc. *Monumenta Alcuiniana*, ap. Bibliotheca rerum Germanicarum, tom. vi, ed. Wattenbach and Dümmler. Berlin, 1873.

Mon. Ang. *Monasticon Anglicanum: a history of the Abbies and other Monasteries . . . of England and Wales . . . originally published in Latin by Sir William Dugdale.* . . . [ed. H. Caley, H. Ellis, and B. Bandinel]. 6 vols. in 8 pts. 1846.

Mon. Mog. *Monumenta Moguntina*, ap. Bibliotheca rerum Germanicarum, tom. iii. Berlin.

Nov. Leg. Ang. *Nova Legenda Angliae* 1516, re-ed. C. Horstman. 2 vols. Oxford, 1901.

P.L. *Patrologiae cursus completus. Patrologia Latina*, ed. J. P. Migne. Paris, 1844–65.

PLUMMER. *Venerabilis Baedae opera historica*, ed. C. Plummer. 2 vols. Oxford, 1896.

POOLE, R. L. *Studies in Chronology and History* . . . collected and edited by Austin Lane Poole. Oxford, 1934.

Priory Hex. *The Priory of Hexham, its Chroniclers, Endowments, and Annals* [ed. J. Raine]. 2 vols. Durham, 1864–5. [Surtees Soc., vols. xliv, xlvi.]

REEVES, W. *Vita S. Columbae auctore Adamnano*, ed. W. Reeves. Dublin, 1857.

—— *On the Céli-dé, commonly called Culdees* (Trans. Irish Acad. xxiv, pt. 3, 1874).

Reg. Dun. *Reginaldi monachi Dunelmensis libellus de admirandis B. Cuthberti virtutibus*, ed. J. Raine. Durham, 1835. [Surtees Soc., vol. i.]

Rep. Min. Women. *The Ministry of Women: a report by a Committee appointed by . . . the . . . Archbishop of Canterbury.* 1919.

Rich. Hex. *Brevis annotatio bonae memoriae Ricardi prioris Hagustaldensis ecclesiae de antiquo et moderno statu eiusdem ecclesiae et de pontificibus eiusdem ecclesiae.*

Rites Durh. *Rites of Durham, being a Description or Brief Declaration of all the Ancient Monuments, rites, and customs belonging or being within the Monastical Church of Durham before the suppression.* Written 1593 [ed. J. T. Fowler]. Durham, 1903. [Surtees Soc., vol. cvii.]

ROGER, M. *L'Enseignement des lettres classiques d'Ausone à Alcuin.* Paris, 1905.

SANDYS, SIR J. E. *A History of Classical Scholarship.* 3 vols. Cambridge, 1903–8 (vol. i, 3rd ed. 1921).

Script. Tres. *Historiae Dunelmensis scriptores tres, Gaufridus de Coldingham, Robertus de Graystanes, et Willielmus de Chambre* [ed. J. Raine]. Durham, 1839. [Surtees Soc., vol. ix.]

SKENE, W. F. *Celtic Scotland.* 3 vols. Edinburgh, 1876–80.

SMITH. *Historia ecclesiastica gentis Anglorum auctore* ... *Baeda* ... *cura et studio Johannis Smith.* Cambridge, 1722.

STEVENSON, J. *Ven. Baedae opera historica minora.* 2 vols. 1841.

SURTEES, R. *History and Antiquities of the County Palatine of Durham.* 4 vols. 1816–40.

Sym. Dun. (S.D.). *Symeonis monachi opera omnia,* ed. T. Arnold. 2 vols. 1882–5 [Rolls Ser., no. 75. vol. i. *Historia ecclesiae Dunelmensis,* &c.; vol. ii. *Historia regum,* &c.].

—— *Symeonis Dunelmensis opera et collectanea* [ed. J. Hodgson Hinde]. Vol. i. Durham, 1868. [Surtees Soc., vol. li.]

Trans. Irish Acad. *The Transactions of the Royal Irish Academy,* vol. i–. Dublin, 1787, &c. *See* REEVES.

TRITHEMIUS, JOHANNES. *De scriptoribus ecclesiasticis.* Basel, 1493.

Vit. Cuth. *Vita Cuthberti auctore Baeda.*

WADDELL, HELEN. *The Wandering Scholars,* 1927.

Will. Malmes. *William of Malmesbury, Gesta regum Anglorum,* ed. T. D. Hardy. London, 1840.

INTRODUCTION

THE 1200th anniversary of the death of the Venerable Bede could not but arouse the keenest interest, not only in the minds of Northern Churchmen, who claimed a direct connexion with the illustrious local saint, but also in all serious students of our ecclesiastical history, and indeed in all who had any understanding of the value of his work. This volume was designed as part of the arrangements for a worthy commemoration of Bede's death in 735, for it seemed to me that the occasion warranted something more considerable and more lasting than services in the churches and historical pageants in the parishes. I desired to connect it with an authoritative estimate of Bede and his work by scholars of indisputable distinction, and so to provide something which would be permanently serviceable to students of the period, and constitute a contribution of real value to our historical literature.

I am under a heavy personal obligation to Professor Hamilton Thompson not only for consenting to act as editor, but also for contributing an essay on 'Northumbrian Monasticism' of great interest and value. Of the other eight essays it may fairly be said that the quality is sufficiently guaranteed by the names of the authors, every one of whom has the character of a specialist on the subject which he handles. The volume as a whole provides in a relatively small compass a treatment of Bede's life and work which is both scholarly and complete.

The more closely Bede's career is studied, the more amazing it appears. In him two streams of spiritual influence seemed to meet and blend—the evangelistic passion of the Celtic missionaries, and the disciplined devotion of the Benedictine monks. He was near enough to the original conversion to have personal links with those who had companied with the missionaries from Iona, and to feel the thrill of their triumphant enthusiasm: and yet he was remote enough to have grown up in another atmosphere, and to have been shaped by the system which disallowed and replaced theirs. He was too near not to know their merits; too generous not to recognize them; too religious not to revere their sanctity; too wise not to perceive their defects. So he stood at the point of new departure—a Benedictine monk in the yet living tradition of Celtic piety, an English student in the rich treasury of Celtic learning, a disciple of Rome inspired by the intellectual passion of Ireland.

It has been the high distinction of Durham to be closely associated with the history of the English Bible. Preaching in Jarrow in 1881, Bishop Lightfoot dwelt on the connexion. between Bede's work as a translator of the Scriptures and the Revised Version of the New Testament, which had just issued from the press. He narrated the moving story of Bede's death (surely one of the choicest gems of Christian biography) and dwelt on its 'true significance' as the 'opening scene' of 'the long, glorious, and eventful history of the English Bible'. We remember that in the sixteenth century it was a dean of Durham, Whittingham, who translated the New Testament in the Genevan Version, and that, in the nineteenth century, among the band of scholars who directly or indirectly were associated with the Revision of the New Testament none were more distinguished or more influential than Bishops Lightfoot and Westcott, who successively governed the Palatine see.

Is it wholly extravagant to perceive in the temperament and achievements of the great Northumbrian Saint a foretaste and a prophecy of what would in the course of time be recognized as the distinctive features of English Christianity—its devotion to Biblical studies, its reverence for sound learning, its firm hold on history, its strong and tenacious patriotism?

It is difficult to realize the full significance of Bede in his own generation, and in the history of Christianity. His death in 735 was parted by no more than a century from the coming of St. Aidan, by less than 150 years from the landing of St. Augustine in Thanet. He belonged to a race which lay outside the confines of ancient civilization, and must have appeared in the eyes of the cultured citizens of Rome and Constantinople as no more considerable than in our eyes are the natives of Uganda. Yet Bede was, and was known in his own lifetime to be, the most eminent scholar of the West. From that semi-barbarous milieu there arises this portent of sanctity and learning. Northern England, at the beginning of the eighth century, holds the intellectual primacy of western Christendom. From Jarrow to York, from York to Aachen, from Aachen throughout the wide reach of Charlemagne's dominion, the light is carried.

In a notable article in the *Hibbert Journal* (April 1935) the influence of Bede is admirably described:

Even during his lifetime his reputation had spread far beyond the frontiers of Britain, and St. Boniface likened his death to the extinction of a brightly burning light. But in the centuries to come he was to exercise an influence far greater than that of any other figure of his time. He has been described as the Father of English History. He was much more than that; he was, in the phrase of a German historian, the Father of all the Middle Ages. In the age of Charlemagne his works were to be found in every cathedral and monastic library in Western Europe. Historians and theologians relied on him implicitly, incorporating large sections of his writings in their own works. His astronomical calculations, his tables for the correct reckoning of Easter, his *Martyrology* and his educational treatises remained for generations the standard and basic works on their subjects. . . . Finally, as a commentator—and his commentaries on Holy Scripture form by far the largest and, as he himself would assuredly have believed, the most important section of his work—as a commentator he came to possess an authority inferior only to that of the four Fathers of the Western Church.[1]

Many circumstances of our time are raising a doubt as to the holding power of Christianity within the communities of modern Christendom. One after another they seem to be casting aside the Christian tradition with a facility which is equally perplexing and minatory. France at the end of the eighteenth century, Russia at the beginning of the twentieth, Germany before our eyes to-day, seem to surrender their spiritual heritage almost without conflict, and without regret. What is the explanation of this strange impotence of Christianity? May we not find the answer to this question in the conditions under which Christendom was originally fashioned? In the pages of Bede's *Ecclesiastical History* we may read the story, learn the method, and take the measure of the primitive conversions. Amid the unquestionable *magnalia Dei*, which must for ever move the wondering praise of the Church, and along with notable examples of individual sanctity, the 'marks of Jesus' on human lives, there is so much that is hollow, and hasty, and unrooted in conscience and reason that the result could never have been more than the thinnest veneer of Christian speech and habit on the unaltered mass of indigenous paganism.

Great in his works, Bede is greater in himself. The example

[1] Vide *H.J.*, 1935, p. 404: 'Bede and Alcuin', by A. L. Maycock, M.A.

of the man is more precious than the achievement of the scholar. Such self-dedication to duty, clearly perceived, loyally pursued, is precious in every age, but never so precious as in an age like ours, beyond all precedent restless, discontented, rootless. As we set in contrast that career of quiet toil and ordered worship in Jarrow which ended in peace and praise twelve centuries ago, and our own fevered and futile course, we cannot avoid the yearning envy which sighs in Matthew Arnold's address to the 'Scholar-Gipsy':

> For early didst thou leave the world, with powers
> Fresh, undiverted to the world without,
>   Firm to their mark, not spent on other things;
> Free from the sick fatigue, the languid doubt
> Which much to have tried, in much been baffled, brings.
>   O life unlike to ours!
> Who fluctuate idly without term or scope,
> Of whom each strives, nor knows for what he strives,
>   And each half lives a hundred different lives;
> Who wait like thee, but not, like thee, in hope.

The age of Bede was but a brief interval between epochs of violence. Close at hand was the terrific disaster of the Danish invasions, which would lay in ruins the homes of Northumbrian piety, and obliterate the fair growths of Northumbrian culture. But the end is not yet. In the Hour-glass of the Eternal the sands run out, and there are again 'times of refreshing from the presence of the Lord'. 'History', runs Bishop Lightfoot's oft-quoted aphorism, 'is the best tonic for drooping spirits.' The fact that, after so many changeful centuries, the memory of the saintly scholar-monk of Jarrow should be recalled with sentiments of pride and praise in the very scenes of his patient labour, is itself profoundly significant. Every circumstance of human living has altered in the course of twelve centuries. The whole aspect and outlook of English society have been transformed; and yet the moral beauty of Bede's life holds us, and we cannot dispute its appeal. What is the key to the paradox? Is it not given in the words of St. John: 'The world passeth away and the lust thereof, but he that doeth the Will of God abideth for ever'?

AUCKLAND CASTLE   HERBERT DUNELM.
26 *May* 1935.

I

THE LIFE OF THE VENERABLE BEDE

IN the year 627, under the influence of King Edwin, Christianity was accepted in Northumbria as the national religion. There was a short-lived pagan reaction after Edwin's death; but the battle of Heavenfield, and the accession of Oswald, made the final victory of Christianity certain. The Angles of the north, as we know them first, were a rude people dwelling chiefly in the river valleys; seafarers, fishers, hunters, and shepherds, with perhaps a few traders. Their religion was full of war, axes, and slaughter; their future hope was a Valhalla of warriors; their superstitions many and gross. Fifty years before Bede was born the religion of Christ was unknown among them: when he died it had exercised its influence for a hundred years, and his lifetime is practically coextensive with the most flourishing period of Northumbrian art and culture.

The earliest Northumbrian churches were of the simplest description, some of wattle, others of timber, like that which Aidan built at Lindisfarne,[1] and Penda burnt down. Finan built another in the same place, 'of hewn oak covered with reeds'; and there were others in divers places.[2] No doubt some of these were of split logs with the smooth faces inwards, like the much later church at Greenstead, in Essex. There were stone churches also, and they increased in number and size. Ninian had built his *candida casa* at Whithorn early in the fifth century. A stone church at York quickly superseded the wooden structure in which Edwin had been baptized; Wilfrid, after he became bishop, repaired and glazed it. At Lincoln Blaecca built a stone church of excellent workmanship,[3] though in Bede's later days it was in ruins. To Wilfrid were due the stone basilica with its columned aisles at Ripon, the great church of St. Andrew at Hexham, and the later church of St. Mary in the same place.[4] For these great churches, as for Wearmouth, masons and other craftsmen were brought from Gaul. Hart, the mother church of Hartlepool, may date back to the seventh

---

[1] *H.E.* iii. 17. [2] *Ibid.*
[3] *Ibid.* iii. 16.
[4] Eddius, xvii, xxii, lvi; Rich. Hex., ap. *Priory Hex.* i. 3, 181, 183.

century,[1] and Escomb[2] and Corbridge probably were in existence in Bede's day.

Monastic establishments increased rapidly. Hilda's first religious house *ad septentrionalem plagam Uiuri fluminis* may have been at South Shields;[3] but she quickly removed to Hartlepool, passed on to become abbess of Whitby, and in the last years of her life founded another house at Hackness. Heiu, who had ruled at Hartlepool, was the foundress of Kaelcacaestir, of which St. John's chapel at Healaugh, near Tadcaster, may mark the site.[4] When Peada was baptized in 653 Utta was abbot of a monastery at Gateshead.[5] Aidan founded Lindisfarne, Chad Lastingham, Wilfrid Ripon, and there were houses at Coldingham, Melrose, Gilling, Watton, and other places.

Ecclesiastical art made great strides. Journeys were made to Rome and other places on the Continent for church fittings, vestments, and pictures. Stone-carvers produced the great ornamented crosses of Bewcastle and Ruthwell, and in this form of art the best seems to have come first.[6] At Hexham we may still see 'Wilfrid's chair', in which Acca or even Wilfrid may have sat,[7] and at Durham wood-carving of the period on the fragments of the ancient coffin of St. Cuthbert.[8] It was the age of the Lindisfarne Gospels, the finest specimens of Northumbrian penmanship remaining to us, and the Stonyhurst Gospel of St. John. The Codex Amiatinus, whether it was written by an Italian scribe at Jarrow[9] or brought from abroad,[10] a view difficult to reconcile with Bede's own statement,[11] must have had considerable artistic influence. Lastly, this was the age which saw Caedmon of Whitby writing the first sacred verse in the English tongue of which knowledge has come down to us.

From the fourth century at least sacred learning and some knowledge of the liberal arts were to be found in the British Church; but racial hostility, embittered by defeat, kept the Britons from intercourse with their conquerors. On the other

---

[1] Baldwin Brown, ii. 457.   [2] *Ibid.* ii. 453.
[3] H. E. Savage, ap. *Arch. Ael.*, ser. II, xix. 47–88.
[4] D. H. Haigh, ap. *Y.A.J.* iii. 349–91.   [5] *H.E.* iii. 21.
[6] Browne, *Ancient Cross Shafts*; Baldwin Brown, v. 289. Collingwood, 114–19, thinks them of later date.
[7] Baldwin Brown, ii. 178.   [8] *Ibid.* v. 404.
[9] F. J. A. Hort, ap. *Academy*, 26 Feb. 1887; H. J. White, ap. *Studia Biblica*, 1890, ii. 285–6.
[10] Howorth, iii. 321–7. Maunde Thompson, 194, 245, says that it is purely Italian in script and decoration.   [11] *H.A.* xv.

hand, British teachers, especially in the fifth and sixth centuries, did a great work among the Irish people. Before the seventh century began the position was reversed, and British scholars flocked to the Irish monasteries, which had become famous for their knowledge, not only of the Scriptures, but of the fathers and the classical authors. Then, through the Celtic missionaries, this influence began to spread to Northumbria. English students also betook themselves to Ireland, and in the time of Finan and Colman many persons, including some of the young nobles, of whom Aldfrid is an example,[1] went thither to study or to enter the religious life, and were willingly and generously received by the Irish monasteries.[2] When Theodore and Hadrian came to England they brought with them the culture of the south, and the school of Canterbury attracted many students. The knowledge of Greek in Ireland had probably been limited to what could be got from glossaries; in Canterbury a wider and deeper mastery could be obtained.[3] Englishmen began to go to the Continent, and even to Rome, in pursuit of learning; Benedict Biscop, for instance, was at Lérins from 665 to 667. For a time a Wessex man, Aldhelm (639–709), was the most famous English scholar: his writings, in spite of their fantastic style, made him famous in other lands. After his death the palm for English learning passed to the north. Of all the Northumbrian scholars the greatest was Bede. While he lived the fame of Wearmouth and Jarrow was widespread; after he died the glory passed to the school of York.

Baeda, or Bede, as he is popularly called by all English-speaking people, was born on the land which was given by Ecgfrid, king of Northumbria, to Benedict Biscop for his monastery,[4] though his birth probably took place before the grant was actually made. At a much later date he was described as a native of an inconsiderable village in the territory of Jarrow, past which sweeps the river Tyne.[5] The traditional place of his birth is Monkton, in the parish of St. Paul, Jarrow. The date is uncertain. Symeon of Durham[6] and the Life ascribed in part to Bede's disciple Cuthbert,[7] say 677; but this seems too late.

[1] Plummer, ii. 263.
[2] *H.E.* iii. 27; Browne, *St. Aldhelm*, 271–86.
[3] Crawford, *Anglo-Saxon Influence*, p. 92. *C.M.H.* iii. 500–13.
[4] 'In territorio eiusdem monasterii.' *H.E.* v. 24.
[5] *Vita Bedae Auct Anon.* Smith, 817.
[6] *Hist. Dun.* i. 8.   [7] *Vita Bed. Ven.* Smith, 791.

Bede says of himself: 'Ex quo tempore accepti presbyteratus usque ad annum aetatis meae LVIIII, haec in scripturam sanctam meae meorumque necessitati ex opusculis venerabilium patrum breviter adnotare, sive etiam ad formam sensus et interpretationis eorum superadicere curavi.'[1] Here follows a list of his own writings. This autobiographical chapter of the *History* begins with a chronological summary which ends with the year 731. Again, the previous chapter[2] definitely states that his description of the condition of Britain refers to the year 731. Now if we are to understand that he finished his *History* in 731, and was then in his sixtieth year, we may place his birth in 672; but if he was only in his fifty-ninth year, then in 673. Mr. R. L. Poole, however, argues that what Bede means in the passage quoted above is that he wrote his commentaries on the Scriptures from his ordination until his fifty-ninth year, that the other books which follow in his catalogue have nothing to do with these chronological statements, and that therefore there is no evidence as to his age when he completed the *Historia Ecclesiastica*.[3] Now Bede gives his list of scriptural works, and adds: 'Item librum epistularum . . . item de historiis sanctorum . . . historiam abbatum . . . historiam ecclesiasticam,' &c. Some of these works, we know, were written during the period when he was composing his commentaries. He wrote this note at the very end of the *Ecclesiastical History*, and though he specially mentions his biblical work, he can hardly mean that he had confined himself to it for twenty-nine years, and had let his historical work stand over until his later life. Everything Mr. Poole says about medieval chronology is of very great weight; but it is difficult to avoid thinking that he takes Bede's words too literally here. Another lesser difficulty arises from the fact that Bede writes: 'Quo tempore [sc. A.D. 729] gravissima Saracenorum lues Gallias misera caede vastabat, et ipsi non multo post in eadem provincia dignas suae perfidiae poenas luebant.' If the latter clause refers to the victory of Charles Martel at Poitiers in 732, and it can hardly refer to anything else, it must be a later addition.[4] There is nothing inherently impossible in this: in fact other additions were made.

Somewhere about the time that Bede was born Benedict Biscop returned from his fourth journey to Rome. It was

---

[1] *H.E.* v. 24.   [2] *Ibid.* v. 23.
[3] Poole, *Studies*, 74.   [4] *H.E.* v. 23; Plummer, ii. 339, 344; Giles, i, p. xlv.

actually his third from Britain, but he had made another journey thither while he was at Lérins.[1] Disappointed of a visit to the West Saxons, he now went north to the court of Ecgfrid of Northumbria, who, influenced by his Queen, Æthelthryth, better known to us as Etheldreda or Audrey, made him a grant of seventy hides of land[2] on the left bank of the Wear. In the second year of the foundation of his monastery Benedict visited Gaul, where he obtained masons from his friend Abbot Torthelm, and before the building was finished he had to send to Gaul for artificers who could glaze the windows of the basilica and monastery.[3] Wearmouth was founded in 674 in the second indiction, and in the fourth year of King Ecgfrid; that is, between September 673 and February 674.[4]

We know nothing of Bede's parents. The Magdeburg Centuriators described him as of lowly origin, but gave no authority for the statement.[5] When he was seven years old his relatives took him to the monastery at Wearmouth and placed him in the charge first of Abbot Benedict, and later of Ceolfrid.[6] Benedict Biscop had just returned from another of his journeys to Rome, this time bringing with him John the Arch-chanter. Jarrow was not yet founded, but it soon would be, and in one or other of the houses Bede spent all the rest of his quiet life. According to Reginald of Durham, he suffered in early life from an impediment in his speech, 'linguae impeditioris impedimento ipsius meritis absolvi meruit', and was cured by St. Cuthbert.[7] Bede himself says, in his preface to his poem on the miracles of St. Cuthbert, that he has not related all: 'Quotidie namque et nova per reliquias eius aguntur, et vetera noviter ab his qui scire poterant indicantur. Ex quibus unum est quod in me ipso, sicut iam tibi dixi, per linguae curationem, dum miracula eius canerem, expertus sum.'[8] According to classical usage *dum canerem* should express the purpose of the miracle; but an impediment in his speech was no obstacle to the writing of verses, and since Bede was not strictly bound by classical usages, one must take his meaning to be that his healing occurred *while* he was writing the verses. Whether or no it was

---

[1] *H.A.* iii; Plummer, ii. 358.
[2] *H.A.* iv; *H.A. An.* vii. says fifty, afterwards increased by the donations of kings and nobles.   [3] *H.A. An.* vii.
[4] Poole, *op. cit.* 46; H. E. Savage, ap. *Arch. Ael.*, ser. II, xxii. 30.
[5] Stevenson, p. iii.   [6] *H.E.* v. 24.
[7] *Reg. Dun.* lxxvi.   [8] Giles, i. 2.

by means of the relics we have no information, but this seems the probable interpretation.

In the year 681 Ecgfrid augmented his former grant by an additional gift of forty hides, and on this land, at the king's desire, Benedict built a monastery, with a church dedicated to St. Paul, at Jarrow. It was not to be a separate community, but the monks of Wearmouth and Jarrow were to form a united body. The author of the anonymous *History of the Abbots*, himself a member of the community, says that ten tonsured monks and twelve other brethren were sent from Wearmouth to the new house. Bede says that seventeen monks were sent; but the anonymous writer has given us the number of both classes, tonsured and untonsured, and the discrepancy may be explained by a confusion between xvii and xxii on the part of some copyist.[1] The work of building lasted three years, and the establishment of the monastery was placed in the hands of Ceolfrid, with the help and direction of Benedict. According to the inscription in St. Paul's, Jarrow, the church was dedicated on 23 April 685.

When he had established his foundation at Jarrow, Benedict took a step which at first sight might seem to endanger the union of the two houses—he made Ceolfrid abbot of Jarrow and Eosterwini abbot of Wearmouth. They were both young men. Ceolfrid was thirty-nine, had been Benedict's chief assistant in the establishment of the monastery, and held an office which we might describe as that of prior. *Prioratus* is the word actually used for his post, though perhaps hardly in the later technical sense.[2] He had suffered much from the jealousy of some aristocratic members of the community who resented his strict rule, and for a short time he retired to Ripon, but was persuaded to return. He had paid a visit to Rome with Benedict, and during their absence Eosterwini had been left in charge. The last-named was now thirty-two years of age, of noble birth, and Benedict's own kinsman; he had been a member of the royal retinue, but had sacrificed his prospects and become a humble monk. The old abbot knew his men and had made a good choice; moreover, he still retained the headship, so that the two might be called vice-abbots. Benedict had done a great work in his day, and he was ageing. He had frequently to be away from home, he was intending to go abroad again, and he knew how quickly even a religious house could get out of hand in the absence of authority. Knowing that he left his monastery in good hands, Benedict set out on his sixth journey to Rome. While he was away calamity fell upon Wearmouth and Jarrow. In 685 there was a terrible outbreak of a pestilence in Britain. At Wearmouth many of the brethren died, and among them Eosterwini. When his illness came upon him and he knew that he could not live, he remained two days in the common dormitory; his last five days he spent *in secretiori aede*, perhaps the monastic infirmary, but more probably some retired cell like that used by St. Cuthbert on Lindisfarne.[1] Just before his death he summoned all his brethren to meet him in the open air, perhaps with a vague idea of precaution against infection, gave them all the kiss of peace, and bade them a tender farewell. He died on 7 March, just as the brethren were finishing matins; and the only possible year to which we can assign the event in 685.[2] In Eosterwini's place the brethren, with the consent of Ceolfrid, chose as his successor a brother named Sicgfrid, a saintly deacon, who appears to have held the office for the rest of his life without proceeding to the priesthood.

At Jarrow all who could read or preach or recite the anti-phons were carried off by the pestilence, with the exception of Ceolfrid and a little boy (*puerulus*). So the abbot commanded that in the daily offices they should go through the psalter, but should omit the antiphons except at matins and vespers. After a week of this he could bear it no longer, and decreed that the antiphons should be restored. All assisted to the best of their power, but the manly voice and the boyish treble bore the burden of the singing until a new choir began to be gathered and trained. The little boy had been 'nourished and taught' by Ceolfrid, and is further described as 'nunc usque in eodem monasterio presbyterii gradum tenens, iure actus eius laudabiles cunctis scire volentibus, et scripto commendat et fatu'.[3] It has generally been believed that it was Bede himself, who in the year 685 would be about twelve years of age.

Benedict Biscop returned from his sixth and last visit to Rome, and he brought with him many treasures for the monastery—relics of the saints, books for the library, pictures for the

[1] Plummer, ii. 362.
[2] *H.A.* viii; *H.A. An.* xiii; Poole, 46–7.
[3] *H.A. An.* xiv.

churches, and two beautiful silken cloaks. These last he afterwards exchanged with King Aldfrid (Ecgfrid had fallen on the
field of Nechtansmere) for three hides of land on the south
bank of the Wear. Of the pictures, some, representing scenes
in the life of our Lord, were hung round the church of our
Lady in the larger monastery,[1] while others, setting forth the
connexion between the Old and New Testaments, were reserved
for St. Paul's.

If Bede was not transferred to Jarrow with the first party of
monks, he went there very soon. In St. Paul's he would see
among the pictures, Isaac with the wood, Christ bearing the
cross, the serpent in the wilderness, the figure of the Crucified.
At St. Peter's he had been familiar with the pictures from the
Revelation of St. John which were on the north wall, and Bishop
Browne supposed[2] that these were the inspiration of the vision
of Drycthelm.[3] But Bede had that story, through Hemgils,
from Drycthelm himself, and there is nothing in it that is not
traditional in earlier Christian literature. Nevertheless, the
pictures in the two churches must have had a formative influence on a thoughtful, pious child. In later life he defended
the use of sacred pictures: 'Cur non licet exaltationem Domini
Salvatoris in cruce qua mortem vicit ad memoriam fidelibus
depingendo reduci, vel alia eius miracula et sanationes . . . cum
horum aspectus saepe multum compunctionis soleat praestare
contuentibus, et eis quoque qui litteras ignorant, quasi vivam
Dominicae historiae pandere lectionem.' His conclusion is:
'Forte parebit non interdictum imagines rerum . . . facere sed
haec idololatriae gratia facere omnimodo esse prohibitum.'[4]

Abbot Benedict was now drawing near to the end of his
arduous career. For three years increasing paralysis slowly
deprived him of the use of his lower limbs; but his mind was
unaffected, and he continued active in prayer and praise, and
in exhortation given to his brethren. Sicgfrid, too, was failing,
irremediabili pulmonum vitio laborantem.[5] Bede was too young
to have been present at the last interview between the two
abbots. Sicgfrid was carried on a litter into the room where
Benedict lay, and placed beside him on the same bed, and
though their heads were on the same pillow, they had not the
strength even to give one another the kiss of peace until the

---

[1] *in monasterio maiore, H.A.* ix.   [2] *Ven. Bede,* 120.
[3] *H.E.* v. 12.   [4] *Temp. Sal.* ap. Giles, viii. 336–7.   [5] *H.A.* x.

loving hands of the brethren assisted them. Two months after this Sicgfrid died, and four months later still Benedict passed away. Before the latter's death he enjoined strict obedience to the rules which he had drawn up after studying those of seventeen Benedictine monasteries, and urged that the library, which he had enlarged with such care, should not be neglected or dispersed. He bade the monks never to choose an abbot for his birth, or from outside the community; but they were to seek out the fittest person of their own number, and to present him to the bishop for his blessing.[1] Bede gives us a touching account of the last scenes of Benedict's earthly life; some of the brethren praying and singing in church all through the winter night, others remaining in the sick man's chamber, the continuous recital of the Gospels through the night, the giving of the viaticum. In the church they sang the psalter through till they came to the 82nd psalm, 'Deus, quis similis erit tibi', and as they were singing these words he passed to his rest. If Bede himself was not present at some of this, and after all Jarrow was not far away and there was continual coming and going between the two houses, at least he must have heard the story told again and again.

When he died Benedict had governed his monastery sixteen years. Jarrow was founded eight years after Wearmouth, and we may assume that the foundation of the monastery came soon after the grant of land in 681: but since Bede says, 'Ceolfridus, iubente pariter et iuvante Benedicto, monasterium beati Pauli apostoli septem annis fundavit, perfecit, rexit',[2] it may even have taken place early in 682. During Benedict's second period of eight years Eosterwini ruled four years at Wearmouth, Sicgfrid three, and Ceolfrid one.[3] But in all these cases we are certainly dealing with round numbers, as is obvious from the dates given for the various deaths. Eosterwini died on 7 March in his fourth year, i.e. 685. Sicgfrid, who is said to have ruled three years, died on 22 August, and the year must be 688, which makes nearly three and a half years. Ceolfrid was made abbot of both houses as successor to Benedict Biscop on 12 May in the third year of King Aldfrid, in the first indiction. This must be in 688. He really ruled much less than a year before Benedict's death, for the latter died on 12 January 689.[4]

---

[1] *Ibid.* xi, xiii.   [2] *Ibid.* xv.   [3] *Ibid.* xiv.

[4] *H.A. An.* xvii; Poole, 46–7. Plummer, accepting the numbers given as

At the age of nineteen years Bede was advanced to the diaconate by John of Beverley, who in 687 had succeeded Eata as bishop of Hexham. The canon law forbade men to be made deacons under twenty-five years of age.[1] A few exceptions are known, all men of outstanding learning and holiness; but Bede's merits in both respects must have been very great indeed to permit the ecclesiastical authorities to anticipate the canonical age by so much as six years. Studious he must have been. 'Recogitate', said Alcuin, writing to the brethren at Wearmouth and Jarrow a century later, 'nobilissimum nostri temporis magistrum Bedam presbyterum, quale habuit in juventute discendi studium.'[2] Of course, too, he had great advantages. Benedict Biscop had collected what in that age must have been a very great library. Archbishop Theodore had so encouraged the study of Greek that it was said that there were many in England who spoke Greek with as much facility as English, and amongst Bede's teachers there were some who had been pupils of Theodore and Hadrian; Trumberct, the disciple of St. Chad at Lastingham, taught him much of his knowledge of the Scriptures. Sicgfrid was a man 'scripturarum studiis abundanter instructum ac singulariter intentum'.[3] Ceolfrid was a scholar, and if the letter to the king of the Picts on the Easter question[4] was composed by him, it would be evidence of the fact; but it is at least possible that Bede is the real author.[5] Some writers have mentioned John the Arch-chanter as one of Bede's teachers; but he was only lent to the English church for a year, and that when Bede had only just come to the monastery as a small boy. But he committed his instructions to writing, and the manuscript was preserved at Wearmouth, where it would be available for study.[6] The special advantage, however, of the great northern monastery lay in the fact that there met all the main streams of learning, from Rome and from the Celtic Church, from Canterbury and from Gaul. Scholars must have been frequent guests, some of whom came from distant parts.

representing complete years, makes the date of Ceolfrid's appointment and that of Benedict's death a year later.

[1] The third council of Carthage (397), council of Agde (506), fourth council of Arles (524), second council of Toledo (531), Quinisext council (680–1), all said twenty-five years. Pope Siricius and Pope Zosimus had both decreed thirty as the age. See Blunt, 541. [2] Alcuin, ep. xiv, 793, ap. P.L. c. 165. [3] H.A. An. xiii; cf. H.A. x. [4] H.E. v. 21. [5] Roger, 304–5. [6] H.E. iv. 18.

All these opportunities were diligently used. It was Bede's pleasure, *dulce habui*, as he puts it, to learn, to teach, and to write.[1] But there were many distractions. A large monastery was a self-supporting institution, and every one had his part in the work; sowing, reaping, threshing, feeding the beasts, gardening, baking, cooking, smith's work, carpentering, and the general menial work of the house. We read how Eosterwini took his share in these labours,[2] and Bede would doubtless do the same. He frequently refers to the necessity for manual work in the monastery, and he praises Ovini, who went to Lastingham not to live idle, but to labour.[3] The novices and other pupils, too, would have to be instructed, to say nothing of visiting students from other monasteries. The scriptorium, even if, as some think, it was not a very large one,[4] would need workers, and Bede would often be seen there, pen in hand. The rule of St. Benedict allowed of much diversity of practice; but the daily recitation of the divine office was insisted on everywhere, and this was one of the duties Bede would not miss. 'Fertur enim magistrum nostrum et vestrum patronum beatum dixisse Bedam: scio angelos visitare canonicas horas et congregationes fraternas: quid si ibi me non inveniunt inter fratres? Nonne dicere habent, ubi est Beda? Quare non venit ad adorationes statutas cum fratribus?'[5]

All Bede's work is redolent of his earnest piety. 'He was a perfect example of the concentration of interests, religious and educational, afforded by the monastic life.'[6] Symeon of Durham says that there used to be shown a little hut (*mansiuncula*) where Bede used to meditate and work.[7] We know that when he lay sick and dying it was in his own cell, and not in the common dormitory. It has been suggested that he was exempted from the general custom of Benedictine houses on account of his studies and the dignity of his position as a teacher,[8] and this may have been true at least of his later days.

At Christmas time in the fourteenth indiction, the Christmas of the year 700 as we should reckon it, though in Bede's reckoning it was 701, certain monks from the community were in Rome, and there procured from Pope Sergius a privilege for the

[1] *Ibid.* v. 24.   [2] *H.A.* viii.   [3] *H.E.* iv. 3.
[4] Plummer, i, p. xx.   [5] Alcuin, ep. xvi, ap. *P.L.*, c. 168.
[6] W. H. Hutton, ap. *Dict. Eng. Ch. Hist.*, s.v. Bede.
[7] *Hist. Dun.* xiv.   [8] Hunt, 187.

protection of the monastery, similar to one which Pope Agatho had granted to Benedict Biscop.[1] There is no evidence whatever that Bede was with them; but a belief grew up that he had at least been invited. Now the Pope had written to Ceolfrid desiring him to send one of his monks to Rome to assist in the examination of certain important ecclesiastical questions, *capitula ecclesiasticarum causarum*. It seems most probable that the matter in question was Wilfrid's business, and that the Pope wished to consult some one who had the necessary local knowledge. William of Malmesbury makes the Pope ask for 'religiosum Dei famulum Bedam, venerabilis monasterii tui presbyterum', and he further says: 'Veruntamen quod Romae fuerit solide non affirmo, sed eum illuc invitatum haud dubie pronuncio: quod haec epistola clarum faciet, simul et quanti penderit eum Romana sedes ut eum tantopere desideret.'[2] After his time it seems to have been gradually accepted that the Pope had asked for Bede by name.[3] But there is an earlier form of this letter among the Cottonian MSS.[4] This makes the Pope ask for 'religiosum famulum dei N. venerabilis monasterii tui'. The Cottonian text does not give the word *presbyterum*; but it gives *Beda*..(the last letter doubtful) in the margin. Giles takes *dei N* as meaning *dei nostri*. This is doubtful, and the words would rather suggest that a copyist was using a defective manuscript, from which a name was omitted, and had inserted N. There is no need to suppose that Malmesbury, whose honesty as a historian is unquestioned, had used the Cottonian text and had wilfully interpolated the words *presbyterum* and *Bedam*. Ussher had in his possession a manuscript in which Bede's name occurs, but in which he is not described as *presbyter*. This lessens considerably the weight which might otherwise be placed on the evidence of the Cotton text. It may be said that Sergius would hardly have asked vaguely for a member of the house without naming some particular person. Still, he may have left the choice of the individual to the abbot. It is not impossible, of course, that he may have heard during Ceolfrid's visits to Rome of a particularly promising young scholar at Jarrow. Again, it has been said that if the reading *presbyterum* is

---

[1] *De Temp. Rat.* xlvii; *H.A.* xv; *H.A. An.* xx.
[2] Will. Malmes., *Gest. Reg.* i. 57, 58.
[3] Cf. *Nov. Leg. Ang.* 107–11.
[4] MSS. Cotton, Tib. A. xv. 50*b*–52*a*.

authentic it puts Bede out of the question, because he was not yet a priest; but the Pope may not have known, or may not even have troubled to inquire about his exact ecclesiastical standing.[1] If the invitation was really sent to Bede, why did he not go to Rome?—for it seems certain that he did not, and one can hardly imagine him refusing a papal invitation. Several writers have supposed that it was because of the death of the Pope in September 701. As we have seen, however, the only monks of Wearmouth and Jarrow who went to Rome about this time were there nine months before Sergius died. Moreover, they seem in all probability to have had some dealings in Wilfrid's affair. Mr. R. L. Poole thinks that they brought back with them the bull relating to Wilfrid, the date of which is nowhere mentioned, and that it was in consequence of this bull that Aldfrid was obliged to summon a council to go into the case again.[2] We know that the privilege they brought back was exhibited before a synod, and confirmed by the signatures of the bishops present and that of King Aldfrid,[3] and Wilfrid's bull may have been considered at the same time.

As far as we know, Bede never left his native shores. In later days, however, strange tales were told of his doings in Italy. One legend relates that he saw on a gate in Rome an inscription:

P. P. P.
S. S. S.
R. R. R.
F. F. F.

and when asked what he was looking at, he replied that it was something his questioner should be ashamed of, and he then read the inscription as:

Pater Patriae Perditus est
Sapientia Secum Sublator
Regnum Romae Ruit
Ferro Flamma Fame.

It was a common literary trick of the time,[4] but we cannot imagine Bede indulging in it. Another story is that the title *Venerabilis* was decreed him at Rome for interpreting S.P.Q.R.

---

[1] Hunt, ap. *D.N.B.*, s.v. Beda; Hardy, introd. to Will. Malmes.; Stubbs, ap. *D.C.B.*, s.v. Bede; Haddan and Stubbs, iii. 248–50.
[2] Poole, 75.   [3] *H.A.* xv.   [4] Browne, *Ven. Bede*, 21.

as *Stultus Populus Quaerit Romam*, with reference to the Goths
swarming thither. It was further added that he died and was
buried at Genoa. There may have been, perhaps, some other
person of the same name buried there; but it certainly was not
the Venerable Bede.[1]

Bede was ordained priest by John of Beverley, bishop of
Hexham. His own statement is, 'Nono decimo autem vitae
meae anno diaconatum, tricesimo gradum presbyteratus . . .
iubente Ceolfrido abbate suscepi'.[2] The canonical age for ordination to the priesthood was thirty, and we may assume that he
had completed that tale of years. His ordination, then, must be
dated 702 or 703, unless we take his words to mean he was
ordained in his thirtieth year; but if so we must similarly interpret *nonodecimo anno*, and understand that he was made a
deacon at the age of eighteen. When he began his career as a
writer we do not know; he gives few indications of the dates at
which his books were written. The two earliest were probably
his *De Orthographia* and *De Arte Metrica*, books of elementary
instruction for his pupils in the monastery. The former is a
glossary arranged alphabetically. The meaning or grammatical
usage of each word is given, sometimes with reference to Greek
parallels, and stress is laid on the signification of words which
closely resemble one another.[3] The *De Arte Metrica* is a collection of examples of verse forms, all of which are carefully
explained. Bede quotes many authors, and expounds amongst
other things the characteristics of hexameters and pentameters,
and the differences between rhythm and metre. In his explanation of rhythmical verse, modern in his day, he admits that by
the old classical rules it is quite incorrect; but it is obvious that
he is interested in it and likes it. He tries to prove the superiority
of sacred poetry over secular, and gives examples from the
Christian poets. The full title of the work is *De Arte Metrica ad
Cuthbertum Levitam*.[4] The last paragraph begins, 'Haec tibi
dulcissime fili et conlevita Cuthberte, diligenter ex antiquorum
opusculis scriptorum excerpere curavi.' From this we may
perhaps conclude that Cuthbert was a pupil of Bede, and
younger, and that the book was written while Bede was a deacon.

---

[1] *Rites Durh.* 234; *Leg. Aur.*, f. ccxx, *Nov. Leg. Ang.* 107–11.   In the two last
he is said to have been buried at Genoa. For other persons named Bede see
Plummer, i. p. lxxviii *n.*
[2] *H.E.* v. 24.   [3] Giles, vi. 1–39.
[4] Giles has *ad Wigbertum Levitam*, though he has Cuthbert in the text.

A short treatise, *De Schematibus et Tropis Sacrae Scripturae*, might be described as an appendix to the *De Arte Metrica*. It is an explanation of the rhetoric of the Bible, and the various rhetorical figures are explained with scriptural examples.[1]

Although at Whitby in 664 the English Church had adopted the Roman rules for Easter, the controversy on that subject had not yet ended, and it was necessary that the correct principles of calculation should be made clear to the clergy. Bede essayed to do this in what was probably his next work, *De Temporibus*, to which he added a condensed chronicle of the six ages of the world, based chiefly on Isidore, but with additions from other sources. In c. xiv he refers to the year 703, and the historical summary ends with the fifth year of the Emperor Tiberius, 702–3. The last two sentences run: 'Tiberius dehinc quintum egit annum, reliquum sextae aetatis Deo soli patet.'[2] It seems certain, therefore, that the book was completed in that year. To Bede's horror it brought upon him a ridiculous charge of heresy.

The accusation was made in the presence of Bishop Wilfrid at a feast. It was said that Bede had denied that the Incarnation took place during the sixth age of the world, and the bishop does not seem to have rebuked the accuser. Bede heard of it by a messenger from a monk named Plegwin. Horrified at the charge and the circumstances of its making, 'quod me audires a lascivientibus rusticis inter haereticos per pocula decantari', he wrote two days later in his *Epistola ad Plegwinum Apologetica*.[3] The accusation is difficult to understand. In the chapter *De Sexta Aetate*, he distinctly said: 'Huius anno xlii Dominus nascitur.'[4] In his epistle he asked what his accusers meant. Did they mean that Christ had not come in the flesh while it was still the sixth age, or that the Lord came in the flesh before the sixth age had begun? Certainly the seventh age had not come, and it is only reason that the sixth age would not have begun with the Incarnation. 'But I understood, whether they meant one thing or the other, they meant to make me a heretic. . . . If I believed the writings of the Evangelists, how could I disbelieve that He was incarnate in the sixth age of the world?' He justified himself by the Scriptures and the fathers, and explained that he had followed the Hebrew chronology and not

[1] *Ibid.* vi. 80–98.
[2] *Ibid.* vi. 138.
[3] *Ibid.* iii. 144.
[4] *Ibid.* vi. 136.

that of the Septuagint. He prayed his friend to show the epistle to their 'religious and learned brother David', that he might be able to read it to their 'venerable lord and father Wilfrid'.

Bede says that the accusation was based on the *De Temporibus*, which he had published (*edidi*) five years previously. If so, the epistle was written in 708; but his scornful reference to the revels has caused some writers to hesitate to refer the occurrence to the greater Wilfrid, and to assign it to the episcopate of Wilfrid II, who was bishop of York from 718 to 732. Some weight is added to the suggestion by some verses of Alcuin:

Hos mentes dapibus, illos sed carnis alebat.
His fovet aetherius, illos carnalibus auget.[1]

If we accept this view the date of the *De Temporibus* must be considerably advanced; but the reasons seem slight. After all, more than one person disapproved of the great state Wilfrid kept.[2] Bede himself did not altogether approve of Wilfrid. In his *History* he omits much that Eddi tells us, and cuts out all his miracles but one, while his biography[3] of Wilfrid is, to say the least of it, meagre. Bede and Wilfrid were on opposite sides: in Wilfrid's eyes some of the men whom Bede admired were ecclesiastical intruders. Bede no doubt disliked Wilfrid's opposition to the division of his see, and, although he speaks of him respectfully enough, his commendations lack somewhat of their usual generosity. But in the present instance the point of the accusation was that a piece of untrue gossip was allowed to go unchallenged.

After writing *De Temporibus* Bede occupied himself for years almost entirely with the study of the Scriptures. His commentaries are mainly based on the works of the four great Latin fathers, Augustine, Jerome, Ambrose, and Gregory. To these he adds comments of his own modelled on their pattern. He used both the Latin and the Itala text, and frequently used the Greek as well. We may suppose that the three books *In Apocalypsin S. Joannis*, which have a prefatory epistle to Frater Eusebius, were written before 716, for in that year Eusebius, better known to us as Huaetberct, became abbot of Wearmouth and Jarrow. It is worthy of note, as illustrating Bede's freedom from narrowness, that he tells us that in this

---

[1] *Carmen de Pontificibus Eccl. Ebor.* i. 1232.
[2] Cf. Eddius, xvii.   [3] *H.E.* v. 19.

commentary he has followed Tyconius the Donatist, whose work he considers of great value,[1] that is to say, when not affected by his heretical views.[2]

After the Apocalypse came *In Acta Apostolorum Expositio*. The prologue to Acca, 'domino in Christo desiderantissimo et vere beatissimo, Accae episcopo', shows that it was written after Acca became bishop of Hexham in 709. To him Bede dedicated a number of his works, always in the most affectionate terms. After his exposition of the Apocalypse, which he had undertaken at the request of Eusebius, he intended to prepare and send to Acca for transcription a commentary on St. Luke's Gospel. This great task, for various troublesome reasons with which his friend was acquainted, he had been unable to undertake as yet; but in the meantime he sent him this little work on the Acts, put forth (*editum*) not many days past. He had prepared it as swiftly as possible, and, not to keep the bishop waiting, he had given it out to be emended in a series of little membranes.[3] It is a little uncertain from the wording whether the commentary on the Apocalypse had been postponed, as well as that on St. Luke; but the general sense seems to be that the former had been finished, though the greater work he had intended to undertake had not been begun. At any rate, we may place the exposition of the Acts before 716.

With the last mentioned he sent at the same time to Acca the fruit of his labours on the First Epistle of St. John.[4] This was afterwards included with the rest of the Catholic Epistles, and to this collection Bede seems to have written a preface which is found only in one extant manuscript, albeit the earliest. It was possibly omitted by later transcribers because it seemed to give the first place among the apostles to St. James, and precedence to the see of Jerusalem over that of Rome.[5] How soon after the First Epistle of St. John the rest of the commentary was written is unknown; but as Bede does not seem to have been in the habit of leaving a work undone which he had once begun, we may perhaps assign it tentatively[6] to the years between 709 and 716.

Perhaps the greatest of the New Testament works of Bede is the *In Lucae Evangelium Expositio* in six books. It was

---

[1] Giles, xii. 338.
[2] *Ibid.* xii. 340.
[3] *Ibid.* xii. 1, 2.
[4] *Ibid.* xii. 4.
[5] *Ibid.* xii. 157.
[6] As Plummer does, ii, p. xxxi.

C

prefaced by an *Epistola adhortatoria* from Acca, who said that
he had often urged Bede by word and writing to undertake the
task when he had finished the Acts; but Bede had shrunk from
attempting to do what had already been so well done by St.
Ambrose. He was afraid that the ancient proverb might be
applied to him:

> In mare quid pisces, quid aquas in flumina mittas?
> Larga sed indignis munera funde locis.

To this objection Acca would briefly reply, 'quia iuxta Comicum
nihil sit dictum quod non sit dictum prius'. It was necessary
that matters should be treated by different authors in different
ways. Bede could explain some difficulties which his predecessors
had passed over, and besides, in a ruder age, the earlier writers
were not easily to be understood by all.[1]

Acca's epistle is followed by an epistle in reply from *Beda,
humilis presbyter*. He has undertaken the task laid upon him,
'in quo (ut innumera monasticae servitutis retinacula prae-
teream) ipse mihi dictator simul notarius et librarius existerem'.[2]
He has a word, too, for his readers: 'Multum obsecro et per
Dominum legentes obtestor, ut si qui forte nostra haec qualia-
cunque sunt opuscula transcriptione digna duxerint, memorata
quoque nominum signa, ut in nostro exemplari reperiunt,
adfigere meminerint.'[3] It is to be feared that the injunction
was frequently disobeyed; consequently it is not always easy
to discover whether a particular comment is Bede's own or
extracted from an earlier writer. In his preface to St. Mark,
also written to Acca, he again requests transcribers to copy
not only the text but the 'annotationem nominum quae supra
in margine apposita sunt'.[4]

Thus he continued working quietly in the peace of the
cloister; but a great bereavement was drawing near, one which
to Bede especially would come as a bitter grief. Ceolfrid had
done a great work at Monkwearmouth and Jarrow. He built
several oratories, added to the furniture of the churches and the
vessels of the altar, enlarged the monastic lands,[5] and doubled
the library. But now, in his seventy-fifth year, he determined,
in June 716, to resign and to go to Rome. He was anxious to
avoid prolonged farewells, and feared lest they should desire to

---

[1] Giles, x. 265–7.   [2] *Ibid.* x. 268.   [3] *Ibid.* xiii. 269.
[4] *Ibid.* x. 2, 3.   [5] *H.A.* xv.

give him presents, for he had made it a rule never to accept one without giving an equivalent in return. When he announced his intention to the brethren they besought him with many tears to remain a little longer. Yielding to their entreaties, he abode with them that day and night; it was the Tuesday before Whit-Sunday, and next morning, attended by many of them, he went to pay a last visit to Jarrow. There he prayed the monks to observe the rule he had taught them, and to continue in the fear of the Lord. He begged them not to try to delay his going, and to forgive him if he had ever transgressed the limits of moderation, as he forgave all who had in any way offended him. So they begged him that he would pray for them at the shrine of the Apostles, or if before that he should pass from this world, he would ever be mindful to intercede for their salvation. He left them that same day, and returned to St. Peter's.

On Thursday morning, 4 June, after mass had been sung in St. Peter's and in St. Mary's, he called all the brethren into St. Peter's church, prayed with them, and standing, with a burning censer in his hand, on the steps from which he had been accustomed to read, he gave some of them the kiss of peace; but some were too overcome with weeping to bear it. Then, still bearing the censer, he went to the oratory of St. Laurence in the dormitory, and as they followed they sang the antiphon and the psalm 'God be merciful unto us and bless us'. Coming forth once more with the incense, he gave his last address, admonishing them to keep peace among themselves and unity between the two houses. Then, resuming the psalm, they went forth towards the river, and on the bank he said a prayer and then embarked. Seated at the prow, with his deacons on each side of him carrying lighted candles and a golden cross, with a full heart he prayed incessantly, 'Christe, miserere illi caetui! Domine omnipotens, protege illam cohortem! Scio autem certissime quia nullos unquam meliores illis et promptiores ad obedientiam novi. Christe Deus defende illos!' So he passed to the other side, quitted the vessel, bowed before the cross and departed.[1]

When he was out of sight the monks returned to the church and commended him to the Lord. After Terce[2] they assembled, and determined to elect a new head as soon as possible. Some

[1] *H.A.* xvi, xvii; *H.A. An.* xxi–xxvii.
[2] 'Completa horae tertiae psalmodia': *H.A.* xviii.

of the brethren from St. Paul's were present, and they and
some of the Wearmouth monks bore tidings of the decision to
Jarrow. On Whit-Sunday, 7 June 716, at a meeting of all the
brethren of St. Peter's together with some of the elder monks
of St. Paul's, Huætberct was elected abbot.[1] The vivid and
detailed description which Bede gives us of all these proceedings
can only be the work of an eyewitness. Knowing all that we do
of Bede, we may wonder why he, the greatest of them all, was
not made abbot. His contemporaries in 716 perhaps hardly
realized his greatness: moreover, a great scholar is not necessarily a great administrator. We may be thankful that he was
not elected, for, in the cares and troubles of much serving in a
community of six hundred monks, he might have been hindered
from his best work, which was yet to come.

Huætberct, the new abbot, had been ordained priest twelve
years previously, had been brought up in the monastery from
boyhood, and had studied in Rome during the pontificate of
Sergius. Bede refers to him thus, 'Huetbertum iuvenem cui
amor studiumque pietatis iam olim Eusebii cognomen indidit',[2]
and in the letter to Huætberct prefixed to his book on the
Apocalypse he adjures him, *Bedae tui semper memor esse*.[3]
Immediately after his election the new abbot and some of the
monks followed after Ceolfrid, who had not yet crossed the sea,
received his approval of the brethren's choice, and gave him a
letter of recommendation to Pope Gregory II. But Ceolfrid
never reached Rome: he died at Langres, and was buried in the
churchyard of the Twin Martyrs, two miles from that city.[4]
He had taken with him presents for the Pope, and one of special
value. He had added to the monastic library 'tres pandectas
novae translationis ad unum vetustae translationis quem de
Roma adtulerat'.[5] One of each of these great codices he left
to the two houses, the third he took with him on his last journey.
Under the name of *Codex Amiatinus* it is still to be seen in the
Laurentian library at Florence.

When Huætberct returned from his interview with Ceolfrid the
monastery at Wearmouth received a visit from Bishop Acca, who
confirmed Huætberct's election with his blessing. On 22 August,
Sicgfrid's birthday, they took up the bodies of Eosterwini and

---

[1] *H.A.* xviii; *H.A. An.* xx.
[2] In Sam. Proph. iv, prooem., ap. Giles, viii. 162.   [3] *Ibid.* xii. 341.
[4] *H.A.* xviii, xxi; *H.A. An.* xxx–xxxii.   [5] *H.A.* xv.

Sicgfrid, the former buried in the entrance porch of St. Peter's, the latter outside the sacrarium towards the south, and, placing them side by side in one coffin, though separated by a partition, gave them their final resting-place in the church near the body of Benedict, which lay east of the high altar.[1] Henceforward the life of the monastery would go on in its accustomed quiet way for the rest of Bede's life.

The first three books of Bede's annotations *In Samuelem* were written before the departure of Ceolfrid in 716. He dedicated the work to Acca, 'most beloved of all the bishops in the world'.[2] In his preface to book IV he said that he had intended to take a rest after the third book, before beginning the fourth; but that space of quiet, if indeed it could be called quiet, since it was a time of unexpected anxiety of mind, had lasted longer than he anticipated, owing to the resignation and departure of the abbot. But now that Huætberct had been appointed, his own peace of mind had returned, and his desire for and delight in the study of the Scriptures. As Bede refers to the resignation but not to the death of Ceolfrid, we may conclude that his book was finished before the news came. During the interval between the third and fourth books Bede had written, in reply to questions by Acca, two epistles to that prelate. One of these is known as *De Mansionibus Filiorum Israel*, the other, *De eo quod ait Isaias, Et claudentur ibi in carcerem, et post multos dies visitabuntur*. In the second of these he apologized for a delay in sending the required information, but explained that he had had to take time to consider his answer.[3]

All we know of the date of his *In Marci Evangelium Expositio* is that it was written long, *plurimos annos*, after Luke. In the accompanying epistle to Acca, Bede said that he had compiled this commentary not only at his exhortation, but at that of many other brethren; and he had done his best to collect whatever he could find on the subject in the Fathers.[4] It was certainly written after his book on Samuel, for he says, 'de qua tota historia pro captu nostro plenius in expositione libri Regum diximus'.[5] It must, then, be later than 716.

Bede's work on Samuel perhaps induced Nothelm, a priest of London, and afterwards archbishop of Canterbury (735–40), to propound to him a number of questions on the books of

<hr>

[1] *Ibid.* xx.   [2] Giles, vii. 369.   [3] *Ibid.* i. 203.
[4] *Ibid.* x. 1, 2.   [5] *Ibid.* x. 37.

Samuel and Kings. In answer there was written *In Libros Regum Quaestionum XXX*;[1] but we have no evidence of the date except that it was before 731. On the whole, however, it seems not unreasonable to suppose that it appeared after *In Samuelem*, and perhaps not very long after. A commentary on Genesis i–xxi. 10, *In Principium Genesis usque ad nativitatem Isaac et ejectionem Ismaelis*, called also *Hexaemeron*, seems to have been his next great biblical work. It is in four books, and has prefixed to it a letter from Bede, *humillimus famulorum Christi*, to his beloved Acca. In his chronological work Bede not infrequently takes examples from the actual year in which he is writing. In the course of his comments on Genesis viii. 16 he says: 'si enim hodierna die, verbi gratia, per Kalendas Apriles esset luna septima decima.' It has, therefore, been calculated that the year in question was 720, and this seems quite a suitable date.[2]

Bede's *Historia Abbatum*, or, more fully, *Vita Beatorum Abbatum Benedicti, Ceolfridi, Eosterwini, Sigfridi atque Hwaetberhti*, was certainly written after the first three books of the commentary on Samuel. It traces the history of the monastery from its foundation by Benedict Biscop, and ends with the death and burial of Ceolfrid, 26 September 716. There is another book by an anonymous writer, a member of the community, which is also known by the title *Historia Abbatum*; but is more correctly entitled *Vita Sanctissimi Ceolfridi Abbatis*, for that is what it really is. It has been described as a commemoration sermon;[3] but it contains comparatively little of a purely homiletic character. If we compare the two, Bede gives us more about Benedict Biscop and the monastery generally, while the anonymous writer gives us details of Ceolfrid's earlier life; and though on the whole his narrative is usually more jejune, he gives the fuller account of the departure of Ceolfrid. It has been sometimes assumed that Bede used this book in the composition of his own: Plummer said without hesitation, 'Bede certainly had the Hist. Anon. before him.'[4] He thought that Bede's account stopped where it did because he 'might naturally feel a delicacy in writing about the administration of Huætberct, now abbot'.[5] There seems, however, something to be said for a different view, namely that the anonymous author was the later. We can

---

[1] Giles, viii. 232.   [2] *Ibid.* vii. 117; Plummer, i, p. cxlix.
[3] Boutflower, 53.   [4] Plummer, ii. 358.   [5] *Ibid.* i, p. cxlviii.

possibly lay too much stress on resemblances in the narratives
Both writers were telling much the same story, they were monks
in the same monastery, they were both writing many things
that were well known in the two houses, and many things they
had seen with their own eyes. Certain texts of each exhibit
interpolations from the other,[1] but apart from this, the verbal
coincidences seem mostly such as we might expect from two
people who were relating the same facts. The anonymous author
gives the reply of Pope Gregory to Huætberct's letter, and
there seems no reason why Bede should not have given it too,
had it arrived before his story was finished. Bede had no prejudice against miracles, so it is somewhat surprising that he
does not mention the miracle at Ceolfrid's grave. When he
wrote, some of the abbot's companions had returned, but some
were still apparently lingering in Gaul. The anonymous author
seems to be writing a considerable time after the abbot's death.
He says, 'The companions of our father used to tell us (narra-
bant), "Mos increbuit eiusdem loci incolis", and "Sed et alia
signa et sanitates ibidem factas fama vulgavit"'.[2] Unless we are
to assume that the whole chapter is a later addition, an assumption for which there appears no ground, we must assign the book
to a date considerably after 716. Further, the reference to the
little boy 'now a priest who both by *written* and spoken words
justly commends the abbot's deeds to all who wish to know
of them',[3] may even be taken as a reference to Bede's book.
We have no proof; it is only a question of the balance of
probabilities; but it seems more likely that Bede's work was
finished soon after Ceolfrid's death, and the other book much
later.

Among the earlier writings of the Venerable Bede was a poem,
De Miraculis Sancti Cuthberti, commonly known as the *Metrical
Life of St. Cuthbert*. Written in hexameters, 'often elegant,
often harmonious',[4] and full of borrowings from other Latin
poets, there is correctness but not much poetical merit in it.
There is a short prose prologue addressed to a priest named
John, who was setting out on a journey to Rome, and Bede is
careful to ask for his prayers when by the protection of God he
should arrive *ad limina apostolorum*. The work is divided into
sections, the twenty-first of which recounts the saint's prophecy

---

[1] Cf. *Ibid.* i. 379 *n.*, 383 *n.*, 394 *n.*, 395 *n.*, 398 *n.*, 400 *n.*
[2] *H.A. An.* xl. [3] *Ibid.* xiv. [4] Ebert.

about the life and reign of King Ecgfrid, and finishes with a
reference to Aldfrid, his successor:

> . . . Novus Josia fideque animoque magis quam
> Annis maturis, nostrum regit inclitus orbem.[1]

Cuthbert died in 687, and Aldfrid reigned from 685 to 705.
The poem, therefore, was composed before the last-named
year, and the reference to Josiah might suggest a date some
years before that.

In the prologue Bede expressed an intention, if opportunity
offered, of recording more of the miracles of St. Cuthbert. In
later years he returned to the subject with *De Vita et Miraculis
S. Cuthberti Episcopi Lindisfarnensis*, a prose work undertaken
at the request of Bishop Eadfrid and the monks of Lindisfarne.
It was certainly written before 721, because it is dedicated to
the bishop, who died that year. In the *Historia Ecclesiastica* he
says that he wrote an account of St. Cuthbert both in heroic
verse and in prose, *ante annos plures*.[2] In *De Temporum Ratione*
he refers to the prose life as writen recently (*nuper*).[3] It can
hardly, then, have been written long before 721. In recognition
of his work the brethren inscribed his name in the White Book
of Lindisfarne, which contained the list of benefactors remembered in their prayers. The prose life is reminiscent of the
language of the poetic version, and the stories are arranged in
almost the same order; yet it is not a mere revision of the old
narrative, but a fresh work. Miracles take up a large part of
the book, which is really a work of hagiography of the type of
Adamnan's *Life of St. Columba*.

The *Vita S. Cuthberti* is not a mere compilation. Bede made
use, though he does not mention it, of a life of the saint by an
unknown monk of Lindisfarne, omitting, however, some of the
details. He frequently names special sources of information,
persons who knew the facts; Trumwine,[4] an unnamed monk,
'one of the most worthy brethren of our monastery',[5] Ingwald,
a priest of Wearmouth,[6] Abbot Sicgfrid,[7] a visitor to Wearmouth who was buried there,[8] Cynemund, a priest still living
and well known,[9] Felgeld, on whose behalf a miracle was performed, and a priest of Jarrow acquainted with the circumstances.[10] When the draft of the book was ready it was submitted

---

[1] Giles, ii. 20.   [2] *H.E.* iv. 28.   [3] Giles, vi. 329.   [4] *Vita. Cuth.* i.
[5] *Ibid.* iii.   [6] *Ibid.* v.   [7] *Ibid.* vi.   [8] *Ibid.* xxxv.
[9] *Ibid.* xxxvi.   [10] *Ibid.* xlvi.

to Herefrid and others, who made some corrections. Bede then took the manuscript to Eadfrid for his judgement, and for two days it was examined by the elders and teachers of the community at Lindisfarne. During his interview with Eadfrid the latter told him many other facts relating to St. Cuthbert, but Bede thought it unwise at this stage to introduce new material. The preface to the 'holy and most blessed father Eadfrid, the bishop', is interesting as showing that Bede once at least visited Lindisfarne.

In his list of his own writings Bede mentions three lesser historical works to which reference may be briefly made here, though their dates are unknown. One was the *Liber Vitae et Passionis S. Anastasii, male de Graeco translatum, et peius a quodam imperito emendatum*. The text of this he had corrected as well as he was able; but no copy is now extant. Paulinus of Nola wrote an account in hexameters of St. Felix of Nola, a confessor of the fifth century. Bede's *Liber Vitae et Passionis S. Felicis* is a prose rendering of this narrative. Lastly there is his *Martyrologium*, in which he has given wherever possible the natal day, that is, the day of the martyrdom, the name of the judge who condemned the martyr, and an account of his sufferings. Founded on early martyrologies, the work, as we have it, has received so much interpolation and supplement that all attempts to distinguish Bede's work from that of others can only have untrustworthy results.[1]

In addition to his metrical *Life of St. Cuthbert* Bede tells us that he wrote two books of verse: *Liber hymnorum diverso metro sive rhythmo*, and *Liber epigrammatum heroico metro sive elegiaco*. Both are lost, and there is special cause for regret in the case of the former, because the combination of metrical and rhythmical poetry in one volume, and the work of one author, would be of great value to the student of the development of the new form of medieval poetry and the breaking away from the old. We have an example of Bede's poetry in his verses on St. Æthelthryth in his *Ecclesiastical History*.[2] It begins with pagan allusions, and in its diction is reminiscent of classical Latin poetry; but there are other references to Christian saints, and the general tone, as we should expect, is entirely Christian. It displays a curious and somewhat wearisome trick of ending

---

[1] H. Thurston, ap. *Cath. Encycl.*, s.v. Bede; Giles, iv 16 ff.; Smith, 327 ff.
[2] *H.E.* iv. 18.

every other line with the first three words of its predecessor, thus:

> *Alma Deus Trinitas*, quae secula cuncta gubernas
> Adnue jam coeptis, *alma Deus Trinitas*
> *Bella Maro resonet*, nos pacis dona canamus
> Munera nos Christi, *bella Maro resonet*.

Much of the verse that has been ascribed to Bede is of doubtful authenticity. The *Cuculus* is an example; a pleasant little poem, but the more one reads of Bede's known work the less likely it seems to be his, and though it cannot absolutely be rejected[1] as the work of Bede, it is much more likely to have been written by Alcuin.[2] *De ratione temporum*, in metrical verse with some rather poor rhymes, *De celebritate quatuor temporum*, and *De variis computi regulis*, all three deal with subjects in which Bede was specially interested. Of the hymns, *Primo Deus coeli globum* seems undoubtedly his, and Alcuin takes it as genuine.[3] Also generally accepted are *Hymnum canentes martyrum*, on the Holy Innocents; *Hymnum canamus gloriae*, on the Ascension; *Praecursor altus luminis*, on St. John the Baptist; and *Salve, tropaeum gloriae* for festivals of the Holy Cross.[4] There seems, then, less difficulty in accepting several other similar hymns in iambic tetrameters.[5] A large part of the poem on the Day of Judgement, *De Die Judicii*, which later appeared in Old English as *Be Domes Dæge*, appears also among works ascribed to Alcuin.[6] Symeon of Durham, however, gives the poem in full under the title of *Lamentatio Bedae Presbyteri*, and adds five lines, which seem to be quite genuine. In them Bede addresses Bishop Acca, and says that he has written the poem at his request.[7] This would appear to decide the question of authorship.

It was said of Bede that he was well acquainted with songs in the vernacular, and it is related how when he was dying he quoted five Old English lines on the departure of the soul from the body.[8] It is certain that Bede knew the Ambrosian hymns,[9] that he knew Aldhelm's verses,[10] and that he had skill in writing hexameters and elegiacs;[11] but, as has been well said, 'He is a

---

[1] Giles, i, p. clxix.   [2] Plummer, i, p. clviii.
[3] *Mon. Alc.*, pp. 748–9.   [4] Julian, *passim*.
[5] Giles, i. 86, 89, 92, 94, 96.   [6] *Be Domes Dæge* (E.E.T.S.), p. vi.
[7] Sym. Dun., *Hist. Reg.* xxvi.
[8] *De Obitu Baedae*, ap. Plummer, i, p. clxi.
[9] *De Art. Met.* xxiv.   [10] Browne, *Ven. Bede*, 208.   [11] Sandys, i. 468.

greater critic than a craftsman: there are cadences in his prose lovelier than anything in his poetry.'[1]

We may now return to Bede's scientific works. One of these is the *De Natura Rerum*, a kind of cosmography, based on Isidore's similar work put forth in 612; but Bede does not follow his predecessor blindly, and he uses also the work of other writers, for example, Suetonius and the younger Pliny. In 725 he wrote *De Temporum Ratione*, the date of which is fixed for us with a fair approach to certainty by the fact that in it he three times refers to that year.[2] The opening words of the preface are as follow: 'De natura rerum et ratione temporum, duos quondam stricto sermone libellos discentibus, ut rebar, necessarios composui. Quos cum fratribus quibusdam dare atque exponere coepissem, dicebant eos brevius multo digestos esse quam vellent.'[3] He felt that this desire for a more expanded treatise was due to their interest in the Easter question, and he had now complied with their wish. Though he mentions *De Temporibus* and *De Natura* here in one breath, as he does also in his list of his works,[4] it would be rash to conclude that they were necessarily written at the same date; all we can say is that the *De Natura* was composed before 725, perhaps a long time before that. The *De Temporum Ratione*, sometimes called *De Temporibus Liber Major*, was dedicated to Huætberct, and was a manual for the right calculation of the dates of the ecclesiastical festivals. With it was incorporated a section, *De Ratione Bissexti*,[5] which Bede refers to in his catalogue of books as an epistle. It was written at an earlier date[6] to Helmwald, a person of whom nothing else is known. The *De Temporum Ratione* is followed by the *Chronicon sive de Sex Aetatibus Saeculi*, which is really a part of the work, though in the folios it was printed separately; and there was appended a table for the calculation of Easter from 532 to 1063. Mindful of the trouble which had arisen over his earlier work, he reasserted his belief that the Hebrew chronology was preferable to that of the LXX. The *Chronicon* was compiled from numerous authors, and at the end Bede added four chapters in which he discussed the time of the Second Advent, the coming of Anti-Christ, the eternal

[1] H. Waddell, *The Wandering Scholars*, 6th ed., 1932, p. 38.
[2] *Temp. Rat.* xlix, lii, lviii, ap. Giles, vi. 244, 249, 256.
[3] Giles, vi. 139. [4] *H.E.* v. 24.
[5] Giles, vi. 222–6. [6] 'Quondam': *ibid.* vi. 222.

Sabbath, and the resurrection of the blessed. It has been frequently said that this treatise first introduced into England the method of calculating dates from the Incarnation, and that this method was carried from England to the Continent by English missionaries. There is reason, however, to believe that the adoption of this era originated rather from the Easter tables than from Bede's *De Temporum Ratione*;[1] but nevertheless Bede's *Ecclesiastical History* is the first historical work to use that method of reckoning.

Before 731, for he mentions it among his *epistolae ad diversos*, Bede wrote *De aequinoctio juxta Anatolium*, addressed to a priest named Wicred, in reply to certain inquiries he had made by letter concerning the paschal canon alleged to have been written by Anatolius, bishop of Laodicea. The Irish clergy relied on a spurious version of this canon, and Bede argued in this epistle that the original canon of Anatolius had upheld the more correct custom.[2] He refers to a visit which he had made to Wicred, expresses himself as 'memor familiaritatis ac dulcedinis, qua, cum illo advenirem, me suscepisti', and adds, 'Sed et quaestionem illam merito famosam . . . super qua me interrogasti praesentem, et cui breviter ut potui respondi, nunc latius etiam literis explanare studui.'[3] Unhappily, as we do not know when the letter was written, or where Wicred lived, or even who he was, we have no clue to the circumstances of this visit.

Between 725 and 731 Bede wrote *In Ezram et Neemiam Prophetas Allegorica Expositio*. The limits of date are fixed by the fact that he refers in it[4] to his account of the fifth age of the world in the chronicle attached to his *De Temporum Ratione*. In his preface to his commentary on Genesis he had expressed his intention of writing this work when opportunity offered, because after writing about the fall of man he would desire to write also about the restoration of the Jews, treating the subject allegorically as prefiguring the restoration of a repentant world to God by the Great High Priest.[5] Next, in all probability, he wrote *De Tabernaculo et Vasis ejus, ac Vestibus Sacerdotum*, an exposition, in three books, of Exodus xxiv. 12–xxx. 21. Another similar work was an allegorical explanation of 1 Kings v–vii and 2 Chronicles ii–v, entitled *De Templo Salomonis*. It was

---

[1] Poole, *Chronicles and Annals*, 25–6; *Studies*, 8, 34.
[2] C. W. Jones, ap. *Speculum*, ix. 50 ff.   [3] Giles, i. 155.
[4] *Ibid.* ix. 4.   [5] *Ibid.* vii. 2.

written after the book on the Tabernacle, because the latter work is referred to in it.[1] In a letter to Albinus, abbot of Canterbury, accompanying a copy of the *Ecclesiastical History*, which he had sent *mox ut consummare potui ad transcribendum*, Bede thanked him for some little gifts, and for the information which he had transmitted to him through Nothelm; also, since Albinus desired it, he was sending for transcription a book which he had lately published (*nuper edidi*) on the allegorical interpretation of the story of the building of Solomon's temple. The work, therefore, cannot have been completed very long before 731.

There are certain scriptural commentaries mentioned in Bede's list of his own works of whose date we have no evidence except that they were written before 731. *In Proverbia Salomonis* is an exposition of the Book of Proverbs. In the folios and some manuscripts the last portion of this is sometimes repeated as a separate tract, under the title *De Muliere Forti*. *In Cantica Canticorum* is in seven books, of which the first is directed against Julian, bishop of Celano in Campania, one of the leaders of the Pelagian party, while the seventh is merely a collection of quotations from Gregory; the other five books are a commentary on Solomon's Song. *In Canticum Habaccuc* is dedicated to some one Bede addresses as *dilectissima in Christo soror*, probably some member of a religious house for women. *In Librum Beati Patris Tobiæ* is another of these undated works. Bede says that the life and character of Tobit set forth mystically the fortunes and history of the people of Israel. Several other books of a similar nature are mentioned in Bede's list;[2] but it is probable that no genuine text of these remains to-day, and the fact that six Old Testament books are each mentioned twice in the list gives rise to a hesitating query whether Bede here was guilty of an inadvertence.[3]

Adamnan, the ninth abbot of Iona, who had been the teacher of Aldfrid of Northumbria, paid that king two visits 'in prima post bellum Ecgfredi visitatione, et in secunda interjectis duobus annis', that is to say, in 686 and 688. On the first occasion he persuaded Aldfrid to give up some Irish captives whom he held,[4] and during one or other of these visits Adamnan was converted to the Catholic usages. His stay in Northumbria, 'observing the canonical rites of the church', must have included

---

[1] *Temp. Sal.* xxiv, ap. Giles, viii. 357.   [2] *H.E.* v. 24.

[3] Giles, vii, pref.   [4] Adamnan, ii. 46.

a visit to Jarrow, and there Bede would see him. Now a certain Arculf, a Gaulish bishop, who about the year 670 had spent some time in visiting the holy places, had been driven by a storm to western Britain, and had stayed at Iona. There Adamnan committed to writing from his own lips an account of what he had seen on his pilgrimage, and on one of his visits to Aldfrid he gave a copy of this book 'On the Holy Places' to the King, who caused further copies to be made and distributed.[1] Bede wrote a summary of Adamnan's book under the title *Libellus de situ Hierusalem sive de Locis Sanctis*, adding information which he had gathered from Josephus and Eucherius, or some predecessor of Eucherius. The chapters on the sacred sites in the *Ecclesiastical History* are taken chiefly from Bede's own book.[2] It might easily be supposed that Bede made his compilation at no great length of time from his first introduction to a subject in which he obviously took great delight, and this will explain why the *De Locis Sanctis* has been dated as early as 701.[3] Bede does not mention it in the list of his works; but he says that readers may find the information they require *in eo, quod de illo dudum strictim excerpsimus.*[4] This, if we take the more common interpretation of *dudum*, must bring the composition of the book much nearer to 731.

Among Bede's publications before 731 he mentions *Omeliarum Evangelii, libri duo*. It seems probable that each of the two books contained twenty-five homilies. Dr. Giles discovered in a library at Boulogne an early manuscript containing fifty, and a comparison with those already published by Mabillon and Martène convinced him that they were all genuine; so he printed them together with a few others.[5] Certain reservations, however, have to be made with regard to them.[6] Four,[7] each a series of brief and dull comments, suffer badly by comparison with the rest, and seem entirely to lack the master's touch: two[8] are simply extracts from Bede's own commentaries on St. Mark and St. Luke respectively; and two[9] are the same sermon with a different opening. But in the remainder we have examples enough to form some idea of Bede as a preacher. He takes the Gospel for the day and expounds it, a sentence or two at a time,

---

[1] *H.E.* v. 15.
[2] *H.E.* v. 16, 17; Plummer, ii. 304.
[3] e.g. Giles, i, p. cxxxiv.
[4] *H.E.* v. 17.
[5] Giles, v.
[6] Plummer, i, p. cliii.
[7] Giles, nos. x, xii, xiii, xiv.
[8] *Ibid.*, nos. xi and xv.
[9] *Ibid.* nos. vii and lvi.

with abundant references to other passages of scripture. There is a sermon for the anniversary of the death of the founder[1] in which, after a careful explanation of his text, *Ecce nos reliquimus omnia,* he expatiates on Benedict Biscop's life and work. Another[2] is for the feast of the dedication, probably of St. Paul's, and in it he draws in great detail a mystical parallel between the temple at Jerusalem and the eternal temple. Mystical interpretation is abundant in these discourses, and so is Bede's learning both sacred and secular. Delivered in the peaceful church of a great monastery, there was no need for oratorical effect; it sufficed for the preacher to explain the scriptures, to inculcate the Christian faith, and to urge his brethren to a holy life.

The *Historia Ecclesiastica Gentis Anglorum* is of all Bede's books that on which his fame rests. His other writings are known to the few scholars; his *History,* 'a work which has nothing to be compared with it on the Continent for learning, breadth and compass',[3] is not only a priceless source of information, but a mine of lovely stories which every English schoolchild knows. His preface to King Ceolwulf shows his constant endeavour to attain accuracy by inquiring of those who might be expected to know the truth. Abbot Albinus, *auctor ante omnes atque adjutor,* sent him information by Nothelm both orally and in writing. Nothelm went to Rome, and with the permission of Pope Gregory II, searched in the papal archives. Bishop Daniel supplied him with materials for West Saxon history. Bishop Cynebert helped him with that of Lindsey. Abbot Esius, of whom nothing is known, was the main source of his knowledge of East Anglian affairs. For the life of St. Chad he went to the monks of Lastingham, for that of St. Cuthbert to the brethren of Lindisfarne. From time to time in the course of the five books we hear of other sources; Deda, abbot of Partney,[4] Bishop Wilfrid 'of blessed memory',[5] and others, while his beloved Bishop Acca, 'Dominus beatissimus et intima semper caritate venerandus,'[6] was able to give him information about St. Oswald,[7] and details about St. Wilfrid. The dedication to King Ceolwulf, manifestly written last of all, shows how the *History* came to its final form. 'Historiam . . .

---

[1] *Ibid.,* no. xxv.
[2] *Ibid.,* no. xlii.
[3] Poole, *Chron. and Ann.* 27.
[4] *H.E.* ii. 16.
[5] *Ibid.* iv. 19.   [6] *De Eo Quod Esaias,* pref.
[7] *H.E.* iii. 13; iv. 4.

quam nuper edideram, libentissime tibi desideranti, rex, et prius ad legendum ac probandum transmisi, et nunc ad transscribendum ac plenius ex tempore meditandum retransmitto.' It was Bede's usual method. How long it took the author to collect all the materials and to write the book, we cannot tell; but, as already shown, the publication may be safely assigned to the year 731.

With the *Historia Ecclesiastica*, the greatest of his books, Bede's life of authorship practically comes to an end. We only know of one more volume written after 731 which is certainly his, the *Retractationes in Acta Apostolorum*. Like St. Augustine, he said, who in later life published retractions of some of the statements he had made in his earlier writings, so he had written this little book to amend his commentary on the Acts written *plures annos ante*. There are two other works ascribed to Bede which, if they really are his, must be assigned also to the last three or four years of his life. One is a letter to Herefrid, perhaps Bede's friend at Lindisfarne, entitled *De Tonitruis*, in which the writer, though afraid of being accused of magical arts, explains the portents expressed by thunder on different days of the year. Most readers of the epistle will agree with one of Bede's biographers; 'Those who love him cannot bring themselves to believe that he wrote it.'[1] The other work is the *Poenitentiale*, 'the only work of the kind appearing under the name of Bede of which the authenticity can be maintained with any probability'.[2] So at least believed two distinguished scholars; but there are many who think otherwise.[3] There seems no certain evidence either way.

Except to go to Wearmouth, Bede seems only to have left his cell on rare occasions. In one of his Homilies he reminds his brethren of the kind welcome they always received from their friends when from any necessity they had to go outside the monastery,[4] and no doubt he took his share in preaching at various places round about. He visited Wicred, he went at least once to Lindisfarne, and in 733 he went to York and stayed with his friend Ecgberct in the minster there, *aliquot diebus legendi gratia*. As old age stole upon him, Bede looked out from his cell upon a darkening world. Politically, Northumbria

[1] Browne, *Ven. Bede*, 230.   [2] Haddan and Stubbs, iii. 326.
[3] Hunt, 216; Thurston ap. *Cath. Encycl.*, s.v. Bede; Plummer, i, pp. clvi, clvii.   [4] Giles, v. 182.

was a scene of factious strife. In 731 Ceolwulf the king, after a reign of barely two years, had been forcibly tonsured and imprisoned in a monastery, though later in the year he was restored to his throne. The religious progress chronicled in the *History* seemed to have come to a halt. There was increasing ignorance and corruption amongst the clergy, kings had impoverished themselves to make monasteries too rich, nobles and rich men had founded too many religious houses, wherein discipline was wholly relaxed. On 5 November 734, Bede wrote to Bishop Ecgberct, who had been consecrated to the see of York that year. Through failing health he had been unable to visit him again, so he must say by letter what otherwise he would have spoken face to face; and he begged him to believe that he was speaking not in arrogance but in all humility. He pleaded with him to follow a high standard of pastoral duty, to ordain learned and sufficient priests, to see that the people were visited and taught. He himself had frequently given unlettered priests a translation of the Creed and the Lord's Prayer. Let him impress on them the importance of confirmation and frequent communion. Scandalous monasteries should be put down, and their wealth devoted to better uses. What was needed most of all was episcopal visitation: consequently there should be an increase of the episcopate, and application should be made to the Pope to raise the see of York to metropolitan rank.[1]

A fortnight before Easter in the year 735 Bede's weakness became more marked, and he had great trouble with his breathing; but not much actual pain. Every day he continued to give lessons to his pupils, and what was left of the day he spent in singing psalms and antiphons. He only slept briefly at night, and his wakeful hours were occupied in prayer and thanksgiving. Words of holy writ were constantly on his lips, and in the Old English tongue, too, he sang to his brethren of that dread journey that all must take, and the judgement that comes after. On one occasion, while he was singing the antiphon for the Ascension Day *Magnificat, O rex gloriae*, when he came to the words *ne derelinquas nos orphanos*, he burst into tears: then after a time recovering himself, he began again from the beginning. Often it was more than they who tended him could bear: they wept while they sang with him, and the voices of the readers in his cell were often heard breaking. Even during this time

---

[1] *Ibid.* i. 106–40.

there were two works which he was anxious to finish, a little book of excerpts from St. Isidore and a translation into English of the Gospel according to St. John. The St. Gallen MS. adds, *usque ad eum locum in quo dicitur* 'sed haec quid sunt inter tantos?': but this hardly agrees with what follows, and seems to be an interpolation.

On Tuesday before Ascension Day he was manifestly worse, yet he taught and dictated cheerfully, saying, 'Learn quickly, I know not how long I shall be with you.' On Wednesday, after a wakeful night, he began very early, and kept them working till the third hour, at which time they had to go forth in the Rogationtide procession, bearing with them the relics of the saints; but one, a boy named Wilbert, remained with him. There was still a chapter to dictate, but the boy hesitated: it seemed hard to trouble the dying man with further questions. But he said, 'No, take thy pen and write quickly.' At the ninth hour Bede sent for the priests of the monastery, that he might distribute his few little possessions among them as parting gifts—a little incense, a little pepper, and some linen napkins. He besought them to say prayers and masses for him, and they wept and lamented for that they should see his face no more; but he rejoiced because the time of his departure was at hand, and he desired to see the King in His beauty. So it drew on to eventide, and Wilbert said, 'Dear master, there is still a sentence which is not written down.' 'Well', said he, 'then write it.' And soon the boy said, 'Now it is written,' and he answered, 'Thou has said the truth. It is finished.' Then at his request they seated him propped up on the floor of his cell, and with his face towards the sanctuary in which he had spent so many holy hours, he sang the *Gloria Patri* and breathed his last breath.

The account of his death was written in a letter which begins, 'Dilectissimo in Christo collectori Cuthwino Cuthbertus condiscipulus.' Cuthbert has been identified with Bede's fellow deacon to whom he dedicated his treatises on the Art of Metre and the Tropes of Holy Scripture; but the writer of the letter calls himself col-lector, which seems to imply that at the time of writing both Cuthwin and he were lectors, and consequently only in minor orders. The Cuthbert who wrote the letter was afterwards abbot of Wearmouth and Jarrow. In a letter to Lullus, archbishop of Mainz, he described himself as *discipulus*

Bedae presbyteri.[1] The earliest date of this letter is 755, and may be later; and there is extant another of his letters of which the earliest date is 767.[2] If he had been made deacon at the canonical age of twenty-five, and was a deacon at the same time as Bede, he would be ninety at least when the latter epistle was written, and perhaps much more. It is not impossible, but it is not very likely; and it seems best to assume that Cuthbert the *con-levita* was not the same person as Cuthbert the *collector*.

Cuthbert tells us that Bede died on Ascension Day, and the ordinary text of his letter inserts *id est vii. Kal. Junii.* The St. Gallen MS. reads *id est vii. Id. Mai.* It is obvious from Cuthbert's letter that the death took place on the Wednesday evening, *diem ultimum usque ad vesperum duxit.* The festival begins on the eve, with the first Vespers, and so it was considered that he died on Ascension Day. The St. Gallen MS. is obviously wrong with its date, 9 May. Ascension Day fell on 9 May in 720 and in 799. If Wednesday, the eve of the Ascension, is counted, it is true that it fell on 9 May in 742, which is still too late. In the letter to Ecgberct written in 734 Bede was too ill to visit, and we should make him live nearly ten years without any recorded work, which in the face of his activity even in his last days, seems impossible. The other reading, the seventh day before the Kalends of June, i.e. 26 May, gives us 735. Again, if the Wednesday be taken as the actual day of his death we are brought to 751, which is even worse than 742. The generally accepted conclusion is the only possible one. According to the civil calendar, he died in the late evening of Wednesday, 25 May 735; but according to the ecclesiastical calendar, he died after the first vespers of Ascension Day, and therefore the day of his death is accounted to be Ascension Day, which fell in that year on 26 May. His festival was, however, ultimately transferred to the 27th, because the 26th is the festival of St. Augustine of Canterbury,[3] but as late as the eleventh century Bede's name was still coupled with Augustine's on 26 May in some of the calendars of southern England.[4] Symeon of Durham says that Bede died at the age of fifty-nine; but he confused the year in which Bede finished his history with that of his death. He also says, 'In cuius, videlicet Bedae, honorem

---

[1] *Mon. Mog.* 300.   [2] *Ibid.* 290.   [3] Baring Gould, vol. May.
[4] *English Kalendars before a.d. 1100,* Henry Bradshaw Society, *passim.*

porticus ad aquilonalem plagam ecclesiae sancti Pauli in Gyrwe consecrata, venerandam fidelibus nominis eius ibidem praestat memoriam.'[1]

So passed away a great scholar and teacher. He had a facility in writing the living Latin of his age, and he did it better than his contemporaries. He had a good knowledge of the Latin poets,[2] a fair knowledge of Greek, and a little Hebrew, and a familiarity with the writings of the early Christian fathers. His knowledge of all these 'n'apparaît pas à quelques expressions, à quelques hémistiches cousus dans sa prose, à quelques épithètes intercalées dans son style, à des fragments de vers réunis en un centon, mais à des habitudes de langue qui correspondent à une réelle culture'.[3] Aldhelm preceded him as a great scholar, but has no permanent connexion with English literature, and was full of a pedantry from which Bede was free.[4] Bede's great delight was in the study of Scripture, and his guiding principle was that the glory of God is the chief end of man. His knowledge of languages and literature all helped in the mystery of interpretation; the rules of prosody and accentuation enabled the psalter to be sung correctly in divine service. Astronomy and the *computus* were needed in order that the right festival days might be kept. He studied ecclesiastical controversies that his pupils might be grounded in the right faith and he wrote history that men might see the wondrous things that God had wrought. Some of his pupils rose to great distinction. Lullus, who completed his studies at Jarrow during Bede's later years, and left there in 732,[5] became archbishop of Mainz. Tradition, for which there is good evidence, makes Ecgberct, afterwards archbishop of York, one of his pupils.[6] At any rate he was a friend, and it is not a far-fetched supposition that Bede's influence indirectly stimulated the growth of the great school of York, to which, through Æthelberht, who succeeded Ecgberct as head, Alcuin owed the foundation of his learning.

Bede's fame spread widely. Copies of his works reached the Continent almost during his lifetime.[7] Boniface and Lullus wrote asking for copies,[8] as did many other continental scholars

---

[1] *Hist. Dun.* i. 14. [2] Manitius, *passim.* [3] Roger, 308–9.
[4] Bright, 336–7. [5] D. A. Haigh, ap. *Y.A.J.* iii. 363, 377.
[6] R. B. Hepple, ap. *Arch. Ael.*, 2nd ser., xiv. 99.
[7] E. A. Lowe, ap. *Eng. Hist. Rev.* xli. 244–6; O. D. Rojdestvensky, ap. *Speculum*, iii. 314 ff. [8] *Mon. Mog.* 180, 181, 250, 288–90, 300.

in the succeeding century and the next. To-day manuscripts of his works are to be found in most of the great libraries of Europe. Hardy calculated 133 of the *Historia Ecclesiastica* alone,[1] and there are others which he missed. Alcuin sang of miracles wrought by Bede's relics.[2] In England the *Ecclesiastical History* was translated into English, perhaps by Ælfric.[3] His feast day was not observed in southern England in the Middle Ages, but it was long honoured at York.[4] It was in Durham that he was best remembered. Thither were brought the bones which Ælfred Westou stole from Jarrow about 1020,[5] and in the great church built by William of Saint-Calais and Ralph Flambard they first found a resting place beside St. Cuthbert. Next to the body of St. Cuthbert they were the abbey's proudest possession. Bishop Hugh Puiset enshrined them in a silver feretory enriched with gold.[6] At the instance of Richard of Barnard Castle this was at a later date removed to the Galilee, and placed on a monument of blue marble supported by five pillars. On Ascension Day, Whit-Sunday, and Trinity Sunday the feretory was carried in procession out of the north door along the South Bailey, and in at the great gate. Bede was represented in at least six windows in the church; of the four bells in the Galilee one was called St. Bede's bell; a mazer, St. Bede's bowl, was kept in the frater house.[7] At the Dissolution his remains are said to have been buried in the Galilee. When the grave was examined in 1831 there were found four bones of the skull, five portions of the arm bones, part of the breastbone, two thigh-bones, and eight small bones of the feet.[8] There are two manuscripts in the Chapter Library each bearing the inscription, *de manu Bedae*, an *Evangelarium* and a copy of *Cassiodorus super Psalterium*. As they were evidently written by different hands they cannot both be his; but the tradition cannot be entirely rejected, and we like to think that Bede wrote one of them.[9] At Monkton is Bede's well, to which sick children were brought for healing as late as the eighteenth century, and in St. Paul's, Jarrow, there is a chair called Bede's chair, parts of which may be genuine. In days

[1] Plummer, ii, p. lxxxvi.
[2] *Carmen de Pont. Eccl. Ebor.* i. 1300–17.
[3] Ker, 310.
[4] Thurston, ap. *Cath. Encycl.*, s.v. Bede.
[5] Sym. Durh., *Hist. Dun.* iii. 7.   [6] *Script. Tres*, 11.
[7] *Rites, passim.*   [8] Raine, *Durham Cathedral*, 79–82.
[9] Hughes, xxxvii, and 21.

II

THE AGE OF BEDE

THE prospects of Christianity and of Western civilization seemed dark in the year 735, when the Venerable Bede died. It is true that he could not, so defective were communications, know the worst. He was ignorant of the triumphant progress of Islam. The Hegira in 622, when Mahomet first raised his standard, was the beginning of victories which subjected half Christendom in little more than a century to a rival religion; and it was within Bede's life, in 732, that Charles Martel inflicted the first serious check upon its advance by his victory in the battle which is usually called that of Poitiers. The whole of northern Africa, from Egypt to Morocco, was subjected to the Caliphate, which as yet was an undivided monarchy; and in Asia the limits of Christianity as the dominant religion were those of Asia Minor, from the Aegean Sea to the Euphrates; Syria was lost to Christendom. For several centuries Asia Minor seemed secure; it was not till the fatal battle of Manzikert, in 1071, that the Turks, who had overthrown the Syrian Caliphate, broke the barrier and began to extirpate Christianity in what had been one of its strongholds. It seems at first sight a strange accident that Theodore, the organizer of the English Church, should have come from a place so remote as Tarsus. But Tarsus was within Asia Minor, which was solidly Christian and orthodox and was in fact through its wealth and its abundant population the chief source of the power of the Emperors who reigned at Constantinople. Savage raids were made from Syria, and retaliation of the same kind was made from Constantinople, but no serious harm was done.

In fact, the solidarity of Christendom was increased, since the formidable bodies of heretics, Monophysite and Nestorian, which had troubled the peace of the Empire were now in the main subjects of the Caliph, and loyalty and orthodoxy coincided. Naturally enough, the Caliphs favoured sects which were hostile to the government of Constantinople; that has always been the Mahometan policy, and as late as the sixteenth and seventeenth centuries the Turks, as masters of Hungary and Transylvania, favoured Lutherans and Calvinists on whose hostility to the House of Hapsburg they could rely. Thus, within the Empire and on its Christian outskirts the only doctrine that prevailed, or of whose existence men were aware, was the normal Catholic orthodoxy. For as yet there was no hatred between Constantinople and Rome. The claim that the authority of Rome is different in kind from that of the other patriarchates had not been made; in fact, stress was laid at Rome on imperial grants as the source of its prerogatives, and soon after Bede's death the famous fiction of the Donation of Constantine was to be invented in support of the same claim. For Rome, till it publicly rejected the authority of the Emperor in 772, was admitted to be a part of the Empire, and during most of Bede's life the popes were orientals, either Greek or Syrian, the latter being members of the orthodox minority in the Caliph's dominions. Between 685 and 753 only one pope out of ten was an Italian. This deference to the Emperor at Constantinople was natural when the Lombards, Arian at first and afterwards almost as hostile when they had become Catholic, were threatening to incorporate Rome in their Italian kingdom. For the Lombards, akin to the Vikings of the north, were among the most savage of the Germanic tribes, and Rome with the other fragments of imperial rule in Italy was compelled in self-defence to be loyal to Constantinople. It was, in fact, only when the emperors could not, or would not, spend the strength which they needed to protect themselves from the Caliphs upon the struggle against the Lombards that the popes changed the course of European history by calling in the Franks to their defence and, as an inevitable consequence, by consenting to the creation of a rival Frankish Empire of the West after the Lombards had been overthrown. As to the Christian subjects of the Caliphate, it must be borne in mind that the Koran forbade compulsory conversion to Mahometanism, and that the special taxation imposed upon Christians was so important a part of the Caliphs' revenues that they were little disposed to press them to abandon their faith. This was especially the case in Spain, where the greater part of the Christians endured humiliation rather than forsake their religion: it was also the case in Syria, where John of Damascus, a younger contemporary of Bede, spent under Moslem tolerance a laborious life in compiling the first system of Christian theology from the Greek Fathers with such success that it has permanently satisfied the orthodox East, which has never advanced into or beyond the scholastic phase, though Albert and Aquinas were willing to take hints from John's Aristotelian exposition of the faith when it was translated into Latin. But, however we may resent the treatment of Christians who were worthy of the name, we cannot doubt that Mahomet's teaching was the source of a genuine revival of religion among his followers, and that this was in great measure the cause of his swift and astonishing success.

While Christendom had suffered so serious a loss in the south —a loss which had not reached its full dimensions around the Mediterranean till after the death of Bede—its increase in north and central Europe had not yet been great. We are not concerned with Teutonic and Slavonic paganism for its own sake; we shall have to consider its effect upon the half-converted populations. But the great shifting of peoples due to the western advance of the Germans was now complete, and the Slavs were in possession of the lands east of the Elbe which had been, and now again are, Teutonic. The Slavs have been Germanized and Germans have migrated eastward. Already in the eighth century the Slavs to the west of the Elbe had been subjected to the Franks, and therefore Christianized, while of the Germans only the fierce and independent Saxons remained pagan, to be converted and conquered by Charlemagne towards the end of the century. Adjacent to them the Frisians, protected by their marshes, were already being won by the mission work which Bede describes.

To the north dwelt the Scandinavians, as yet untouched by Christianity though influenced, and in a sense civilized, by commercial contact with Constantinople and with Persia. They had opened communication by way of the great Russian rivers with the Black Sea and the Caspian. Though they had not yet discovered the possibilities of aggression by sea that were to make the Vikings so terrible throughout western Europe in the ninth and following centuries, they were already savages in temper. They had laws and customs akin to those of our ancestors, but little regard for human life. Interments on the Volga have shown that the Scandinavian Russians practised that horrible rite of sacrificing companions for the dead which Herodotus had found in use among the Sarmatians of the same region. But they had also, unlike the other Teutonic races, a strong and definite religion, or rather fatalism, which found expression in a most striking literature which served as a pattern to the other Northern races. The English epic of *Beowulf* and the German *Nibelungenlied*, which was put into its permanent shape so late as about 1200, are Scandinavian in character and manner.

When the first Teutons became Christian it was under the influence of Constantinople, and at the time when Arianism was dominant there. They believed that they were being admitted into Christianity in its most authentic form—that to which the Emperor himself adhered. They had no suspicion, and made no conscious choice between one type and another of the faith. But their adhesion to Arianism, given first by the Goths and then in succession by the several tribes when they submitted to what was the creed of civilization, was to be fatal. They conquered the various provinces of the western half of the Empire, but they could not amalgamate with their population. They remained an alien aristocracy and a minority which steadily diminished till each Arian kingdom succumbed in turn either to a revival of the Empire's force or to a kindred race which had been fortunate enough to postpone its conversion till orthodoxy was dominant in the world. The one exception was Spain, where after a severe internal struggle the Goths accepted the Nicene doctrine. In Italy, though the Lombards towards the end of their domination made the same change, the bitterness engendered by their tyranny could not be overcome, and the Franks were called in to rescue the people from a rule against which Constantinople could not, or would not, protect them.

The Franks are the worst instance of a political conversion. Clovis, baptized on Christmas Day 496, was in the middle of a successful career of which assassination had been one of the chief methods. He had the wisdom to choose Paris for his capital and united for the time the greater part of what was to become France. He had the statesmanship to be aware of the dislike of the Catholics and their bishops for their Arian rulers; and the orthodox bishops were very tolerant of his crimes. For Clovis was as murderous and treacherous after his conversion as before; for him and his followers the acceptance of catholic Christianity meant no change in morality, and the history of the time as recorded by Gregory of Tours, himself a bishop of Latin descent, shows how men, themselves not unworthy of their calling, could narrate as a matter for no special reprobation a string of the wildest crimes. His dynasty may be said to culminate in the strife between Brunhild and Fredegund, with the barbarous fate of the former. Gregory the Great was in frequent and friendly intercourse with Brunhild, urging her to hold councils for the reform of the Gallican Church and to forward the mission of St. Augustine, whom he was sending through her territories towards England. Popes have often found it necessary to ask the assistance of very strange allies.

Whether English history may not have had forgotten stains of the Frankish kind we cannot say. There is a grim example, perhaps one among many, in the pages of Bede. The Isle of Wight was the last harbour of English paganism, and King Cædwalla of Wessex determined to annex it. He was no pagan, but, after the custom of the time, an unbaptized Christian, and he made a vow that, if he were successful, he would give a third part of the land and the booty to Christ. He was successful, and according to Bede he exterminated the people and replaced them with West Saxons; but ancient stories of extermination are always doubtful. Bishop Wilfrid, who was holding the see of Sussex, accepted his share of the land. Two *regii pueri*, brothers of Arvald, king of Wight, had escaped from the slaughter and found refuge at Stoneham on the mainland. They were betrayed to Cædwalla, who commanded them to be slain. The abbot of Redbridge, in the neighbourhood, interceded for the lads, and asked for time to instruct and baptize them. He did baptize them, and rendered their entrance into the kingdom of heaven sure. 'When the executioners came upon them, they gladly underwent the temporal death whereby they were certainly assured that they would pass into eternal life.'[1] Bede tells the story without any sign of abhorrence, and as though it were a normal incident. We are reminded of the tale, as well authenticated as most that concern St. Patrick, of the maidens Ethne and Fedelm whom Patrick instructed and baptized on the bank of the Shannon. In Dr. Bury's rendering it runs that the saint taught them the faith: 'with one voice and with one heart the two king's daughters said "Tell us with all diligence how we may believe in the heavenly King that we may see Him face to face, and we will do as thou sayest."' After they had made their confession of faith, the story continues: 'Then Patrick baptized them in the fountain and placed a white veil on their heads, and they begged that they might behold the face of Christ. And

[1] *H.E.* iv. 14.

Patrick said "Until ye shall taste of death ye cannot see the face of Christ, and unless ye shall receive the sacrifice." They answered "Give us the sacrifice that we may see the Son, our bridegroom." And they received the Eucharist, and fell asleep in death. And they were placed in one bed, and their friends mourned them.'[1] This has been interpreted as a case of religious suicide. However that may be, and Bury quotes similar instances from Ireland, in any case it relieves Bede from the suspicion of having indulged in pious verbiage when he speaks of rejoicing in the prospect of death. We must remember that, apart from the points of discipline in which he condemned Irish practice, Bede had a deep reverence for Irish piety and shared the credulity of his age.

That credulity was beyond measure. In part it was the survival of a paganism that had never been extirpated: of which, indeed, we still see such remnants as the dropping of pins into wells that once were sacred to forgotten deities. The penitential writers constantly find occasion to denounce sacrifices, and to provide appropriate penances for them; and pagan notions are common in literature. The pagan hell of the north was frozen; that was a terror more present than the furnace of the south, and quite late in the Anglo-Saxon period was used in the Blickling Homilies to intimidate sinners, while in the Irish Apocalyptic legends the lost oscillate between freezing and burning torments. But the continuity with the past was not limited to details. In impressive poetry such as *Beowulf*, put into its present shape within the Christian period, the whole range of pagan moral and philosophical ideas is expounded, lightly coloured by some Christian allusions. And the general tone of Anglo-Saxon poetry is pensive, and even melancholy, so profound is the sense of man's helplessness against an inexorable fate. The practical morality of retaliation is assumed as the rule of life.

With these reminiscences of paganism there persisted in Christian minds a multitude of strange and sometimes mischievous notions that received their death-blow not at the Reformation, but in the course of the Civil War. John Aubrey, the father of English folk-lore, lays stress on the disappearance after the Restoration of superstitious ideas and practices which till then had been accepted without doubt. This momentous change

---

[1] Bury, 140, 307 *n.*

meant the abandonment of the whole traditional view of nature which culminated in the encyclopaedia of Vincent of Beauvais. The science of nature, or of what passed for nature, had taken the form of accumulations of instances. True observations and, equally with them, the absurdest of falsehoods were uncritically heaped together. It occurred to no one to examine them. There was no standard of probability, and impossibilities in the natural order excited no more doubt than the strangest and least edifying of miracles. Human thought had been steadily deteriorating for many generations. The elder Pliny belonged to a lower order of mind than Aristotle, and from Pliny downwards thought grew feebler and feebler. No one was more characteristic of this decadence than Gregory the Great, or more influential in depressing the intelligence of the generations which followed him.

But there was a special cause for this credulity. The one literary impulse of the time was derived from monasticism, and among monks and their admirers it was a point of honour to be credulous. Each body of monks, and sometimes each individual monk, was eager to cap the wonders which surrounded his or their rivals. This competition was never more grotesque than in the days when monachism was a novelty ; and in obedience to the general thought of ages which regarded the past as superior to the present and therefore made it a point of honour to reproduce the phenomena of the past so far as might be possible, the standard of eccentricity was sedulously maintained. It had been set in the region where improbability was most in vogue. It is not an accident that Egypt, the land where Herodotus collected his wildest and often most indecorous incidents, was also the birthplace of monasticism. Herodotus listened to the tales of the priests, Christian pilgrims to those of or about monks and hermits, and there is a startling resemblance, in all respects save that of propriety, in the narratives collected from the two singularly different types of religionists. They were equally capable of developing profound religious ideas and of inventing stories which might be frivolous. For these Egyptians were far from the Greek standards of thought which prevailed at Alexandria ; monasticism is the one contribution to civilization made by the Copts, and they were able to make it in part because the grotesque attire in which they clothed it caught the imagination of a decadent age.

For in the course of the fourth century a passion for visiting the monks of Egypt developed. The first pilgrim who set down his experience in writing was a bishop named Palladius from Asia Minor who composed the *Historia Lausiaca*, an account of his travels dedicated to a certain Lausus. It had an extraordinary influence, for it is ably written and touchingly sincere, whether he is recording wise words and mystical piety or feats of astonishing abstinence, or again when he relates visions and miracles, some of which came under his own observation. Occasionally they remind us of the wonders of Eastern magic or anticipate the feats of the Egyptian Hall. In any case they fixed in the general mind the conviction that the supernatural was a customary element in monastic life, which therefore was higher than any other human activity.

Thus a type of religion which in its lower phases reminds us of Dr. E. B. Tylor's observation that among certain negroes the sense of reality is so feeble and the dreams so vivid that they are never thoroughly awake or quite asleep spread from Egypt both to the East and the West. Everywhere it excited emulation. Cassian's *Collations* did for the Latin-speaking world what the Lausiac History had done for the Greek, in spite of the hostility of St. Augustine, who regarded him as a semi-Pelagian. He, like Palladius, had visited the Egyptian deserts in the search for examples of Christian perfection, and no books were more widely circulated and copied than his throughout the Middle Ages. They are, of course, full of miracles, visions, and the like, and mark a turning-point of thought. Towards the end of the fourth century St. Hilary of Poitiers, a philosopher as well as a great theologian, made the observation that miracles in his day had ceased. In the days of persecution, he allowed, they had abounded; yet in the authentic *Acta Martyrum* none are recorded, which is a fact that Hilary has not called to mind. His explanation of the change is that in an age of security miracles were no longer necessary for the encouragement of the faithful. A generation later, when Coptic thought had overwhelmed Alexandrian, miracles once more abounded. Credulity came into vogue. It had no exponent so impressive and so convinced as Gregory the Great. He was always looking for displays of the supernatural, and he was not critical in his examination of sources. A good ghost story which he tells was anticipated, though he certainly did not know it, by the younger Pliny and by Lucian in his *Philopseudes*. Yet we must bear in mind that this deterioration of mind was not specifically Christian; the decadent paganism of the age was equally haunted by un-accountable phenomena.

Monasticism coloured the whole Christianity of those times. It stands to the credit of Egypt that it not only produced the most striking of hermits, whose pattern was copied in the West, but that St. Pachomius, a Copt in all his characteristics, framed the first scheme for an organized religious life and carried it out with such success that St. Basil in the East and St. Benedict in the West professed themselves his disciples. He first devised those agglomerations of scattered buildings within a surrounding wall, of which the remains are still found in Ireland; but it is still more to his honour that he banished from his communi-ties the besetting sin of competition in austerity. Not that he was lax in his life; the stone couch of St. Pachomius in *The Monastery* is one of the recondite pieces of erudition that are often to be found in Scott. But the life was to be uniform: all were to conform to the same rule, which with him meant a level of life which a healthy peasant might maintain. The same standard was set by St. Benedict, who strictly forbade any boast-ing on the part of visitors to Monte Cassino of austerities achieved elsewhere. This they held was demoralizing; their purpose was uniformity in work, study, and worship, and Pachomius was again an innovator in opening this life to women as well as to men.

The chief difference between this life and that lived by later monks was that the Eucharist had but a small part in it. The original hermits, whose glory was their isolation, were necessarily destitute of the privilege, and since their solitude was their pride, and in the eyes of their admirers was part of their merit, they cannot have regarded the deprivation as a loss. So much of this mind still remained at the end of the fourth century that by the Rule of St. Pachomius no monk might be ordained priest, though priests might be admitted into the community and would naturally exercise their function within it. The rule that monks of due age must enter Holy Orders dates only from the days when the assumption had been generally accepted that bishop, priest, and deacon correspond to the Jewish ministry of high priest, priest, and levite, and have the biblical right to tithe. That comparison between the ministries of the Old and the New Covenant was never accepted in the East, where the patristic canons know nothing of a right of the clergy to tithe; in the West, it served as a justification for depriving the local clergy of an endowment to which monks, provided they were in the higher orders, had an equal claim. But this line of thought, which St. Ambrose probably had the chief share in propagating, had not gained authority in the lifetime of Bede.

In regard to the inner life, the accurate verbal knowledge of Scripture was, and continued to be, a character of the monk. It may have begun in the general ignorance of devout peasants, who learned by heart what they were unable to read. When the custom began of adopting children into the vocation, the Psalter was the beginning of their training, and it is evident that the profit was great. The passages best fitted to express their mind were present in their memory, and there are striking resemblances between their utterances and those of devout Presbyterians as recorded or imagined in the serious Scottish fiction of the last generation. The possession of so elevated a vocabulary for the expression of their thoughts was in itself a spiritual education. This perhaps was especially a characteristic of the solitaries; but in the convents the hours devoted to study and thought were fruitful in developing a practical philosophy. The practical psychology which was worked out, with its classification of mental states and especially of vices, was to be the starting-point of all casuistry and of much scholasticism. Yet we may be tempted to suspect that the elaborate arrangement of scales of sins, possible and impossible, with their appropriate penalties, was to some extent a game of patience devised to enliven the monotony of monastic life. We certainly have no right to think that it represents what was the actual experience of monastic communities. The Penitentials, in which it was put into shape, had a vogue for some centuries, and reached England with Theodore of Tarsus. When the Middle Ages developed a thought of their own, this very unattractive literature lost its position. But in the age of Bede it was at the height of its authority, and reigned equally among Celtic and among Latin Christians, both having learnt it from the same source.

In another respect monastic practice was to influence all later Christian observance. The monk, aiming at perfection, was introspective. He wished to know what progress, if any, he was making, and in an eminently social life, where all were interested in the welfare of others and all were under authority, there ought to be no secrets. Confession and penance hitherto had been concerned only with outrageous breaches of the Divine Law; sensitive consciences within the monastery wished to reveal their subjective failures and to gain strength through correction and through guidance. But the monks were the model Christians of their age, and the thought spread that what was good in their case must be of general value. There is reason to believe that it was first in England that the practice of confession, of private penance, and of guidance arose in the case of persons living godly lives in the world, and that by the time of Bede the custom was well established. It was not, however, till the General Council of 1215 that it was made obligatory for all to make confession at least once a year before receiving communion. The minimum became the general rule in both respects, and undoubtedly its observance tended to become perfunctory.

If we turn from the modes of thought in the eighth century to the organization of its life, we are struck by the fact that its leaders were not like the first preachers of Christianity, below the higher levels of their time, nor, like modern missionaries, superior in education to those whom they aspired to convert, but on exactly the same level. Gregory the Great, for instance, was influential because he was the average man of his age, taken at its best. The tendencies of the time were uniform both in the East and in the West, and Gregory, as a practical man, obeyed and inculcated them. The movement was towards what came to be known as feudalism; not that it was yet organized or named. In Asia Minor and throughout the Eastern Empire great landlords were securing their position, and so also in the West. Among them were the great churchmen. The bishops, and especially the Pope, were entrusted by the State with large powers of government and with judicial authority. The Church was placed by the State in their hands; each was the sole responsible officer in his diocese, the only person who could hold property or receive income on its behalf. The clergy were absolutely under the bishop's control, and had no rights against any arbitrary action on his part; on the other hand, he was bound to maintain any whom he ordained, and they were unable to seek a position in another diocese. To meet the charges upon them the bishops could look, at any rate before the collapse of the Western Empire, to considerable subsidies from the State.

But their main dependence came to be on endowments, which were liberally bestowed. Wealthy families of Latin descent tended to die out, and the Church was a frequent legatee. The consequence was that the greater prelates came to be land-owners in many provinces: the popes, especially, drew revenues from all parts of the Empire, and we know that while Milan was under the Arian Lombards, who saw to it that their own bishop received that portion of the income of the see which was drawn from Lombard lands, his orthodox rival was maintained by rents from southern Italy which was under the rule of the Emperor at Constantinople. In England it was not till 1836 that 'peculiar' jurisdictions were abolished. They rose from the fact that forgotten benefactors, before the Norman Conquest, had endowed English sees with lands outside their dioceses, and that the bishops, whether voluntarily or in obedience to a custom too strong to be disobeyed, endowed the ministry in those places. The local bishop had contributed nothing, and it may be assumed that his diocesan fund was relieved to the extent of the endowment; it seemed therefore to the patron— the advowson was always attached to the endowment—that the bishop had no right in the place. The grantor claimed a 'peculiar' jurisdiction, which often was fiercely disputed. Harrow in Middlesex was, for instance, part of a Canterbury peculiar, and the bishops of London resented what they re-garded as an encroachment on their rights. The correspondence of Gregory the Great contains many instructions to his agents in distant provinces concerning ecclesiastical affairs which came within his cognisance as landlord, not as pope. But this irregularity, as it seems to us, was not confined to the western provinces of what had been the Empire. It had invaded the East, and reached its extreme development in Ireland, where episcopacy was reduced to insignificance and bishops came to be subject to abbots, though there is no reason to doubt that in the beginning of Irish Christianity there was an effective episcopal government. But throughout the Dark and the Middle Ages the machinery of government was inefficient, and in the England of Bede bishops regarded themselves as at liberty to offer their services where they seemed to be needed, without respect to conventional limitations. It is not till after the puri-fication which followed the Danish raids that we can look for regularity of administration. Nor can we find much evidence for ecclesiastical order within the dioceses. The first known English archdeacons appear after Theodore's arrival. Before that, all we can discover is that the more earnest bishops made missionary tours among a quite unorganized body of clergy and an uninstructed laity. When Peada, the son of the heathen king Penda, desired a Christian bride and sought her in Northumbria, he was told that if he and his people would be baptized he should have his wish. He agreed, and after some instruction he with all his company, his earls, knights, and their attendants, was baptized. Four priests were sent to complete the work, and the whole people of the South Angles became Christian without hesitation. We may doubt whether the instructions were adequate. We know from Bede that in Kent it was not till some fifty years had passed since the arrival of St. Augustine that King Earconbert enforced the destruction of idols and made the observance of Lent compulsory; we cannot imagine that this act of violence, even if it were maintained long enough to produce a considerable effect, succeeded in abolishing the survivals of paganism. On the other hand, Bede also tells how Pippin of Heristal bribed the Frisians 'with great advantages' to become Christian; here also we must doubt the heartiness of conversion.

If the problems were complicated in the case of secular converts and the clergy charged with them, they were simpler in regard to the beginnings of monasticism. If a handful of earnest people chose to live a devotional life in each others' company, and without expense to the bishop, most of them, if not all, being laymen, what right had the bishop to meddle? It could only be on the ground that he was, by the letter of the law, the authorized holder of trusts for religious purposes. But the founders of such religious houses had no wish, sometimes for strong reasons, to vest their foundations in the bishop; and the consequence was that patronage often lapsed to the family of the founder. No form of trust had as yet been devised for securing perpetuity, and the best that the heir could do was to maintain for his own life, if he wished, the religious use, and leave to his own heirs the responsibility of continuing, if they chose, this employment of a part of their inheritance. In course of time formulae, more or less efficacious, came to be devised, the earliest being such maledictions as Sterne has imitated in his curse of Ernulphus. But for England our information begins with the arrival of Theodore, no documents concerning church endowments having survived from the earlier period.

One strange abuse which dates, so far as we know, from the later years of Bede, who laments it in the latest of his writings, the Epistle to Ecgberct, bishop, afterwards archbishop, of York, is that of fraudulent monasteries. It was not peculiar to England: it is recorded at the same period in the Eastern Empire, when social conditions in regard to the predominance of the land-owning class resembled those in western Europe, and also in the parts of Europe adjacent to England. Grantees of land would profess to devote them to monastic purposes, which meant that they were exempt from certain public charges to which other lands were liable; and would then enjoy this exemption and at the same time keep the whole profit for themselves. Things, Bede says, had come to such a pass that Northumbrian kings could no longer find land at their disposal for grants to noblemen. Since the condition of such charters or grants of land, called 'bookland' in the south and 'sunderland' in the north of England, was that the holders should furnish a number of soldiers proportionate to its value for the king's service, the fraudulent monasteries were an injury to the state, and, from a date which Bede gives as about 705, the kings had connived at the abuse by selling such grants for an immediate personal profit, well knowing how they would be employed, while bishops had assented. Nominal monasteries for women were established on the same terms. Nor can we assume that more regularly administered monasteries were above reproach. There was much laxity, and especially that constant temptation of medieval monks, indulgence in field-sports, already prevailed. But all this was swept away by the invasions of the Northmen, and the monasticism which revived under Alfred and his successors made a fresh start, and was hardly affected by the traditions of its predecessor.

Of endowments internal to the parish it is needless to speak at length. There is no doubt that parochial glebe passed unchanged, with the same rights and the same liabilities, from the last pagan to the first Christian priest. This needed no public sanction. The priest of either creed was the 'man' of his lord, and the process whereby he became the bishop's 'man', in days much later than Bede's, is an important chapter in history. The priest's glebe throughout the Teutonic countries was normally twice as large as that of the ordinary copyholder (to borrow a later word) and he was free from the servile tasks with which the other subjects of the manor were burdened. But this obligation was not confined to England. It is found in all countries where Teutons were at home or became settled, from Scandinavia to Tyrol and Lombardy, with some parts of Spain. A detailed study of the places where the special servitude of providing male animals for the flocks and herds of his parishioners was, or was not, imposed upon the parish priest would furnish a good test of the extent to which different localities fell under Teutonic influence. It seems, for example, to have prevailed in eastern more than in western France. In England a few rectors were still providing a bull and a boar in the earlier years of Queen Victoria. The other chief source of clerical income, tithe, had not become a compulsory or even a general payment in the eighth century, for the doctrine that the Christian ministry, designed after the analogy of the Jewish with three grades, had therefore inherited the Mosaic right to maintenance from tithe, was as yet only a matter of private opinion.

By the time of Bede's death a beginning had been made of a parochial system, though it was only approaching completeness towards the end of the Anglo-Saxon period, when public opinion seems to have required the holder of five hides to provide a church and priest for his tenants. But even after the Norman Conquest there were instances of parishes, if they should be so called, of enormous acreage and value, such as Whalley in Lancashire, Scarborough in Yorkshire, Luton in Bedfordshire, and Bosham in Sussex. They had become mischievous anomalies, but they represent the primitive condition when priests were very few. They were quasi-ecclesiastical family endowments, and by annexation to abbeys or otherwise they were brought within the lines of ordinary ecclesiastical administration.

The office of the bishop was of extraordinary importance. He was recognized as the representative of a higher civilization than that of the invading tribes. In the old Roman cities on the Continent his judicial office was more important than it had been while the Empire survived, for he was now the sole exponent of Roman legal ideas. In regard to the traditional law of the Teutonic tribes, certainly in England and probably elsewhere, it was under Christian influence that it was put into writing, and made more rational and merciful in the process.

The bishops made the most of their position, and were justified in so doing by the opportunity it gave them of guiding kings and chiefs into humanity and purity. It seems safe to assume that as the minor chiefs in the pagan period had each his priest, without whom his status would have been defective, so the king had his chief priest, whose counsel he was expected to receive. That he had more than one such chief priest is not probable. As the parish priest of the Christian Teutons took the place of the pagan priest, so the pagan high priest was the predecessor of the Christian bishop. That he was localized is unlikely; wherever the king reigned the bishop exercised his function, and in Scandinavia, where primitive conditions lasted longest, dioceses with definite frontiers were not established till the middle of the twelfth century, when Cardinal Nicholas Brakespear, the future Pope Hadrian IV, was charged with the northern legation. Till then, the bishops, who had a great share in establishing the power of the kings over the nobles, had been attached to the kings and had moved about with them.

In England the first bishops were equally connected with the kings. St. Augustine was sent with a papal letter to the king of Kent, and the other bishops who founded missions also were associated with kings, and the conversion of subjects was perilously rapid when kings led the way. Little attempt was made, or perhaps could have been made, to instruct before baptism. Bede in his latest writing, the Epistle to Ecgberct, says that he has translated the Lord's Prayer and the Apostle's Creed into English for the convenience of illiterate priests, that they might teach them to their flocks; if then priests could not execute so simple a task for themselves, we may doubt whether they could understand the Latin services which they repeated. He speaks of monks and clerics who are ignorant of Latin, leaving us to assume that priests had some knowledge of the language. This ignorance was certainly universal among the laity, and this increased the responsibility, and the power, of the higher clergy who were called into the king's counsels.

In Kent, the kingdom first converted, the authority of the clergy was dangerously excessive. In the earliest English laws, those of St. Augustine's convert Ethelbert, the status of the clergy was higher than that of the king. Rank in primitive England, as in other Teutonic countries, was indicated by the fine for injuring property. Ethelbert and his wise men ordained a twelvefold compensation for wrong done to the archbishop, elevenfold to the bishop—the only bishop in Kent was at Rochester, and the existence of a second see in the kingdom is proof that its unity was incomplete and somewhat modern— ninefold for the king and clergy, with more modest scales for humbler folk. We can only assume that in their enthusiasm for the new creed and in their confidence in its exponents, the men of Kent offered this distinction, and that it was accepted because the recipients were confident that they could make good use in the interest of religion of the homage to their character which it indicated. Often enough Christian missionaries have used opportunities of the same kind; the Jesuits in Paraguay are an instance of an experiment in the use of authority which was not allowed to develop, and in the last generation an English (not an Anglican) missionary in the Pacific made so full a use of the authority entrusted to him by his converts that a British gunboat had to be sent to fetch him away. There are no later examples in Anglo-Saxon laws of bishops set above kings. There are one or two of equality; but as time went on kings grew scarce and finally were reduced to one, and under Alfred we find bishops classed, with the aldermen of counties and other dignitaries, as king's thegns.

The office of bishop was intended in England by Gregory the Great to be held by monks. This, an innovation rendered possible because monks had recently become an organized class, is a peculiarity of the English Church which was rarely imitated elsewhere and then under the influence of the English example. Yet it came to Gregory only as an afterthought. When he dispatched Augustine and his party from Rome, their head received only the indefinite title of *praepositus*, or 'leader'. But when they grew discouraged on their journey and sent a deputation back with the petition that they might be released from their dangerous quest, Gregory refused this, and to encourage Augustine gave him a more definite position and a higher authority by constituting him abbot over his company. This did not mean that they were turned into monks, whether they would or no, for the entrance into monasticism was a voluntary act. It meant that Augustine was to receive from all, whether or not they had taken vows, the obedience which followers of St. Benedict owed to their abbot. And in fact there is evidence that till the Norman Conquest the chapter of Canterbury was a composite body, including both monks and seculars; and doubtless there were both in the original company, which numbered forty, according to the tradition which Bede had received.

Though in course of time these composite bodies became wholly monastic or wholly secular, there is no doubt that Gregory designed that their heads should be monastic. And, at any rate in monastic circles, this aspiration remained. When Bede, in his Epistle to Ecgberct, was sketching an ecclesiastical policy for northern England, he advised Ecgberct, the last bishop of York, to take the step, which he actually took soon after Bede's death, of asking the Pope to confer upon him the *pallium*, or token of archiepiscopal rank, and, when he had received this, to use his new power by consecrating bishops and dividing his province into several dioceses. Provision for them, Bede said, could be found in existing monasteries: we have seen that Bede advocated the abolition of useless houses of the kind. Let the king of Northumbria increase the endowment of the monasteries he selected for the purpose that it might be adequate to maintain a bishop and his staff as well as the monks. The latter might resent the loss of independence they would suffer when they came under the control of a bishop: in compensation for this, let them have the right of electing the bishop out of their own number.

This was probably no more than a devout imagination. The evidence, so far as it goes, is against such election. We hear of nomination by the king, as indeed we might expect, since the bishop stood to the king in the same relation as the parish priest stood to the lord of the village. We hear sometimes of election of a bishop by the laity of the diocese. The office was, in fact, of such political importance that the characteristic virtues of a devout monk were not those that would be of most avail in so disorderly a world. And the tenure might be very precarious. Bishops might offer themselves to kings who accepted their service without credentials and without reference to Canterbury. One stray prelate from Gaul, of whose antecedents Bede knows nothing, was the first bishop of Winchester, when Wessex was divided between two sees. The king, Coenwalch, after a few years dismissed him as casually as he had received him. So Wini, the bishop, betook himself to the king of Mercia and from him he 'bought with a price' the bishopric of London, in which he ended his days. Bede narrates all this without comment or condemnation; it was innocence itself in comparison with what Gregory of Tours has to tell concerning bishops and bishoprics in Gaul.

It is evident that the mission of St. Augustine in less than a century and a half had quite broken down. Little control was exercised from Canterbury, and still less from Rome. To some extent this want of discipline may be due to Irish precedents; most of it must have been caused by the general lack of self-control and of governing capacity. In the Penitential of Theodore the first enactment is that if a bishop or other cleric be an incorrigible drunkard he must be deposed; and Bede in his Epistle to Ecgberct states as a fact in the cognizance of them both that there were drunkards among the bishops. As to Ecgberct himself, Bede has nothing worse to charge against him than undue jocularity and uproariousness in debate. We may judge what the standard of life must have been among the lower clergy, whose duty was to repeat forms of words the efficacy of which was above all doubt. It is true that in the middle of the seventh century we find kings enforcing Christianity upon their subjects, destroying idols and making the observance of the Lenten fast compulsory. But these external props are a poor evidence of strength, and we may best judge of the state of the English Church by the fact that its episcopate, like that of the Nonjurors of the eighteenth century, was on the point of extinction when Theodore of Tarsus came to inspire our Christianity with a new life. Yet Theodore was too late; it needed the terrors of invasion by the heathen Norsemen to purify the Anglo-Saxon Church, and the character and genius of the statesmen and churchmen, of whom Alfred was the greatest, to inspire it with new ideals and produce a wave of progress that would not be exhausted for several generations.

It was under the influence of Theodore that Bede wrote. Disordered as the England was which he undertook to reform, Theodore succeeded at last in creating an ecclesiastical administration. Bishops—and bishops were as authoritative as under the Rome of Constantine—had hitherto been excessively few, and even good ones, like Wilfrid, resented any increase of numbers as an encroachment on their prerogatives. But very soon their protests were overcome, and bishoprics became on the whole moderate in extent. It was equally important that steps were taken towards making diocesan administration

uniform. At his council of Hatfield Theodore had produced an
elementary set of canons selected from the standard councils,
to which the English bishops gave their sanction. In future it
would be impossible for them to plead that they did not know
what the law was; and provision was made for recurrent
councils at which questions, as they rose, should be settled.
Whether this machinery, had the Norsemen not come, could
have been made effectual may be doubted, so incorrigibly
unbusinesslike were the minds of the time. We can recognize
from the canons that survive that sound sense and a healthy
temper did not fail to show themselves. Yet the difficulties of
communication over decaying Roman roads and along unregu-
lated rivers were too great to allow of effectual visitation,
diocesan or provincial; and the position of the parochial clergy,
subordinate to the lay patrons of their parishes, made it difficult,
even if the attempt was made, for the bishop to exercise any
practical control over the clergy, whom at the request of the
patrons he had admitted to orders. The process by which the
parish priest became the bishop's 'man' was a long one which
had hardly begun in the time of Bede. As to diocesan officers we
can only say that the first known English archdeacons appear
after the arrival of Theodore. As yet they had no local sphere
within the diocese. The archdeacon, or archdeacons, might be
set to any task at any point within the diocese when the bishop
thought that an archdeacon could be of service. Local archdeacons do not appear before the Norman Conquest, but soon
after 1100 the whole country seems to have been divided into
archdeaconries within definite bounds. Whether rural deaneries,
of course local, are early is a moot point. It seems clear that
some of them corresponded in area to the 'hundreds' of civil
organization: there are instances where the rural deanery
appears to preserve boundaries which have been modified in a
rearrangement of hundreds. But there are grave authorities who
refuse to believe in a system of hundreds older than the Norse
invasions.

There was, then, no more than a very rudimentary organization of Church and of State even after the reforms of Theodore,
for these demanded a regularity of administration that was not
forthcoming. One of the most striking advances made by
Theodore was the introduction of Greek culture into England. In
the days of Bede there were to be found a few venerated old

men who had transmitted this to a second generation. But they had no successors. If there was this lack of vitality in education, we cannot wonder that there was a corresponding defect in practical and even in devotional life.

We have seen that Bede frankly recognized this in his letter to Ecgberct. His experience corresponded with that of all contemporary missions. Immature Christians had been left to face temptations and difficulties to which their forces were not equal, and the inevitable result followed. It has been the same in modern missions. Their leaders have been able to describe in glowing terms the lives and deaths of their early converts; but soon sad experience has brought disillusion, and they have had to justify their work as preparation for a harvest that later generations must reap. Bede himself is a most striking instance of this early perfection. He is always sincere, and free from that conventionality which is a besetting sin of ecclesiastical historians. He may tell us strange things, but he tells what he believed he saw. His literary task, outside his historical writings, was that of a compiler, for he had full confidence in the authorities from whom he drew, and would have regarded it as presumption to criticize them. But as an historian he deserves the highest praise for the choice he made among his materials. Alone among the historians of his age, he had the statesmanship to know what was of permanent importance, and the skill to record it clearly and fully. We must regret that there were aspects of the age so familiar to him that he did not realize that they could be perplexing to future generations, and therefore has left us to infer, as best we may, from what we know of the subsequent northern invasions, what must have been the processes of mutual influence and ultimate amalgamation which reduced the mixed populations of the England he knew to their ultimate uniformity.

E. W. WATSON.

III

NORTHUMBRIAN MONASTICISM

I

IN the document known as the *Catalogus Sanctorum Hiberniae*
written about the middle of the eighth century, the second of
the three orders of saints described followed the age of episcopal
saints inaugurated by St. Patrick.

'The second order was that of Catholic priests; for in this order
there were few bishops and many priests, in number three hundred.
One Head they had, our Lord: they followed various liturgies and
various rules, they had one Easter on the fourteenth of the month
after the equinox, one tonsure from ear to ear. They rejected the
ministry of women, banishing them from the monasteries. . . . They
received their liturgy from David the bishop and Gildas and Cadoc
the Britons.'[1]

The saints of this period, which covered the second half of the
sixth century, were founders and members of monasteries; and
the list of twenty-five representative names in the *Catalogus*
includes St. Finian of Clonard, St. Finian of Moville, St. Brendan
of Clonfert, St. Iarlath of Tuam, St. Comgall of Bangor, St.
Coemgen of Glendalough, St. Ciaran of Clonmacnoise, St. Canice
of Kilkenny, and St. Columba of Hy. These were the patriarchs
of the monastic system which played so large a part in the
Christianizing of the Northumbrian kingdom and, although unable to maintain itself against the influence of the rule of St.
Benedict, survived into the lifetime of Bede.

In its origin this form of the religious life was Gallo-Roman.
Its ultimate source was in the religious communities established
by St. Martin in the latter part of the fourth century at Ligugé
(*Locoteiacus*) near Poitiers and at Marmoutier (*Majus Monasterium*) close to Tours. Some two years before St. Martin's death
(397) Ninian, a native of the district north of the Solway who
had been brought up as a hostage at the court of Theodosius
the Great, was consecrated bishop and sent to evangelize his
fellow countrymen in the Roman province of Valentia. On his
way from Rome to Britain he visited Marmoutier, and his own

---

[1] H. and S. ii. 292.

Magnum Monasterium at Whithorn (*Candida Casa*) in Galloway was founded upon the model of St. Martin's famous house.[1]

There is some probability that St. Ninian visited the north of Ireland, and that in this way Celtic monasticism established outposts there before the coming of St. Patrick.[2] It was, at any rate, under the influence of Whithorn that the three British saints mentioned in the *Catalogus* brought Celtic customs into Ireland; for David, Gildas, and Cadoc belonged to families of Scottish origin whose migration to Wales took place in the course of the fifth century.[3] In spite of its debt to St. Martin, the Church founded by St. Ninian in Scotland was built up by native converts without the aid of Gaulish missionaries, and the abandonment of Britain by the Romans and the subsequent Teutonic invasions cut it off from foreign contact. Thus the Celtic Church developed upon its own lines in the west of Britain and in Ireland, which lay beyond the frontier of the Roman Empire. The natural outlet for its energies was in Ireland, peopled by inhabitants of Scottish race who spoke the same language, and the age which saw the second order of Irish saints marked the absorption of the Church established by St. Patrick and his Romano-Celtic followers within a system which was a purely Celtic growth. The episcopal government which St. Patrick had founded was superseded by a form of government controlled by a monastic organization.

The peculiarity of this system is summarily described by Bede in his account of Columba's monastery at Hy.[4] 'The island is accustomed to have as its ruler always an abbot who is a presbyter, to whose jurisdiction the whole district and even its bishops, by an unusual state of affairs, are duly subject, after the pattern of their first instructor, who was not a bishop but a presbyter and a monk.' The process by which the abbots of Irish monasteries obtained this jurisdiction is obscure. How far St. Patrick may have encouraged the religious life is uncertain; but there can be no doubt that his ecclesiastical system was founded upon episcopal jurisdiction and there is good reason for assuming that the bishops whom he consecrated were ordained after the usual fashion to definite sees.[5] St. Ninian, as already said, may have planted the seeds of monasticism in Ireland before St. Patrick's coming, and Ninian himself was both bishop

---

[1] *Hist. Ch. Ireland*, i. 61 ff. [2] *Ibid.* i. 69–72. [3] *Ibid.* i. 75, 131.
[4] *H.E.* iii. 4. [5] Bury, 181.

and abbot like his exemplar St. Martin. But the monastic system in Ireland developed on lines independent of any scheme of diocesan organization. It is certain that the multiplication of bishops after St. Patrick's death does not imply a corresponding number of dioceses with sees at fixed centres. The order of bishops was still regarded as the highest ecclesiastical rank with special gifts whose maintenance was essential to the Church, but it was dissociated from jurisdiction. Its qualification was saintliness of life, not administrative ability. Bishops were found in large numbers, living in monasteries or following the anchoretic way of life without diocesan duties. While episcopal government, as it was known on the Continent, was the model on which the Irish Church was founded, it was overshadowed in the course of the sixth century by the monastic system which came into being under leaders of Celtic birth and adapted itself closely to Celtic tribal customs.

The monastery in fact was an ecclesiastical replica of the tribe in whose territories it was founded. Its abbot stood in the position of a tribal chieftain to the community: he himself was in many instances a member of the local ruling family, and the monks who formed his *familia* within the monastic precincts would naturally be drawn from converts in the immediate neighbourhood and recognize in his authority the Christian counterpart of that which prevailed outside their settlement. Further, the succession to the headship of the monastery followed the tribal principle. It was confined to members of the family to which the first abbot belonged: when an abbot died, it passed to the *coarb* or kinsman who had the right of succession, and, if that family was also that of the local tribal king, it furnished a series of *coarbs* to fill the dignity. For the failure of a suitable *coarb* in the 'tribe of the saint' or in the 'tribe of the land' the Brehon Laws provided a regular entail of succession among the members of the monastery and its dependent foundations until another abbot of founder's kin should be eligible.[1]

It is unnecessary to point out the close interweaving of local interests, temporal and spiritual, which was thus created, and the influence which the tribe of Christian converts, devoted to the service of God and to peaceful occupations and protected by the instinctive dread of the guilt of sacrilege inseparable from hallowed sites, exercised in the Christianizing of its pagan neigh-

[1] Skene, ii. 64–75.

bours. The essential point is that the quasi-hereditary succession of abbots was dissociated from any idea of episcopal succession. There were abbots, like St. Iarlath of Tuam, who were also bishops: there were possibly here and there diocesan bishops of the old régime who were not monks. But within the monastery the union of jurisdiction and episcopal order in the same person was exceptional. Not that the episcopal office was undervalued. The age of St. Patrick had been rich in saintly bishops: tradition numbered 350 episcopal saints, 'illustrious, holy and full of the Holy Spirit',[1] and it would seem that a superior holiness of life and detachment from worldly affairs inconsistent with the practical cares of administration were regarded as special qualifications for episcopacy. Nor does the number of bishops seem to have diminished appreciably in the new age. We read of monasteries in which there were many bishops among the monks: every monastic family or *muintir* probably included a certain proportion, large or small, of bishops. Their duties, however, were wholly spiritual, duties inherent in their order; and, where everything outside these was concerned, they, in common with all members of the *muintir*, were subject to the jurisdiction of the abbot, who was normally a priest.[2]

From this it follows inevitably that the monastic bishop was not a diocesan. Ireland, outside the pale of the Roman empire, was without the *civitates* and provincial capitals of Romanized lands which provided ready-made sees for Christian bishops. If, as we have said, St. Patrick consecrated bishops to work in jurisdictional areas, we have no certain knowledge of any see which he established apart from his own see of Armagh, and for the time being diocesan organization on the continental model found little root in a society so different from that in which it had been developed. It would seem also that in the post-Patrician monastic age the primacy of Armagh had no place in the ecclesiastical scheme. The Church which had 'one Head, Christ, and one leader, Patrick'[3] still acknowledged the one Head, but no one leader. Bishops might be sent out upon missionary journeys and even found new monasteries, but they remained subject to the jurisdiction of their abbots, and the monasteries founded by them and by other monks were incorporated in the parent community. Such diocesan organization

---

[1] H. and S. ii. 292.   [2] Skene, ii. 42–4.

[3] H. and S. ii. 292: 'Unum Caput Christum, et unum ducem Patricium.'

as there was was purely monastic. Each monastery with the communities founded from and dependent upon it, often at long distances, formed one united family over which its abbot exercised supreme jurisdiction.

The monastic Church thus constituted followed no uniform rule of life: the few individual rules which have come down to us from various monasteries enforce a severe standard of asceticism with a competitive austerity.[1] They were strongly affected by that penitential system which played so large a part in the enforcement of Christian civilization upon a barbarous and heathen society to which horror of sin was a foreign notion. The most effective means of impressing this idea upon converts was by an assessment of penalties graduated in proportion to the heinousness of a minutely enumerated series of offences. The denizens of monasteries were themselves in the first instance converts from heathenism whose attitude to sin and its remedies was in the natural course of things elementary, and for whom such a penal code with all its crudity was as necessary as for the untonsured sinner in the outer world. The *muintir* was a family with many members. The normal number of monks in a single community was 150, but in the great monastery of Bangor on Belfast Lough and its dependencies there are said to have been 4,000.[2] In any case the maintenance of a rigid standard of discipline must have been a difficult problem which was met by the prescription of rules of singular harshness. It is not surprising that the rule imposed by Columbanus, the greatest son of Bangor, upon the monasteries which he founded on the Continent, was unable to hold its own permanently against the practical wisdom and the knowledge of human frailty with which the rule of St. Benedict inculcated the love of God as the supreme motive of the religious life.[3]

On the services which such monasteries as Bangor and Kells rendered to learning and art we need not dwell here. It is their

[1] On the severity of such rules see *Hist. Ch. Ireland*, i. 173. On the rule of St. Columban (*P.L.* lxxx, 207 ff.) see Hauck, i. 246 ff.

[2] Skene, ii. 60, 61.

[3] See Hauck, i. 282–4, for the supersession of the Rule of St. Columban by that of St. Benedict: 'Hier sind alle die Fragen beantwortet, welche in Columbas Regel unerledigt bleiben. . . . So bot die Regel Benedikts das, was Columbas Regel vermissen liess: ein höchst brauchbares Statut für jeden Mönchsverein.' The impermanence of the Rule of St. Columban was the unadaptability of its precepts to the ordinary man: 'Die ganze Regel ist zugeschnitten für eine Herrschernatur wie Columba, der alles dies selbst regelte und ordnete.'

missionary character which principally concerns us. Before no long time had passed, their influence was felt in the regions across the Irish Channel from which they derived their origin. Farther afield, it penetrated with remarkable success into the dominions of the Merovingian kings, where, face to face with a powerful diocesan organization, the mission of Columbanus originated a large number of famous monasteries which subsequently adopted the Benedictine rule.[1] But the impetus which the Celtic monastic system was to give in the seventh century to Northumbrian Christianity came from the monastery founded by St. Columba in Hy, the Ioua which by a literary error is known to later ages as Iona.[2]

II

The monastic movement which so profoundly affected the Irish Church had reached it through missionaries from North Britain. The debt thus incurred was paid by Columba, Irish-born and a striking example of the close union between the tribe and the monastic ruler, for he came of the royal house of Niall of the Nine Hostages.[3] Born, as is now generally agreed, about 521, the first forty years of his life were spent in Ireland, first in the monastic schools of Moville, Clonard, and Glasnevin, and afterwards in monasteries of his own foundation, Derry, Durrow, and Kells. His departure from Ireland is said to have been hastened by the battle of Culdreimhne, in which the cause of contention is attributed to Columba's indignation with the Ard-Righ Diarmait, who had endowed the monastery of Kells and subsequently had incurred his enmity. Columba summoned his kinsfolk, the Clan Niall, to avenge him: they were victorious, but Kells was in the kingdom of Diarmait, and Columba narrowly escaped excommunication from a synod which met under the king's protection. The story of these events is beset with legend, and the motive which induced Columba to leave Ireland is variously explained.[4] He found at any rate an outlet for his missionary energy on the west coast of Britain and in a district peopled by his kinsfolk.

[1] On the influence of Luxeuil upon the growth of monasteries, see Hauck, i. 273–82.
[2] On the name of the island see Reeves, *Adamnan*, 258–62, and summary note in *Adamnan*, ed. Fowler, 58, 59.
[3] See the genealogical table of the abbots of Iona, *ibid.* 83.
[4] See the summary account, *ibid.* 55–7.

It is hardly necessary to point out that in the time of Columba and till much later Ireland was commonly known as Scotia, and that the present Scotland derived its name from Scotia Minor, the coastal area which early in the sixth century had been colonized from the kingdom of Dalriada in north-eastern Ireland.[1] The greater part of North Britain or Alba was inhabited by the heathen Picts, formidable neighbours who, at the time of Columba's coming, threatened to overwhelm the Scotic colony and had wellnigh destroyed its Christianity. To Columba is due the revival of a faith which spread to the heathen race of the inland country, and the conversion of the Pictish king, Brude, at his court on Loch Ness.[2] Of the form which the Christianity previously imported from Ireland had taken we know nothing; but the story of the two bishops who attempted to hinder Columba from settling in Hy seems to indicate that it was that of the Patrician age, before the jurisdiction of abbots succeeded that of bishops.[3]

Bede states that Columba after the conversion of Brude received the gift of Iona from the Picts.[4] The Irish story, however, that the island was bestowed upon him by his kinsman the Dalriadan king, Conall, is not improbable, in which case the donation mentioned by Bede merely marked the acquiescence of the dominant race in his right of possession.[5] The date of his arrival is given by Bede as 565, but it was probably a year or two earlier. Between this and his death in 597 his time was spent in missionary labour and journeyings, extending the colonies of Iona in Scotland and returning from time to time to take part in the affairs of the Irish Church.

Although no complete picture of an Irish monastery of the Columban age remains, details of its general plan and of the life led within its precincts can be gathered from the biography of

---

[1] Reeves, *Adamnan*, 433. See *H.E.* i. 1: 'Brittania post Brettones et Pictos, tertiam Scottorum nationem in Pictorum parte recepit; qui duce Reuda de Hibernia progressi', &c.

[2] *H.E.* iii. 4; for incidents connected with Columba's visit to Brude see Adamnan, i. 1, 37; ii. 33-5.

[3] *Old Irish Life of St. Columba*, trans. Hennessey, ap. Skene, ii. 491.

[4] *H.E.* iii. 4.

[5] See the discussion in Reeves, *Adamnan*, 434-6. His conclusion is: 'Columba probably found Hy unoccupied and unclaimed, Conall kindly promised not to disturb him, and when the Picts were converted, Brudeus, the supreme lord, of course gave to the infant institution all the right and title which the weight of his sanction could confer.' See also Plummer, ii. 131, 132.

St. Columba written by Adamnan, the ninth abbot of Hy (697–704), to whom Bede devotes a chapter of the *Historia Ecclesiastica*.[1] Adamnan's collection of anecdotes of the saint is full of allusions which enable us to see Hy and its kindred monasteries as they were, the walls of dry-built stone with which they were girded, the space so enclosed in which stood the huts or cells of the abbot and his brethren, the church or oratory with its lateral chapels or sacristies, the *magna domus* or common refectory, the *hospitia* which afforded lodging to guests.[2] We must not think of the orderly plan of church, cloister, and outer court which was developed in the Benedictine monasteries of the Continent: the Celtic monastery much more nearly resembled the groups of hermits' cells in the East from which the isolation of early monachism gradually found its approach to the life of an organized community. Outside the common services in church and the common meals in the refectory the brethren lived in their cells. Adamnan refers frequently to Columba's hut set upon a knoll within the enclosure and raised upon a substructure of planks.[3] He alludes more than once to the work of writing and copying carried on by the abbot and his monks, which at Kells and Durrow and Lindisfarne produced masterpieces of Celtic art.[4] But side by side with this the monks were engaged in field-labour and in the various occupations necessary for their maintenance, under the charge of a *dispensator operum*.[5] It is from the self-supporting monastery, dependent upon the labour of its inmates, at once a place of prayer and contemplation, an active centre of labour, a training-school for the religious life, and a home of sacred learning, that ideal pictures of medieval monastic life have been frequently drawn; and although in later times this ideal was partially revived, notably by the Cistercian order, its fullest realization was in these Celtic monasteries founded in the midst of a turbulent and uncivilized society and affording a sanctuary to the oppressed and an example of peaceful and concentrated activity to their whole neighbourhood.

But with the monastic life was combined the work of evangelization which led Columba and his chosen companions into

---

[1] *H.E.* v. 15.

[2] The evidence for the buildings and economy of the monastery supplied by Adamnan is fully collected by Reeves, 357 ff.

[3] See Adamnan, i. 25, 35; ii. 16; iii. 15, 22.

[4] e.g. *ibid.* i. 23. For Columba's own diligence in writing see i. 25; ii. 16; iii. 15, 23.   [5] *Ibid.* i. 37.

regions distant from their home. No detailed account of his journeyings can be gathered from Adamnan. We know of his visit to the Pictish king, probably not the only occasion on which he penetrated the defiles of Drumalban, the central ridge of northern Britain.[1] His presence seems to have been required from time to time in Ireland, not only on ecclesiastical grounds but on political business, for his influence was used for purposes of mediation between his relations the kings of Dalriada and the Pictish kingdom.[2] So far as is known, the monasteries which he founded as daughters of Hy were on neighbouring islands, two on Tiree and one or more on the island of Hinba, not identified with certainty.[3] Such daughter communities, ruled by provosts, formed with Hy his 'diocese' or group of monasteries under his rule. They were, in fact, like Benedictine priories in later time, integral parts of the parent monastery. Hinba and Campus Lunge in Tiree, where Baithene, Columba's successor as abbot, was provost, were employed as places of retreat for penitents.[4] It has been conjectured that the term *primarius*, used in one place by Adamnan in conjunction with *praepositus*,[5] implies a grouping of the provosts of these small monasteries under superiors; and it may be that where, as at Tiree and Hinba, more than one of these cells existed on a single island, the provost of one of them exercised a general oversight. At the same time, it is more likely that the two words are equivalent in meaning and that *primarius* merely defines *praepositus*.

Both in Iona and the island Eilean Naoimh, which has been identified with Adamnan's Hinba, there are remains of beehive cells built of stone; but it seems probable that most of the buildings were of wood or wattles. The church at Iona is called indifferently *ecclesia* or *oratorium*,[6] and, if the first of these terms usually implies a church of stone, while the second may be more fittingly applied to an oratory of wood, the distinction does not seem to exist here. At the close of Columba's life, he had a vision

[1] Adamnan, i. 34: 'Alio in tempore trans Britanniae Dorsum iter agens' (cf. ii. 31); ii. 27: 'cum vir beatus in Pictorum provincia per aliquot moraretur dies' (of one of his visits to Loch Ness).

[2] *Adamnan*, ed. Fowler, 54, 55.

[3] For Tiree (*Ethica insula*) see Adamnan, i. 19; ii. 15, 39; iii. 8; for Hinba, i. 21, 45; ii. 24; iii. 5, 17, 18, 23.

[4] *Ibid*. i. 21, 30.   [5] *Ibid*. i. 35. See also i. 17.

[6] *Ibid*. i. 8: 'ad ecclesiam, ipso sancto praesule praeeunte, ocius currunt. . . . Et post modicum intervallum egressus oratorium.' Here the one building is obviously called by the two names.

of an angel *intra ipsius oratorii parietes*, who, having looked down upon the community present at mass within the church and blessed them, disappeared *per parasticiam ecclesiae*.[1] Here *oratorium* and *ecclesia* are obviously identical, and, although *parasticia* has been explained as a roof or vault,[2] it is more likely to be a synonym of *paries*, an enclosure which might be either of wood or stone. In both cases Adamnan's phraseology is not technical, and he appears to use synonyms in order to avoid the monotony of repetition. In this context, the evidence of Bede with regard to Finan's church of Lindisfarne, that it was built *more Scottorum*, not of stone but of hewn oak, carries weight.[3] We know at any rate that large quantities of timber were brought by sea to Hy for the construction of the *magna domus*, and on another occasion for the repair of the buildings.[4]

While the task of spreading the gospel involved intervals of considerable length, during which Columba and a chosen band of companions were absent from their monastery, and while the monastic life, so largely spent in the formation of a Christian Church amid a heathen population, was restrained by no conditions of stability or strict enclosure, we may note that from time to time monks, and even abbots, left their monasteries to adopt the hermit life. Adamnan more than once tells us of Cormac Ua Liathain, abbot of Durrow, who thrice went sailing in search of a desert island.[5] That for such wanderings the licence of an abbot was necessary is illustrated by the tale of one of the voyages of Cormac which failed because he had in his company a monk who had left his monastery without his abbot's leave.[6] At this date the impulse to the hermit life was strongly at work in the Celtic Church, and, at the time of St. Columba's death, the age of hermit saints was already taking the place of the age of that holy priesthood which had exercised its mission from monastic centres.

III

In the year of Columba's death, Augustine and his companions landed in the Isle of Thanet and began that work of Christianization which, twenty-eight years later, planted for the time being an outpost in the Northumbrian kingdom. Apart from its zeal for the conversion of the heathen, the mission of Augustine

---

[1] *Ibid.* iii. 23.   [2] See Reeves, *Adamnan*, 229–30 *n*.
[3] *H.E.* iii. 25.   [4] Adamnan, ii. 45.
[5] *Ibid.* i. 6; ii. 42.   [6] *Ibid.* i. 6.

had nothing in common with the Celtic monastic system. Although the band of missionaries was composed of monks over whom Gregory the Great had set Augustine as abbot, they did not form a monastery. In their settlement at Canterbury they lived as a bishop and his household, imitating the apostolic life of the primitive Church in constant prayers, watchings and fastings, preaching the word of life to whom they could, shunning the things of this world, and depending for their bare necessities upon the alms of their converts.[1] While Augustine in the course of his labours founded the Benedictine monastery of St. Peter and St. Paul at Canterbury, his own metropolitical church was governed rather by the example of St. Augustine of Hippo and was an active centre of diocesan effort ruled by himself, not as abbot but as bishop.[2] The fundamental difference in fact between the Roman Church in the south and the Celtic Church in the north was that the constitution of the first was based upon a diocesan episcopate, while that of the second was controlled by the jurisdiction of abbots ruling groups of monasteries.

The mission of Paulinus to Northumbria in 625 was similar to that of Augustine. He came as a consecrated bishop with the express purpose of founding a see at York, whose traditions as a Roman provincial capital still survived. He had been one of the *cooperatores ac verbi ministri* who with Laurentius the priest and Peter the monk had brought the pall to Augustine in 601.[3] There is no indication that he himself was a monk, and of the clergy who formed his *familia* we know only by name James the deacon, the constant companion of his missionary journeys and the solitary continuator of his work after his flight from Northumbria.[4] Nor were the churches with which his name was associated founded upon a monastic pattern, so far as is known: at York he founded no monastery like St. Augustine's abbey at Canterbury. In a diocese whose frontiers moved with the extension of Edwin's kingdom the time was not yet ripe for the formation of new sees, and the picture of it which we obtain from Bede is one of a large and uncertain area, with a city and

---

[1] *H.E.* i. 26.

[2] See J. Armitage Robinson, 'The Early Community at Ch. Ch. Cant.' (*Journ. Theol. Stud.* xxvii. 225–40); M. Deanesly, 'The Familia at Ch. Ch. Cant.' (*Essays in Med. Hist. presented to T. F. Tout*, 1–13).

[3] *H.E.* i. 29.

[4] *Ibid.* ii. 16, 20; iii. 25; iv. 2.

church from which a travelling bishop derived his jurisdiction and with outposts of evangelistic work in which permanent churches were few.[1]

The defeat and death of Edwin at Hatfield in 633 abandoned the southern part of the Northumbrian kingdom for the time being to paganism; and when about a year later the victory of Oswald over Cædualla at Heavenfield restored the northern part, Bernicia, to Christianity, it was under a new influence. The conquest of Northumbria by Edwin in 617 had been achieved at the expense of Æthelfrith, king of Bernicia, who had dispossessed him of his kingdom of Deira. The seven sons of Æthelfrith sought refuge in North Britain among the Scots and Picts and there embraced Christianity. After Edwin's death Bernicia was restored to Eanfrid, the eldest of the family, while Osric, a cousin of Edwin, became king of Deira. Both, however, returned to paganism, and both within a year were slain by Cædualla.[2] As a result of his victory, Oswald again united the two kingdoms, fixing the seat of his rule at Bamburgh, the Bernician royal town which had been founded by his great-grandfather Ida. Although he completed the stone church at York which Edwin had left unfinished,[3] the see abandoned by Paulinus was left unfilled, and the neighbourhood of Deira to the hostile Mercian kingdom of Penda was a menace to its independence. Consequently, during Oswald's reign, York played no part in the conversion of Northumbria, and the centre of Northumbrian Christianity was transferred to the neighbourhood of the royal residence.

It is generally accepted, although it is nowhere precisely stated, that Oswald had resided for some time among the monks of Iona.[4] It was at any rate to Iona, the chief Scottish monastery in northern Britain, that Oswald applied for a bishop. The person chosen for the task, a severe ascetic, proved unequal to it, and in his stead was sent Aidan, who was consecrated probably by the bishops who were members of the monastery. To

[1] For the extent of Edwin's kingdom see *ibid.* ii. 9. Of places visited by Paulinus Bede mentions Lincoln, Tiouulfingacæstir on the Trent (ii. 16), Ad Gefrin in Bernicia, Cataracta (Catterick) on the Swale, and Campodonum in Deira.

[2] *Ibid.* iii. 1.   [3] *Ibid.* ii. 14.

[4] Bede says (*ibid.* iii. 3) that Oswald sent for a bishop 'ad majores natu Scottorum, inter quos exulans ipse baptismatis sacramenta cum his qui secum erant militibus consecutus est'.

his island see of Lindisfarne he brought a body of Scottish monks and there he instituted the monastic life which was continued without a break till the Danish invasion of 793.

The choice of Lindisfarne as a settlement for Aidan and his monks was in keeping with the tradition of Iona and its cells, missionary centres on remote islands. Bede's account of the life of Aidan, from which all others are derived, seems to indicate that the position of the episcopal founder with regard to the monastery of Lindisfarne was different from the subordination of bishops to the abbots of Scottish monasteries.[1] It is of course possible that a hundred years later Bede's conception of Aidan's episcopate was coloured by his inability to dissociate the bishop from the diocesan. He equates Aidan's diocesan and monastic relations with those of Augustine of Canterbury, quoting Gregory the Great's instructions to Augustine to the effect that a bishop, although trained in a monastery, should not separate himself from his secular clergy, but live with them according to the pattern of the early Christians who had all things in common.[2] At Lindisfarne, he says, it was the ancient custom for the bishop to live with his clergy and the abbot with his monks, yet in such a way that the monks were in the bishop's charge after the manner of a household.[3] He implies again that, while those who accompanied or followed Aidan into Northumbria were for the most part monks, some of them were seculars. He speaks of the *clerici* who came with Aidan to Oswald's table and distinguishes between the *adtonsi* and *laici* who went with him upon his preaching tours.[4] Aidan further recruited his household and monastery from his Anglian converts: Eata, afterwards abbot of Melrose and bishop of Lindisfarne, was one of the twelve English boys whose Christian education he undertook at the beginning of his episcopate.[5] Thus Bede's picture is that of a

---

[1] *H.E.* iii. 5.   [2] *Ibid*. iv. 25; cf. i. 27.

[3] *Ibid*. iv. 25. See also the important passage in *Vita Cuth*. xvi: 'una eademque servorum Dei habitatio utrosque (sc. episcopum et abbatem) simul tenet, imo omnes monachos tenet. Aidan quippe qui primus ejusdem loci episcopus fuit, monachus erat et monachicam cum suis omnibus vitam semper agere solebat. Unde ab illo omnes loci ipsius antistites usque hodie sic episcopale exercent officium ut regente monasterium abbate quem ipsi cum consilio fratrum elegerint omnes presbyteri, diaconi, cantores lectores ceterique gradus ecclesiastici monachicam per omnia cum ipso episcopo regulam servent. Quam vivendi normam multum se diligere probavit beatus Gregorius', &c.

[4] *H.E.* iii. 5.

[5] *Ibid*. iii. 26.

bishop dwelling among a group of immediate followers, but with supervision over the monastery which he had founded. He frequently took up his abode at Bamburgh, where he had a church and a lodging, as a convenient centre for his preaching journeys, and where he died;[1] while he also was in the habit of visiting the Farne Islands for retirement and meditation.[2]

It is clear that Aidan did not relinquish his jurisdiction into the hands of the abbot whom he set over Lindisfarne, nor is there any trace at Lindisfarne of a number of monks in epis-copal orders. The position of Aidan was definitely that of a diocesan bishop, the source of jurisdiction as well as of order, and in this respect the custom of the Scots was abandoned. It has been suggested that, when Bede speaks of the Scottish im-migrants who came to take part in Aidan's work, his limitation of the ministry of the sacrament of baptism to those who were endowed with *sacerdotalis gradus* implies that episcopal order was necessary for the rite.[3] But it is not at all certain that Bede attached such a meaning to *sacerdotalis* in this context.[4] It may also be noticed that he gives no indication of the spread from Lindisfarne of a monastic 'diocese' such as developed out of the great Irish monasteries and Iona. In his description of Aidan's work in the north the building of churches for the ministry of the Word takes the first place, the endowment of monasteries by royal munificence the second;[5] and, although these monasteries, centres of regular discipline and of education for the young, would naturally be attached where possible to the new churches, it does not follow that Aidan's diocese was simply a group of monasteries subordinate to Lindisfarne.

The successors of Aidan, Finan (651) and Colman (661), were both monks of Iona. Finan was responsible for giving Lindis-farne a church befitting an episcopal see, although in accordance with Scottish practice, it was built of timber.[6] During his

---

[1] *Ibid.* iii. 17.   [2] *Ibid.* iii. 16.

[3] *Ibid.* iii. 3: 'Exin coepere plures per dies de Scottorum regione uenire Brittaniam . . . magna deuotione uerbum fidei praedicare et credentibus gratiam baptismi, quicumque sacerdotali erant gradu praediti ministrare.' See the note in Plummer, ii. 126, 127, who thinks that the reference is to non-diocesan bishops from Scottish monasteries.

[4] On Bede's use of *sacerdos* in this sense see Plummer's note (ii. 55, 56) on *sacerdotum* in *H.E.* i. 28.

[5] *Ibid.* iii. 3.

[6] *Ibid.* iii. 25: 'quam tamen more Scottorum non de lapide, sed de robore secto totam composuit, atque harundine texit.'

episcopate the influence of Lindisfarne was carried beyond the southern limits of Northumbria. Penda, the heathen king of Mercia who had defeated and slain Edwin at Hatfield and Oswald on the Maserfeld, lost his life at Winwæd in 655, where his army was routed by Oswiu, the brother of Oswald. The alliance of Oswiu's son Alchfrid and daughter Alchfled to the daughter and son of Penda, Cuniburh and Peada, two years before Winwæd, was preceded by the baptism of Peada at the hands of Finan.[1] This event[2] led to the conversion of Mercia. Penda himself had been tolerant to Christianity where he saw that conduct corresponded to profession,[3] and, when Mercia became tributary to Oswiu, the way was already prepared by the priests whom Peada had brought home from the royal vill Ad Murum. In 656 Finan consecrated the Scot Diuma to be bishop of the Midland English and the Mercians, and of the three bishops who rapidly succeeded him, Ceollach, a monk of Iona, was also consecrated by Finan, while Trumheri, an Englishman by birth, and Jaruman received Scottish consecration.[4] Similarly, the friendship between Sigberct, king of the East Saxons, and Oswiu brought Sigberct to receive baptism from Finan, and in 654 the Anglian Cedd, one of Peada's four priests, was called from Mercia to be bishop in the East Saxon kingdom, and was consecrated at Lindisfarne by Finan and two other bishops.[5] Thus the influence of Lindisfarne spread southward as far as the estuary of the Thames.

Thirty-three years, however, after the coming of Aidan, the link between the Northumbrian Church and Iona was broken by the declaration of the council of Whitby in favour of the Roman Easter. At Whitby Colman of Lindisfarne and Cedd appeared as defenders of the Scottish observance; but, while Cedd accepted the decision, Colman and his clerks retired to Iona. With him went all the Scottish monks of Lindisfarne and about thirty of Anglian birth.[6] Already Englishmen had begun to find their way to the monasteries of Ireland, and it was not surprising that their loyalty to the source of their Christianity

---

[1] *H.E.* iii. 21.

[2] The names of Alchfrid and Cuniburh occur among the runes incised upon the Bewcastle Cross: see Baldwin Brown, v; Browne, *Cross Shafts*.

[3] *H.E.* iii. 21: 'Nec prohibuit Penda rex quin etiam in sua . . . natione uerbum, siqui uellent audire, praedicaretur. Quin potius odio habebat et dispiciebat eos quos fide Christi inbutos opera fidei non habere deprehendit. dicens contemnendos esse eos et miseros qui Deo suo in quem crederent oboedire contemnerent.'   [4] *Ibid.* iii. 21.

[5] *Ibid.* iii. 22.   [6] *Ibid.* iii. 25, 26; iv. 4.

prompted them to adhere to the party which maintained the thesis ironically propounded by Cummian: 'Rome is in error, Jerusalem in error, Antioch in error: only the Scots and the Britons know what is right'.[1] The seceders from Lindisfarne eventually found a home with Colman in the island of Inisboffin, off the west coast of Ireland; but here a dissension was caused by the Scots, whose habit was to quit the monastery at harvest-time and leave the Angles to gather in all the provisions for the winter, and in consequence of this dispute the monastery of Mayo was founded to be colonized by Anglian monks.[2]

Yet Lindisfarne still continued to derive its chief strength from its connexion with the Celtic Church. Tuda, the successor of Colman, was consecrated in the south of Ireland, where he had been educated and where the Roman Easter was accepted.[3] Shortly after his consecration, however, he died of the plague, and the episcopal succession at Lindisfarne came for the time being to an end; for the consecration of Wilfrid in 664 as bishop in Northumbria and that of Chad in the same year led to the revival of the see of York. Meanwhile the monks who remained at Lindisfarne were placed, it was said by the special request of Colman, under the jurisdiction of Eata, abbot of Melrose, who, as has been said already, had been one of the Anglian boys chosen by Aidan for instruction in Christianity.[4] The foundation of the monastery of Melrose is ascribed to Aidan, and Eata is the first abbot whose name has come down to us. He was abbot in 651 when Cuthbert entered the monastery: subsequently Alchfrid, the son of Oswiu, put him in charge of a monastery at Ripon, to which he brought a colony of monks from Melrose, including Cuthbert.[5] When Alchfrid under the influence of Wilfrid gave the monks of Ripon the choice of adopting the Roman Easter and tonsure or leaving their monastery, they returned to Melrose.[6] After Whitby, however, they seem to have conformed to the Roman practice, and it says much for Colman's wisdom and for the estimation in which he was held by Oswiu that, although he himself could not conscientiously stay at Lindisfarne, he could recommend that king to entrust it to monks who were of its spiritual lineage.

[1] Letter of Cummian to Seghine, abbot of Iona (*P.L.* lxxxvii, 974): 'Quid autem pravius sentiri potest de Ecclesia matre quam si dicamus, Roma errat, Hierosolyma errat, Antiochia errat, totus mundus errat: soli tantum Scoti et Britones rectum sapiunt.'   [2] *H.E.* iv. 4.   [3] *Ibid.* iii. 26.
[4] *Ibid.* iii. 26.   [5] *Vita Cuth.* vii.   [6] *Ibid.* viii.

Eata combined the abbacy of Lindisfarne with that of Melrose. Under him at Melrose Boisil, whose name survives in that of the neighbouring village of St. Boswells, was provost or prior, and was succeeded on his death by Cuthbert. After some years Eata sent Cuthbert to be provost of Lindisfarne, where in time his name was to become even more famous than that of Aidan.[1] During this period Wilfrid was exercising jurisdiction as bishop, at first over the northern part of Northumbria, later, after the translation of Chad to Lichfield, at York over the whole kingdom.[2] But in 678 the growth of ill feeling between him and Ecgfrid, the son and successor of Oswiu, brought about the expulsion of Wilfrid, and Theodore of Tarsus, coming north from Canterbury, arranged the division of Northumbria into three dioceses and consecrated three bishops at York.[3] Of these, Eata was chosen to rule the diocese of Bernicia with his see divided between Lindisfarne and Hexham, an arrangement which prevailed until in 685 the joint see was separated and Cuthbert was called from his hermitage on Farne Island to become bishop of Lindisfarne.

The fame of Cuthbert as monk and provost, although many of his miracles are connected with that period of his career, is somewhat eclipsed by the reputation which he won as an anchorite. Obeying that impulse to the solitary life which had become so characteristic of the monk nurtured in Scottish traditions, he retired from Lindisfarne to Farne Island, and when at the synod of Twyford on the Aln, held under the presidency of Theodore, he was elected bishop, he yielded only to the persuasion of Ecgfrid, who with Trumuine, bishop of the Picts, and a company of representative nobles and churchmen and the monks of Lindisfarne visited him in his solitude.[4] It was intended that he should rule at Hexham and Eata at Lindisfarne; but Cuthbert preferred the second of these. Of the exemplary character of his short life as bishop, in which he signally inculcated his precepts by his practice, Bede, his contemporary, speaks with enthusiasm.[5] Of the saints and heroes of the Northumbrian Church he achieved the most lasting celebrity. But before his death he retired once more to his favourite

---

[1] *H.E.* iv. 25.

[2] On the chronology of Wilfrid's episcopal career see Poole, *Studies*, 56–81.

[3] *H.E.* iv. 12.　　　　　　　　　　　　　　　　　　　[4] *Ibid.* iv. 26.

[5] *Ibid.* iv. 26: 'Et, quod maxime doctores iuuare solet, ea quae agenda docebat ipse prius agendo praemonstrabat.'

hermitage, the dwelling from which every prospect but the heaven for entry into which he thirsted was shut off by the earthen rampart that surrounded it.[1] Of the spiritual bond which united him with Hereberct, the anchorite of Derwentwater, of their last meeting at Carlisle and of their simultaneous death, granted in answer to their mutual prayers, Bede tells the affecting story.[2] Cuthbert lived to see the fatal blow dealt to the power of Northumbria by the Pictish victory at Nechtansmere,[3] but, living on the verge of its decline, he inherited all the energy and zeal which characterized its golden age, and his name, cherished by the faithful custodians of his body who after many vicissitudes brought it three centuries later to its final resting-place at Durham, remained the most permanent reminder of the debt which the English Church owed to the Scottish mission.

IV

Of the monasteries which owed their existence to Lindisfarne some are mere names. Such was the monastery *Ad Caprae Caput*, with little doubt at Gateshead, of which Utta was abbot,[4] and the monastery of Pægnalæch, of quite uncertain identity, at which Tuda was buried.[5] The foundation of Melrose is attributed to Aidan, as has already been said, and he also is said to have founded Coldingham, of which more presently. After his consecration as bishop of the East Saxons, it was Cedd's custom to pay occasional visits to Northumbria, where his preaching won the heart of Æthelwald the son of Oswald, who seems for a time to have disputed the kingdom of Deira with his uncle Oswiu. From Æthelwald he obtained the gift of land for a monastery at Lastingham, in the northern moorlands of Yorkshire, where he introduced the rites and discipline of Lindisfarne, retaining it with his bishopric. Cedd died here, and when later on a church of stone was built in the monastery, his body was translated to the right-hand side of the altar.[6] He was succeeded at Lastingham in 664 by his brother Chad, who very

---

[1] *Vita Cuth.* xvii: 'Est autem aedificium situ paene rotundum, a muro usque ad murum mensura quatuor ferme sive quinque perticarum distentum; murus ipse deforis altior longitudine stantis hominis: nam intrinsecus vivam caedendo rupem multo illum fecit altiorem, quatenus ad cohibendam oculorum simul et cogitatuum lasciviam, ad erigendam in superna desideria totam mentis intentionem pius incola nil de sua mansione praeter caelum posset intueri.'

[2] *H.E.* iv. 27. [3] *Vita Cuth.* xxvii. [4] *H.E.* iii. 21.
[5] *Ibid.* iii. 27. [6] *Ibid.* iii. 23.

soon afterwards was promoted to the see of York. It is a curious fact that, upon the death of Cedd, a large body of monks from the East Saxon monastery in which he had lived, either at the Roman station of Othona (*Ythanceastir*) or at Tilbury, migrated to Lastingham in order to live and die near his body. They were well received, but their prayer to be buried with him was answered sooner than they expected, for the whole body of monks was carried off by the plague which ravaged Northumbria before the end of 664.[1] This, however, was not the end of the monastery, for Chad seems to have held it after his consecration and retired to it after he resigned his bishopric.[2] It is possible that he retained it when in 669 he was called to the see of Lichfield, but after that time we hear no more of it. Local tradition not unnaturally has connected the interesting crypt beneath the chancel of the church at Lastingham with the stone church of St. Mary in which Cedd was eventually buried. The architectural evidence produces nothing in support of this, and there is no doubt that the fabric belongs to the period at which, a few years after 1080, the Benedictine monks who seceded from Whitby found an abode at Lastingham before their eventual settlement at St. Mary's, York.[3]

Reference has already been made to the monastery at Ripon, first colonized from Melrose, with which Eata and Cuthbert were for a while connected. The actual founder was Alchfrid, the son of Oswiu, whose whole-hearted conversion to the Roman side in the Easter controversy soon led him to change his mind and transfer the foundation to the care of Wilfrid. It is probable that Wilfrid, with his zeal for the rule of St. Benedict, altered the constitution of the monastery. However this may be, he received at Ripon monks who had been brought up in Scottish traditions but were ready to conform to Roman practice. Æthelwald, who succeeded Cuthbert in his hermitage on Farne Island, was for many years a monk of Ripon.[4] Wilfrid also invited to Ripon monks from the monastery of Ingætlingum, usually identified with Gilling in Richmondshire, which had been founded in memory of Oswin, the young king of Deira, treacherously slain there in 651 after the disbanding of the army which he had gathered to oppose Oswiu.[5] The first abbot of Ingætlingum was Trumheri, who was related to Oswin and became, as has

---

[1] *H.E.* iii. 23.   [2] *Ibid.* iv. 3.   [3] See below, p. 100.
[4] *Ibid.* v. 1.   [5] *Ibid.* iii. 14.

been said already, bishop of the Mercians in 659.[1] He seems to have been succeeded by Cynefrid, a man of noble birth, who, going to study the scriptures in Ireland, committed his monastery to his kinsman Tunberct. Under Tunberct Ceolfrid, the brother of Cynefrid, learned monastic discipline; and, when the pestilence of 664 carried off Cynefrid and depopulated Ingætlingum, Tunberct and Ceolfrid with some of the surviving monks joined the community at Ripon.[2] Thus, after Wilfrid had obtained possession of Ripon, the monastery contained a strong element of Scottish tradition, and it was from Ripon that Willibrord, the apostle of Frisia, went to improve his learning in Ireland.[3] Ceolfrid left Ripon to join Benedict Biscop at Wearmouth: Tunberct presumably remained at Ripon until 681, when, during the period of Wilfrid's first expulsion from Northumbria, he was consecrated bishop of Hexham by Theodore.[4]

The rule of Wilfrid as abbot at Ripon marks the transition of monasticism in Northumbria from Scottish custom to a life in conformity with Benedictine practice. After his consecration as bishop, Ripon remained his see until in 669 he administered the whole of Northumbria from York; but he still kept Ripon in his hands. It was taken from him in 678, when Eadhæd, bishop of Lindsey, was translated to Ripon. On Wilfrid's return from exile about 686 he did not recover the see of York, but was at Ripon until his second expulsion in 691. On his second return to the north in 705 his see was fixed at Hexham, where about 670 he had founded his second and equally famous monastery. During this period, however, he retained Ripon, and there he eventually was buried on the south side of the altar of the church which he had built and whose crypt, like that at Hexham, remains to the present day.[5]

Of the later history of the monastery of Ripon and of its sister at Hexham we shall speak presently. But of the religious houses founded in the reigns of Oswald and Oswiu under the influence of the Celtic mission none were more remarkable than St. Hilda's monastery at Whitby. Aidan inaugurated the religious life for women in Northumbria by consecrating Heiu to be abbess of Heruteu, now Hartlepool.[6] He is also said to have founded the monastery of Coldingham in Berwickshire, of which Æbba, the

[1] *Ibid.* iii. 24.
[2] *H. A. An.* 2, 3.
[3] Alcuin, *Vit. Willibrordi*, 3, 4.
[4] *H.E.* iv. 12.
[5] See Poole, *Studies, ut sup.*
[6] *H.E.* iv. 23.

half-sister of Oswiu, was abbess.[1] Here Æthelthryth, daughter
of the East Anglian king, Anna, and wife of Oswiu's son Ecgfrid,
retired from her husband's society, subsequently leaving Northumbria for the monastery of Ely in her native country.[2]
Æbba, although herself blameless, according to the Irish monk
who prophesied the destruction of Coldingham by fire from
heaven, was no disciplinarian, and the disaster which after her
death fulfilled the monk's warning was ascribed to the vengeance
of Heaven upon the laxity and corruption of the monastery.[3]
Ebchester on the Derwent, which, as well as St. Abbs Head on
the Berwickshire coast, preserves the name of Æbba, was probably the site of another monastery ruled by her.

The failure of Æbba was redeemed by Hild, daughter of
Hereric, a nephew of Edwin. She was one of the company who
with Edwin received baptism from Paulinus. Her sister Heres-
with married Æthelhere, an East Anglian prince who succeeded
his brother Anna on the throne, but, anticipating the behaviour
of her niece Æthelthryth, seems to have left her husband for a
more congenial life at the monastery of Chelles in Gaul. Hild
proposed to follow her there and stayed for a year in East Anglia
with this intention. She was recalled, however, by Aidan, and
for another year dwelt in a small monastery on the north bank
of the Wear. Still under the diligent supervision of Aidan, she
succeeded Heiu, who had removed to a monastery near Tadcaster on the Wharfe, as abbess of Hartlepool. Here she remained
from 649 to 657, when she undertook the construction and
ordering of a monastery at Streaneshalch, now Whitby, which
at her death in 680 she had ruled for twenty-three years.[4]

Streaneshalch is the most famous example of a community
consisting of monks and nuns under the supervision of an abbess.
Such communities had formed no part of the organization of the
Scottish mission and appear to have been modelled upon originals
in Gaul. Bede tells us, for instance, of the nunnery of Faremoûtier
in Brie, in which the brethren had separate quarters from the
sisters.[5] Symeon of Durham describes a similar arrangement
at Coldingham.[6] It seems quite clear that it prevailed at Hartlepool,[7] and Bede speaks of the *locus virorum* in a Lincolnshire

---

[1] *H.E.* iv. 19.   [2] *Ibid.* iv. 19.   [3] *Ibid.* iv. 25.   [4] *Ibid.* iv. 23.   [5] *Ibid.* iii. 8.

[6] S.D. *Hist. Dun.* ii. 7: 'Erant siquidem in eodem loco diversis tamen
separatae mansionibus monachorum sanctimonialiumque congregationes.'

[7] Oftfor, bishop of Worcester, was educated under Hilda 'in utroque monasterio', i.e. at Hartlepool and Whitby.

nunnery,[1] of the nuns' dwelling at Barking set apart from the men's house,[2] and of the brethren at Ely.[3] The necessity of priests to administer the sacraments and of monks or lay brothers to do manual labour which was too hard for women to perform unaided accounted, as they did in later days, for these experiments.[4] Of Hilda's monastery Bede implies that its 'regular discipline' was after the example of the primitive church, a life in which all property was held in common, but in which apparently no formal rule derived from an external source was followed.[5] Not merely was Hilda the nominal mother of the community: her personality was the driving force which made her monastery famous throughout Britain. Under her guidance its inmates were trained in works of righteousness and encouraged in the study of the Scriptures. It is probable that the choice of Streaneshalch as the meeting-place of the famous synod in 664 was suggested by the wisdom and learning of Hilda and her followers, and their conversion from the Scottish to the Roman Easter cannot have been without weight in the victory of Wilfrid's party. Two years before Hilda's death, one of her monks, Bosa, was consecrated bishop of York, and apparently in the year of her death Tatfrith was elected bishop of Worcester. Subsequently Ætla became bishop of Dorchester, John was consecrated by Theodore to the see of Hexham in 687, and Oftfor by Wilfrid, then bishop of the Middle Angles, to that of Worcester in 692; while John, upon his retirement from the see of York in 718, consecrated another of Hilda's *alumni*, Wilfrid II, as his successor.[6] More celebrated than these distinguished names is that of the lay brother Cædmon whose divinely inspired gift of song brought him into the company of the monks and was employed in the versifying of sacred history for their edification and delight.[7]

Through the picturesque legend of the vision of Hilda's death seen by the nun Begu, we are acquainted with the monastery

[1] *H.E.* iii. 11.

[2] *Ibid.* iv. 7: 'eam monasterii partem qua ancillarum Dei caterua a uirorum erat secreta contubernio.'

[3] *Ibid.* iv. 19: 'iussitque [sc. Sexburg abbatissa] quosdam e fratribus quaerere lapidem de quo locellum in hoc facere possent.'

[4] See *Rep. Min. Women*, 145–64 (app. viii).

[5] *H.E.* iv. 23: 'ita ut in exemplum primitiuae ecclesiae nullus ibi diues, nullus esset egens, omnibus essent omnia communia, cum nihil cuiusquam esse uideretur proprium.'

[6] *Ibid.* iv. 23; see also iv. 12; v. 3, 5.   [7] *Ibid.* iv. 24.

founded by Hilda at Hackness, between Whitby and Scarborough.[1] Of another nunnery of uncertain foundation at Uetadun, identified with Watton in the East Riding of Yorkshire, we have information in one of the miracle-stories recorded by Bede of St. John of Beverley.[2] John himself, as we have seen, was one of the bishops trained at Streaneshalch. Consecrated bishop of Hexham in the year of Cuthbert's death and in succession to Eata, he lived a life not unlike that of Cuthbert, retiring from time to time with a few companions to the oratory of St. Michael on the north bank of the Tyne at the place now called St. John Lee.[3] When Wilfrid in 705 returned to the north and settled down as bishop in the church which he had founded at Hexham, John became bishop of York. But he is specially associated with the monastery which he instituted *in silva Derorum*, Inderauuda, and which was in later days succeeded by the minster of Beverley, so closely connected throughout the Middle Ages with the see of York. Here, surrounded by his *familia* of monks, he finally retired in 718 and died three years later; and we derive our knowledge of his life from Bercthun, his successor as abbot, upon whom Bede drew for information.[4]

In these and other monasteries ruled by abbots and abbesses who had been nurtured in Scottish traditions the influence of Aidan's mission was never wholly superseded by continental influences, nor is there any evidence that, with the adoption of the Roman Easter and the Roman tonsure, the Benedictine rule was formally introduced in place of previous rules or customs. On the other hand, Wilfrid, in spite of his early training at Lindisfarne, was as zealous a supporter of Benedictinism as of other forms of continental practice at a time when in the monasteries of Gaul the rule of St. Columban was yielding to that of St. Benedict. Wilfrid introduced Benedictinism into the north of England,[5] and we may regard his churches at Ripon and Hexham as the homes of communities which, if not wholly abandoning local customs, grafted the rule upon them. At the

---

[1] *H.E.* iv. 23.   [2] *Ibid.* v. 3.   [3] *Ibid.* v. 2.   [4] *Ibid.* v. 2–5.

[5] Eddius, xiv: 'regionem suam rediens cum regula sancti Benedicti instituta ecclesiarum Dei bene meliorabat.' Bede no doubt implies this among other things in *H.E.* iii. 28: 'et ipse perplura catholicae obseruationis moderamina ecclesiis Anglorum sua doctrina contulit.' See also iv. 2: 'qui primus inter episcopos qui de Anglorum gente essent catholicum uiuendi morem ecclesiis Anglorum tradere didicit.' This, characterized by Plummer (ii. 206) as an 'extraordinary statement', becomes intelligible if his influence upon monastic life is taken into account.

same time they had a double aspect as sees of a bishop as well as monastic churches. As we have seen, the peculiar system of Celtic monasteries under which bishops were merely members of a community and were distinguished from the rest only by their superior orders repressed the growth of diocesan jurisdiction. But this system had not taken root in Northumbria, and Aidan at Lindisfarne had this in common with Augustine and his successors at Canterbury, that his jurisdiction as bishop of the local kingdom was independent of any superior officer. If the foundation of new monasteries marked the progress of diocesan expansion, the bishop with his clerical *familia* occupied a position apart from the monastic *familia* attached to his church; and thus from the beginning there grew up, in the north as well as in the south of England, the custom which in time produced a virtual separation of the bishop and his clerks from the domestic life and polity of the chapter of a monastic cathedral church, as strongly marked as that which existed between the bishop and the chapter in dioceses where the cathedral was a secular foundation.

Thus, while Wilfrid's connexion with his monasteries was still of the closest kind, his work as diocesan bishop and missionary had an individual character which overshadowed his monastic profession. The real development of Benedictinism in Northumbria was the work of his friend and associate Biscop Baducing,[1] better known as Benedict Biscop, the founder of Wearmouth and Jarrow.[2] A member of the court of Oswiu, he attached himself to the Romanizing party led by Alchfrid and Wilfrid. Soon after Wilfrid's departure for Rome in 653 he followed him with the same purpose of examining monastic life as it prevailed at the Holy See. He joined Wilfrid in Kent and, when Wilfrid stopped on the way at Lyons, preceded him to Rome. This first journey was followed by another undertaken at first in company with Alchfrid, who was recalled, however, by his father Oswiu for reasons of state. The date of this is uncertain, but it was probably soon after the synod at Whitby in 664. From Rome Biscop went to the famous monastery of Lérins, where the Benedictine observance had recently been introduced by Aygulf of

---

[1] Eddius, iii: 'ducem nobilem et admirabilis ingenii, quendam nomine Biscop Baducing.' In *H.E.* v. 19 he is called 'nomine Biscop, cognomento Benedictus'. See the note in Plummer, ii. 355.

[2] His journey in company with Wilfrid, not recorded in *H.A.*, is told in Eddius, iii, and in *H.E.* v. 19.

Fleury, one of the monks who in 653 had brought the remains of St. Benedict to Fleury from Monte Cassino.[1] Here Biscop received the tonsure and remained two years. It is probable that now, upon his entry into religion, he took the name Benedict. His return to Rome coincided with the death of Wighard, who had been sent there by Ecgberct, king of Kent, for consecration to the see of Canterbury, and with the consecration of Theodore of Tarsus in his stead. In 668 he accompanied Theodore to England and for two years remained in his diocese as abbot of the monastery of St. Peter and St. Paul which Augustine had founded at Canterbury. On resigning this post he went for a time to Rome and returned to Britain laden with books of sacred learning which he acquired there and in Gaul. For a time he proposed to settle in Wessex, attracted by the friendship of its king, Cœnwalh. But Cœnwalh died in 672, and Benedict betook himself to his native Northumbria, where he found a ready friend in Ecgfrid, the successor of Oswiu. In 674 he founded upon territory given him by Ecgfrid, on the left bank of the Wear, the monastery of Wearmouth, dedicated to St. Peter.[2]

The history of Benedict's doings at Wearmouth belongs largely to that of the fabric of his church there, which forms the subject of another essay in this volume. It will be seen that, unlike Wilfrid, who had been an inmate of Lindisfarne, he had no first-hand experience of the monastic life of the Scottish mission. His training was wholly Benedictine, his ideals of ecclesiastical organization and monastic discipline were Roman, and he brought them to a country in which the outstanding points of difference between the Scottish and Roman parties had been settled and the traditions inherited from Iona had been tacitly abandoned. Some time after the foundation of Wearmouth Benedict began to build the sister monastery of St. Paul at Jarrow, united with it in one inseparable society under two co-equal heads, as was indicated by the division between the two houses of the joint dedication to the Apostles.[3] Of Ceolfrid, the first abbot of Jarrow, mention has been made already. Entering the monastic profession at Ingætlingum, he had migrated to Ripon, where he was ordained priest by Wilfrid; and later had visited Kent and St. Botolph's monastery at Icanho in the East Anglian kingdom. At Wearmouth he became Benedict's right-hand man and accompanied him on his fifth visit to Rome which took place

[1] *H.A.* ii.   [2] *Ibid.* iii, iv.   [3] *Ibid.* vii.

about 678. It was not until after their return that Jarrow was founded in 681 or 682, when Benedict appointed his cousin Eosterwini abbot of Wearmouth and Ceolfrid abbot of Jarrow, and returned to Rome for a long visit from which he brought back fresh treasures to his monasteries.[1]

Bede himself entered the monastery of Wearmouth shortly before this period and his life at Jarrow began with its earliest years. Thus the *Historia Abbatum* was written with the fullest personal knowledge of Benedict's latest days and of the abbacy of Ceolfrid. Its details, however, need not be recounted here, as they belong more properly to an account of his life. It is sufficient to say that the death of Eosterwini occurred shortly before Benedict's last return from Rome, probably in 686. His successor Sicgfrid died in August 688 or 689, and Benedict, long afflicted with paralysis, died in the following January.[2] Before Sicgfrid's death the two monasteries were united under the rule of Ceolfrid,[3] which lasted until 716 and during which they flourished with all the freshness of youth. In June 716 Ceolfrid resigned and departed with the intention of seeing Rome once more before he died. The scene of his departure is drawn graphically by Bede: the company who, with golden cross and burning tapers, accompanied him to the river bank and watched him cross the ferry and ride away southward, saw him no more, nor did he obtain his desire, but died on the way at Langres. As he waited for his ship at some English port, news was brought to him of the election of Huætberct as his successor, which he confirmed.[4]

The rest of the life of Bede was spent under Huætberct, and after Bede's death in 735 the history of Benedict's double monastery is a blank. Even in Bede's lifetime the rapid decline of the Northumbrian power had brought with it a decline in ecclesiastical discipline, and it was only for a brief time that monastic life survived the increasing tendency to laxness and disorder. The foundation and prosperity, however, of Wearmouth and Jarrow, if followed by a period of eclipse, were a signal manifestation of the success of the Benedictine rule over the somewhat haphazard organization of Celtic monasteries in the north. Benedict Biscop and Ceolfrid ruled with different ideals from those of the Scottish abbots. Their monasteries were not established as centres of missionary work whose abbots were constantly engaged in visits to outposts which might serve as points of

[1] *Ibid.* vii.   [2] *Ibid.* xi–xiv.   [3] *Ibid.* xiii; *H.A. An.* xvi.   [4] *H.A.* xvii.

departure for further effort. They were homes of prayer, learning, and culture, in whose churches the divine office was celebrated in the beauty of holiness. They had no connexion with the growth of dioceses: there was no bishop within their walls, but their diocesan came to visit them from outside, as when Acca of Hexham came to Wearmouth to give his episcopal blessing to Huætberct.[1] That tendency to association with a particular tribe or family which was characteristic of Celtic monasteries and is seen here and there in earlier Northumbrian communities was eliminated from them. If Eosterwini was related to Benedict, yet Benedict himself, addressing his brethren shortly before his death, warned them emphatically against preferring considerations of family to piety and moral worth.[2] Their conversation was governed by the statutes which regulated their internal affairs and by the rule of St. Benedict; and when, three centuries after they had been laid desolate by Danish pirates, Aldwin of Winchcombe and his companions came to search for the vestiges of monasticism in the north of England, it was at Wearmouth and Jarrow that the long interrupted current of Benedictinism was resumed.

V

The letter which in the last year of his life Bede wrote to Ecgberct, bishop of York, deals freely with the decline of the religious life in his own day. Since the death of Aldfrid, the brother and successor of Ecgfrid, in 705, things had gone from bad to worse. Monasteries had fallen into the hands of married laymen, officers of the king and courtiers. There were some men who, without experience of any probation, were tonsured and became abbots at once. A number of nominal monasteries had come into being in which there was no monastic life to speak of. Under the pretence of founding religious communities worldly-minded laymen had bought lands from the king for themselves and their heirs in which they placed creatures of their own or monks who had been expelled or enticed from genuine monasteries. These institutions were abodes of sloth and vice. They were ruled by married men with families, whose wives were sometimes heads of *soi-disant* nunneries. In fact, the usurpation of monasteries by the laity was a scandal which needed reform. The object of Bede's letter was to urge upon

[1] *H.A.* xx.　　　　　　[2] *Ibid.* xi.

Ecgberct the desirability of establishing new bishoprics in ful-filment of the wish of Gregory the Great to create a province of York with twelve suffragan sees, corresponding to the ideal which he proposed for Canterbury. Bishops for such sees might well be found in monasteries, either among the monks themselves or with their advice and by their choice. But, amid the general deterioration, this was impracticable. Monastic reform was the first need: those royal grants which had filled the kingdom with spurious monasteries must be revoked and the monasteries be brought back by synodical authority to continence and piety of heart.[1]

This recognition by Bede of the advantages of a monastic episcopate was not a revival of the Celtic ideal of the monastic bishop subordinate to the jurisdiction of an abbot. The monas-tery is regarded as part of his diocese and within his cure of souls. At the same time, it was through the monastery that Bede saw the best opportunity for the extension of the influence of the Church. Through the spread of monasteries the Anglian Church had grown: with the decay of monasticism its own was closely involved. With these convictions, it is possible that Bede did not wholly understand the nature of the religious communities whose growth he deplored, and that he put an entirely adverse construction upon a system which followed no recognized rule and made little of celibacy. As a matter of fact, secular clergy were beginning to enter into competition with monks. We have seen already how the anchoretic movement was leavening Irish and Scottish monasteries even in the days of Columba. Monks were retiring from community life into solitude, and in the Celtic Church the age of anchorites was succeeding that of monks.[2] The same tendency was noticeable among the followers of Columbanus upon the Continent, where, however, the develop-ment of Benedictinism arrested the disintegration of monas-teries. To the life of the anchorite and hermit a notion of special sanctity was attached. He left the world with a special object which combined the ascetic taming of the body with the desire to enter into mystical communion with God. It is during the period of monastic decline in Ireland, when the holiness which had distinguished the life of monasteries was a thing of the past, that the term *Cele Dè*, the equivalent of the Latin *Servus*

[1] *Ep. ad Egb.* ix–xiii.
[2] See *Catalogus Sanctorum*, ap. H. and S. ii. 293.

Dei, appears to have come into use with a special application to missionaries who came with a message of reform and to those who, whether in hermitages or in religious communities, sought to adopt a stricter mode of life. Although *Servus Dei* in its earlier use was a term specially given to monks, its connotation was never exclusively monastic, and the *Cele Dè* or Culdee of the tenth and following centuries, whether anchorite or monk, was a member of no particular order.[1]

Anchorites obviously freed themselves from monastic observance and formed a separate element in the life of the Church which required organization, not only at this period but for long after. Side by side with these, especially upon the Continent, there were priests serving cures of souls or engaged in the services of particular churches whose life was guided by no rule, but who were frankly seculars, living in and mixing with the world. Some ten years after the death of Bede, Chrodegang, bishop of Metz, brought together the clergy of his cathedral church into a community for which he composed a rule of life.[2] Its basis was the organization of community life on a strict observance of the canonical precepts of the Church which constituted its common law. Thus members of such societies became known as canons, occupying an intermediate position between monks on the one hand and secular clergy upon the other. During the second half of the eighth century the rule of Chrodegang became widely known, and the Council of Aachen in 817 attempted to impose its observance upon all seculars. Although this endeavour met with no general success, it had the effect of multiplying communities of canons. The ultimate divergence between the secular canons of cathedral and collegiate churches and canons regular who adopted the rule of St. Augustine does not concern us here. It is enough to say that, so far as the north of England is concerned, the canonical life superseded the strictly monastic life and that the monasteries condemned by Bede indicate the decay of Benedictinism and the transition to a less exacting form of life, which as yet was controlled by no rule.

The movement which during the generation succeeding the

---

[1] 'Culdee is the most abused term in Scotic church history' (Reeves, *Adamnan*, 368 *n.*). The origin and implications of the term are fully discussed by Reeves in *Trans. Irish Acad.* xxiv (see Bibliography). See also Bellesheim, i. 24 ff.; *Hist. Ch. Ireland*, i.   [2] See *P.L.* lxxxix. 1057, 1120.

death of Bede made headway upon the Continent had its reper-
cussion upon the Scottish and Irish Churches, and seems to have
reached Ireland from Scotland early in the ninth century. Of
its introduction into England nothing is certain except that
canonicae begin to emerge somewhat dimly a century later from
the darkness of the period of Danish invasion and conquest, and
that some of these were established in old seats of monastic life
such as Ripon and Beverley.[1] But Bede, in urging upon Ecgberct
the reform of monasteries and their employment in the work of
diocesan extension, was addressing a prelate whose church at no
time in its history had conformed, so far as we know, to the
Benedictine rule. York was the seat of a bishop with his clerical
familia: neither under Wilfrid nor St. John of Beverley, whose
monasteries were elsewhere, had the church of York adopted a
monastic organization. The church of York under Ecgberct and
his successor Æthelberht, the first archbishop, of which Alcuin,
himself trained in Benedictinism, has left us a description, was
a centre of piety, art, and learning on which the example of
Wearmouth and Jarrow doubtless had its influence; but its
parallel is found, not in regular monasteries, but in such episcopal establishments as that of St. Chrodegang. It is certain
at any rate that its subsequent development, as well as that of
its closely allied churches at Ripon and Beverley, was upon the
lines of the Lotharingian system inaugurated at Metz, whose
traces long survived in the constitution of the chapter of
Beverley.

It may be noted here that in England the early association of
anchorites in communities, which is noticeable in Scotland and
Ireland after the introduction of the canonical system and left
its mark upon the constitution of the primatial church of Armagh
until a late date,[2] cannot be traced with any certainty, unless we
may assume that *canonicae* such as Beverley and Southwell, as
is quite possible, were founded on such a basis. But it is significant that the *Deicolae* or *Ceile Dè* of Celtic countries, terms
specially applicable to anchorites, became, through the latiniza-
tion of their Celtic name, the *Colidei* or Culdees whose churches
were establishments of canons, and that this term was used in
England with the same connotation and is definitely applied to

---

[1] See the introductions to *Mem. Ripon*, ii, *Bev. Chapter Act-Book*. i, and
Vis. and Mem. Southwell.
[2] See Reeves, *Culdees*, 128–37, 216–23.

the canons of the church of York at the period of the Norman Conquest.[1] The old fable which discovered in the Culdees a species of esoteric community, preserving a primitive sacred tradition which was hostile to the claims of Rome upon ecclesiastical obedience, has long been proved to be without foundation; and the contexts in which the term is used clearly show that it is nothing more than a synonym for secular canons leading a common life with a church as its central object.[2]

Meanwhile, whatever dangers and abuses beset the monastic life in 735, it still continued in the old centres. The sanctity of Lindisfarne was guarded by the memory of St. Cuthbert. In 740 died his disciple Æthelwald, who had succeeded him in his hermitage and had been called thence to be abbot of Melrose. Consecrated bishop of Lindisfarne in 721, he caused that cross to be made in memory of Cuthbert which accompanied the saint's body through its subsequent wanderings and was at last set up in the churchyard at Durham.[3] The retirement of the Northumbrian king Ceolwulf, to whom Bede dedicated the *Historia Ecclesiastica*, to Lindisfarne in 737, was a notable event in the history of the monastery. In so doing, Ceolwulf followed the example of some of his nobles, who took advantage of the peace that succeeded the early troubles of his reign to leave the practice of arms and transfer themselves and their families to monasteries.[4] This, however, which Symeon of Durham records with favourable comment, unquestionably led to the state of things which Bede deplored among his contemporaries, and Ceolwulf in his religious zeal can hardly be acquitted of encouraging a dangerous habit which was easily abused.

Materials for the later history of the monastery of Lindisfarne are scanty. It survived its sack in 793 by the Danish pirates who in the following year plundered Jarrow,[5] and it was not until

---

[1] Hugh the Chanter, ap. *Hist. Ch. York*, ii. 107, 108, describes the changes achieved in the constitution of the church of York by Thomas of Bayeux. The pre-Conquest clergy of York are called Culdees, *ibid*. iii. 162, in a document (1246) relating to St. Leonard's hospital: 'Qui omnes jurati veniunt et dicunt super sacramentum suum quod quidam rex ante Conquaestum tempore Englescherie dedit illis qui deservierunt ecclesiae Sancti Petri Eboracensis, qui vocabantur tunc Kaladeus, qui modo dicti sunt canonici, de singulis carucis junctis totius comitatus Eboracensis unam travam bladi.'

[2] As in the passage from the Register of St. Leonard's Hospital ap. *Mon. Ang.* vi. 608, 609, referring to the Culdees of York Minster: ' ministris dictae ecclesiae, adtunc dicti Colidei.'   [3] S.D. *Hist. Dun.* i. 12.

[4] *Ibid*. i. 13, 16.   [5] *Ibid*. i. 20.

after the great Danish invasion in 870 that the island was finally abandoned. That invasion, which eclipsed monasticism in the north and east of England for a long period, did not touch Lindisfarne. But the disaster of 793 had reduced the number of monks, and subsequently kings of Northumbria who cared nothing for its sacred traditions had robbed the monastery of possessions which their predecessors had granted. Moreover, the old race of monks had died out, and their successors, persons who had been brought up under monastic tuition and had taken the clerical habit, were no longer professed monks, and the only link which bound them to past observance was the unbroken recitation of the divine office.[1] But the body of Cuthbert, interred in their cemetery, remained their palladium to be guarded from sacrilege by the survivors of his congregation. In 875 their bishop Eardwulf and their abbot Eadred determined to disinter the body of the saint and other sacred relics and transfer them to some place of safety.[2] The sequel is well known and need not be recounted at length here. Attempts have been made to trace the course of that odyssey which ended after more than seven years in the settlement at Chester-le-Street, and a list of English churches dedicated to St. Cuthbert which was drawn up at Durham in the fifteenth century has been taken without foundation of fact to supply an itinerary of wanderings which led Eardwulf and his companions westward to the mouth of the Cumbrian Derwent, thence to Whithorn in Galloway, and finally to Crayke in the North Riding of Yorkshire, where the remnants of a monastery still existed.[3] There it is said that the abbot Eadred was ordered by St. Cuthbert in a vision to go to the army of the Danes, bereft of its leader Halfdene, demand from them the surrender of the Anglian prince Guthred, and proclaim him king at the place called Oswiesdune.[4] With the accession of Guthred and the departure of the Danish army for the time being to seek new spoil across seas, the guardians of the body took up their abode at Chester-le-Street in 883. It was at this time that the territory between Wear and Tyne became the patrimony of St. Cuthbert and that special privileges of sanc-

[1] *Ibid.* ii. 6: 'sed qui inter eos ab aetate infantili in habitu clericali fuerant nutriti atque eruditi, quocunque sancti Patris corpus ferebatur secuti sunt, moremque sibi a monachis doctoribus traditum in officiis duntaxat diurnae vel nocturnae laudis semper servarunt.'

[2] *Ibid.*

[3] *Ibid.* ii. 11–13.

[4] *Ibid.* ii. 13.

tuary were granted to the precincts of his shrine.[1] But, after more than a century of quiet, fear of the Danes once more in 995 drove Bishop Ealdhun and his congregation from Chester-le-Street to Ripon for three or four months, and it was on their return that they had the inspiration, accounted for by miraculous incidents, of choosing the natural fortress of Durham as the final home of their precious and restless charge.[2]

The migratory band which entered Durham with their bishop in 995 was a very different body from the monastic body to which they could trace their origin. As has been said, the persons who left Lindisfarne with Eardwulf were mainly secular clerks. They still formed a loosely knit community whose head, formerly a monk and abbot of Carlisle, still bore the title of abbot:[3] their custom of reciting the hours, the fundamental duty of the religious life, was maintained all through the long period which separated them from their coming to Durham. But they were under no vows, and it is perfectly clear that the rank and file were not celibate. It was a mixed company of men, women, and children which accompanied the body of Cuthbert from Lindisfarne. Worn by pestilence and famine, many died or fell out by the way to dwell where they could, until the multitude was reduced to the bishop and abbot and the seven chosen bearers of the sacred coffin, sworn to protect their ark of the covenant from the sin of Uzza.[4] From four of these bearers, whose families doubtless remained with them, Hunred, Stilheard, Eadmund, and Franco, the aristocracy of the Haliwerfolc, St. Cuthbert's subjects, were proud to derive their origin. Their office was hereditary, and, in default of other evidence, it may well be assumed that this body of seven clerks, a number frequently associated with a secular minster, and their successors formed the clergy of the churches of Chester-le-Street and of Durham in its early days. Although there were monks among the first

---

[1] S.D. *Hist. Dun.* ii. 14. This was in obedience to the command of St. Cuthbert, revealed to Eadred in his vision at Crayke.

[2] *Ibid.* iii. 1.

[3] *Ibid.* ii. 6: 'Eadredus quoque monachus et abbas; Ascito ergo probandae sanctitatis viro Eadredo, qui ab eo quod in Luel monasterio dudum ab ipso Cuthberto instituto educatus officium abbatis gesserit Lulisc cognominabatur.'

[4] *Ibid.* ii. 10: 'Nec tamen sacri corporis loculum nec in quo ferebatur vehiculum passim cuilibet attingere licitum fuerat, sed observata tantae sanctitati reverentia ex omnibus specialiter septem ad hoc ipsum constituti fuerant, ut si quid in his cura vel emendatione indigeret praeter ipsos nemo manum apponere auderet.'

community at Durham, yet they formed only a part of it, and Ælfred Westou, famous as a collector of relics of saints to do honour to St. Cuthbert and as the pious spoiler who brought the remains of Bede from Jarrow to Durham, was not a monk, but a secular, diligent in ringing the bells for matins and in instructing youth in reading, song, and divine service.[1]

It is true that the tradition prevailed that successors to the see of Cuthbert and Aidan should be monks. Thus Eadmund, consecrated bishop in 1020, became a monk. Where he was professed is not certain, but on his way from his consecration at Winchester he called at Peterborough and took with him thence a monk named Ægelric to be continually with him and teach him regular discipline.[2] On Eadmund's death at Gloucester in 1041, Eadred, the secular who was *post episcopum secundus* at Durham, bought the bishopric from Harthacnut. He did not long survive his act of simony, and after his sudden death his place was taken by Ægelric. The seculars, however, refused to receive Ægelric as their bishop and expelled him. Restored to his see by the instrumentality of Siward, earl of Northumbria, he surrounded himself with monks, chief among them his brother Ægelwin, who busied themselves in helping him to secure the money and treasure of the church and transfer them to Peterborough, where he eventually retired, leaving Ægelwin to succeed him.[3]

The old position was thus reversed. The secular clerks clung to the church in opposition to the bishop and his *familia* of monks. Some credit may be given to Ægelric for the work of rebuilding in stone the church of Chester-le-Street, which hitherto had been of timber,[4] and it is possible that he intended to found a monastic chapter here to counteract the seculars of Durham, just as, long after, Antony Bek, at variance with the monks of Durham, set up secular chapters at Auckland, Chester-le-Street, and Lanchester. Ægelwin pursued his brother's policy of robbing his church, though under the stress of the disturbances of 1069 and 1070 he became its defender and, during the Conqueror's wasting of the north, led the brief and hasty migration in which the body of St. Cuthbert revisited Lindisfarne.[5]

---

[1] *Ibid*. iii. 7.   [2] *Ibid*. iii. 6.   [3] *Ibid*. iii. 9.
[4] *Ibid*.: 'Placuerat eidem antistiti ecclesiam in Cunecaceastre . . . de ligno factam destruere et . . . aliam de lapide fabricare.' But he appropriated the treasure found in digging the foundations and sent it to Peterborough.
[5] *Ibid*. iii. 15.

But Ægelwin had more to fear from the Conqueror's wrath than the saint, who already had frustrated a first visit contemplated by William and presumably could repeat the miracle.[1] After his return to Durham, he endeavoured to escape abroad with part of his stolen treasure, but was driven back to the coast of Scotland, and eventually was captured by William's officers and died in prison.[2] Meanwhile Walcher, a secular clerk well disposed to the monastic life, was made bishop. Finding that the seculars of Durham were using the mixed rites and customs inherited from the last days of Lindisfarne, he reorganized them upon the lines of a secular community.[3] But before his tragic death at Gateshead in 1080, the result of his negligence in the administration of his bishopric and the earldom of Northumberland in which he atoned for the cupidity of his ministers, he contemplated the introduction of monks and had begun to build a cloister at Durham.[4]

The days of seculars were numbered. Walcher had apparently been unable to change their way of living. His successor, the Benedictine William of Saint-Calais, could call them neither monks nor canons. They were simply secular clerks, living upon old traditions founded on the decay of monastic observance. The new bishop, eager to restore the monastic discipline which, as he heard, had prevailed under Aidan and Cuthbert at Lindisfarne and taking little account of the devotion which had preserved the sacred relics through so many vicissitudes, brought to Durham monks from the recently revived houses of Wearmouth and Jarrow and gave the seculars the choice of staying as monks or departing. All chose to depart with the exception of

---

[1] S. D. *Hist. Dun.* iii. 15: The first visit of William, to take vengeance upon the murderers of Robert Cumin, was prevented by a dense fog at Northallerton, attributed to the agency of St. Cuthbert.

[2] *Ibid.* iii. 17.

[3] *Ibid.* iii. 18: 'primus post Aidanum ex clericali ordine ipsius ecclesiae suscepit praesulatum, sed vitae laudabilis conversatione religiosum praeferebat monachum. Qui cum clericos ibidem inveniret, clericorum morem in diurnis et nocturnis officiis eos servare docuit; nam antea magis consuetudines monachorum in his imitati fuerant sicut a progenitoribus suis, ut supradictum est, qui inter monachos nutriti et educati extiterant, hereditaria semper traditione didicerant.'

[4] *Ibid.* iii. 22: 'Hic quoque, si diuturniora sibi hujus vitae tempora extitissent, monachus fieri et monachorum habitationem ad sacrum corpus beati Cuthberti stabilire decreverat. Unde positis fundamentis monachorum habitacula ubi nunc habentur Dunelmi construere coepit, sed heu proh dolor morte praeventus quod disposuerat perficere nequivit.'

their dean, who was persuaded with difficulty by his son, already a monk, to make his profession.[1] It is possible that he was a widower, and it can hardly be doubted that among his companions there were some who had wives and families.[2] Indeed, the supersession of *clerici* by *monachi* at Durham was the substitution of celibates for a secular married clergy who retained certain monastic customs.

In relating the end of the descendants of the congregation of St. Cuthbert, we have anticipated the revival of the two foundations from which Benedictine Durham was colonized. But, before arriving at their history, we must examine the fate of the two monasteries founded by Wilfrid. It has already been said that the Danish invasion of 870, falling upon a kingdom which had lost its pre-eminence and become practically moribund, blotted out monasticism in the north. Whitby disappeared, Wearmouth and Jarrow disappeared, then if not earlier. Some small monasteries such as that which we have noticed as existing at Crayke in 883 may have escaped the storm, but it is improbable that they retained a distinctively monastic character. There can be no doubt that the first ravaging of northern monasteries by the Danes in 793 and 794 marks a dividing line in their history: weakened by plunder and massacre, the diminished communities relaxed a discipline for which no adequate means of guidance were left. At Hexham the bishopric came silently to an end after the death of Tidferth in 821.[3] If the monastery continued to exist, Halfdene's invasion put an end to it in 875. There is some evidence that early in the tenth century it was restored for a time, but this cannot be taken as a certainty.[4] All that we know is that the bishops of Chester-le-Street seem to have annexed the church of Hexham to their see, regarding themselves as successors of the bishops of Hexham, and administered it by provosts and priests, the first of whom had charge of its temporalities, while the second had cure of souls.[5]

---

[1] *Ibid.* iv. 3.

[2] See *Arch.* xlv. 386, where Dr. Fowler, describing the excavations made in 1874 on the site of the chapter-house at Durham, says that, 'below the level of the graves of the bishops, the earth was full in all directions of interments of men, women, and children, the adult skulls being of a distinctly long-headed type, and so, as is believed, marking a cemetery belonging to the period previous to the expulsion of the secular married canons . . . in 1083'.

[3] On the end of the see of Hexham see *Priory Hexh.* i, introd., pp. xl, xli.

[4] *Ibid.*, p. xlix.

[5] See the document quoted *ibid.*, app. p. vii: 'Post illud tempus episcopi apud

Both offices were hereditary, the provostship descending in the family of Hunred, who has been mentioned as one of the original guardians of St. Cuthbert's body. From the time at any rate of Edmund, the second bishop of Durham, the priesthood was held, like a prebend in a secular college, by members of the community at Durham who served the cure by deputy. Ælfred Westou, the indefatigable relic-hunter, who was probably a member of a younger branch of the house of Hunred, was sacrist at Durham and priest of Hexham. The priesthood descended to his son Eilaf, treasurer at Durham.[1] The events of 1069 and 1070, as we have seen, left the Conqueror master of the north and were followed by the flight of Bishop Ægelwin from Durham. At this point the provost Uctred seems to have bethought him of the early connexion of Hexham with Wilfrid, whose possession of Hexham while he was bishop of York had been granted him by Ecgfrid's queen Æthelthryth. In the vacancy of the see of Durham, Uctred suggested to the new archbishop of York, Thomas of Bayeux, that he should annex the wasted lands of Hexham to his domains.[2] Thus Hexham and Hexhamshire passed under the sway of the primate and obtained that immunity from the jurisdiction of the bishops of Durham which they possessed for several centuries. Eilaf still held the priesthood and his office at Durham. But in 1083, when Benedictine monks were introduced at Durham, Eilaf was one of the expelled clerks. He now went to the archbishop and was confirmed in the priesthood of Hexham, which passed upon his death to his son, another Eilaf.[3] In the meantime, however, Thomas of Bayeux annexed Hexham to a prebend in the church of York, and both Eilafs retained merely the cure of souls and part of the endowments.[4] Their status in fact was changed from

Sanctum Cuthbertum illum locum tenuerunt, et ibidem, scilicet in Hagustald', suos presbiteros statuerunt et praepositos.'

[1] Ibid., app. p. viii: 'Eluredus, Westou sune, secretarius Dunelmensis ecclesiae dono domini sui Edmundi episcopi tenuit ecclesiam de Hagustaldaham; et postea posuit in ea presbiterum Gamel elde et postea . . . Gamel iunge. . . . Post Eluredum filius ejus Eylaf Lawreu, thesaurarius Dunelmensis ecclesiae, tenuit ecclesiam . . . ponens ibi presbiterum Sproh.'

[2] Ibid.   [3] Ibid.

[4] Rich. Hex., ibid. i. 51: 'Sed non multo post idem archipraesul eam, cum quadam villa nomine Holm, dedit in praebendam Eboracensi ecclesiae cuidam canonico ecclesiae Sancti Johannis Beverlacensis qui Ricardus de Maton vocabatur. Sub quo quidem presbyter nomine Aeillavus, praedicti Aeillavi filius, eidem ecclesiae sumministravit et pro suo servitio quandam partem beneficiorum habuit.'

that of rectors to a curacy in which they were deputies of the pre-bendary. Finally in 1113 Archbishop Thomas II restored Hexham to the monastic life, introducing a prior and convent of canons regular into the church and compensating the prebendary with a share in the commons of the canons of York.[1] Eilaf II, how-ever, was allowed to remain as parish priest. The two Eilafs deserved some gratitude for their efforts to repair and rebuild the church, and it is also interesting to note that Ælred, the son of Eilaf II, bearing the name of his great-grandfather, be-came a monk and abbot of Rievaulx and thus the greatest of English Cistercians traced his descent through the clerks of Durham back to the chief of the bearers who carried the remains of St. Cuthbert from Lindisfarne.[2] It was hardly by accident that, when monks of Rievaulx colonized the first Cistercian abbey in Scotland, they settled at Melrose, the scene of Cuth-bert's novitiate and profession.

At Ripon the monastic observances introduced by Wilfrid long survived his death. The history of the church, however, during the Danish inroads is very obscure. The same may be said of the churches, so closely allied with it, of York and Beverley. Æthelstan, on one of his visits to the north, probably that in 925, is said to have visited all three. The famous story preserved in the chartulary of St. Leonard's Hospital at York relates how the king found Culdees serving the church of York and in return for their prayers granted them of his regality a thrave of corn annually from every plough in Yorkshire from which to maintain hospitality.[3] His name was also connected with a similar grant of thraves from the East Riding to Beverley and of privileges of sanctuary and immunity from taxation both to Beverley and Ripon; but, although the strength of tradition seems to rest upon some substructure of fact, the evidence was compiled at a much later period.[4] Nor is there any evidence with regard to the constitution of either church at this period. Whatever form of religious life survived at Ripon, it was brought

---

[1] *Ibid.* i. 54, 55.

[2] The delivery by Eilaf II of the interest which he retained in the church, when nearing his end, to the prior and canons, was witnessed by William, first abbot of Rievaulx, and Ælred, 'monachus eius et filius ipsius Aeilavi' (*ibid.* i. 55). See Ælred's tract *De Sanctis ecclesiae Hagustaldensis, ibid.* i. 173–203.

[3] *Mon. Ang.* vi. 608, 609.

[4] See texts, *Mem. Rip.* i. 90–3, and *Bev. Chapt. Act-Book*, ii. 280–7.

to an end by the punitive expedition of Eadred to Northumbria about 948, when he avenged himself upon Archbishop Wulfstan for his treasonable dealings with the Danes by a campaign of fire and slaughter in the course of which Ripon, one of the archbishop's possessions, was laid waste. When Oda, archbishop of Canterbury, came to Ripon a few years later, he found Wilfrid's monastery a solitary ruin, and took the opportunity of removing the remains of its founder, with the exception of a small portion, to Canterbury. There were, however, two versions of this story into whose relative merits we need not enter, and in the long run the claim of Ripon to possess the bones of St. Wilfrid gained popular credence. When Oda's nephew Oswald, after his accession to the see of York in 972, visited Ripon, the church was still untenanted, and what relics Oda had left behind him were apparently in confusion, but Oswald caused a shrine to be made in which he placed such as were supposed to be those of Wilfrid.[1]

A somewhat ambiguous passage in the anonymous life of Oswald has been taken by some to record his reintroduction of monks to Ripon. The place, however, to which reference is made seems from the context to be one of the sees which he held simultaneously,[2] and it is much more likely that of these not York but Worcester is meant. For, while Oswald played a leading part in the work of monastic reform promoted by Dunstan and Æthelwold, his activity belonged mainly to the southern province and especially to the revival of monasteries in his diocese of Worcester. Of his tenure of the see of York almost nothing is known, and it is certain that he left no permanent impression upon religious life in this district. At York he is merely a name, whereas at Worcester, where he was buried, he gave a powerful impetus to ecclesiastical reform.[3]

At the same time, there can be no doubt that Oswald's visit to Ripon was followed by the renewal of divine worship there. At Ripon the body of St. Cuthbert rested for some time during

---

[1] The passages from various chroniclers relating to these events are collected in *Mem. Rip.* i. 36–46.

[2] *Ibid.* i. 42: 'De loco in quo ejus pontificalis cathedra posita est, quid referam quidque dicam? Nonne in eo quo quondam mansitabant dracones et struciones fecit Deo servire monachos?'

[3] See the essay on St. Oswald by the late bishop of Worcester in *York Minster Hist. Tracts.*

the migration from Chester-le-Street to Durham.[1] It is unknown what type of community gave hospitality to the body and its bearers, but the later history of Ripon indicates that it was more probably a body of seculars, akin to that which it presumably entertained, than one of monks. Ripon was one of the churches specially connected with the see of York. Of three of these, York, Beverley, and Southwell, we know something in the period before the Norman Conquest. The tradition of Culdees or secular clerks at York goes back, as we have seen, to the days of Æthelstan. At Beverley and Southwell, during the eleventh century, successive archbishops did much in the way of beautifying the churches and building houses for the local communities,[2] and of Beverley it may be said that it was a church of secular canons organized upon the Lotharingian model. The same model probably had its influence upon Southwell, and, when Thomas of Bayeux in 1070 found the seculars of York dispersed, he made temporary use of it in gathering together the clergy of the church as a preliminary to the establishment of a chapter upon the Norman pattern which was familiar to him.[3]

Ripon at all events after the Conquest appears as the home of a body of seculars who were called canons and developed into a chapter whose constitution received important alterations in the thirteenth century and was not finally settled until about 1300.[4] With Beverley and Southwell it may be reckoned among the *monasteria* of secular clergy whose prevalence in England at the time of the Conquest is witnessed by Domesday Book.[5] It is interesting to notice how to such churches the title minster has clung through all their later history, so that *monasterium* in their case does not imply the existence of monks, but that of a community of seculars as distinct from the regular communities of abbeys and priories.

The old monastic life of the Northumbrian kingdom had thus given way in the period between the Danish invasions and the Conquest to the adoption of a loosely knit organization of secular clergy in certain centres. Not until 1069 was a Benedictine monastery founded in a district which for some two

---

[1] S.D. *Hist. Dun.* iii. 1.

[2] *Chron. Pontif. Ebor.*, ap. *Hist. Ch. York*, ii. 343, 344, 353, 354.

[3] Hugh the Chanter, *ibid.* ii. 108.

[4] See documents in *Mem. Rip.* ii. 2, 3, 25.

[5] See W. Page, 'Some Remarks on Churches of the Domesday Survey' (*Arch.* lxvi. 61–102).

centuries had lost its connexion with the regular religious life. Then Selby Abbey grew out of the hermitage of a monk from Auxerre on the right bank of the Ouse some distance below York.[1] But the revival of Benedictinism in the north was the work of a monk from the diocese of Worcester, Aldwin of Winchcombe, who, edified by the rumour that Northumbria had once been full of monasteries, set out with two companions from Evesham to explore their remains. At York the sheriff, Hugh Fitz Baldric, who had been a good friend to Selby, provided them with a guide who led them to the Tyne.[2] Their quest was obviously inspired by the study of Bede and perhaps also by traditions which the close association of the dioceses of York and Worcester for a time under one bishop had fostered. After a short residence on the site of the Roman *Pons Aelii*, known as Monkchester on account of some old monastic settlement there,[3] they eventually reached the goal of their journey at Jarrow. There, favoured by Bishop Walcher, they remained, raising new buildings: the twin monastery of Wearmouth was revived, and in 1083 William of Saint-Calais called the monks of Wearmouth and Jarrow to form his convent at Durham. In the meantime, however, Reinfrid, one of the three companions, had left Jarrow, and, after living for a time at Hackness, founded the abbey of Whitby on the headland where Hilda's monastery had stood.[4] A band of monks who seceded from Whitby took up their abode for a time at Lastingham, where Cedd had been abbot, and about 1085 colonized the famous abbey of St. Mary outside the ramparts of York.[5] Thus Wearmouth and Jarrow, the scenes of the first complete experiment of Benedictine observance in Northumbria, became the cradle of revived Benedictinism in the north of England. In no small degree this revival may be attributed to the fame of the works of Bede, the historian of the age of missionary activity in which monasticism

---

[1] See *Historia Selebiensis Monasterii*, ap. *Coucher Book of Selby* (Yorks. Rec. Ser.), i. [1]–[54].

[2] S.D. *Hist. Dun.* iii. 21; *Hist. Reg.* sub anno 1075 (Surt. Soc. li. 94 ff.).

[3] Munekeceastre is mentioned by S.D. only in *Hist. Reg.*, where he identifies it with Newcastle. As it is mentioned nowhere else, and there is no record of any early monastery at Newcastle, it is not improbable that the name may have been coined in consequence of Aldwin's settlement there. The identification with Newcastle is open to some doubt, and the editor of the Surt. Soc. volume was inclined to suggest Wallsend as an alternative.

[4] *Whitby Chart.* i. 1, 2.

[5] *Mon. Angl.* i. 545.

played so great a part. It was fitting that from Wearmouth and Jarrow, so intimately connected with his life and labours, the rule of St. Benedict should be brought to the church in which Cuthbert lay in state and to which the remains of Bede himself had not long before that time been removed.

A. HAMILTON THOMPSON.

MONKWEARMOUTH AND JARROW

THERE are two places in the county of Durham where buildings which may claim to have been standing in Bede's lifetime still exist, Monkwearmouth and Jarrow. For the history of both he is the primary authority. It has often been repeated, and here it will not be necessary to do more than give the bare outline, on which a description of what now remains may be based.

Benedict Biscop, founder of the monastery of Wearmouth, was by birth an Angle of good family, who as a young man was taken into King Oswiu's service, and in due course received a grant of lands sufficient to keep up his position. In his twenty-fifth year he gave up his worldly prospects, in order to be free to go to Rome, and on his return thence occupied himself with study and preaching. Alchfrid, son of King Oswiu, wishing to make the journey to Rome, chose him as his companion, but was forbidden by his father to leave the country. Benedict, however, made the journey, and on the way back from this second visit to Rome went to the monastery at Lérins, where he was duly professed a monk, and for the next two years lived as one of the community. But the attraction of Rome was too strong for him, and he again set forth, this time in a merchant ship which had called at the monastery. While he was in Rome, Wighard, the elect of Canterbury, sent by King Ecgberct of Kent to receive consecration at the Pope's hands, arrived with his companions, but died there before he could be made bishop. In his place the Pope chose Theodore of Tarsus, and giving him as colleague and adviser the abbot Adrian, sent him to Britain, ordering Benedict to return with them. The three landed in Kent in May 669, and Benedict was made abbot of the monastery of St. Peter and St. Paul at Canterbury.

After two years, however, he revisited Rome, and returned with a number of books, intending to go to the court of Cœnwalh, king of the West Saxons, who had shown him friendship. But the king died as soon as Benedict arrived, and he went back to his native Northumbria, where King Ecgfrid welcomed him, and granted him lands on the north bank of the mouth of the river

Wear, that he might build a monastery there, This was in the year 674. A year was spent in preliminaries, and then Benedict went to Gaul to find masons who should build him a stone church, after the Roman fashion to which he was devoted. With their help the work went so quickly that within a year from the start the roofs were on and the church of St. Peter in use. As the building neared completion, Benedict sent to Gaul for glassmakers, craftsmen hitherto unknown in Britain, to fill the windows of the church, the porticus and the refectories (*caenacula*). The glassmakers did more than this, they taught the art of making lamps to light the *claustra* of the church, and vessels suitable for divers purposes. For the rest, the holy vessels and vestments, and all things necessary for divine service, were brought from abroad, since they could not be found in Britain. But Gaul could not supply everything, and so once more Benedict journeyed to Rome in the company of Ceolfrid on his fifth visit, and brought back books, relics, and paintings, and with them John, the arch-chanter of St. Peter's Church and abbot of St. Martin's, Rome, to teach the right methods of singing. The paintings were on boards, and they were set up in St. Peter's Church as follows: our Lady and the twelve Apostles were set round the *media testudo*, the boarding extending from wall to wall; the Gospel history was on the south wall of the church; the Apocalypse of St. John on the north wall. So that all who entered the church, whether they could read or no, might see, whithersoever they turned, the faces of Christ and His Saints, the birth of the Lord, or the Last Judgement.

King Ecgfrid was so pleased with Benedict's administration that he gave land for the foundation of a second monastery, to be closely connected with Wearmouth, at Jarrow. Seventeen monks, with Ceolfrid as abbot, were sent to colonize it; it was dedicated to St. Paul. This was in 683, and Benedict, in order to obtain further ornaments for his two monasteries, went for the sixth time to Rome, leaving Eosterwini abbot in Wearmouth and Ceolfrid in Jarrow. Eosterwini died before Benedict returned, and Sicgfrid was chosen to succeed him, but fell sick shortly after his consecration. Benedict himself had not long been back when he became paralysed and it was evident that neither he nor Sicgfrid had long to live. Ceolfrid was therefore made abbot of both monasteries, and so remained till June 716, when he resigned in order to make the pilgrimage to Rome.

Benedict had brought with him, from his last journey, a number of books and many paintings. To adorn the church of St. Mary which he had built at Wearmouth (*monasterium majus*) he had bought a set of pictures of the Life of our Lord, which went all round the walls, and for the church of St. Paul at Jarrow, and for the monastery also, he had brought sets of types and antitypes from the old and new Testaments.

He had also brought two silver pallia, with which he bought from King Aldfrid a piece of land near the mouth of the Wear.

Benedict died in the year 690, having ruled Wearmouth for sixteen years. Ceolfrid, as abbot of both houses, continued to enrich them with books and vestments, and built several chapels: in his time the monastic possessions greatly increased by gifts and purchases of land. The story of his departure for Rome gives some evidence of the buildings then standing at Wearmouth. After mass in the church of St. Mary and in that of St. Peter, all the convent assembled in St. Peter's, and the abbot standing on the steps before the altar, with a censer in his hand, gave them the kiss of peace. From the church they went to the oratory of St. Laurence, which was in the dorter, and thence to the bank of the river where Benedict embarked on a boat which took him to the other side, where a horse awaited him. The monks of Wearmouth at once met to choose a successor, taking those of Jarrow into their counsel, and Huætberct was chosen without any dissent, so that it was possible for him to go to Ceolfrid where he awaited the ship that was to take him overseas, to receive confirmation of his election, and to entrust to him a letter to Pope Gregory.

Ceolfrid, we are told, was in the monastery of Ælbert, in a place called Cornu Vallis, and the only evidence for its position is based on the statement that his journey to Gaul was to be by way of the mouth of the river Humber.

Acca, bishop of Hexham, was brought to consecrate Huæt-berct abbot of the twin monasteries, and the new abbot made it his first business to translate the bodies of Eosterwini and Sicgfrid into the church of St. Peter, and to bury them in one coffin next to the body of Benedict. Benedict had been buried in the porticus of St. Peter, to the east of the altar: Eosterwini in the entrance porch (*porticus ingressus*) of St. Peter's Church, and Sicgfrid outside the sanctuary (*foris sacrarium*) to the south. As it seems unlikely that the high altar in the church should not have been that of St. Peter, and equally so that there should have been a second altar of St. Peter in a porticus (taking the word to mean a side chapel), it looks as if the eastern apse is here referred to as the porticus of St. Peter, and that Benedict was buried here, to the east of the high altar, Eosterwini and Sicgfrid being brought to the same place in 716. The translation took place on the *dies natalis* of Sicgfrid, and Uitmær, dying on the same day, was buried, we are told, in the place where the abbots had formerly lain. This is obscure, seeing that they had not originally been buried side by side, but perhaps it may be assumed that the western porticus is meant.

So much in respect of the buildings of Wearmouth and Jarrow it is possible to obtain from Bede's writings—incidentally the existence of a common dormitory and a common refectory is deducible from the fact that Eosterwini preferred to take his meals and to sleep in the same place as the monks after he had been made abbot, and not separately, as it was open to him to do. From other contemporary monasteries it can be assumed that there were separate buildings for the novices, and separate infirmaries for the sick, and that the members of the community lived in small houses like those mentioned at Coldingham, and of which remains have been found at Whitby. Bede himself, as we know, died in his *casula* at Jarrow.

Both monasteries were laid waste in the last years of the ninth century by the Danes and so remained till near the end of the eleventh, when they were once more brought into use. Some measure of occupation may have existed between these dates, but nothing that could be called a community remained at either place.

In the time of Bishop Eadmund of Durham, 1022-45, there was in the monastery a priest named Ælfred, son of Westou, who being specially devoted to the relics of the saints, went about Northumbria collecting such as he could find. In this manner he dug up—and placed in shrines—the bones of the anchorites Balther and Bilfrid, of Acca and Alchmund, bishops of Hexham, of King Oswiu, and of the abbesses Æbba and Ethelgitha. Parts of all of these he brought to Durham and put them with St. Cuthbert's body. From Melrose he brought the bones of St. Boisil, and set them in a shrine near St. Cuthbert's, and going to Jarrow on several occasions, on the anniversary of Bede's death, he was accustomed to stay there, and eventually contrived to abstract the saint's bones and bring them secretly to Durham, putting them into St. Cuthbert's coffin.

In the time of Simeon of Durham, who wrote his *History of the Church of Durham* at the beginning of the twelfth century, a porticus was still shown on the north side of St. Paul's Church at Jarrow, dedicated to the memory of Bede, and the site of his cell —*mansiuncula*—was also pointed out. This of course was after the reinstatement of the monastery by Aldwin. In the devastation of the north by King William in 1069 the church of St. Paul in Jarrow is said to have been burnt, so that there was something more than a ruin there before Aldwin's time. Aldwin was sent with his companions to Jarrow by Bishop Walcher, who held the see of Durham from 1071 to 1080, and found at Jarrow the remains of many buildings, with some half-destroyed churches. Shortly afterwards he went on to Wearmouth, where also ruined buildings remained, and in both places he repaired the churches and added accommodation for monks, such as may still be seen on the south side of the church at Jarrow.

It now becomes necessary to consider what, at this time, may have survived of the buildings which Bede himself had known.

It is recorded that in addition to the church of St. Peter there was a church of St. Mary at Wearmouth, and also an oratory of St. Laurence in the dorter.

There is abundant evidence for the existence of several churches in these early monasteries, and in more than one it is possible to establish the fact that they were built on the same axis, in a line from east to west. At the present day the early work at Wearmouth is at the west, while at Jarrow it is at the east, but there is at the latter place complete evidence that there existed an early western church, larger than that now remaining at the east and on the same axis with it. What Aldwin did was to throw these two churches into one, much as Wulfric did at St. Augustine's, Canterbury, in the middle of the eleventh century, with the churches of St. Mary and St. Peter and St. Paul. The whole length, therefore, of the western church at Jarrow became that of the nave of the monastic church, and a description printed in Hutchinson's *History of Durham* shows what it looked like. It was 28 paces in length—84 feet—and only six paces—18 feet—in width. The side walls were nearly 30 feet high, so that 'the edifice had a very singular appearance'. The existing nave at Wearmouth is 65 feet long by 19 feet wide,

and some 27 feet high to the wall plate. At the west end of
Wearmouth is a porch of entrance, and the same feature occurred at Jarrow. We can hardly be wrong in seeing in this as
much as has come down to us of the churches of St. Peter at
Wearmouth and St. Paul at Jarrow, with a second church to
the east at Jarrow, and evidence that a similar church existed
at Wearmouth. This latter can hardly have been other than the
church of St. Mary, built by Benedict Biscop, and the existing
chancel at Jarrow, which is the nave of a small church, may well
be due to Abbot Ceolfrid, and in that case must date before the
year 716.

Taking Monkwearmouth first, what is now left to us may be
identified as the west wall of the nave of St. Peter's Church,
begun about 675, with a two-story west porch which is not
bonded into the wall of the nave, but is probably part of the
original design. Abbot Eosterwini was buried in the porch of
entrance in or about 684.

The west wall of the nave is sufficiently preserved to show its
original width and height to the wall plate, with the pitch of the
nave roof. The walling is in small irregular courses, with a
little herring-bone masonry, and the original quoins at the
north-west angle, which show traces of fire, are of good size
though not megalithic, nor do they show any tendency to the
long-and-short technique of later pre-Conquest masonry. The
south-west angle is not original, nor is there anything in the
south wall of the nave that looks like early masonry. What we
can gather from this is the width and height of the nave of
Benedict's church of St. Peter, built with the aid of his Gaulish
masons in 675–6. The west doorway remains, having a single
upright stone in each jamb, with horizontal stones at the springing of the arch, tailing nearly 3 feet into the wall on either side.
The semicircular arch is built with eight voussoirs of the full
thickness of the wall, cut back on the east side to give room for
the opening of the door. Above is the doorway opening to the
chamber over the west porch, with modern stonework on its
east face, but having on its west face an original semicircular
head cut in a single stone. High up in the wall are two round-
headed windows with splayed jambs, into the lower parts of
which are set four baluster shafts. The west porch is not bonded
into the nave wall, but on the evidence of the doorway above
the west door of the church was prepared for from the first, and

there seems no reason to consider it as other than part of the original building. It was of two stories with a gabled roof, and its details are of careful and even ornate workmanship. In its north and south walls are doorways in the same technique as the west door of the church, while the western entrance to the porch is an open archway of more remarkable character. It is 4 ft. 10 in. wide, with a semicircular arch of nine voussoirs once recessed on each face, and worked with a small roll on the arris. The chamfered imposts have similar edge-rolls and rest on pairs of baluster shafts, below which are carved on the face of the jamb two intertwined long-billed creatures. The craftsmanship is that of skilled masons, and the string-course above the archway is of equally careful execution, showing the weathered remains of small animals in low relief between cable mouldings. In the upper story of the porch, the floor of which is carried on a stone barrel vault, there is a wide west window, round-headed with a chamfered arris, but modernized, and over it is a chamfered string marking the base of the original gable of the porch, the masonry of which is clearly distinct from the later work above. On the gable are traces of a standing figure, some 6 feet high, between two rounded corbel stones, and it is reasonable to suppose that a rood between our Lady and St. John completed the design. The ornamental details of this porch are confined to its western face, and in its north and south walls, in addition to the doorway already mentioned, there is only to be noted a small blocked window in the south wall of the upper story, perhaps original, and a blocked square-headed doorway in its north wall which looks like an insertion. At a recent repair search was made, but in vain, for traces of buildings flanking the porch on north and south, to which the side doorways would have given access. Such are the remaining parts of the church of Wearmouth which we may suppose that Bede himself must have seen. The porch has been carried up as a tower, the details of the work making it probable that it is part of Aldwin's repair late in the eleventh century. Coeval with it is the chancel arch which, as already suggested, may mark the eastern end of Benedict's church of St. Peter.

At Jarrow the modern nave stands on the site of the original church of St. Paul dedicated, according to the inscription still preserved, on 23 April 685. What is known of it derives from a drawing dated 1769 in the British Museum, and the account in

Hutchinson's *History of Durham* (ii. 475), published in 1785, two years after it was pulled down. On neither document would it be safe to base any conclusions: a blocked arcade is shown in the north wall, and that a church of this age may have had aisles is possible, on the analogy of Brixworth; but since no critical examination is possible, we must be content to repeat Hutchinson's statement that 'it was not to be distinguished to what age any particular part of it belonged'. The high narrow nave and western porch must in comparison with Wearmouth be part of Ceolfrid's church, and that is perhaps as far as it is safe to go.

The present chancel, which is the nave of a small church built directly to the east of the church of St. Paul, measures 41 ft. 6 in. by 15 ft. 9 in. and is built of squared stones, more angular than the masonry of Wearmouth, with large quoin-stones at all four angles. In its south wall are three original windows with round heads cut from single stones, bonding stones at the springing, and single upright stones in the jambs. Within they are splayed, and on the splays of the eastern windows of the three is a coat of plaster, showing traces of a dark red paint, which from the appearance of its junction with the mortar of the walls is possibly coeval with the building. Two of the three windows have roughly pierced stone slabs—the third was pulled out by Sir Gilbert Scott—flush with the outer face of the wall, and it is evident from the eastern window that the slab is not later than the plaster, which is carried over its edge without any break. If then the plaster is original, the slabs must also be original. In the middle of the north wall is an original doorway, and traces of another in the south wall: the west wall having been removed, there is no evidence for a west doorway. That there was a chancel to the east is shown by the remains of the jambs of its western arch, but the plan has not been recovered and is probably destroyed by later burials.

Such are the evidences from which we may recover for ourselves a picture of the surroundings in which the greater part of Bede's life was spent. He lived in one of a number of small stone houses set round the principal church of the monastery and its chapels. Nothing in the nature of a cloister existed, but certain buildings larger than the rest served as dormitories and refectories, and perhaps also as infirmaries. At Wearmouth we know that the dormitory was on the south of the church on

V

BEDE AS HISTORIAN

'Semper aut discere aut docere aut scribere dulce habui.'—Bede, *H.E.* v. 24.

WHEN Bede began to write, there was a decline of historiography everywhere in the western world; the historical heritage of Antiquity was not only diminishing but, moreover, had
ceased to be productive. There had been several continuations
of Eusebius' Chronicle as translated by Jerome: hardly one was
added after the sixth century; the same thing happened to the
annals affixed to the *Fasti Consulares*. In Italy, only the *Liber
Pontificalis*, the official collection of the Lives of the Popes, put
forth new germs. In the kingdom of the Franks, the later part
of the sixth century had seen the Histories of Gregory of Tours,
which, combining the records of State, Church, and the lesser
circles of society, were unparalleled for a long time in abundance
and vividness. The compilation of the so-called Fredegarius,
partly connected with them, is already on a lower level in its
different strata, the last of which stopped in 658: not before 726,
in Bede's time, followed a new, even poorer attempt at Frankish
history. In Spain, the compendious Chronicles of Isidore of
Seville (†636) and his unimportant histories of the peoples
settled there mainly mark the end of historiography; alone the
unique history of the rebellion against King Wamba written by
Julian of Toledo with its vehement, prejudiced eloquence, shows
that the faculty of writing history was not yet quite extin-
guished. But this work stands as an exception: only after the
Saracen conquest and under the influence of an oriental model
was Isidore's *History of the Goths* continued for the last
time (754). The Celts of the British Isles had produced no
historiography of distinction: Gildas is no historiographer at all,
and whatever of the unwieldy materials of Nemnius' *Historia
Britonum* may go back to the seventh century is not worth while
considering; in the Irish and British records of later times short
annals of earlier origin are to be recognized. While at the end
of the seventh century hagiography was cultivated everywhere
in Christendom, other forms of historiography in the West were
in decay. Bede gave it fresh impulse and a new model.

Historical studies form the smaller part of his work: coming

to the front gradually, they derived their independent value
from two roots belonging to the theological province of his age,
chronology and hagiography. The oldest life of a saint written
in England is symptomatic of this process: the unknown monk
of Lindisfarne who wrote about 700 the anonymous *Life of
St. Cuthbert*, prefixed to it a prologue, whose sentences he
borrowed from predecessors of two different kinds; from Victorius' letter introducing his Paschal table and from a few of the
most frequently read lives of saints, St. Antony of Egypt and
St. Martin of Tours.[1] So he shows the learning then usual in
the monasteries of Northumbria, in which young Bede participated; and at the root of Bede's historical studies are the
science of computing dates and the cult of saints.

I. CHRONOLOGY AND CHRONICLES

Bede began his literary work by giving instruction to his pupils;
later on he believed that his manuals should be supplemented
and illustrated by the spoken word.[2] So his first manuals were
written to be 'helps for students', to assist the memory; his
little work *De temporibus*[3] of 703 and the similar manual *De
natura rerum*[4] were text-books for his monks, to be interpreted
by the teacher.[5] Bede did not intend to expose new results of
research but to sum up lucidly traditional knowledge, closely
following the other great scholar of the early Middle Ages,
Isidore of Seville. But he was not satisfied to refer his pupils to
the summaries which Isidore had given in his book *De natura
rerum* and in the large cyclopaedia *Etymologiae* or *Origines*: he
went back to more original sources to increase and to illustrate

[1] See Levison, *MGH. Script. rer. Merov.* vi. 181 f.; Colgrave, p. 150.

[2] *De temporum ratione*, ch. 16 (Giles, vi. 182): 'Multa hinc dici poterant, sed
haec melius a colloquente quam a scribente fiunt'; ch. 20 (p. 189): 'Quae
profecto omnia melius colloquendo quam scribendo docentur'; ch. 55 (p. 253):
'Sed innumera huiusce disciplinae, sicut et ceterarum artium, melius vivae
vocis alloquio quam stili signantis traduntur officio'.—I am quoting throughout
the edition of Giles, if no special edition of a work is mentioned.

[3] Giles, vi. 123–38.

[4] *Ibid.* 99–122. The time of origin is unknown (see Plummer, i, p. cxlix), but
most likely about 703. Both books are coupled by Bede in the preface of
De temporum ratione (Giles, vi. 139), in *H.E.* v. 24, and in the verses prefixed
to the *Liber de natura rerum* (p. 99): 'Naturas rerum varias labentis et aevi
Perstrinxi titulis tempora lata citis.' See also J. Hoops, *Reallexikon d. germani-
schen Altertumskunde*, i (Strassburg, 1911), 192 ff.

[5] *De temporum ratione*, preface (Giles, vi. 139): 'Quos [libellos] cum fratribus
quibusdam dare atque exponere coepissem, dicebant eos brevius multo digestos
esse quam vellent, maxime ille "De temporibus".'

the teaching of his predecessor.[1] In his own work on the Nature
of Things which he expanded chiefly from Pliny's *Natural
History*, the theory of sun and moon led him to questions of
chronology; but he treated them separately in the special book
of 703 just mentioned. Certainly it was not only out of a sense
of proportion that he was dissatisfied to deal with the doctrine of
time within the limits of a general description of the world; a
more momentous reason for a special treatment of the principles
of chronology was the Paschal controversy, which had divided
the Church of Northumbria nearly up to Bede's day. It was
still kept alive by the neighbourhood of the Celts who clung to
their forefathers' practice, different in some respects from the
Alexandrinian rules of reckoning Easter adopted by the Roman
Church in the sixth century. The controversy thus resulting
between the Roman party and the Irish missionaries in England
came to an end in 664 at the Synod of Whitby, but even after
half a century no incident of the eventful life of Wilfrid, the
advocate of the Roman cause, is celebrated in his epitaph at
such length as his victory in the Paschal question:[2]

> Paschalis qui etiam sollemnia tempora cursus
> Catholici ad iustum correxit dogma canonis,
> Quem statuere patres, dubioque errore remoto,
> Certa suae genti ostendit moderamina ritus.

About the year 700 the Britons, the northern Scots, and the Picts
still maintained the Celtic custom. Bede's own monastery and
his abbot Ceolfrid succeeded in partially winning over their
opposition. Adamnan, the famous abbot of Iona, was first converted (probably in 686), numbers of Scots following him.
About 710 the Picts joined the ranks of the Roman party; in
716 Iona itself and the dependent congregations renounced the
native observance of Easter. Thus the Paschal question, com-
prehending in itself several problems of difference, may have
been the origin of Bede's chronological interest. Isidore had

---

[1] On the sources of Bede's *De natura rerum* see Karl Werner, *Beda der
Ehrwürdige und seine Zeit* (Vienna, 1875), pp. 107 ff.; M. Manitius, *Geschichte
der lateinischen Literatur des Mittelalters*, i (Munich, 1911), pp. 77 f. I refer to
both works henceforth generally without naming them specifically. On Pliny,
cf. K. Welzhofer, 'Beda's Citate aus der naturalis historia des Plinius' (*Abhandlungen aus dem Gebiet der klassischen Altertumswissenschaft Wilhelm von
Christ dargebracht*, Munich, 1891, pp. 25–41); M. L. W. Laistner, 'Bede as a
classical and a patristic scholar' (*Transactions of the Royal Historical Society*,
4th series, xvi, 1933, pp. 75, 77, 86). [2] *H.E.* v. 19.

separated the Paschal cycle from his survey of chronology.[1] Bede treated the matter combined with the rest of the doctrine of time; no less than five of the twenty-two chapters constituting the *Liber de temporibus* are given to the Paschal theory (ch. 11–15).

Bede, the chronologer, became at the same time chronicler. For his work combines a manual of mathematical-astronomical and technical chronology with a survey of the history of mankind (ch. 16–22);[2] here as in other respects he is depending on the Etymologies of Isidore, who, in the same way, had concluded his chronological summary with a short history of the world.[3] Like Isidore, Bede proceeds from the smaller to the larger units of time, from days, weeks,[4] months, seasons, through years to ages of the world: 'Tempora momentis, horis, diebus, mensibus, annis, saeculis et aetatibus dividuntur' (ch. 1). But although owing much to his model, he is no slavish copyist; here also he recurs to older authorities, as Pliny and Macrobius, augmenting and supplementing the exposition of his forerunner, not only in the chapters on Easter-time. There, naturally, he uses above all the *Liber de paschate* of Dionysius Exiguus, who had led the Paschal use of Alexandria to victory in the Roman Church; illustrating the rubrics of the Paschal table, Bede shows the practical scope of his work. No less does the theologian reveal himself by explaining the *sacramentum*,[5] the mystical sense of the mobility of Easter (ch. 15), being in this respect also a man of his age, always seeking mysteries even behind external things. As to his description of facts, what has been said of his doctrine of the *saltus lunae*[6] may be stated in general: his information usually is 'clear, correct and calculated exactly'.

It has been suggested above, how, proceeding from the smaller

---

[1] *Etymologiae* (ed. Lindsay), v. 28–39 and vi. 17.

[2] Bede's *Chronica minora*, published separately together with his *Chronica maiora* by Th. Mommsen, *MGH. Auctores antiquissimi*, xiii (1898), 223–354. I refer to this edition.

[3] Isidore, *Chronica minora* (=*Etymologiae*, v. 38, 39), ed. Mommsen, *ibid.* xi (1894), 391–506, printed beneath the *Chronica maiora* of Isidore.

[4] What he says here (ch. 4, Giles, vi. 124) and in *De temporum ratione*, ch. 8 (*ibid.* 161 f.) of the *feriae*, depends on the legendary *Actus Silvestri*, which he used also in his Martyrology with regard to the martyr Timothy (H. Quentin, *Les martyrologes historiques du moyen âge*, Paris, 1908, p. 92). See Levison, 'Konstantinische Schenkung und Silvester-Legende' (*Studi e Testi*, 38, Rome, 1924, p. 168, n. 4, and p. 214, nn. 2, 3).   [5] See Plummer, i, pp. lvi f.

[6] Eduard Schwartz, *Christliche und jüdische Ostertafeln* (=*Abhandlungen der Gesellschaft der Wissenschaften zu Göttingen*, Philol.-hist. Klasse, Neue Folge viii, 6), 1905, p. 62; cf. p. 93, n. 1, pp. 99 and 102.

units of time to the larger ones, Bede from chronological studies arrived at historical research; the theory of the greatest units, *aetates mundi*, the ages of the world, induced him, like Isidore, to add a Chronicle exhibiting the duration of the single ages of history. He had a predilection for this doctrine to which he often refers in his writings,[1] an echo of the eschatological expectations of the early Christian communities; though altered, they gained new strength through Bede. The conception that a thousand years are like a day in the sight of God had involved the comparison of history with the days of the week of Creation and, further, with the well-known periods of the individual human life. The temporal world is thought to last 6,000 years, the Incarnation of Christ taking place in 5,500; hence come endeavours to find out how many years have passed since the Creation, to know at the same time what length of time remains till the Judgement-day and the end of things below. The founders of Christian chronography in the third century, Sextus Julius Africanus and Hippolytus, were adherents of this belief, disproved after all by experience in the sixth century. But even Bede had to reprove with scornful sadness 'rustics' asking how many years of the last *miliarium saeculi* were left over, as he relates in 708 in his letter to Plegwin,[2] when he had to defend his *Liber de temporibus*, written five years previously, against the reproach of heresy. There he mentions having seen, when a boy, the book of a heretic chronographer, who allotted to the world 5,500 years before the Incarnation and 500 after it, of which 300 and some more were then past[3]—perhaps Bede had read the book of Q. Julius Hilarianus of 397 maintaining that opinion.[4] Bede rejected such a primitive belief;

[1] See Plummer, i, p. xli, n. 6. On this doctrine cf. also H. Hertzberg, 'Ueber die Chroniken des Isidorus von Sevilla' (*Forschungen zur deutschen Geschichte*, xv, 1875, pp. 327 ff.); E. Bernheim, *Lehrbuch der historischen Methode*, 3rd and 4th eds. (Leipzig, 1903), pp. 63 ff.; H. Grundmann, 'Die Grundzüge der mittelalterlichen Geschichtsanschauungen' (*Archiv für Kulturgeschichte*, xxiv, 1934, pp. 326 ff.); as to England, Max Förster, 'Die Weltzeitalter bei den Angelsachsen' (*Die Neueren Sprachen*, 6. Beiheft: *Festgabe Karl Luick dargebracht*, 1925, pp. 183–203).

[2] Giles, i. 152. On the writings of Augustine used in the letter, see Laistner, *loc. cit.*, p. 88.   [3] *Ibid.* 151 f.

[4] Ed. C. Frick, *Chronica minora*, i (Leipzig, 1892), pp. 170 ff. Not very likely Bede thinks of the *Prologus paschae* of 395, published from a MS. of Cologne by B. Krusch, *Studien zur christlich-mittelalterlichen Chronologie* (Leipzig, 1880), pp. 227–35 (cf. pp. 32 ff.), where ch. 5 (p. 232) the same opinion is expressed in brief. Cf. the various readings of an Oxford MS. ed. Krusch, *Ein Bericht der päpstlichen Kanzlei* (see below, p. 118, n. 5) pp. 57 f.

frequently he affirms, like Augustine, that the time of Doomsday is hidden from mortal eyes. But though disapproving of the idea that men could know the duration of these things, he is fond of the comparison of history with the six days of Creation and the six phases of human life and consequently fond of the division of history into six *aetates mundi*. Therein he is following the authority of Augustine, who had fixed with biblical arguments the epochs of these ages in the closing chapter of his work on the City of God and in other writings, viz. on the Creation, the Flood, Abraham, David, the Babylonian Captivity, and the Incarnation. Isidore had introduced this doctrine into historio-graphy in the little Chronicle which concludes his survey of chronology in the Etymologies. Bede follows him from the summary at the beginning of the Chronicle up to the last sentence: 'Residuum sextae aetatis tempus Deo soli est cogni-tum' (Isidore); 'Reliquum sextae aetatis Deo soli patet' (Bede). Using frequently the very words of his model, he exhibits a mere skeleton of history, for the most part nothing but the succession of the generations and rulers of the Bible, that is, their names and durations, and finally the series of the Roman emperors, which he continued beyond Isidore to his own time with the help of a catalogue of them. The Biblical element prevails; moreover, the beginnings of kingdoms and some important events are recorded in the way definitely usual since Jerome. Bede did not add much to Isidore, taking what he did partly from the greater Chronicle of the same author. In fact, he gives a survey which is rather poor in design and performance; the time of single events is not settled distinctly, the duration of generations and reigns is given only to make out the length of the ages.

But in one respect Bede shows already in this work an inde-pendence of mind: he differs from Isidore in calculating the *aetates*. For he does not borrow simply the numbers of the Old Testament from his prototype and so indirectly from the Greek version of the Septuagint, the numbers of which Eusebius and his translator Jerome in the Chronicle had often admitted and transmitted to Isidore. Bede purposely preferred to substitute the numbers of the Vulgate, Jerome's famous Latin translation of the Hebrew text.[1] He thus adopts to a certain extent a principle

---

[1] In neglecting this view Mommsen's text, § 87 (p. 262), has the impossible reading *XL annis*; it has to be changed into *XXXII annis* (=MS. P) or

of modern historical research, in preferring primary sources to derived ones: he appreciates the *Hebraica veritas* (as given by Jerome) more than the Greek translation. It is unnecessary to discuss here the value of the texts on which the Septuagint and the Vulgate are based: in any case the critical sense of Bede is striking, as well as his readiness to carry through the principle in contradiction to the authority of men like Eusebius, Jerome, and Isidore.[1] The duration of the first and the second ages of the world was greatly shortened by this proceeding, as was the length of the fourth age in a smaller degree, so that the five ages ending with the Incarnation fell far short of the traditional 5,000 (or 5,500) years. The result was a charge of heresy against which Bede defended himself in the letter to Plegwin mentioned above by explaining his method of reasoning and by denying every kind of chiliasm. In his theological writings also he shows appreciation of textual criticism.[2]

The Chronicle at the end of the manual on chronology was no work of historiography, not even a substantial table of human history in the narrow limits set by Biblicism and the tradition of Christian chronography. The whole book was too short; especially the chapters of the Paschal reckoning required a more detailed treatment in the opinion of Bede's brethren. So after twenty-two years, when already a real historian, he wrote in 725 his second book on the same matter, *De temporum ratione*, as it is usually called, a manual more than thirteen times larger than the sketch of 703;[3] he incorporated a letter he had written in the meantime on a special, pertinent question.[4] The order of the earlier work is retained in general, but the subjects are expounded in detail and new chapters are introduced by going back to the same sources and by making use of new ones; the quotations are more numerous. Throughout Bede seeks

---

(= Giles, p. 134) *XXXII annis, non XL* (I do not know the documentation of Giles's text by MSS.).   [1] See also Augustine, *De civitate Dei*, xviii. 43.

[2] Cf. Plummer, i, pp. liv ff.

[3] Giles, vi. 139–342. Bede himself calls the book *De temporibus librum I maiorem* (*H.E.* v. 24). The usual name is taken from the mention of the earlier book in the preface of the later (p. 139): *De natura rerum et ratione temporum* &c. influenced by Rufinus' *Historia ecclesiastica*, i. 1, § 6 (ed. Mommsen, p. 9): 'in chronicis, id est in eo opere quod de temporum ratione conscripsimus'.—A new edition by a young American scholar, Charles W. Jones, is expected.

[4] The letter to Helmwald *de bissexto* (ed. Giles, *Anecdota Bedae, Lanfranci et aliorum*, Caxton Society, 1851, pp. 1–6; cf. Plummer, i, p. xxxvii, n. 1) is reproduced without the preface in ch. 38 and 39 of *De temp. rat.* (pp. 222–6).

Biblical analogies and above all the spiritual figures of things.[1]
He expounds copiously that Creation began on 18 March
(ch. 6); the days of Creation are compared to the ages of the
world in a most artificial way (ch. 10). But not only does he
repeat the sentences of the Fathers and condense them ade-
quately, retaining in this way many erroneous views of his time,[2]
he learns also here and there from contemporaries and from
observation of nature. He notes the ebb and flow of the British
sea (ch. 29),[3] he illustrates celestial phenomena by the experience
of daily life, such as burning candles in a church on a martyr's
day (ch. 26). As to Greek months, he obtains his information
from other literature[4] and from a *computus annalis* transmitted
lately from Rome (ch. 14), viz. the calendar of Polemius Silvius;
he inserts the inscription of a Christmas candle seen and copied
there by his brethren in 701 (ch. 47). Nor does he only tell of the
months of the Hebrews, Romans, and Greeks, he manifests a kind
of national feeling by treating also the English months and seasons:
'neque enim mihi congruum videtur aliarum gentium annalem ob-
servantiam dicere et meae reticere' (ch. 15); discussing the bearing
of the names upon heathenism, Bede praises Christ who had converted his nation from the sacrifices of victims to *sacrificia laudis*.

For those ignorant of reckoning he prefixes a table on the
lunar movement (ch. 19, 20, 23), with the purpose of giving not
mere theory but also help for practical life. Hence his extensive
exposition of the calculation of Easter-tide and the detailed
explanation of the columns of the Paschal table. Dionysius
Exiguus had drawn up his table only for the period of five lunar
cycles or 95 years (A.D. 532–626); Bede was not satisfied to continue it for a few more cycles like Felix Ghyllitanus (627–721),[5]

---

[1] On Bede's allegorical method see Plummer, i, pp. lvi ff.

[2] Cf., e.g., Browne, *The Venerable Bede*, pp. 220 ff.

[3] He owes the idea of *rheuma* (see also Bede's *Vita Cudbercti prosaica*, ch. 17,
and *H.E.* v. 3) to Vegetius, *Epitoma rei militaris*, iv. 42 (ed. Lang, 1885, p. 161),
used also in the preceding chapter 28 (p. 200; cf. Vegetius, iv. 35, 36, pp. 152 f.)
and *H.E.* i. 5 (cf. Vegetius, i. 24, p. 26), as Ch. W. Jones has shown, 'Bede and
Vegetius' (*Classical Review*, xlvi, 1932, pp. 248 f.); cf. G. Macdonald, *ibid.* xlvii,
1933, p. 124.

[4] Cf. Jones, 'Polemius Silvius, Bede, and the names of the months' (*Speculum*,
ix, 1934, pp. 50–6).

[5] On Felix see Poole, *Studies in Chronology and History*, pp. 32 f., 36 f.
To the literature on Dionysius mentioned by him add B. Krusch, 'Ein Bericht
der päpstlichen Kanzlei an Papst Johannes I. von 526' (*Papsttum und Kaiser-
tum, Forschungen ... Paul Kehr dargebracht*, Munich, 1926, pp. 48 ff.), where
p. 53 the missing word after *Wentonia* is to be read *ciuitate* (cf. plate II).

but put in front of his work the complete table extended to 28 lunar cycles or $19 \times 28 = 532$ years, from A.D. 532 to 1063.[1] There may be some doubt whether, as has been supposed, he was, after Victorius, the first to calculate the entire table;[2] certainly he furthered its wide spread by his work and thus promoted the rise of the new Frankish annals based on Easter-tables. Bede knows and mentions a good many literary products of the Paschal controversies, genuine and forged.[3] The actuality of the Paschal question made him argue against other systems, especially that of Victorius, whom he is addressing directly (ch. 51)[4]—one imagines hearing him deliver a lecture!

Bede's larger work on chronology also ends with a chronicle of the world, but this time of a copiousness which made it a favourite of the chroniclers of the Middle Ages. For the imita-tion of Isidore's short survey a work is substituted, based on an abundance of sources, which Mommsen has indicated in his edition of these *Chronica maiora*;[5] they seem to suggest partly that Bede was already collecting materials for his *Ecclesiastical History* finished six years later.[6] The Chronicle of Jerome with

[1] *De temporum ratione*, ch. 65 (p. 270). There exists as yet no edition of the genuine text of Bede's Paschal table. Lately Paul Lehmann has given the elucidation of the continental descent of a Paschal table, written in Northum-bria not before 703, with curious entries about Roman emperors and with annals of Northumbria and Kent (till 690) in close relation to Bede; in one of the MSS. at least, the Kassel MS. of the oldest Annals of Fulda, the table is prefixed to Bede's *De temporum ratione*. Cf. Lehmann, 'Fuldaer Studien' (*Sitzungsberichte der Bayerischen Akademie der Wissenschaften*, Philos.–philol. und hist. Klasse, 1925, No. 3, pp. 23 ff., and 1927, No. 2, pp. 50 ff.).

[2] See Ceolfrid's letter to Naitan, king of the Picts, written about 710, perhaps, as has been suggested, by Bede himself, and inserted in *H.E.* v. 21: 'Quibus (the cycles of Dionysius) termino adpropinquantibus, tanta hodie calculatorum exu-berat copia, ut etiam in nostris per Brittaniam ecclesiis plures sint, qui, mandatis memoriae veteribus illis Aegyptiorum argumentis, facillime possint in quotlibet spatia temporum paschales protendere circulos, etiamsi ad quingentos usque et xxx duos voluerint annos. . . . Ideo autem circulos eosdem temporum instan-tium vobis mittere supersedimus, quia de ratione tantum temporis paschalis instrui quaerentis, ipsos vobis circulos paschae catholicos abundare probastis.'

[3] I refer only to Krusch, *Studien zur christlich-mittelalterlichen Chronologie*, cf., e.g., pp. 304 f., 315 f., 328 (p. 316 on Bede's criticism of Anatolius in the letter to Wictheda *de aequinoctio vernali*, Giles, i. pp. 155 ff., cf. pp. clxxiv f.), and Mommsen, *Auct. ant.* xiii. 228 f. On Anatolius see also Jones, 'Polemius Silvius', *loc. cit.*, pp. 51 ff.

[4] See now Jones, 'The Victorian and Dionysiac Paschal Tables in the West' (*Speculum*, ix, 1934, pp. 408–21), on Bede, pp. 409 (nn. 6, 7), 417 f., 420.

[5] See above, p. 114, n. 2. Cf. also Georg Wetzel, *Die Chronicen des Baeda Venerabilis* (dissertation of Halle, 1878).

[6] In this respect perhaps might be mentioned the Papal letters, used by Bede, §§ 532 and 541. Cf. below, p. 138, n. 5.

the continuations of Prosper and Marcellinus Comes is one of
the foundations amplified from the greater Chronicle of Isidore,
from Jerome's book *De viris inlustribus* continued by Gennadius,
from a Latin Josephus, and Rufinus' adaptation of Eusebius'
History of the Church, from Eutropius and Orosius for Roman
history, from Gildas for British events.[1] When Isidore had
ended, Bede drew amply from the *Liber Pontificalis*, the official
Lives of the Popes; he had obtained a copy of the second
recension of the text, continued even in the lifetime of the
ruling Pope, Gregory II.[2] I shall pass over the Paschal literature, genuine and false, also used here; the *Dialogues* of Gregory
the Great, one of Bede's favourites; some lives of saints;
and only mention the interest shown in the Persian martyr
Anastasius (§§ 537, 539, 540), whose *Passio* Bede himself had
adapted.[3]

Here also Bede shows the same care for what he believes to
be the real dates, and applies the same method of criticism to the
numbers given by the Septuagint, for which he substitutes the
readings of the *Hebraica veritas*, as found in the Vulgate.[4] From
the third age onwards he follows mostly Jerome, adding 1948
years to the years since Abraham reckoned by his predecessor
in order to obtain the years of the world; but here also he
corrects him now and then in conformity with the Vulgate or
Josephus. The years of the world are annotated in the margin
at the close of the reigns and similar sections, not at the time
of the single events. The years of the Incarnation, the series of
which could be read in the prefixed Paschal table and therefore
had been treated by Bede in connexion with the elements of
Easter-reckoning (ch. 47), are not employed in the Chronicle
itself to mark the years, save in a few exceptional cases (§§ 518,
586). Notwithstanding the greater abundance of the contents,

---

[1] I would, like others, strike the *Historia Britonum* of the so-called Nennius
or rather Nemnius out of Mommsen's list of sources (pp. 115, 132, 228). See
F. Lot, Bibl. de l'École des Hautes Études, 263, 1934, p. 72.

[2] See Mommsen, *Auct. ant.* xiii. 227 f. and *MGH. Gesta pontificum Romanorum*,
i (1898), p. cv. Bede used the *Gesta pontificalia*, as he calls them, also in the
H.E. (cf. Plummer, ii. 82 and below, p. 135, n. 2; p. 136, n. 1), and in his
Martyrology (see Quentin, *loc. cit.*, pp. 102–4, 117). The monk of Whitby also,
who wrote the first Life of Gregory the Great, had a MS. of the second class
of the *Liber Pontificalis* (ed. Gasquet, *A Life of Pope St. Gregory the Great*,
Westminster, 1904, p. 2, l. 1, and p. 46, ll. 9–12, chs. 1 and 32).

[3] See below, p. 125.

[4] Cf. especially §§ 17 and 19 (pp. 251 f.) on the much discussed question of
Methuselah.

profane history does not prevail here, but sacred and ecclesi-astical history;[1] anyhow, Bede records the beginning and end of the realms of the Assyrians and Sicyonians, the years of the Latin, Roman, and Persian kings, of Alexander the Great and the Ptolemies, of the Roman emperors—the dependence on earlier Christian chronography is so evident that one might at times call the book a compressed Jerome. Bede tells us com-paratively much of literature, of the dogmatic controversies of the seventh century, of the invention and translation of relics. But though he proves himself in many respects a theologian here also, the predilection for Church and universality is tempered by a special liking for country and nation, as has been already manifested as regards the Anglo-Saxon calendar;[2] many reports from the time of Caesar onwards relate to Britain and so, from the fifth century, to the history of the English peoples—the outlines of the future historian of the Church of England begin to appear. In these sections, though not in them alone, Bede gives more than short notes, combining brevity with circum-stantial clearness. In the fashion of his time he borrows freely from his sources, where possible retaining the very words[3] with-out harm to the plainness of the narration, for he is averse to any pompous style.

Special attention is necessary for the last chapters (ch. 67–71), in which the theological element of his work chiefly manifests itself. It has already been stated what importance Bede ascribes to the doctrine of the ages of the world, derived from Augustine and his predecessors, and transmitted by Isidore; how, in fact, his proceeding from the smaller units of time to the greatest and the statement of their duration was for him the very reason for inserting chronicles in his chronological books. Dealing with the week in the work of 725 (ch. 10), he had compared, as mentioned above, the week of Creation with the six ages; but going farther than Isidore's Chronicle and following Augustine,[4] in consideration of God's rest-day, he

---

[1] What he says about the universal synods, § 561 (p. 315), seems to depend on Isidore, *Etymol.* vi. 16, §§ 6–9, and on the acts of the Council of Hatfield (Bede, *H.E.* iv. 17, p. 240), supplemented by Bede, not entirely without mistakes.   [2] See above, p. 118.

[3] On Bede's borrowing from precedent writers, with quotation and without, see Plummer, i, pp. xxiii f. Cf. also Laistner, 'Source-marks in Bede manu-scripts' (*Journal of Theological Studies*, xxxiv, 1933, pp. 350 ff.).

[4] Cf. Augustine, *De Genesi contra Manichaeos*, i. 23–5 (*P.L.* xxxiv. 190 ff.); *Sermo* 259, cc. 1, 2 (*ibid.* xxxviii. 1196 ff.); the end of *De civitate Dei*.

added a seventh and an eighth age. The seventh age is the
sabbath of the blessed souls in the unseen world, contemporary
with the other six ages, from the death of Abel until the resurrection of bodies at the last Judgement; then, after the end of this
world, the eighth age begins, everlasting with eternal happiness
and eternal damnation. To these eschatological ideas, based
on Biblical revelation and patristic tradition, Bede devoted the
entirety of the last five chapters; though not belonging to
history in the modern sense, they are a constituent part of his
historical conception.[1] He, who divided history according to the
days of Creation, who started the sixth and last age of this world
with the Incarnation, naturally had to answer the question as
to the end of the *aetates*—so Bede's Chronicle does not finish in
chiliasm, but in eschatology. Again he denies the six thousand
years' duration of the world: no age has lasted exactly one
thousand years, they have been now longer, now shorter, so God
alone knows the duration of the sixth age (ch. 67). Following
a letter of Augustine,[2] he goes further in discussing when the
Lord will return, whether soon or late (ch. 68); he records the
signs which will announce the approach of Antichrist (ch. 69),[3]
and then treats Doomsday itself (ch. 70).[4] So the end of the
sixth age is reached, and the last chapter deals with the seventh
and with the eighth ages, when, after the unsteady and agitated
flowing of this time, the eternal stability and the stable eternity
with no end will arrive. The work thus finishes in sublime
devotion. The reader who omits these last chapters[5] gets only
an imperfect knowledge of Bede's mind. He stands at an important point in the line which starts from Augustine and
reaches its highest level in Bishop Otto of Freising. He has
been content to substitute for Augustine's sketch of the ages
'a chronicle of the world consolidated more chronologically and

---

[1] Cf. Grundmann, *loc. cit.* (above, p. 115, n. 1).

[2] Letter 199 to Hesychius *de fine saeculi* (ed. Goldbacher, *Corpus script.
eccl. Lat.* lvii, 1911, pp. 243–92); cf. c. 13, §§ 52–4 (pp. 289 ff.). Even the
beginning i. 1 (p. 243): 'ut salvatoris nostri *diligatur et desideretur adventus*'
shows Bede's indebtedness; cf. *De temp. rat.*, ch. 68 (Mommsen, p. 322): 'Cuius
quidem *adventus* horam merito sancti omnes *diligunt et* citius adesse *desiderant*'.
Cf. also Bede's Commentary on Luke, ch. 17 (Giles, xi. 250).

[3] At the end of the chapter he refers to Jerome's Commentary on Daniel,
ch. 12 (*P.L.* xxv. 579). Cf. also Bede's letter (xv) to Acca (Giles, i. 203 ff.).

[4] He quotes Augustine, *De civitate Dei*, xx. 25, and Gregory, *Homil. in evang.*
i. 1, § 6 (*P.L.* lxxvi. 1081).

[5] In the edition of the Chronicle by J. Stevenson (1841), p. 206, the last four
chapters are missing.

better fitted out with historical facts'.[1] He has not yet tried
to perceive the inner meaning of the course of history as a whole,
like Otto with his theory of the Two Cities, influenced even
more by Augustine; but he leads in this direction, connecting
in one chronicle the events of the visible world with the ideas
of the last things and the παρουσία, a theologian even when
writing history.

II. HAGIOGRAPHY AND BIOGRAPHY

Chronology was one starting-point of Bede's historiography;
hagiography, the literary expression of the cult of saints, was
the second. Lives of saints and, inseparable from them, ecclesiastical biographies were the only branch of historical writing,
as before stated, that put forth many new shoots in the western
countries about 700. The young Christian civilization of Bede's
nation also participated therein, the Northumbrians first of
all.[2] In the front rank stands the Life of St. Cuthbert, written
about 700 by a monk of Lindisfarne. Soon after 710 Aeddi-
Stephanus describes at Ripon the varied vicissitudes of Bishop
Wilfrid's life, a work one-sided and partial, but remarkable in
shape and contents for the time. A monk of Wearmouth writes
a biography of his abbot Ceolfrid after 716. In the same decades
the oldest legend of Gregory the Great may have originated at
Whitby.[3] With Felix's Life of the hermit Guthlac of Crowland
this first series of English hagiology, different as it is in value
and form, comes to an end, shortly before the middle of the
century.[4] The number of names shows how much this kind of

[1] So, on the historiography of the early Middle Ages, Moriz Ritter, *Die
Entwicklung der Geschichtswissenschaft an den führenden Werken betrachtet*
(Munich, 1919), p. 83.

[2] See, e.g., E. Bishop, 'English Hagiology' (*Dublin Review*, 3rd series,
vol. xiii, 1885, pp. 123–54).

[3] P. Ewald (*Historische Aufsätze dem Andenken an Georg Waitz gewidmet*,
Hannover, 1886, pp. 17 ff.), Plummer (i, pp. clxv ff.; ii. 389 ff.) and Gasquet
(see p. 120, n. 2) thought that this first *Vita Gregorii* was a source of Bede's
H.E. I am convinced that the Life was written before the great work of Bede
existed; but there are momentous arguments that he never saw the little work
of Whitby, and that the two authors wrote down the national traditions independent of each other. See H. Moretus, 'Les deux anciennes vies de S. Grégoire
le Grand' (*Analecta Bollandiana*, xxvi, 1907, pp. 66–72); W. Stuhlfath,
'Gregor I. der Grosse, sein Leben bis zu seiner Wahl zum Papste' (*Heidelberger
Abhandlungen zur mittleren und neueren Geschichte*, 39), 1913, pp. 63 ff.; below,
p. 140, n. 5.

[4] About 748 according to F. Liebermann, 'Ueber ostenglische Geschichts-
quellen (*Neues Archiv*, xviii, 1892, pp. 245 f.). I could not obtain Walter de Gray

124 BEDE AS HISTORIAN

composition was already within the province of English literature and within reach of Bede's mental sphere.

From Bede's Martyrology one may guess how many *Passiones martyrum* and *Vitae sanctorum* he read. Its contents were previously uncertain, but have been determined, together with its sources, in an excellent book by the late Dom Henri Quentin.[1] Bede's Martyrology, which belongs to his later life (probably after 725, certainly before 731),[2] was fundamental for the development of this literature, initiated in the West a century earlier by the questionable compilation of the so-called *Martyrologium Hieronymianum*.[3] Bede had a copy of it, similar to the manuscript of the abbey of Echternach, the foundation of his countryman St. Willibrord, the Northumbrian apostle of the Frisians. But he was not satisfied with the dry and more or less confused series of mere dates and names; his historical sense required fuller information, so he endeavoured, as he has said himself,[4] to set down all martyrs that he could find, and 'not only on what day, but also by what sort of combat, or under what judge they overcame the world': on 114 days of the year he thus added to the names of the martyrs short histories, derived from their Acts or other sources; he combined, when necessary, the evidence of different authors into summaries of the saints' lives. He started thus the 'historical', as Quentin has called them, or rather 'narrative' martyrologies.[5] The traditional dates are repeated by him exactly, nor has he supplied missing ones arbitrarily, in contrast with Ado of Vienne, who in the next century exercised such a disadvantageous influence upon the further evolution of the martyrologies. Naturally, being a child of his time, he does not censure the legends, though

Birch's *Memorials of S. Guthlac of Crowland* (Wisbech, 1881), nor B. P. Kurtz, *From St. Antony to St. Guthlac*, Berkeley, 1926 (= *University of California Publications in Modern Philology*, xii, No. 2, pp. 103–46).

[1] Quentin, *loc. cit.* (see p. 114, n. 4) pp. 17–119. In the MS. to which the existing copies go back, the death of St. Boniface (754) had been interpolated. A. Ehrhard, *Byzantinische Zeitschrift*, xvii (1908), pp. 508 f., has shown that Bede used a Greek calendar also.

[2] The borrowings from Prosper seem to have come through the medium of Bede's Chronicle of 725; cf. Quentin, pp. 87 f. and 108.

[3] See now the edition and commentary of H. Delehaye and H. Quentin, *Acta sanctorum Novembris*, Tomus II, pars posterior, Brussels, 1931. Bede mentions the 'liber martyrologii, qui beati Hieronymi nomine ac praefatione attitulatur', in his *Retractatio in Actus apostolorum* (Giles, xii. 99). [4] *H.E.* v. 24.

[5] Cf. also H. Delehaye, *Cinq leçons sur la méthode hagiographique* (*Subsidia hagiographica*, 21), Brussels, 1934, pp. 59 f.

showing a certain discretion in repeating miraculous particulars, a tendency strengthened no doubt by the desire for space and symmetry. Besides other sources Bede used about fifty hagiographical texts.[1]

No wonder that Bede himself, with such wide reading, tried his hand at Lives of Saints. Here also he does not start as an historiographer, he does not at first give an original relation of a saint's history; the elegant writer of a clear Latin style endeavours to give a new shape to existing texts for the edification of readers. The Passion of the Persian martyr Anastasius (†628), to whom a church was dedicated outside Rome,[2] had been ill translated from the Greek and worse amended, as Bede says, by an ignoramus; he corrected it with regard to the sense.[3] His adaptation of the text has not been as yet discovered; his interest in the subject is manifest by the copiousness with which he relates Anastasius' martyrdom in the second Chronicle and in the Martyrology.[4] Paulinus of Nola had dedicated to the glory of Felix, the saint of his native town, poems which are by no means clumsy or awkward, but lengthy owing to poetical accessories. Bede translated them into prose for the benefit of many plain readers.[5]

[1] Bishop Acca of Hexham, Bede's contemporary, also collected the relics of apostles and martyrs as well as *historias passionis eorum*; cf. *H.E.* v. 20. In another part of England Aldhelm's books *De virginitate* show a similar knowledge of this literature; see R. Ehwald, *MGH. Auct. ant.* xv, pp. xxi f.

[2] At present S. Vincenzo ed Anastasio. See P. Kehr, *Italia Pontificia*, i (Berlin, 1906), pp. 170 f.; Chr. Huelsen, *Le chiese di Roma nel medio evo* (Florence, 1927), p. 173.

[3] *H.E.* v. 24. The Greek acts of the martyr were no doubt the *Acta m. Anastasii Persae* published for the first time by H. Usener in a Bonn University Paper of 1894; cf. *Bibliotheca hagiographica Graeca* (1909), no. 84.

[4] Mommsen, pp. 310 f., §§ 537, 539, 540; Quentin, p. 106. It is not necessary to dwell on the rhythmic *Passio Iustini martyris* (Giles, i. 38–49), recognized as spurious (cf. Plummer, i, p. clviii) and published lately by K. Strecker, *MGH. Poetae Latini*, iv. 2 (1923), pp. 841–56.

[5] Giles, iv. 173–201 (with English translation). The sentence p. 198, l. 4: 'coeperunt quaerere divinum, ubi humanum cessabat auxilium', depends on Rufinus' *Historia ecclesiastica*, i. 5, § 5 (ed. Mommsen, p. 119). Bede's *Vita Felicis* is not based on all the pertinent poems of Paulinus, but only on nos. 15, 16, 18, 28 (ed. Hartel, *Corpus script. eccl. Lat.* xxx. 51–81, 96–118, 291–305), because he had a MS. similar to the *Petropolitanus* (G) and *Palatinus* (R), which contain besides the poems mentioned only nos. 27 and 17 of Paulinus (*ibid.* pp. xxviii f., xxxiii). The verses of this poet quoted by Bede in his book *De arte metrica* (see H. Keil, *Grammatici Latini*, vii, 1878, p. 610) and in his Commentary on Luke, ch. 21 (Giles, xi. 12) belong to the same small collection. Cf. also R. Davis, 'Bede's Early Reading' (*Speculum*, viii. 1933, p. 191). Bede used his *Vita Felicis* himself in the Martyrology; see Quentin, pp. 106 f.

His Lives of St. Cuthbert, too, were composed principally with regard to the form. There already existed a Life of the anchoret and bishop of Lindisfarne (†687), mainly a collection of *virtutes* or miracles, written by a monk of his monastery between 698 and 705 in a plain and unpretentious style.[1] Bede the poet here preceded Bede the prose-writer. He had translated the verses of Paulinus into a prose *Life of St. Felix*; on the other hand, the *Vita Cudbercti* became the basis of Bede's largest poem which we possess,[2] of nearly a thousand hexameters, produced between 705 and 716, when Bede himself had experienced the saint's healing power on his sore tongue; on account of the similar circumstances the poetical moulding of the writings about St. Martin by Paulinus of Périgueux and Venantius Fortunatus has been compared with Bede.[3] In the preface he promises a second work on the subject; his *Life of St. Cuthbert* in prose, which he finished before 721, was the result.[4] Sedulius' *Carmen* and *Opus paschale*, much read and familiar to Bede also, were the model for the twofold treatment; Bede himself mentioned it, when speaking of Aldhelm's double work on Virginity.[5] The epic concerns Bede the poet more than the historian. Here he gives an even less complete life of the saint than his anonymous predecessor; one miracle follows the other,

[1] The *Vita Cudbercti auctore anonymo* has been printed by Stevenson, *Bedae Opera historica minora*, pp. 259–84, and by Giles, vi. 357–82; a new edition of it and of Bede's *Vita Cudbercti prosaica* is being prepared by Bertram Colgrave. Cf. Heinrich Hahn, *Bonifaz und Lul* (Leipzig, 1883), pp. 175 f., who suggests that Herefrid is the author. On the sources of the preface, see above, p. 112. On the *Actus Silvestri* as the model of Cuthbert's portrait cf. Levison, 'Sigolena' (*Neues Archiv*, xxxv, 1910, pp. 227 f.); 'Konstantinische Schenkung und Silvester-Legende', *loc. cit.* (see above, p. 114, n. 4), p. 213.

[2] Bede's *Vita Cudbercti metrica*, ed. Stevenson, *loc. cit.*, pp. 1–43; Giles, i. 1–34. A new edition by Werner Jaager, a pupil of Karl Strecker, has just appeared in the collection *Palaestra* (no. 198, Leipzig, 1935), the introduction being at the same time a dissertation of Berlin University. On the date of the poem see Manitius, *loc. cit.* i. 84, who refers the end of ch. 21 to the reign of King Osred of Northumbria; he has also noted some poetical reminiscences, 'Zu Aldhelm und Baeda' (*Sitzungsberichte der philos.-hist. Classe der Wiener Akademie*, 112, 1886, pp. 616 f.). [3] Werner, *loc. cit.*, p. 104.

[4] Bede's *Vita Cudbercti prosaica*, ed. Stevenson, pp. 45–137; Giles, iv. 202–357 (with translation). On the time of origin see Plummer, i, p. cxlviii. Bede has mentioned both his works on St. Cuthbert in the *Chronica maiora*, § 570 (pp. 316 f.), and *H.E.* iv. 28, 30, 31; v. 24.

[5] *H.E.* v. 18. On Bede's knowledge of Sedulius, see Plummer, i, p. lii; Davis, *loc. cit.*, p. 191. Bede's model was afterwards imitated by his countryman Alcuin in the double *Vita Willibrordi*, Alcuin again in the new adaptation of the same subject by Thiofrid of Echternach; cf., e.g., *Script. rer. Merov.* vii. 95 and 110.

designed in vaguer outlines. Many proper names are omitted to suit the exigencies of the verses, so that the local colours have frequently faded. However, the poem is no mere adaptation of its model to a metrical form; the proximity of time and place has given the author the opportunity to add some particulars and several new stories mostly referring to the later and the posthumous life of his hero.

This can, moreover, be said of the book in prose. Bede, like the first biographer, wrote it at the request of Bishop Eadfrid of Lindisfarne, and it was certainly his principal aim to give a more pleasing form to that simpler biography.[1] In fact, he showed here also his talent for lively and vivid narration, though there are certain lengthy passages, due to biblical quotations, devout meditations, comparisons with the Legend of St. Antony,[2] Possidius' *Life of St. Augustine*,[3] and above all with the favourite *Dialogues* of the 'English apostle' Gregory the Great,[4] who provides Bede, as in his other writings, not only with facts but also with handsome phrases.[5] He seems, as has been said,[6] 'to take delight in altering the language for the mere sake of alteration'; here also he drops names of persons and places to make his tale more readable. But there are merits which indicate Bede's historical sense. He relates the progress of Cuthbert's life more clearly than his predecessor, noting in due

---

[1] He never mentions his source except in the preface of *H.E.*, perhaps out of delicacy.

[2] Ch. 19; cf. *Vita Antonii*, ch. 25 (*P.L.* lxxiii. 149). Cf. also Cuthbert's last speech, ch. 39: 'Cum illis autem . . . vobis sit nulla communio', and *Vita Antonii*, ch. 41 (col. 157): 'Cum Arianis vobis nulla sit coniunctio'. On Bede's knowledge of this legend cf. Laistner, 'Transactions', *loc. cit.*, pp. 83 f.

[3] At the end of ch. 38; cf. *Vita Augustini*, ch. 29 (*P.L.* xxxii. 59). Bede used it also in *Chronica maiora*, § 480 (p. 302).

[4] Ch. 14, 19, 20; cf. *Gregorii Magni Dialogi*, i. 6; ii. 10, 5, 8 (ed. U. Moricca, *Fonti per la storia d'Italia*, Rome, 1924, pp. 42, 97, 88, 91 f.). Bede also frequently relied on the Dialogues in other works, in the second Chronicle, §§ 510, 514, 529 (Mommsen, pp. 306 f.), the Martyrology (Quentin, pp. 102, 104), and *H.E.* Cf. Hans Hecht, *Bischof Waerferths von Worcester Uebersetzung der Dialoge Gregors des Grossen* (Grein and Wülker, *Bibliothek der angelsächsischen Prosa*, v. 2), Hamburg, 1907, pp. 13–18, whose examples of borrowed phrases in *H.E.* can be augmented without difficulty. Cf. also Bede, *De orthographia*, ed. Keil, *Grammatici Latini*, vii. 594, &c.

[5] I refer only to the pages and lines of Stevenson's and Moricca's editions: Stev., pp. 99, 23; 106, 26; 125, 2; 131, 27; 133, 5; cf. Mor., pp. 292, 18; 64, 26; 132, 13; 133, 7; 252, 17–20. There may be more of this kind than I have casually noticed.

[6] Plummer, i, p. xlvi; cf. p. xxviii, n. 1 on an anecdote of the older Life spoiled by Bede.

order his domiciles, his preaching in the Highlands (ch. 9), describing more exactly the situation of places[1] and buildings; he not only omits names of localities but also supplies one (ch. 28). The new narratives are for the most part the same as in the metrical Life; here the extensive record of Cuthbert's death (ch. 37–40) is a masterpiece, vividly described by Bede according to the report of an eyewitness, abbot Herefrid.[2] Given, as he is, to the belief in miracles, he nevertheless endeavours to ascertain the truth of the related facts. He let Herefrid and other men who had known Cuthbert personally verify his first draft (*schedulae*), and corrected it before he sent a fair copy (*membranulae*) to Lindisfarne for approval,[3] and while he omits the names of witnesses of his predecessor, he mentions his own authorities all the more, adopting a principle of Gregory the Great, which he repeats more literally in the *Ecclesiastical History*:[4]

Dialogi, preface (p. 16): 'Sed ut dubitationis occasionem legentibus subtraham, per singula quae discribo, quibus mihi haec auctoribus sint conperta, manifesto.'

Vita Cudbercti, preface: 'Quin potius primo diligenter exordium, progressum et terminum gloriosissimae conversationis ac vitae illius ab his qui noverant investigans, quorum etiam nomina in ipso libro aliquoties ob indicium certum cognitae veritatis apponenda iudicavi. . . .'

H.E., preface: '*Ut* autem in his *quae scri*psi vel tibi vel ceteris auditoribus sive *le*ctoribus huius historiae *occasionem dubita*ndi *subtraham, quibus haec* maxime *auctoribus* didicerim, breviter intimare curabo.'

Moreover, the conscientious and scrupulous narrator distinguishes

[1] On his interest for the *rheuma* see above, p. 118, n. 3.

[2] In ch. 16 Bede quotes a sentence from the famous replies of Gregory the Great to Augustine's questions (*MGH. Epist.* ii. 331–43) which he afterwards inserted nearly complete into *H.E.* i. 27. Lately M. Müller, 'Zur Frage nach der Echtheit und Abfassungszeit des "Responsum b. Gregorii ad Augustinum episcopum"' (*Theologische Quartalschrift*, 113, 1932, pp. 94–118) has given important arguments against the genuineness of the letter, trying to show that it was forged probably in the last decade before 731; but being cited in the Life of St. Cuthbert (as Plummer ii. 46 has noted), it must be at least older than 721.—In ch. 42 Bede repeats nine distichs of a lost poem on Eadbert, to which he alludes also in the metrical Life, ch. 39; it may be a fragment of his *Liber epigrammatum heroico metro sive elegiaco* (*H.E.* v. 24) as Plummer, i, p. cliv, has suggested. See also Jaager, *loc. cit.*, p. 50.

[3] He relates this in the prefatory letter of dedication. Cf. the preface to *H.E.*, which he sent to King Ceolwulf at first *ad legendum ac probandum*.

[4] Cf. Hecht, *loc. cit.*, p. 14.

between witnesses who have seen the details related with their own eyes and those who have heard it only from others. I may quote a few instances from many:

Ch. 5: 'Haec mihi religiosus nostri monasterii, quod est ad ostium Wiri fluminis, presbyter nomine Ingvald . . . ab ipso Cudbercto iam tunc episcopo se audisse perhibuit.'

Ch. 6: 'Sicut religiosus ac veteranus Dei famulus et presbyter Sigfridus solet attestari, qui eidem Boisilo haec dicenti inter alios adstabat. . . .'

Ch. 23: 'sicut ipsa [Aelfled] postea reverentissimo Lindisfarnensis ecclesiae presbytero Herefrido et ille mihi referebat.'

Thus, in repeating even an 'aretalogy', as the Life of St. Cuthbert may be characterized, Bede manifests an endeavour at clearness of arrangement, continuity, and lucidity as well as care for the reliability and trustworthiness of an historian.

The transition from hagiography to history is completed by the work which Bede devoted to the lives of the first abbots of his own double monastery of Wearmouth and Jarrow—during those periods when official canonization did not exist, it is especially difficult to distinguish between Lives of saints and ecclesiastical biographies. Here also Bede had a precursor, probably a monk of Wearmouth, who seems to have been present when abbot Ceolfrid resigned his office there in 716 and started on his pilgrim's journey to Rome, whence he did not want to return: nor did he do so. The author, who was also there at the election of Huætberct, Ceolfrid's successor, in the same year, wrote soon after, before 725, the anonymous *Vita Ceolfridi*, the Life of the venerated abbot.[1] It is usually called *Historia abbatum auctore anonymo* in contradiction to the tradition of manuscripts; but it is throughout a Life of Ceolfrid: the doings of Benedict Biscop and of others are only considered so far as they are connected with Ceolfrid's activities. In fact, the *Vita sanctissimi Ceolfridi abbatis* contains the history of his life but no collected miracles; only in the last chapter are miraculous

---

[1] Edited by Plummer, i. 388–404. The Life was not written before 717 (cf. ch. 38, l. 3 *postea*) and existed in 725; for, as a few words show, Bede in his *Chronica maiora*, § 590 (p. 320) then used this *Vita*, ch. 32, 36, and especially 37, not his own *Historia abbatum*. With regard to Gangvulf, in whose manor the dying abbot found hospitality and his last resting-place (ch. 35, 36, 38), see *Script. rer. Merov.* vii. 142 ff. (in supplement to Plummer, ii. 376); on the author's (ch. 36)—and Bede's (*Hist. abbat.*, ch. 23; Quentin, pp. 62 f.)—knowledge of Warnacharius' *Passio sanctorum Ter Geminorum*, see *ibid.*, p. 144, n. 5 (on the cult of them cf. *MGH. Scriptores*, xxx. 2, 1934, pp. 1347 f.).

apparitions at his tomb shortly mentioned.[1] The tale is brief, but of rich content and important for the monastic history of Northumbria and the cultural intercourse with Gaul and Rome. The aim of the new learning in the world of Bede is manifested by the mention of books, brought from Rome by Benedict (ch. 9) and written at home in his monasteries (ch. 20); the very verses are reproduced with which Ceolfrid accompanied the famous *Codex Amiatinus*, his pilgrim's gift for the Church of Rome (ch. 37). The impression of the latest events caused disproportion: the whole earlier life of Ceolfrid occupies less space (ch. 2–20) than the vivid tale of his last journey with its preparations and aftermath (ch. 21–40). A concentrated direct description of his character (ch. 19) has the usual form of ' eikonismos', the asyndetic and rather monotonous enumeration of attributes,[2] though the indirect description through the deeds of the hero prevails. One sees the author's liking for documentation; not only privileges of the popes Agatho and Sergius for the monasteries (ch. 16, 20) and letters of recommendation by the Frankish King Chilperich II (ch. 32) are mentioned, but the whole wording of Abbot Huætberct's letter of introduction for Ceolfrid to Gregory II (ch. 30) and of the Pope's reply (ch. 39) are also inserted.[3] The author is fond of exactitude in fixing times, he mentions even days and hours; he computes dates by the regnal years of the Northumbrian kings (ch. 7, 17) and by indictions (*ibid.* and ch. 35), but he distinguishes the time of the foundation of Wearmouth (674), in addition, by means of the year of the Incarnation (ch. 7), the era created by Dionysius Exiguus. Bede had already touched on it in his chronological manual of 703 (ch. 13, 14); he went back to it, as stated before, in his larger book on time-reckoning in 725, where the prefixed Paschal table gave practical value to this kind of dating. We

---

[1] The author here employs a few phrases of Gregory's *Dialogues*; cf. Plummer, i. 404, ll. 3 ff. and 8 with *Dial.* iv. 16, 17 (ed. Moricca, pp. 253, 255): ' *subito* caelitus *lux* emissa . . . *miri* est *odoris flagrantia* sub*secuta* . . . is qui subsecutus est odor *remansit*', ' *subito flagrantia miri odoris* aspersa est', and iii. 11 (p. 157): ' *ut p*atenter omnibus *daretur intellegi*'.

[2] Cf. S. Hellmann, 'Einhards literarische Stellung' (*Historische Vierteljahrschrift*, xxvii, 1932, pp. 86 f.); Hilde Vogt, *Die literarische Personenschilderung des frühen Mittelalters* (*Beiträge zur Kulturgeschichte*, ed. W. Goetz, 53), Leipzig, 1934, pp. 8, 25, 37, &c.; S. Cavallin, *Literarhistorische und textkritische Studien zur Vita S. Caesarii Arelatensis* (= *Lunds Universitets Årsskrift* N. F. Avd. 1, vol. xxx, No. 7), Lund, 1934, pp. 27 f.

[3] H. Hahn, *loc. cit.*, pp. 216 f., conjectured that Abbot Huætberct himself wrote the *Vita Ceolfridi*.

shall see that Bede introduced this into historiography in his *Ecclesiastical History*—the biographer of his abbot Ceolfrid is thus his precursor in this regard.

We have here reached the province of real history and, at the same time, Bede's own circle. But the *Life of Ceolfrid* was for him also the foundation of a new biographical work: he wrote the history of the abbots of his double monastery.[1] Though ending like his predecessor in 716, he seems to have completed it not very long before his famous book of 731, enumerating there together with his other writings[2] *Historiam abbatum monasterii huius, in quo supernae pietati deservire gaudeo, Benedicti, Ceolfridi et Huaetbercti in libellis duobus.* In fact, he wrote a history of the abbots, using Ceolfrid's Life freely, but supplementing it from tradition and personal experience. He goes back beyond the abbacy of Ceolfrid and relates at first the life of Benedict Biscop, the real founder of the monasteries (ch. 1–14), whose merits he also praised in a homily for his anniversary.[3] Bede therein celebrated Benedict's journeys to Rome, the books and other goods of civilization he brought with him from beyond the sea; in the History of the abbots he deals more in detail with the six journeys, he mentions the books again and again (ch. 4, 6, 9, 11), he dwells more fully on the end of Benedict (ch. 11–14). The lives of his fellow abbots Ceolfrid, Eosterwini, and Sicgfrid are treated only so far as they are connected with the history of Benedict, but a warm-hearted picture of the second's character is included (ch. 8). As Benedict dominates the first part, so does Ceolfrid the second. But there is again a kind of disproportion, perhaps on purpose owing to the existing Life: Bede glides in one chapter over the quarter of a century (690–716) during which Ceolfrid ruled both monasteries alone (ch. 15); all the rest (ch. 16–23) is devoted to his last pilgrimage and death and to Huætberct's beginnings.[4] He there omits some traits given by the anonymous biographer, not all unimportant, possibly for symmetry's sake; he repeats Huætberct's letter, but drops the answer of Pope Gregory, perhaps because its text, at least as given in the *Vita Ceolfridi*, is partly corrupt. Nor does he

[1] Edited by Plummer, i. 364–87.   [2] *H.E.* v. 24.
[3] Giles, v. 179–85; (shortened) Stevenson, *loc. cit.*, pp. 335–8. Plummer, ii. 356–9 and 363, gives extracts.
[4] Bede mentions Ceolfrid's departure and the election of Huætberct also in the preface to the fourth book of his *Allegorica expositio in Samuelem*, written no doubt in the very year 716 (Giles, viii. 162; Plummer, ii. 366 f.).

record the miraculous apparitions related there in the last chapter; he concludes impressively by praising the Holy Triplets, in whose monastery near Langres Ceolfrid was buried.[1] On account of the position of his community Bede lays even more stress on the papal privileges, mentioning their confirmation by kings and bishops (ch. 6, 11, 15). He not only repeats the year of the Incarnation for the origins of Wearmouth (ch. 4), but gives it also for the time of Ceolfrid's death (ch. 23).

The *Historia abbatum* is a work of real historiography; it represents a part of the history of the English Church within the frame of monastic life, a further step towards Bede's masterpiece, to which he owes his glorious name of historian, the *Historia ecclesiastica gentis Anglorum*.

III. THE ECCLESIASTICAL HISTORY

Bede, no doubt, himself thought much of his *Ecclesiastical History*, seeing in it a kind of culmination of his work; for it was to this very work that he appended his autobiography with a list of his writings (v. 24). There were several models for the idea of an autobiography[2] in the literature known to him. Jerome and Gennadius had concluded their books on ecclesiastical authors, *De viris inlustribus*, with a chapter on themselves, and Gregory of Tours closed the continuous catalogue of the bishops of his see, added to the last book of his Histories, with a summary of his personal activities, episcopal and literary.[3] Bede seems to have made the acquaintance of this work only in later life; he quotes it solely in the *Liber retractationis in Actus apostolorum* (ch. 28), probably written after 731;[4] Gregory thus may have influenced the design of his not unworthy Anglo-Saxon successor in historiography.

Bede was impelled by Abbot Albinus of Canterbury[5] to write the *Historia ecclesiastica Brittaniarum et maxime gentis Anglorum*,

[1] Cf. above, p. 129, n. 1.
[2] Bede's autobiography is shortly mentioned by Friedrich von Bezold, 'Ueber die Anfänge der Selbstbiographie und ihre Entwicklung im Mittelalter' (*Zeitschrift für Kulturgeschichte*, i, 1894, p. 158, n. 18; also in v. Bezold's collected papers: *Aus Mittelalter und Renaissance*, Munich, 1918, p. 414, n. 422 to p. 208).   [3] Ed. Arndt, *Script. rer. Merov.* i. 448 f.
[4] Giles, xii. 156, referring to Gregory, *Hist.* v. 34 (p. 226); cf. Laistner, 'Transactions', *loc. cit.*, p. 78 f. Bede, when writing the *Liber retractationis*, no doubt had Augustine's *Retractationum libri* in mind, where the latter's earlier books are enumerated and criticized. Bede's list less closely compares with the *Indiculus* of Augustine's writings appended to his Life by Possidius (*P. L.* xlvi. 5 ff.).   [5] Letters to Albinus and Ceolfrid (Plummer, i. 3, 6.).

as he calls it at the beginning of his autobiography. His chief model was, no doubt, the work which was to him the Church History κατ' ἐξοχήν, the Ecclesiastical History of Eusebius as translated, adapted, and continued by Rufinus. He mentions this first history of the Christian Church very often, sometimes giving the name of the author, otherwise calling it simply *Historia ecclesiastica*;[1] the second work on ecclesiastical history much read in the West during the Middle Ages, Cassiodorus' *Historia tripartita*, seems to have been unknown to Bede. Eusebius and Rufinus comprehend, at least in idea, the whole Christian world, the scene changing from one leading Church to another; Rufinus reports also, for instance, the beginnings of Christianity among Indians and Iberians, but they do not speak of Britain in this respect. It was Bede's intention to add a British and Anglo-Saxon supplement to the older work, and he thus produced the first special ecclesiastical history of an occidental people. He did not know of tribal histories like Jordanis' and Isidore's Histories of the Goths;[2] only the work of Gregory of Tours can have been, in this connexion, a kind of model to him, which, in spite of its wider frame, becomes more and more a history of the Franks and, at the same time, includes so much ecclesiastical matter that some manuscripts call it *Historia ecclesiastica*.[3] But there may have been no need for a model at all. Notwithstanding Roman example,[4] the Anglo-Saxons were the first Germanic people to write down laws and annals in their mother tongue. So Bede, in spite of his consciousness of the universality of the Church and his desire for unity with Rome, manifests a kind of national feeling (though certainly not in a too narrow modern sense). As stated above (p. 118), he does not omit the English months and seasons in his

[1] Plummer, i, p. li (under *Eusebius* and *Historia ecclesiastica*); cf. Mommsen, p. 228; Quentin, pp. 98 f., 108. See also Laistner, *loc. cit.*, pp. 77, 83, 91.

[2] According to E. F. Jacob, 'Some Aspects of Classical Influence in Mediaeval England' (*Vorträge der Bibliothek Warburg*, 1930–1, Leipzig, 1932, p. 6), who may have adopted a conjecture of L. Traube, *Vorlesungen und Abhandlungen*, ii (Munich, 1911), p. 176, Bede was familiar with Isidore's History of the Goths. But I have found no proof in support of this opinion. Cf. Mommsen, *Auct. ant.* xi. 265.

[3] See the various readings *Script. rer. Merov.* i. 31 and 33. Bede (*loc. cit.*) calls Gregory's work by the right name: *Gregorius in libro Historiarum suarum quinto*. With reference to Gregory's inset of ecclesiastical history, see S. Hellmann, 'Gregor von Tours' (*Historische Zeitschrift*, 107, 1911, pp. 8 f.).

[4] Ethelbert's laws are written down *iuxta exempla Romanorum* (Bede, *H.E.* ii. 5).

book *De temporum ratione*; in the Chronicle belonging to it many British and English events are recorded. For the instruction of the people he made an English version of the Creed and Lord's Prayer.[1] He not only knew the native songs, but also, even on his death-bed, he composed English spiritual verses and began to translate St. John's Gospel and some extracts from Isidore's book on the Nature of Things.[2] So the idea of writing an English Church History cannot have been far from the thoughts of Bede, who had already treated parts of the subject in the Lives of St. Cuthbert and the History of his abbots.

At first he laid the foundation for it by a conscious collecting of material and a real work of research. At the end of his book he briefly mentions his sources (v. 24): 'prout vel ex litteris antiquorum vel ex traditione maiorum vel ex mea ipse cognitione scire potui', and he gives them more explicitly in his letter of dedication to King Ceolwulf of Northumbria.[3] His written sources, as far as we can recognize them, are indicated by different types in Plummer's admirable edition. For the first chapters, from Caesar until before Gregory the Great, Bede had to draw for the most part upon older narrative works, from which he borrowed whole pages, more or less word for word. His knowledge of these times is derived principally from three sources: he picked out matter relating to Britain from Orosius' Histories against the Pagans (i. 2–6 and 8–11); the querulous book of Gildas (ch. 7, 12–16, 22) and Constantius' Life of Bishop Germanus of Auxerre[4] (ch. 17–21) were the links with

---

[1] Bede's letter to Archbishop Ecgberct of York, ch. 5 (Plummer, i. 409; cf. ii. 381).

[2] Cuthbert's letter *de obitu Baedae* (Plummer, i, pp. clxi f.; cf. pp. lxxiv f.). On the verses cf. R. Brotanek, *Texte und Untersuchungen zur altenglischen Literatur und Kirchengeschichte* (Halle, 1913), pp. 150–94, 201 f. (I have collated the Vienna MS. 336, not mentioned there; cf. *Script. rer. Merov.* vii. 696). As to the extracts from Isidore the reading of some MSS. (Plummer, p. clxii, n. 8; cf. p. lxxv, n. 6) *de libris rotarum* (Plummer corrected *notarum*) is true; cf. Gustav Becker, *Isidori Hispalensis de natura rerum liber* (Berlin, 1857), p. v; Manitius, *loc. cit.* i. 54 f.

[3] Plummer, i. 6 f.

[4] Plummer used the second much interpolated Life of St. German. I have myself published Bede's source, the original Life, *Script. rer. Merov.* vii. 225–83; cf. my article: 'Bischof Germanus von Auxerre und die Quellen zu seiner Geschichte' (*Neues Archiv*, xxix, 1904, pp. 95–175). In Plummer's edition the end of ch. 18 (from p. 36, l. 25, *ubi Germanus* onwards) does not depend on the Life of St. German (cf. *loc. cit.*, p. 262), but on the third *Passio Albani*, ch. 21 and 22 (see below, p. 135, n. 4). In ch. 21 the words, p. 40, ll. 5–7, *qui erat* to *verbum praedicabat* have been inserted from the Life of Bishop

Anglo-Saxon times. He supplemented his large excerpts with additional matter scattered here and there. To the narrations of Orosius he added details taken from the Breviary of Eutropius (ch. 3, 8);[1] from the *Liber Pontificalis* he took over the misunderstood history of the correspondence of Pope Eleutherius with the 'British' King Lucius (ch. 4), who, in fact, had been a king of Edessa.[2] The existence of a *Passio Albani* as the source of Bede's narration of St. Alban's martyrdom (ch. 7) had long been assumed,[3] before the late Wilhelm Meyer discovered and published it, together with even older forms of the legend.[4]

Bede borrowed a few items also from Prosper's and Marcellinus Comes' continuations of Jerome, which he had already employed in his larger Chronicle.[5] But he had, too, at least one other annalistic source, now lost but recognizable with certainty. At the close of his work he added (v. 24) a table of annals, summarizing shortly *ob memoriam conservandam* of the principal

Lupus of Troyes, ch. 11 (ed. Krusch, *Script. rer. Merov.* vii. 302), which Bede also used in his *Martyrology* (Quentin, pp. 81 f.).

[1] On an addition from Vegetius in ch. 5, see above, p. 118, n. 3.

[2] The story of *Lucio Brittanio rege* in the Life of Eleutherius (*Liber Pontificalis*, ed. Mommsen, i. 17) has been admitted by Bede also into his second Chronicle, § 331 (p. 288). A. Harnack, 'Der Brief des britischen Königs Lucius an den Papst Eleutherus (*Sitzungsberichte der Berliner Akademie der Wissenschaften*, 1904, pp. 909–16), has given the ingenious and convincing explanation that *Brittanio* owes its origin to a misinterpretation of *Britium* (= *Birtha*, castle) of Edessa, and that the notice is to be referred to King Lucius (Abgar IX) of this kingdom. Bede used the *Liber Pontificalis* also in i. 23 and ii. 1, 4; cf. Plummer's *Addenda*, i, p. clxv, and above p. 120, n. 2.

[3] I mention only Plummer, ii. 17, and what I have written myself, *Neues Archiv*, xxix, pp. 148 ff. My suggestion that the end of ch. 18 depends on the same *Passio Albani* as ch. 7 has been confirmed by W. Meyer's discovery of the source.

[4] 'Die Legende des h. Albanus des Protomartyr Angliae in Texten vor Beda' (*Abhandlungen der Göttinger Gesellschaft der Wissenschaften*, Philol.-hist. Klasse, N. F. viii, No. 1), 1904. Bede used the third Passion (*ibid.*, pp. 37–47 and 48–62), transmitted in a Paris MS. Neither this text nor its source, the second text, an extract from the first, gives the date of St. Alban's martyrdom, which is ascribed to the time of the Emperor Severus (193–211) in the first Passion. Gildas, who read the same text as Bede, conjectured that St. Alban suffered in the time of Diocletian (ch. 10, ed. Mommsen, *Auct. ant.* xiii. 31: 'supradicto *ut conicimus* persecutionis tempore'); Bede took this supposition for certain in his second Chronicle, § 406 (p. 295), and in the Martyrology (Quentin, p. 105) as well as in the Ecclesiastical History. On his authority the Middle Ages accepted this more than questionable date.

[5] Bede used Prosper in chs. 10, 13, and 17 (beginning; see Plummer, ii. 32). Marcellinus was Bede's source not only in ch. 13, as Plummer has noted, but also at the end of ch. 21 (p. 41) on the fall of the Western Empire; he has there partly adapted passages of Marcellinus, A.D. 454–5 (*Auct. ant.* xi. 86), as in his *Chronica maiora*, § 493 (p. 304 f.). On Bede's employment of Marcellinus' Chronicle in his Commentaries, see Laistner, 'Transactions', *loc. cit.*, pp. 77 f.

events narrated at full length in the preceding books, a *recapitulatio chronica totius operis*, as it is called in the heading of the chapter. In fact, he cannot have taken a part at least of these annals from his finished work; he must have collected the notes, either wholly or in part, beforehand, as a kind of skeleton and guide for his narration, because there are some records of events not even mentioned in his History, which therefore, I think, might be explained only as remnants of preparatory work.[1] A few of these happenings belong to recent decades in the history of Mercia (675, 697) and Northumbria (698, 711). Only three refer to an earlier time: one concerns the reign of Ida, the ancestor of the Northumbrian kings (547); the other two are eclipses of the sixth century, whose mention appears rather strange in this place:

'Anno DXXXVIII. eclypsis solis facta est XIIII. Kalendas Martias ab hora prima usque ad tertiam.

Anno DXL. eclypsis solis facta XII. Kalendas Iulias, et apparuerunt stellae pene hora dimidia *ab hora diei tertia*.'

The notes, as has been long observed, are nearly correct, the only inexactitude being that the eclipse of 538 occurred on the 15th, not on the 16th February. But both eclipses were invisible in England and could only be observed in the Mediterranean countries.[2] Bede apparently here copied annals brought over from Italy and connected in some way with the *Consularia Italica*, as Mommsen has called them, or Annals of Ravenna, according to the older designation. For the second note corresponds not alone in substance but partly in the very words to a similar passage in the St. Gall excerpts from the said Annals.[3] The passage, on account of its incorrect date, has been hitherto referred, now to 539, now to 540,[4] but no doubt belongs to the latter year, as the comparison with Bede shows:

'tenebrae factae sunt *ab hora diei III*. usque in horam IIII. die Saturnis'.[5]

---

[1] One may adduce in this respect also the words referring to the year 167, *XV annos*, which depend on the *Liber Pontificalis*, but are missing in the narration, i, 4, and the title of the Pope in 430, *papa*, corresponding to the source (Prosper, *H.E.* i. 13, *pontifice Romanae ecclesiae*, differs).

[2] Cf. Oppolzer, *Canon der Finsternisse* (*Denkschriften der Wiener Akademie der Wissenschaften*, Mathematisch-naturwissenschaftliche Classe, lii), 1887, pp. 166, 168 and plates 83, 84; F. K. Ginzel, *Spezieller Kanon der Sonnen- und Mondfinsternisse . . . bis 600 n. Chr.* (Berlin, 1899), p. 96 and map xv.

[3] Ed. Mommsen, *Auct. ant.* ix. 334 (with n. 1); C. Frick, *Chronica minora*, i (Leipzig, 1892), p. 422.

[4] See also O. Holder-Egger, *Neues Archiv*, i (1876), pp. 236, 366.

[5] June 20th in 540 was a Wednesday, not a Saturday.

Probably Bede did not see a copy of the Italian Annals themselves; he may have had a Paschal table, of Victorius or Dionysius, in whose margin some notes extracted from the Annals were written.[1] Other events may have been added in England; one feels inclined to include among such entries Bede's record of the eclipse of the first (he gives erroneously the third day) of May in 664,[2] an eclipse which indeed could be especially well seen in Northumbria.[3] The conclusion is that annals, now lost, were among his sources, and may have provided him with several of his dates.[4]

But with regard to the later books of Bede, works of real historiography, like those used in the introductory part, did not exist. He could draw a few words from the *Liber Pontificalis*; he collected historical matter from the writings of Gregory the Great for the short biography of this apostle of England, which he inserted into his second book (ii. 1).[5] There were some pertinent Lives of saints, the *Vita* of the Irish visionary St. Fursa[6] (iii. 19) and the *Life of St. Cuthbert* written in prose by Bede himself[7]

---

[1] Two entries in the *Chronica maiora*, §§ 512 and 527 (pp. 307 f.), referring to the years 525–26 and 569 and corresponding a little with the Chronicle of Marius of Avenches (*Auct. ant.* xi. 235, 238), may be of the same origin, as also Mommsen (*ibid.* ix. 752) thought before; but he recognized Bede's source afterwards in Marius himself (*ibid.* xiii. 227), reserving to Paschal tables a part of § 469 (p. 300; cf. p. 227). L. Schmidt, *Neues Archiv*, ix (1884), pp. 197–200, referred the two entries mentioned first to the Annals of Ravenna themselves, which Mommsen, *loc. cit.* ix. 253, rejected.

[2] *Chronica minora*, § 284, *maiora*, § 553 (p. 313); *H.E.* iii. 27. Cf. Plummer, ii. 194.

[3] See Oppolzer, *loc. cit.*, p. 180 and plate 90; J. Fr. Schroeter, *Spezieller Kanon der zentralen Sonnen- und Mondfinsternisse, welche innerhalb des Zeitraums von 600 bis 1800 n. Chr. in Europa sichtbar waren* (Kristiania, 1923), pp. 2, 79, and ix (map 9 b).

[4] I abstain purposely from asking which earlier English annals might be recognized in Irish and Welsh compilations and in the Saxon Chronicle, and refer only to A. G. van Hamel, *De oudste Keltische en Angelsaksische geschiedbronnen*, dissertation of Amsterdam University, 1911.

[5] I add only borrowings which Plummer has not indicated: p. 74, ll. 7–12 from the Dialogues, preface (ed. Moricca, p. 14, ll. 6–13); p. 74, l. 34 (*monasterio*) to p. 75, l. 17 (not only from l. 8) mostly from the letter to Leander prefixed to the *Moralia* (*MGH. Epist.* i. 353 ff.); p. 75, ll. 26 and 29 to p. 76, l. 11 from *Moralia*, xiv. 56, §§ 72–4 (*P. L.* lxxv. 1077 ff.); p. 77, ll. 6–13, from the letter to Leander, ch. 5 (*loc. cit.*, p. 357).

[6] Krusch, *Script. rer. Merov.* iv. 423 ff. (cf. vii. 837 ff.) has given a new edition of the *Vita Fursei*, but omitted the visions of the saint. Bede refers to the *libellus de vita eius conscriptus*.

[7] Cf. above, pp. 127 f. Where chapters of Bede's fourth book have a double numbering in Plummer's edition, I use, like others, the higher number for quotations.

(iv. 27–31). He read the voluminous, one-sided biography which Aeddi-Stephanus had devoted to the agitated life of Bishop Wilfrid of York several years before, and knowing also the standpoint of Wilfrid's adversaries, he used it here and there with discretion (iii. 25, 28; iv. 2, 3, 12, 13), giving, moreover, a continuous, cautiously written survey of the bishop's stormy career (v. 19).[1] Miracles of the monastery of Barking, known to us only through Bede's extracts (iv. 7–11), likewise belonged to the literature recently born in England and accessible to him.[2] But this completes the list of narrative sources available to Bede; he had to look round for other material.

At first he endeavoured to obtain documentary evidence, that is, letters and synodal proceedings. It may have been the example of Eusebius and, in a smaller degree, of Gregory of Tours, if indeed he needed a model at all, that induced him to include the whole wording of such documents in his work, of which they constitute nearly a seventh part. It was a practice widespread in the Middle Ages to give a mixture of chronicle and chartulary, when authors often lacked the ability to condense their proofs into a continuous narrative.[3] Bede had this ability, he knows how to give a summary of a document;[4] but we must be grateful to him that, nevertheless, he has thus preserved important texts which would otherwise be lost without his documentation. Bede himself tells how the presbyter Nothelm of London searched the archives of the Roman Church for relevant letters of the Popes and brought copies of them to him,[5] transcribed from the registers of the Papal chancery: the copies thus transmitted by Bede have been an important factor in elucidating the form and arrangement of these

[1] On the differences between Stephanus' and Bede's accounts of Wilfrid, I refer only to one of the latest essays, that of Reginald L. Poole, 'St. Wilfrid and the see of Ripon' (*Eng. Hist. Rev.* xxxiv. 1919, pp. 1–24; reprinted in Poole's *Studies*, pp. 56–81).

[2] Bede mentions this source in chs. 7, 10, and 11. It may be doubted that he knew a written source on Ninian (iii. 4, p. 133). Cf. now K. Strecker's edition of the *Miracula Nynie episcopi* (*MG. Poetae Latini*, iv. 2, pp. 943 ff.) and his article, *Neues Archiv*, xliii (1922), pp. 1 ff.

[3] Cf. M. Ritter, *loc. cit.*, p. 117.

[4] Cf. *H.E.* ii. 18, where Bede gives a good summary of a letter as well as the letter itself.

[5] *H.E.*, preface (p. 6). Nothelm seems to have copied the letters before 715. See Mommsen, 'Die Papstbriefe bei Beda' (*Neues Archiv*, xvii, 1892, pp. 387 f., Mommsen's *Gesammelte Schriften*, vi, Berlin, 1910, p. 620).

registers.[1] Some of his texts may have come from another source, such as the originals of letters sent to England and preserved there.[2] Letters of the popes prevail among the documents inserted by him (i. 23, 24, 27–32 ; ii. 8, 10, 11, 17–19 ; iii. 29), mostly belonging to the first period of the mission in England, but extending from Gregory I to Vitalian (about 666). Bede gives only two letters of other origin. About 605 Archbishop Laurentius and his co-bishops had written in vain to the Irish clergy to win them over to the Roman rite ; a part of this letter is inserted (ii. 4). A century later Abbot Ceolfrid wrote, with more success, to the Pictish King Naitan ; Bede produces this letter, possibly written by himself,[3] at full length (v. 21)—the topical interest of the selection is evident.

Apart from the letters included in his work, he knew others which he worked up shortly in his narrative ;[4] coming nearer to his own times, tradition and personal experience provided him with richer material, so that he was able to do without the incorporation of entire documents. After the letter of Pope Vitalian (iii. 29) alluded to above and besides that of Ceolfrid on the Paschal question just mentioned, Bede inserted only proceedings of the first two synods of the English Church: the synodal letter of Archbishop Theodore containing the decrees of Hertford in 672 (iv. 5),[5] and parts of the official record of the

---

[1] I refer only to H. Bresslau, *Handbuch der Urkundenlehre*, i, 2nd ed. (Leipzig, 1912), pp. 116, n. 4 (where the literature on the subject is indicated), and E. Posner, 'Das Register Gregors I.' (*Neues Archiv*, xliii, 1922, pp. 274 f., 283 ff.).

[2] Gregory's reply to the questions of Augustine (Bede, i. 27 ; cf. ii. 1), which seems not to be derived from the Papal registers (cf. Posner, *loc. cit.*, pp. 285 ff.) and the genuineness of which is at least questionable (see above, p. 128, n. 2), and the *libellus synodicus* of 595, quoted in *H.E.* ii. 1 and used also in the *Chronica maiora*, § 530 (p. 309), are transmitted only in collections of canon law. Cf. *MGH. Epist.* i. 362 ; ii. 331 f. (cf. *ibid.*, pp. xxvi f.).—The detailed rubrics of the letters of Pope Boniface V to King Edwin and his wife (ii. 10, 11), containing official titles used at Rome, seem to suggest that copies made in the Papal chancery were here at Bede's disposal.

[3] See Plummer, ii. 332. See p. 151.

[4] Bede mentions letters of Archbishop Laurentius to the Britons (ii. 4, p. 88) and of the Popes Boniface IV (*ibid.*), Boniface V (ii. 7, p. 94), Honorius I (ii. 19 ; iii. 7), Vitalian (iv. 1) and Agatho's privilege (iv. 18) ; cf. above, pp. 130 and 132 ; cf. Jaffé, *Regesta pontif. Roman.* (2nd ed.) i, nos. 1999, 2000, 2005, 2022, 2023, 2094, 2106. Bede used also the lost proceedings of a Roman synod of 610 (ii. 4) ; cf. Jaffé, p. 221.

[5] On the year 672 (not as Bede says 673), see Krusch, 'Die Einführung des griechischen Paschalritus im Abendlande' (*Neues Archiv*, ix. 1884, p. 160) ; Poole, *Studies*, 41 (with n. 4).—The formula in the beginning *regnante in*

council of Hatfield in 680 (iv. 17).[1] Anyhow, the included texts manifest Bede's aim to tell a documented story. In the same manner he repeated sepulchral inscriptions, not only of Bishop Wilfrid, copied at Ripon (v. 19), and of the Archbishops Augustine and Theodore of Canterbury (ii. 3; v. 8), but also epitaphs transcribed at Rome, of Gregory the Great (ii. 1) and King Cædwalla of Wessex (v. 7)—Bede may owe these to a corpus of Roman inscriptions collected by pilgrims.[2]

Bede not only collected written sources, but sought also to learn the oral traditions of the different parts of England. In the dedicatory letter to King Ceolwulf, he enumerates the helpers who, in the various districts, had communicated to him personally or in writing their knowledge of regional history, drawn from tradition and records. But Bede does not only mention his authorities summarily in the preface; in the narrative also he often refers to his informants.[3] As in the prose Life of St. Cuthbert,[4] he distinguishes sometimes between indirect accounts and reports of eyewitnesses, e.g.:

ii. 16. 'De huius fide provinciae narravit mihi presbyter et abbas quidam vir veracissimus de monasterio Peartaneu vocabulo Deda retulisse sibi quendam seniorem. . . .'

iii. 15. 'Cuius ordinem miraculi non quilibet dubius relator, sed fidelissimus mihi nostrae ecclesiae presbyter Cynimund vocabulo narravit, qui se hoc ab ipso Utta presbytero, in quo et per quem conpletum est, audisse perhibebat.'

He frequently suggests by *fertur*, *ferunt*, *perhibetur* or similar words that he had obtained the story from hearsay.[5] He was

perpetuum . . . may depend on the proceedings of a Roman synod; cf. the *decretum* of 595 (*MGH. Epist.* i. 362).

[1] The records of Roman synods were the model at Hatfield, except that years of English kings (*imperantibus*!) were substituted for years of the emperors. Cf., e.g., Levison, 'Die Akten der römischen Synode von 679' (*Zeitschrift der Savigny-Stiftung für Rechtsgeschichte*, xxxiii, 1912, Kanonistische Abteilung, ii. 259 ff.).

[2] The *sylloge* of Cambridge, published for the first time by me, *Neues Archiv*, xxxv (1910), pp. 350 f., and supplemented from a Canterbury MS. *ibid.* xxxviii (1913), pp. 645 f., 652 f., ends just in Bede's time with the epitaph of Pope John VII (†707).   [3] Plummer, i, p. xliv, n.3.   [4] Above, pp. 127 f.

[5] Plummer, i, p. xlv. He indicates by expressions of this kind (p. 79, l. 25, *opinio quae . . . traditione maiorum ad nos usque perlata est*; l. 28, *Dicunt*; p. 80, l. 3, *ut aiunt*; p. 81, l. 4, *iuxta opinionem quam ab antiquis accepimus*) that the famous tale of the English slaves in the Roman market depends on tradition, not, as has been suggested, on the Northumbrian Life of Gregory the Great (cf. above, p. 123, n. 3). What he gives of royal genealogies (i. 15; ii. 5, 15) may also have been obtained from hearsay.

conscious of the uncertainty of rumour and expressly requested the reader, if he should find any untruth in his book, not to impute it to the author, who, *quod vera historiae lex est*, for the instruction of posterity had faithfully committed to writing what he could gather from common report.[1] In fact, he did not rely entirely on oral tradition; as far as possible, he tried to verify it from documentary evidence, as we have seen.

And now, what has the historiographer made out of all his research? The result is the *Ecclesiastical History*. The five books, though not of the same size, do not differ in the number of chapters and length so much as to give the reader a sense of disproportion. The fact that there are five books is, perhaps, not due to chance; Bede may just have selected half of the number of books into which Gregory of Tours divided his Histories. As we have seen, he has in common with Gregory an autobiography and list of writings at the end of the work; further, both prefix to the main subject a kind of introductory history. Gregory, in a short sketch, goes back to the beginning of things at the Creation; after a few pages he reaches, with Caesar, Roman times, and soon, with the persecutions of the Christians, Gaul, the principal scene of his tale, where the Franks appear shortly afterwards. So Bede does not go straight to his proper theme, to the time of Gregory the Great and the origins of the English Church, but commences with Caesar and the first contact between Britain and Rome in a preliminary section (chs. 2–22), which leads him at once, through the story of the alleged British King Lucius[2] (ch. 4), to the vicissitudes of the early British Church and gradually to the end of the Roman domination and the coming of the English. Bede goes back even beyond Caesar to the immigration of the first inhabitants of Britain. For just as Orosius had prefixed a description of the *orbis terrarum* to his Histories, so Bede, even beginning with

---

[1] Preface to Ceolwulf (Plummer, i. 8). Plummer, ii. 3 f., compares Bede's Commentary on Luke, ch. 2 (Giles, x. 333): 'Neque enim oblitus evangelista, quod eam de Spiritu Sancto concepisse et virginem peperisse narrarit, sed *opinionem vulgi exprimens, quae vera historiae lex est*, patrem Ioseph nuncupat Christi'. Bede's sentence was sometimes quoted in the Middle Ages from the preface to Ceolwulf, e.g. by Hincmar of Reims (preface to *Vita Remigii*, ed. Krusch, *Script. rer. Merov.* iii. 253). Cf. Marie Schulz, 'Die Lehre von der historischen Methode bei den Geschichtschreibern des Mittelalters' (*Abhandlungen zur Mittleren und Neueren Geschichte*, xiii), Berlin, 1909, pp. 36 ff.

[2] See above, p. 135, n. 2.

Orosius' first words on Britain,[1] gives a description of the British Isles as a prelude; he supplements the latter's information from Pliny, Solinus, Gildas and, not least, from his own knowledge in this first chapter, concluding with an ethnographical survey of the languages and peoples of the Isles. Later also he shows an interest in geographical facts, already manifested in his prose Life of St. Cuthbert;[2] he notes, for example, the size and situation of the Isles of Wight, Thanet, Man, and Anglesey, he mentions arms and currents of the sea, he displays a topographical sense by indicating distances between places—the ancient authors may have strengthened his natural instinct for observation in this respect. He likes to speak of relics of the past, of British defences, of Roman earthworks and walls, of ruined churches, of Horsa's tomb, and so forth.

The division into books[3] is, at least in part, well thought out. Bede relates in the first book, after the introductory chapters, the beginnings of the English Church until just before Pope Gregory's death (605 instead of 604), which initiates the second book; the latter also comes to a convenient end with the fall of King Edwin and the break-up of the first Northumbrian church (633), and not less congruous is the conclusion of the third book immediately before Archbishop Theodore's arrival on the scene (668). The fourth book covers the times of this archbishop, so important for the development of the English Church, and though finishing chronologically with the year of St. Cuthbert's death (687), includes his translation (698) and miracles. The fifth book comprises the rest, from 687 to 731. Thus Bede selected as dividing limits two momentous years, 633 and 668, and the striking ends of men like Gregory and Cuthbert. Within these frames the time-sequence generally determines the arrangement of the narrative and the change of scene and subject; distinct dates or phrases, such as *His temporibus, Eo tempore, Ipso etiam anno*, mark the commencement of a new subdivision.

The idea of apostolic and episcopal succession had been fundamental for the development not only of the Church itself, but also of ecclesiastical historiography. Bede's models, Eusebius and Rufinus, express in their very first words the intention

---

[1] Orosius, *Historiae adversum paganos* (ed. Zangemeister), i. 2, § 76: 'Britannia oceani insula. . . .' Cf. Plummer, ii. 5, who has not seen the origin of Bede's *oceani.*   [2] See above, p. 128.   [3] Cf. Plummer, ii. 66 f.

of demonstrating this succession, and Bede himself had no less the purpose of giving as completely as possible the succession of the English bishops, even his words being reminiscent of Rufinus' initial sentence.[1] It is significant that he sometimes notes not only the day of the death[2] and the burial place of a bishop, but also, within the limits of his knowledge, the day of his ordination and the names of the consecrators. William of Malmesbury, who, four centuries later, wrote the *Gesta pontificum Anglorum* anew, treated the history and the episcopal succession of one diocese after the other, from the origin of each to his own times. Bede, with his historical sense, took the history of the English Church as a united whole and, with regard for synchronism, did not separate simultaneous happenings. Thus, for instance, in the third book he speaks of the development of the Church in Northumbria, Wessex, Kent, in East Anglia and among the Middle Angles, in Essex and Mercia—only in this way could he present a real picture of the progress of the Christian mission, its vicissitudes and dependence on political events, ending with a survey of the contemporary English bishops (v. 23).[3]

His synchronization occasionally separated coherent matters. So Bede inserts in the story of southern England, at the end of the first book, incidents from Northumbria (i. 34), at the end of the third events from Essex (iii. 30), referring in the preceding chapter (iii. 29) to the next book, there (iv. 1) to the penultimate chapter, in order to provide the connecting link. But he does not over-emphasize the synchronization: the time of Cuthbert's death is the boundary between the fourth and fifth books, but, as stated above, Bede, notwithstanding, includes in the fourth

---

[1] Rufinus, *H.E.* i. 1, § 1 (ed. Mommsen, p. 7): '*Successio*nes sanctorum apostolorum et tempora, quae a Salvatore nostro *ad* nos *usque* decursa sunt, *quae*que et qualia in his *erga* ecclesiae statum *gesta sint*, qui etiam insignes viri in locis maxime celeberimis ecclesiis praefuerunt. . . .' Cf. Bede's preface (p. 6): '*Exinde autem usque ad* tempora praesentia, *quae* in ecclesia Cantuariorum per discipulos beati papae Gregorii sive *successo*res eorum . . . *gesta sint*', and below (p. 7): 'At vero in provincia Lindissi *quae sint gesta erga* fidem Christi, quaeve *successio* sacerdotalis extiterit. . . .'

[2] We do not know how far Bede himself used obituaries. Cf. *H.E.* iv. 14: 'Quaerant in suis codicibus, in quibus defunctorum est adnotata depositio. . . . Requisivit in annale suo et invenit eadem ipsa die Osvaldum regem fuisse peremtum.'

[3] The phrase there used, 'Hic est in praesentiarum universae *status* Brittaniae' may be compared with the end of Eutropius' *Breviary*, x. 18, § 3, 'Is *status* erat Romanae rei. . . .'

book the translation and later miracles of the saint (iv. 30–32). The arrival, the episcopal election, or the death of famous men gives him the opportunity to insert small continuous biographies: of Gregory the Great (ii. 1), Fursa (iii. 19), Cuthbert (iv. 27–32), and Wilfrid (v. 19). He likes to give whole series of homogeneous narrations, the miracles of Oswald (iii. 9–13), of Aidan (iii. 15, 16), of the monastery of Barking[1] (iv. 7–11), stories of Hilda and her monastery (iv. 23, 24), of Bishop John of Hexham (v. 2–6), or the sequence of some visions of the other life (v. 12–14), showing the influence of the widespread *Visio Pauli* and of the fourth book of Gregory the Great's *Dialogues*, which is known to have so strongly affected the precursors of Dante, among whom Bede must be reckoned as regards these chapters.[2] A liking for episodes leads him a little away from his subject, when the history of Abbot Adamnan of Iona induces him not only to mention the latter's work on the Holy Places, but also to insert into the Church History of England entire sections of his own adaptation of the book (v. 16, 17), which are really out of place.[3] Bede the theologian is therein manifested. He says more than once that the purpose of edifying the reader has determined him to admit such and such a miracle or vision—even in his dedicatory letter he emphasizes the moral effect of historical learning:

'Sive enim historia de bonis bona referat, ad imitandum bonum auditor sollicitus instigatur; seu mala commemoret de pravis, nihilo minus religiosus ac pius auditor sive lector devitando quod noxium est ac perversum, ipse sollertius ad exsequenda ea, quae bona ac Deo digna esse cognoverit, accenditur.'

In addition to the edificatory intention, it may have been the naïve joy of the poet in his work that caused him to add to the tale of St. Etheldreda his own hymn in her honour (iv. 20).

Certainly he did not take the composition of his narrative easily. Perhaps there are a few traces of rearrangement, remains of earlier efforts. In his chapter on Bishop Aldhelm (v. 18) a real continuity is established only by removing the sentences on his writings, which seem to have been added by Bede sub-

---

[1] Cf. above, p. 138.

[2] These chapters were copied separately from the ninth century onwards and added to collections of other Visions. Cf. Plummer, ii. 295, 299, and my notes, *Neues Archiv*, xxxii (1907), p. 382, and *Script. rer. Merov.* v. 374 (l. 32); vii. 606, 609, 659, 668.

[3] Bede's *Liber de locis sanctis*, compiled from Adamnan, Eucherius, and Hegesippus, has been published by Paul Geyer, *Itinera Hierosolymitana saeculi IIII–VIII* (*Corpus script. eccl. Lat.* xxxix), Vienna, 1898, pp. 299–324.

sequently.[1] It has been noticed that he says, in the *Historia
ecclesiastica* (iv. 18), of Benedict Biscop, *cuius supra meminimus*,[2]
without previous mention, and in the *Historia abbatum* (ch. 2), of
Pope Vitalian, *cuius supra*, though his name does not appear
before in the book. I should like to conjecture that these
incongruous words are vestiges of an earlier plan rather than
slips of memory: perhaps Bede at first intended to give the
history of his monasteries within the frame of the general work,
but afterwards saw that there was not room enough for an
adequate treatment in a well proportioned book.

Unevenness of this or any other kind is very seldom to be
found. Generally the work is symmetrical, and Bede knows how
to tell his tale, which is animated by frequent use of direct
speech, a device which gives vivacity also to the work of Gregory
of Tours.[3] His language is lucid and clear, void of all pompous-
ness and bombast. In this respect he shows the way to the
Northumbrian school, very different from Aldhelm's circle of
Wessex with its inflated style.[4] Narrations such as those of
Pope Gregory in the slave-market of Rome, of the conversion
of the Northumbrians with the decisive Witenagemot and the
speeches of Coifi and the alderman, of the humility of King
Oswine, or of the bard Cædmon are pearls of story-telling and will
be appreciated as long as any interest in medieval life endures.

Certainly his tale is as unequal as the information he obtained;
he knows, for instance, less of Wessex than of Kent and his
native Northumbria.[5] There are some small mistakes, as when
he adopts Gildas' conjecture on the time of St. Alban's martyrdom,[6] or when he assigns the see of Arles erroneously to a
bishop of Lyons;[7] there are contradictions and slips in his

[1] Cf. Plummer, ii. 313. The words, *ibid.* i. 321, l. 14, *Quibus episcopatum
administrantibus* almost certainly refer to p. 320, l. 29, so that p. 320, l. 29,
Denique to p. 321, l. 13, *eruditus* seem to be a later insertion; also the reference
p. 321, l. 9 (*ut dixi*), to p. 320, l. 29, may be a mark of it.

[2] He uses the same words of Benedict in v. 19.

[3] Cf. S. Hellmann, *Gregor von Tours* (see above, p. 133, n. 3), p. 16.

[4] See, e.g., M. Roger, *L'Enseignement des lettres classiques d'Ausone à Alcuin*
(Paris, 1905), pp. 293 ff., 309 f.; Plummer, i. p. liii f.; Laistner, *Thought and
letters in western Europe A.D. 500 to 900* (London, 1931), pp. 119 ff.

[5] Cf. Werner, *loc. cit.*, p. 211 f.; van Hamel, *loc. cit.*, pp. 182 ff.

[6] See above, p. 135, n. 4.

[7] *H.E.* i. 24, 27, 28, on Aetherius. On Bede's derivation of the *Angli* from
Angulus (i. 15) and on the odd archaism in calling the Danes *Danai* (v. 9, p. 296)
see Elis Wadstein, 'The Beowulf poem as an English national epos' (*Acta
philologica Scandinavica*, viii, 1933–4, p. 279 f.).

synchronisms and dates. In the selection of his material he is a child of his times, as in his predilection for the miraculous, and the importance he attaches to the Paschal question. We should like to hear more from him about the controversies and struggles of the last generations round the person of Wilfrid, about which he gives less but more discreet information than we have reason to believe he possessed.[1] One has only to imagine Bede's work as non-existent to realize how much our knowledge of early English history, political as well as ecclesiastical, is dependent on him, and this holds, not only for England itself, but also for the beginnings of the Anglo-Saxon mission on the Continent, among Frisians and Saxons.[2] He is not free from sympathies and antipathies. Pagans and heretics are *perfidi* in his eyes;[3] he detests the Celtic rites, so that he calls the army of the Britons a *nefanda militia* (ii. 2). But he abstains from 'odious invectives against the vanquished cause'[4] and manifests a real sense of fairness and justice. The unjust, unprovoked war of his own King Ecgfrid against the 'innocent' Irish people is, in his opinion, the reason for the King's fall (iv. 26), and though always objecting to the Paschal reckoning and to the other special rites of the Celtic churches, he nevertheless defends them against unfounded accusations (iii. 4, 17) and highly praises the virtues of the Irish monks formerly working in Northumbria, notwithstanding their ecclesiastical peculiarities, which he definitely opposes. The words he devotes to Aidan do honour to himself just as much as to the subject of his admiration (iii. 17):

'Scripsi autem haec de persona et operibus viri praefati, nequaquam in eo laudans aut eligens hoc, quod de observatione paschae minus perfecte sapiebat, immo hoc multum detestans, sicut in libro quem de temporibus conposui manifestissime probavi; sed quasi v e r a x h i s t o r i c u s simpliciter ea, quae de illo sive per illum sunt gesta, describens et quae laude sunt digna in eius actibus laudans atque ad utilitatem legentium memoriae commendans: studium videlicet pacis et caritatis, continentiae et humilitatis, animum irae et avaritiae victorem',

---

[1] Cf. above, p. 138.

[2] *H.E.* v. 9–11; cf. Bede's *Chronica maiora*, § 566 (p. 316), and on the two Hewalds, also the Martyrology (Quentin, p. 105 f.). See, e.g., my introduction to Alcuin's Life of St. Willibrord, *Script. rer. Merov.* vii. 81 ff.

[3] See Plummer, ii. 18 f., 78.

[4] Gustav Hübener, *England und die Gesittungsgrundlage der europäischen Frühgeschichte* (Frankfort, 1930), p. 125.

and so on. The principle of sincerity and veracity thus marks him as a real historian, within the limits of his times.

His liking for exact statement of sizes and distances has been mentioned; but it is necessary to return here to his sense of chronology and to throw it into higher relief, as the introduction of the era of the Incarnation into historiography is especially due to his Church History. Two centuries before, Dionysius Exiguus had created it in order to substitute in his Paschal table a Christian starting-point in the numbering of years for the era named after the persecutor Diocletian. Bede had naturally retained the invention of Dionysius in the complete Paschal cycle from 532 to 1063, prefixed to his work *De temporum ratione*,[1] and he thus unconsciously laid the foundation for a new kind of annals, based on the Easter table with its Christian framework of years: the latter was soon afterwards written separately to receive annalistic entries alone.[2] Bede had also theoretically treated this system of numbering, in relation to the Paschal table, in both books on chronology, but had as yet actually practised it only in exceptional cases.[3] In the Roman Empire, when there were no more consuls, time was reckoned by means of the imperial years, for which in the Germanic kingdoms the regnal years of the kings were substituted. The practice of the fifteen-year period of indictions, coming from Egypt into the West, also spread with the Church; Archbishop Theodore's synodal letter of Hertford in 672 is dated in this way:[4]

'Convenimus autem die XXIIII. mensis Septembris, indictione prima, in loco qui dicitur Herutford'.

But the dating was not very distinct, the numbers recurring every fifteen years. The Anglo-Saxons, like the other Germanic peoples, employed the regnal years of their kings; Bede gives many examples of this.[5] In Northumbria the black year of the pagan kings Osric and Eanfrid (633) was added to the years of the succeeding King Oswald,[6] and in Bede's monastery of Jarrow the fifteenth year of King Ecgfrid (685) can to-day still

---

[1] See above, pp. 118, 119.
[2] I mention only the sketch given by Poole, *Chronicles and Annals* (Oxford, 1926).   [3] See above, pp. 120, 130, 132. Cf. Poole, *Studies*, p. 33 f.
[4] *H.E.* iv. 5. Cf. above, p. 139, n. 5.   [5] Cf. Poole, *Studies*, pp. 40 ff.
[6] *H.E.* iii. 1, 9. Cf. Earle and Plummer, *Two of the Saxon Chronicles parallel*, ii (Oxford, 1899), p. cix f.

be read in the dedication inscription of the church.[1] But what, then, if inhabitants of several of the little Anglo-Saxon kingdoms came together and had to date a document without being content with the indiction? The answer is given in the decrees of the synod of Hatfield in 680, formed after the model of a Roman council, but with the names of the Emperors superseded by the names of the kings to whose realms the attending bishops belonged:[2]

'In nomine domini nostri Iesu Christi Salvatoris, imperantibus dominis piissimis nostris Ecgfrido rege Hymbronensium anno x. regni eius, sub die xv. Kalendas Octobres, indictione VIII; et Aedilredo rege Mercinensium anno sexto regni eius; et Aldvulfo rege Estanglorum anno XVII. regni eius; et Hlothario rege Cantuariorum regni eius anno VII; praesidente Theodoro gratia Dei archiepiscopo Brittaniae insulae et civitatis Doruvernis. . . .'

This kind of reckoning was troublesome and, at the same time, did not correspond to the unity of the English Church, which then formed one province, though politically divided. In order to indicate the years in the history of this Church Bede chose Dionysius' era of the Incarnation as the most applicable to all parts of England, employing it from the very beginning of his work. Even when relating Caesar's invasion of Britain, he adds to the year after the building of Rome found in his source, the date reckoned backwards from the Incarnation (i. 2; v. 24): 'anno ab Urbe condita DCXCIII, ante vero incarnationis dominicae tempus anno LXmo' and he thus uses this era throughout, also dating the annals of his *recapitulatio* (v. 24) in this way.[3] Just as the Paschal table at the front of his second chronological book prepared the way for annals,[4] so too his *Ecclesiastical History*

---

[1] Hübner, *Inscriptiones Britanniae Christianae*, no. 198; Plummer, ii. 361; Quentin, p. 128.   [2] *H.E.* iv. 17 (p. 239). Cf. above, p. 140, n. 1.

[3] Also the words at the end of *H.E.* ii. 18, added to the dates of a Papal letter: 'id est anno dominicae incarnationis DCXXXIIII', have been no doubt supplied by Bede and should not have been printed in italics in Plummer's edition. It is not necessary here to examine the beginning-point of Bede's year of the Incarnation. Cf. Poole, *Studies*, pp. 8 ff., 40 ff.

[4] See above, p. 119. Bede's compatriot, Willibrord, used the era in 728 in an entry of his calendar, fol. 39 v. Cf. H. A. Wilson, *The Calendar of St. Willibrord* (Henry Bradshaw Society, vol. lv), 1918; *Script. rer. Merov.* vii. 92; Franz Flaskamp, *Die Anfänge friesischen und sächsischen Christentums (Geschichtliche Darstellungen und Quellen*, ix), Hildesheim, 1929, p. 81, and plate II. The author of a Frankish chronological treatise of 737, not dependent on Bede, gives the era among the other elements of the system of Dionysius, but not as the 'name' of the year; cf. B. Krusch, 'Das älteste fränkische Lehrbuch der Dionysianischen Zeitrechnung' (*Mélanges offerts à M. Émile Chatelain*, Paris, 1910, p. 242.)

spread the use of the Christian era in England, as well as on the Continent, where some of the oldest existent manuscripts of the work were also written. The era came into use now in English charters and synodical documents.[1] The first continental example of such dating in an official text is especially significant; it heads the decrees of the first Frankish synod, assembled in 742 under Anglo-Saxon influence, at a time when the Frankish throne was vacant and the regnal years could not well be used.[2] It is not necessary to follow here the further, and in part rather slow, spread of the era: to-day nearly the whole Christian world has adopted Bede's practice.

But his influence as historian was not confined to this; a great part of medieval historiography is indebted to him. Most of what was known in the Middle Ages of early English history depended on his principal work, on the Continent nearly all of it; but in England also, from the ninth century onwards, when the Saxon Chronicles were compiled, their authors drew richly from the *Ecclesiastical History* and especially from the Recapitulation, which, having itself been immediately continued, had already given origin to further annals in the generation following Bede's time. I mention Alfred the Great's translation, not to speak of the later English historians who relied more or less on Bede. The wide diffusion of the work is demonstrated not only by the great number of existing manuscripts, but also by the fact that Bede's death is often noted in medieval annals in 731, the concluding year of the History.[3] Another significant example. The chronicler Sigebert of Gembloux wants to give an English column beside the royal names and regnal years of other countries; but he is able to do so only so far as Bede's narrative stretches: 'Abhinc regnum Anglorum annotare supersedeo, quia hystorias maiorum, quas sequar, non habeo'[4]—not until after the Norman Conquest does he again take up the thread. The style was as attractive as the matter; imitators and plagiarists very soon appeared. Before the end of the eighth century Bede's hymn on St. Etheldreda, inserted

---

[1] See, e.g., Earle, *A Hand-book to the Land-charters and other Saxonic documents* (Oxford, 1888), pp. xxix f. See also p. 151.

[2] The *capitulare* of the so-called *Concilium Germanicum* (*MGH. Capitularia*, i, 24, and *Concilia*, ii. 2). But Boniface, the leader in the reform of the Frankish Church, did not yet know Bede's works directly; of. his 75th, 76th, and 91st letters (ed. M. Tangl, *MGH. Epistolae selectae*, i. 1916, pp. 158, 159, 207).

[3] See Plummer, i, p. lxxi, n. 3. [4] *MGH. Scriptores*, vi. 331.

in his History, was excerpted at Nivelles in Belgium in a rhythmical piece in praise of St. Gertrude.[1] Shortly afterwards the monks of Saint-Wandrille, in Normandy, read the 'admirable work' so ardently that the phrases copied from Bede for their Lives of Saints and the Chronicle of their house sometimes constitute a mosaic extending to whole chapters.[2] So much for the *Ecclesiastical History*.

The *Historia abbatum* was not known outside England. But his other historical writings had an even greater influence than the *Ecclesiastical History*. His *Martyrology* with its narrative parts gave material and, what is more, direction and character to all the literature of this kind. The lucidity and clearness of both books on chronology made them favourites for centuries, as the multitude of manuscripts demonstrates.[3] They were a mine of information to the later computists.[4] In particular, the Chronicles joined to these manuals, narrow as their contents may seem to the modern historian, largely answered the needs of the Middle Ages. Certainly the chroniclers did not forget Jerome and his continuations, but they seized no less upon the shorter and handier text-books of Bede, which were transcribed until the fifteenth century, the appended chronicles being copied separately, summarized,[5] augmented, and continued.[6] Authors

---

[1] *Virtutum S. Geretrudis continuatio*, ch. 3 (*Script. rer. Merov.* ii, 473). The dependence on Bede has been recognized by the late Paul von Winterfeld; see my note, *Neues Archiv*, xxxiii (1908), pp. 558 f.

[2] See, above all, *Vita Vulframni* (*Script. rer. Merov.* v. 662–673), but also *Vita Ansberti*, chs. 11 and 34 (*ibid.* 626, 639), *Condedi*, ch. 1 and 12 (*ibid.* 646, 651), *Eremberti* (*ibid.* 654–56). On the Chronicle of Saint-Wandrille see Anton Rosenkranz, *Beiträge zur Kenntnis der Gesta abbatum Fontanellensium* (dissertation of Bonn, 1911), pp. 74 ff., and what I have said myself, *Revue Bénédictine*, xlvi (1934), pp. 246 f., 249 ff., 255, 257 f.

[3] See Mommsen's edition of the Chronicles and Laistner, 'Transactions', *loc. cit.*, p. 93, on the MSS. of *De temporum ratione*. On medieval catalogues of books see M. Manitius, *Neues Archiv*, xxxvi (1911), pp. 762 ff.; xli (1918), p. 715 f.

[4] I mention only the computistical collection of the eighth century, treated by Karl Rück, *Auszüge aus der Naturgeschichte des C. Plinius Secundus in einem astronomisch-komputistischen Sammelwerke des 8. Jahrhunderts* (= *Programm des Kgl. Ludwigs-Gymnasiums*, 1887–8), Munich, 1888, and Byrhtferth's Manual (A.D. 1011), edited in 1929 by the late S. J. Crawford, Early English Text Society, O.S., no. 177. See also p. 151.

[5] So in the little *Chronicon de sex aetatibus*, edited as *Generationum regnorumque laterculus Bedanus* by Mommsen, *Auct. ant.* xiii. 346–54.

[6] So the *Chronicon universale* to 741; cf. Mommsen, *ibid.*, pp. 237 ff., 334–40. Cf. the same, *Neues Archiv*, xxii (1897), pp. 548 ff. (= *Gesammelte Schriften*, vi. 643 ff.). On the time of the compilation (after 768) see *Script. rer. Merov.* vii. 776, n. 2.

of new chronicles, like Frechulf of Lisieux,[1] Ado of Vienne,[2] and Regino of Prüm[3] and many of later times, made more or less copious extracts from them. Augustine's doctrine of the ages of the world owed its continuous existence in historiography largely to Bede.

He shows his creative powers most conspicuously in the History of the Church. As for the rest of his historical writings, his own comment on one of his earliest writings may be quoted to some extent:[4] 'Haec tibi . . . diligenter ex antiquorum opusculis scriptorum excerpere curavi et, quae sparsim reperta ipse diutino labore collegeram, tibi collecta obtuli'. But where he lacks originality, he surpasses all others of his time in the manner in which he has transmitted traditional knowledge to posterity, 'a brilliant example to all who, in dark ages, set themselves the task of handing on the glimmering torch of learning to coming generations'.[5] Through the *Ecclesiastical History*, moreover, he himself lighted a new flame.

WILHELM LEVISON.

[1] See Aem. Grunauer, *De fontibus historiae Frechulphi episcopi Lixoviensis* (Vitoduri, 1864), p. 52 f.

[2] Cf. Wilhelm Kremers, *Ado von Vienne, sein Leben und seine Schriften*, i (dissertation, Bonn, 1911), pp. 78 ff.

[3] See the edition of Fr. Kurze, *Reginnis abbatis Prumiensis Chronicon* (*Script. rer. Germ.*), Hannover, 1890.

[4] Bede, *De arte metrica*, ed. H. Keil, *Grammatici Latini*, vii. 260.

[5] Schwartz, *loc. cit.* (see p. 114, n. 6), p. 104.

ADDITIONAL NOTES

Page 139. Note 3. The famous sentence of Plato on kings and philosophers at the beginning of the letter depends upon Lactantius: *Divin. Inst.* iii. 21, 6 (ed. Brandt, *Corpus script. eccles. Lat.* xix. 249); on other renderings of the sentence see P. *Rutilius Lupus*, ed. D. Ruhnken (Leiden, 1768), pp. 21 f.

Page 149, Note 1. M. Treiter, 'Die Urkundendatierung in angelsächsischer Zeit' (*Archiv für Urkundenforschung*, vii, 1921, pp. 68 f., 78 f., 92 f.).

Page 150, Note 4. See also Jones, 'Polemius Silvius', *loc. cit.*, pp. 54 f.

BEDE AS EXEGETE AND THEOLOGIAN

I

THE Venerable Bede, dying in 735 at the age of sixty-two, left a name which is still acclaimed after 1,200 years as that of the Father of English History. Yet it may be doubted if in his own view or in that of his younger contemporaries or of those who followed for many centuries the *Historia Ecclesiastica Gentis Anglorum* was either his most notable achievement or the means through which the influence of his life's work was chiefly to be felt. The task to which he set himself on his ordination to the priesthood at the age of thirty for the satisfaction of his own needs and the needs of those around him was the interpretation of Scripture and its illustration from the writings of the Fathers; and the well-known list of works completed by the time that he had reached the age of fifty-nine, which he added to the last chapter of his History, supplies both a canon of his writings and singular evidence of his industry. As Dr. Charles Plummer, to whom all lovers of Bede owe grateful acknowledgement, has pointed out, that list is not entirely complete; nor is it in chronological order. But it is not an accident that Bede places first his treatises on biblical subjects, for, though he is one of the most modest of scholars in his account of what he has tried to do, such studies have to his mind an importance to which no others should be preferred.

Four books on the beginning of Genesis to the birth of Isaac and the ejection of Ishmael are followed in the list by three more on the Tabernacle and its vessels and the garments of the priests, with which may be compared the two books on the allegorical exposition of the building of the Temple and the single book in which Tobit is interpreted of Christ and the Church. *Capitula lectionum* on the Pentateuch, Joshua and Judges, and the treatise in three books on the first part of Samuel to the death of Saul, of which the sequel provides a pathetic paragraph of Bede's own biography, like the thirty *Quaestiones* on Kings and other works on Kings and Chronicles and Ezra and Nehemiah, give us an insight into the writer's method of handling the historical and quasi-historical materials that he finds in the Old Testament and into the purposes for which he regards them as useful. It is indeed one of Bede's merits as a commentator that that practical aim is never long absent from his thoughts, and this explains a feature which, however disappointing it may be at times to ourselves, is entirely characteristic. We should always be glad to know what Bede himself thinks of a passage, and sometimes he tells us; but that opinion is in his own eyes for the most part of secondary importance. He was one to whom tradition spoke with impressive emphasis and, while by no means a slavish traditionalist, he would probably have accepted readily as descriptive of his own attitude Bishop Creighton's words to Dr. Hodgkin: 'I always like to keep very close to my authorities.' We are conscious as we read of sharing the privilege of admission to a student's workshop and of watching the student at work. We may wish that he had expounded more fully his own reflections on the prophet Isaiah: from his point of view it is even more important to prepare in handy form materials possibly for future work, certainly for present edification, by making excerpts from the blessed Jerome on Isaiah, Daniel, the Twelve Prophets, and part of Jeremiah, or transcribing in an orderly scheme from the writings of St. Augustine any notes that he can find for the interpretation of 'the Apostle', who for him as for Augustine is of course St. Paul. He is exercising his learning and, it must be added, his ingenuity in a different field when he turns to the book of 'the blessed Father' Job or to the Song of Habakkuk or to Proverbs, Ecclesiastes, or above all to the Song of Songs, in relation to which he performs, four centuries before St. Bernard, some of the most astonishing feats of exegesis in all theological literature. Of a less elaborate kind are letters on biblical and kindred topics, including one on the Six Ages of the World, another on the Halting-places (*mansiones*) of the children of Israel on their way to the Promised Land, and a third on Isaiah xxiv. 22, 'And they shall be shut up there in prison: and after many days they shall be visited.'

For the New Testament the list includes, besides what has been mentioned, four books of commentary on St. Mark and six on St. Luke, as well as two of Homilies of the Gospel, a commentary on the Acts of the Apostles in two books, an explanation of each of the seven Catholic Epistles, and three books on the Apocalypse of St. John. Lastly we may mention *Capitula lectionum* for the whole of the New Testament apart from the Gospel, and a little work of a special kind dealing with what may be called the 'style' and rhetorical figures of Scripture, a subject in which, as his commentaries show, Bede took a more than occasional interest, since it seemed to him to have no small importance in determining the principles of interpretation.

It is probable that most of the works enumerated above are still extant somewhere, though one or two have not been identified with certainty. The list does not include a large number of exegetical treatises which have come down to us under the shelter of Bede's name and which are generally rejected by editors as spurious or at least doubtful. Some of these are Bede-worthy in subject but hardly in treatment, and the whole could certainly not find a place in the interval between the composition of the list *c.* A.D. 731 and the death of Bede. At the latter date, according to Cuthbert's story,[1] which has been well described as 'not inferior in beauty and pathos to any of Bede's own', he was engaged upon a translation of the Gospel of St. John; and we must add to the list of his works on Scriptural subjects one on the Holy Places and the important *Liber Retractationis* on the Acts of the Apostles, which are indisputably genuine, and just possibly (although this has been challenged on good grounds) the commentary on St. Matthew.

A curiously interesting if imperfect impression of the course of Bede's exegetical work is derived from the prefatory letters to several of the books. In that prefixed to the 'Explanation of the Apocalypse' and addressed to a *frater dilectissimus* Bede states his view of the construction of the work in seven sections, and then proceeds to enumerate in detail the seven celebrated rules of interpretation formulated by the Donatist Tyconius[2] to which his attention had probably been drawn in the first instance by his study of Augustine. They are rules by which, in Bede's estimation as in Augustine's, students are greatly helped to understand Scripture, and it would be worth while if space allowed to dwell upon them, for no one who considers carefully Bede's exposition of Tyconius and the illustrations that he gives and then turns to Bede's own commentaries can

---

[1] For the Latin see Introduction to Plummer, i, pp. clx–clxiv, and for an English translation, *op. cit.*, lxxii–lxxviii.

[2] Cf. Burkitt, F. C., *The Book of Rules of Tyconius* in Cambridge *Texts and Studies*, iii. 1 (Cambridge University Press, 1894).

fail to observe the marked influence which the rules have exercised upon his whole method. Not only in the Apocalypse, he tells us, but in every canonical Scripture and especially in prophetic literature any careful observer will find these same rules in force; and in reference to the Apocalypse he announces his intention of following Tyconius, omitting some things for the sake of brevity, but superadding so far as he could attain either from the tradition of his master or from recollection of his reading or even from the grasp of his own understanding a good many things which to Tyconius as a man of ability and one who, as was said of him, flourished 'like a rose among thorns' seemed clear and not worth seeking after. In justification of his procedure Bede alleges the command that the talent he had received should be rendered to the Lord with usury—a maxim which might well be taken as the motto of his whole life. The work is to be divided into three books, since, as the blessed Augustine says, 'for some reason the attention of the reader is refreshed by the end of a book in the same way as the traveller's labour is by an inn'. None the less, that finding might be made easier for seekers, the same unbroken series of chapters according to that which in the book itself Bede had distinguished by *praeposita brevia* seemed necessary to be preserved throughout; for, he adds, 'Thinking to consult the slothfulness of our race of the Angles, which not so long ago in the days of the blessed Pope Gregory received the seed of the Faith and cultivated it, so far as reading went, lukewarmly enough, I have determined not only to elucidate meanings but express statements tersely, since plain brevity rather than prolix disputations is wont to stick in its memory.' We can hardly doubt that he had here the motive for those short pithy sentences which still delight a race which may not have wholly lost its preference for what is easily remembered nor ceased to mistake a slogan for an argument.

In the letter to Bishop Acca prefixed to his exposition of the Acts of the Apostles Bede mentions that he had sent the work on the Apocalypse to Acca to be copied, and had been exhorted not to allow the keenness of his mind to grow torpid or to sleep, but to give all the exertion of which he was capable to an explanation also of the blessed Evangelist Luke, following in the steps of the Fathers. He says that the immensity of the task completely terrified him and that he was hindered by the constraint of conflicting causes of which Acca is aware, but in order that the authority of the Bishop's request might not seem to be despised, he had done what he could meanwhile and has sent a little work on the Acts only finished a few days before and corrected with the utmost speed. In this he has tried to make clear things which seemed either 'mystically wrought or somewhat obscurely expressed' with the help of very many writers of the Catholic Faith, especially of Arator, a subdeacon of the Holy Roman Church. Arator's heroic verse with its 'flowers of allegory' has proved less attractive to later scholars than to Bede, who clearly admired it greatly. He adds that he is sending also a tiny little explanation of the Epistle of the most blessed Evangelist John, the greater part of which as a *compendiosus abbreviator* he had taken from homilies of St. Augustine diffused with broad-spreading sweetness, weaving in also some things at the end by his own exertion. Fortunately for learning, Acca was not a man easily to be turned from his purpose, and the receipt of the Exposition of the Acts served only to whet his desire that Bede, whom he now addresses as *presbyter*, and *reverendissimus in Christo frater et consacerdos*, should carry out the project of expounding St. Luke's Gospel which he had often urged upon him both by word of mouth and by letter. He shows himself quite unmoved by Bede's excuses, first that the task is difficult, and secondly that it had been already done by the most holy and learned Bishop Ambrose, and Bede's letter in sending him the commentary when at last completed shows how he triumphed over difficulties. Acca became bishop of Hexham in 709, so that none of these works nor the treatise on Solomon's Temple addressed to the *dilectis-simus antistitum*, if that be Acca, not Nothelm, can be earlier than that date. The commentary on St. Mark, as we learn from another letter to Acca, was produced many years later than that on St. Luke, and the very valuable *Liber Retractationis* on the Acts of the Apostles, in which Bede, following the example of Augustine, gave to the world a series of comments by way of addition and correction in relation to his earlier work, was written many years after the work thus revised. It contains in its comment on *sudaria et semicinctia* (Acts xix. 12) a note of considerable historical importance. 'Many of us', says Bede, 'are ignorant of the meaning of *semicinctia*; but Gregory, who is now Bishop of the Apostolic See, while he was still archdeacon, when a friend from Britain made inquiries of him, wrote back this among other things that it is a kind of napkin (*sudarium*) which the Hebrews use on their head.' The fact that Gregory II had been archdeacon is unnoticed in the *Dictionary of Christian Biography*, but he became pope in 715. We need have little hesitation either as to the identity of the 'friend from Britain' or in placing the exposition of Acts before that date, while the *Liber Retractationis*, as we have seen, is possibly and even probably later than 731. The matter is one of greater importance than might at first appear, for Bede was a scholar who died learning, and one of the most difficult questions in regard to him is the extent of his knowledge of languages other than Latin.

Certainly no one who studies the works of Bede with care is likely to doubt that he was a much better Greek scholar at the time he wrote the *Liber Retractationis* than he had been when he composed his earlier works including the commentary on Acts. If the critic feels obliged to add that even in his latest years Bede was far from being what would now be regarded as a finished Greek scholar, he will in fairness remember the difficulties which had to be overcome by a student in England in the eighth century and be inclined not to belittle but to admire his achievement. And every one will admit that Bede supplied delightfully human means for criticism of himself.

In the *Liber Retractationis* after calling attention to an addition in the Greek of Acts vi. 8 he adds:

'I wrote in the previous book that Stephen means "crowned", nor is what I wrote far from what is true. But, learning more accurately, I have found that Stephen signifies in Greek not "crowned" but "a crown", for this name *corona* is, among the Greeks, of the masculine gender and therefore appropriate to a man; but that one who is crowned is called *stephanephoros*, i.e. bearing a crown. Further, in the Psalm where we sing "Thou shalt bless the crown of the year of thy goodness" (Ps. lxiv [lxv]. 11) that verse among the Greeks begins thus: "Eulogeseis ton stephanon". Eusebius, explaining beautifully the meaning of this name, speaks of him as "immediately after his ordination having been stoned by those who slew the Lord also, whereby there was given by Christ a crown to one who was by his name a crown." But "crown" among the Greeks is also in the neuter gender *stemma*. I have thought this worthy of commemoration, because we often find this name [sc. Stephen] occurring in Latin books too.'

The lexicographical hints to be found here and elsewhere are always interesting: to regard them as puerile or superfluous is merely to show ignorance of the conditions of the time. But it must be admitted that in the later work he finds nothing to amplify or to correct in his former comment on Philip's opening his mouth (Acts viii. 35), that 'Philip is interpreted "mouth of the lamp" and the meaning is a beautiful one: the 'Mouth of the Lamp opens his mouth in bringing the dark things of prophecy to the light of knowledge'. When we remember that the interpretations 'Os lampadis' or 'Os manuum' were accepted by Jerome we can hardly blame Bede; but others besides transatlantic readers may allow themselves a smile when he continues by saying that the circumlocution 'Philip opened his mouth' might also be taken to indicate that his discourse at that time would be somewhat lengthy.

Bede's observations when he is consciously acting as instructor are sometimes delightful. On Acts ii. 1, he notes in the *Liber Retractationis* that some codices wrongly have 'Dies Pentecosten', and proceeds to decline Pentecostes = Quinquagesima, pointing out that Pentecosten is not genitive but accusative. In a note of some interest to liturgists he adds: 'But indeed in the prayers of the same day it has to be said "Et diem sacratissimam Pentecosten celebrantes (i.e. quinquagesimam)"'; from familiarity with this word the solemnity of this day is thought by some who do not know the Greek language proper to be known even in the nominative case as 'Pentecosten'. And we cannot help wondering if the person whose *mumpsimus* had provoked the remark lived to read it. There is an indication a little later that Bede himself was perhaps a little sensitive to criticism. On Acts ii. 7, 8 he says:

'I know that I have been blamed by some because I said that this sentence [sc. 'Behold, are not all these that speak Galileans? And how have we heard every man our own tongue wherein we were born?'] could be understood in two ways, or rather inquired in what way it should be understood. To these I briefly reply that what I wrote about this same sentence in my previous volume, I did not put forth from my own understanding, but took from the words of a master holy and in all things unreprovable—Gregory Nazianzen.'

The passage as we now read it gives us no hint that it is due to any one but Bede himself, but if it were originally identified by Gregory's initials in the margin the note must have been overlooked by copyists even at so early a date. Probably the misunderstanding was one of those which led to the procedure referred to in his preface to St. Luke's Gospel. Cheerfulness is restored when we read as a comment on Acts ii. 20, 'the sun shall be turned into darkness', that the Greek is singular but that the Latin translator could not write *tenebram* and so necessarily wrote the plural *tenebras*. 'I have thought it necessary', Bede says, 'to note this, that any one of the race of the English who reads it may not think it incumbent on him by reason of the authority of the Latin tongue to express *tenebras* by a plural in his own language, but rather in the singular, since this is equally allowable for him of course by the Greek authority from which it was translated into the Latin scripture.' Are we confronted with another reminiscence of the provoking person who would offend the scholar's ear by talking about 'Pentecosten'?

Readers of Dr. Plummer's masterly introduction to the *Historia Ecclesiastica*, which contains so much that subsequent writers can scarcely avoid covering part of the same ground, will recall the remarkable catalogue of Latin and Greek authors quoted or referred to in Bede's writings. When every deduction has been made of cases in which the reference is possibly or even probably at second hand, the list remains what Dr. Plummer calls it, 'a stately one'. The student has opportunities of seeing Bede legitimately annoyed at finding himself to have been misled by an authority upon whom he had every reason to rely and, even though that authority be Jerome, making without hesitation what he considers a necessary correction. Nor will the modern reader reasonably complain if a further study of an author leads Bede to include an additional piece of information even where his former statement had been correct. In his first book on Acts, he had written 'following Plinius Secundus' that Mitylene (Acts xx. 14) is 'an island over against Asia'. We look for the passage and find it not in the first book but in the *Expositio de nominibus locorum*, which we are there-fore justified in regarding as Bede's and as once part of his commentary on Acts, though now printed separately. But he adds in the *Liber Retractationis*: 'the same Pliny also writes in another place that Mitylene is a city in the Island of Cyprus,' and Bede has of course to point out that this cannot be the place intended. And Acts xxvii. 16 provides occasion for a more elaborate rectification. 'In the first book,' he says, 'following Isidore we wrote that *scapha* is a light little vessel woven of

rushes and covered with undressed skin.' Turning back we find
that, though Isidore is not indeed mentioned, Bede has made
quite a lengthy note. Not only does he tell us that the crew let
down ropes from either side to which anchors might be fastened,
'just as in our, that is, the Britannic sea, they are wont to
fasten millstones behind the stern to rein in the ship,' with a
further explanation from Sallust of the meaning of 'Syrtes',
but he adds to the observation as to *scapha* or *catascopos* that it
is so called in Greek from 'contemplating', because with such
a mode of sailing sailors or pirates are wont to prospect lands
and coasts. Now, however, in the *Liber Retractationis* he says:
'But subsequently in going through the writings of others we
have found that the name *scaphae* applies to little vessels also
hollowed out of single trees which the Greeks call *monoxula.*'
One of the two long notes with which the *Liber Retractationis*
ends is a disquisition on the nature of the disease from which
the father of Publius was suffering (Acts xxviii. 8) illustrated by a quotation from the *Aphorisms* of Hippocrates, and
we may conjecture that it was from Hippocrates rather than
from Xenophon that Bede derived the previous note on
monoxula. But it is curious that in his comment on Acts xv.
39 no reference is made to the Greek *paroxusmos*, which is
inadequately represented by *dissensio* and might well have
interested him, if he found it afterwards in Hippocrates, as
much as it did William Laud nine centuries later, as his copy of
that author in Lambeth Palace Library shows. However, Bede's
own note seems to go beyond what *dissensio* would suggest,
for he says: 'Do not think that this is a delict. For to be
thoroughly upset or put out (*commoveri*) is not an evil thing, but
to be thoroughly upset irrationally and when no just business
demands it'; and again we wonder if there is some personal
reflection behind the comment. The suggestion is at least as
plausible as that made elsewhere that it was the Apostles'
singing which *terram carceris commovit.*

The following passage may be taken as illustrative both of
Bede's attitude to his authorities and the degree of facility with
which he used them. He gives on Acts i. 13 the Greek rendering
and order of words, and then continues in reference to the
Apostles:

'The histories in which are contained the Passions of the Apostles and
which are regarded by very many as apocryphal relate that these

(i.e. Simon Zelotes and Judas Jacobi) preached in Persia and there underwent a glorious martyrdom, having been killed by the *pontifices* of the temples in the city of Suanir. And with this agrees the book of the Martyrology which is known by the name and preface of the blessed Jerome, though he is not the author of the book but the translator (*interpres*), the author being narrated to be Eusebius. Further Isidore thinks that this is the Simon who after James the Lord's brother governed (*rexit*) the Church of Jerusalem and under Trajan was crowned with the martyrdom of the cross when 120 years old: whom we ourselves also formerly followed in the first book of the Acts of the Apostles, not discussing too scrupulously what he said but simply listening to his words, thinking that he had learnt them from assured histories of the ancients. And even now we do not dare to deny it, especially since the writer of the aforesaid Passions has most assuredly betrayed himself to have written things uncertain and false; for he says that the eunuch Candacis whom Philip had baptized in Judaea was in Ethiopia at the time when Matthew taught there and lent him aid as he taught, though it is clear that Candaces is the name not of a man but of a woman, not of the eunuch but of his mistress, viz. the queen of the Ethiopians, who, as we have learnt from the "monuments" of the ancients, were all of old time wont to be so called.'

The most credulous of hagiologists would find himself hard put to defend the credibility of the 'Apostolic History of Abdias', and, thanks to Père Delehaye and other members of the distinguished little company of modern Bollandists, hagiography has become austerely scientific. But the above criticism deserves to be noted to the credit of Bede, and it is on a par with his vehement denunciation of some of the apocryphal literature relating to the Blessed Virgin. In the present extract he continues:

'I have written, too, in the same work, following the commentary of Jerome also concerning Jude the brother of James who was also called Thaddaeus, that he was sent to Abgar king of Osroene, as the Ecclesiastical History had handed down; but inspecting subsequently the Ecclesiastical History itself more diligently I found that it was not written there that it was Thaddaeus the Apostle, one of the Twelve, but Thaddaeus, one of the seventy disciples, who was sent to the aforementioned king.'

And then follows what one may venture to regard as an observation of some importance in its self-revelation: 'But I do not think that error ought to be imputed to me when following the authority of great doctors I thought that I ought to adopt without scruple what I found in their works.' Bede's was not the temperament which leads a man to try to pick holes in established reputations; but we can scarcely doubt that he was seriously annoyed at what had happened as the result of quoting an authority at second hand. It is easy to imagine the keen anticipation which would be caused by the arrival of a manuscript of an author either known hitherto only in extracts or now more faithfully represented by the new text. An interesting question, however, suggests itself whether Bede knew some or any of the works of Eusebius in Greek as well as in the Latin version of Rufinus or of Jerome. We may judge that he used ordinarily the former's Latin version of the History and the latter's version of the Chronicle, but it may be doubted if a close examination of all the references to the works of Eusebius can be said to make knowledge of the Greek certain. Even the notable passage in the Epistle to Plegwin, in which he tells how he showed that Eusebius in his 'description of times' did not follow in all things either the *Hebraica veritas* or the edition of the LXX, does not absolutely prove it. On the other hand it is quite clear that the library accessible to him did come in course of time to possess a number of Greek manuscripts other than biblical, and that Bede not only found himself using them with increasing facility, but also feels a certain ingenuous pride in being able to show that he can do so and to add lexicographical notes for the benefit of other students, like that, for example, on 'Theomachos' and 'Theomachia' in reference to Acts v. 39. But what are we to make of such a comment as this on Acts xvi. 16 in the *Liber Retractationis*? 'As for what I wrote in the former book that "Fythona" in Hebrew could mean "mouth of the abyss", I wrote what I found in the "Book of Hebrew Names". But the reader should know that this name is Greek and violently interpreted according to the Hebrew language—a fact which Jerome himself the interpreter of Hebrew names did not omit to mention, as though it were called "Fythona"; for the Hebrews have not the letter P, but in foreign (*barbaris*) words use F for it.' It is to be feared that if Jerome had seen the note, and also Bede's original comment, which contained no reference to himself and to his warning that the violence of the interpretation in the case of this and other names would be perspicuous to the reader, his observations on Bede's linguistic ability would have been at least subacid and probably acerb. The fact would seem to be that Bede's interest in names was concerned with edification rather than phonetics. He finds Jerome, for example, saying that *Hebraice* Eutychus is *amens*, but in Greek it means *fortunatus*: he states this, without reference to Jerome, as the basis of the note on Acts xx. 9: 'the one [sc. *amens*, i.e. senseless] is appropriate to him who through the sensuality of adolescence has fallen from the peak of virtues, the other [sc. *fortunatus*] to one who owing to the condescension of the preacher has returned to the heights of virtues'. We are justified in challenging any one who desires to establish the contention that Bede was a student of Hebrew to produce any evidence for it which cannot be explained as taken from the writings of other authors. The famous passage in Isa. v. 7: 'I looked that he should do judgement (*mesphat*) and behold iniquity (*mesphaa*); and do justice (*sadaca*) and behold a cry (*saaca*)', as Bede explains it in the *De schematibus et tropis*, s.v. *Paronomasia*, is simply Jerome abbreviated. His avowed preference in the preface to the *De temporum ratione* for the *Hebraica veritas* would not seem, when its exemplifications are examined, to demand first-hand knowledge, and the same may be said of other references. On the other hand Bishop Stubbs in the *Dictionary of Christian Biography* credits him with some knowledge of Hebrew, and Dr. Charles Singer in *The Legacy of Israel* expresses the opinion that 'his acquaintance with the language, though exceedingly elementary, was real', and contrasts him with Alcuin who had no knowledge of Hebrew, adducing in support of these judgements S. Hirsch's *Book of Essays*, which hardly proves them.

It is unnecessary to reproduce the valuable series of references given by Dr. Plummer to the types of biblical text with which Bede can be shown to have been familiar. But of one great codex at least something more should be said, viz. the Codex Laudianus (E) of Acts which is usually assumed to have been among the books brought to England either by Benedict Biscop and Ceolfrid *c.* 650 or by Theodore of Tarsus in 668, and almost certainly used by Bede. There is evidence that he knew it when he composed his original commentary on Acts, although, e.g. on Acts xiii. 6, he clearly prefers the authority of Jerome. But it is scarcely temerarious to suggest that the greater importance attached in the *Liber Retractationis* to the reading of the Greek text and the more frequent references to a *Graecum exemplar* are due to the fact that years of increasing familiarity with its Greek text and the parallel Latin rendering had led him to form a much higher opinion of its value, and it may even be that from his use of it, e.g. on Acts xxviii. 2, we may be justified in conjecturing with a fair degree of certainty its reading in a part of the manuscript which is now no longer extant. If few great manuscripts have had a more interesting history of wandering, from Sardinia to England, from England to Germany, from Germany after the sack of Würzburg by the Swedes in 1631 to England, where Archbishop Laud gave it to Bodley's Library in 1636, the most interesting chapter in its history is its association with Bede.

There is a very notable passage in the preface to the *Liber Retractationis* on Acts which no textual critic would wish to overlook, whatever inference he may draw as to Bede's attitude to the problems in which he is himself interested. Bede says that he has taken the opportunity given by this revision to make brief notes of some things which he has found set down in the Greek either differently or in a plus or minus form. Whether these things were omitted or differently said by the negligence of the interpreter or depraved or left by the carelessness of copyists (*incuria librariorum*) Bede has not yet been able to ascertain. For, he says, 'That the Greek exemplar has been falsified I do not dare to suspect. Wherefore I admonish the reader that where we have done these things he should read for the sake of erudition but should not insert them in his own volume as though intending to make a correction unless perchance he has found them so interpreted of old in the Latin codex of his own edition. For Jerome too explains several *testimonia* of the Old Testament as the *Hebraica veritas* has them; but none the less he did not wish either himself to interpret them in this way or that we should so correct them. For example: "I shall not behold a man further and an inhabitant, my generation is at rest" (Isa. xxxviii. 11, 12); and "His sepulchre shall be glorious" (Isa. xi. 10); and "From the ends of the earth we have heard praises" (Isa. xxiv. 16); and "Every one who shall have killed Cain shall be punished sevenfold" (Gen. iv. 15). These passages Jerome says are in Hebrew "shall pay seven punishments" and "from the wings of the earth" and "his rest shall be glorious" and "an inhabitant of quiet, my generation has been taken away". These things as he testifies that they are found among the Hebrews he wished the reader to know for the sake of erudition only, but not of emendation'. Any one who takes the trouble to compare this with the Hebrew and LXX and Jerome's commentary upon Isaiah will read it with mingled feelings; and at any rate he will probably conclude that Bede's attitude to problems of criticism was very different from that of the modern student, and that while Bede frequently insists that the Latin version that he used was drawn from the Hebrew fount or represented the Hebrew verity he was little likely to trouble himself with verification, even if he had been able to do so, or to judge differences to be important which he deemed the blessed Jerome to have regarded as no more than of interest to the learned. But the passage as a whole shows that Bede has in view more than one class of possible reader of his own works.

Reference has already been made to the practical aim which Bede tried to keep before his mind and the minds of all his readers. The tendency of modern investigation has been on the whole to limit rather than to extend the area of his personal experience of the outer world, but that would not necessarily mean that a man with so numerous communications with that world and opportunities of converse as well as correspondence with men to whom its affairs were an everyday concern would not know a great deal about it and be able to form fairly shrewd judgements. It is natural to look for these in the *Ecclesiastical History*, nor are they altogether wanting among the other features which give to that most remarkable work so great a value to students. But any one who will take the trouble (and it is no light labour) to read and re-read the other works which can with certainty be attributed to Bede will hardly fail to observe that, so far from being merely the product of a discursive mind seeking stimulus in variety and heaping together masses of recondite learning, they have a definite purpose and method and are subject to self-imposed limitations in order that the purpose may be achieved. When in his commentary on Prov. xiii. 23 *multi cibi in novalibus patrum*, we find the text used as a ground for commendation of patristic studies, it is noteworthy; but it is evidence of the general impression left by his work that it does not surprise us to note the added warning that, apart from practical use, such studies may be wasted. On Prov. xv. 31 he says that the disciple who submits obediently to the admonitions of those who teach him frequently by his proficiency ascends to the *cathedra decoris*. He instances St. Paul's advance to apostleship, but we wonder if he is thinking of pupils of his own. Yet in any case what he has in mind is certainly not worldly advancement. He need fear comparison with no writer of earlier or later date in regard to his estimate of the position of the teacher, its responsibility and the opportunity which it affords. There is a very human touch in the interpretation of Prov. iv. 3, 4, where Bede says that there is nothing which lifts the mind more to the hope of obtaining (*percipiendae*) wisdom than the remembrance that those at whose present distinction we marvel were once little and unlearned; and on xv. 23 he adds that it is human for any one to rejoice in his own opinion as stated with prudence, but the true wise man seeks with diligence not only the things to speak, but the suitableness of place or time or person to whom he speaks. The faithful preacher, he says on Prov. xiv. 4, both refreshes his hearers by his word and is himself refreshed by the same refreshment with the Lord. No reader of Bede can fail to observe his insistence, repeated and manifold, on the blessing which attends preaching—a blessing not only for the hearers but also for the preacher himself. Not only is this to be found in the reward of faith and confession from them, but in his own inward growth and at last in the Master's praise of the good and faithful servant. He warns of course against the kind of preaching which is designed to win the praises of men, and both on Proverbs and in the commentary on Cant. ii. 14 has strictures of those who change their words according to the wish of the hearers. And on Prov. xii. 9, where the Vulgate differs widely from the Hebrew and the LXX, he comments: 'Better is a stupid (*idiota*) and simple brother who, working the good things he knows, merits life in heaven, than one who being distinguished in learning of Scripture or even having filled the place of a "doctor" lacks the bread of love'; and he adds that a man who holds back from labouring for the salvation of his soul will be reproved among the foolish, even though he now seems to be famous either in divine or human wisdom, and 'his speech is not otherwise made fruitful to a "doctor" unless he himself first does the good things which he teaches', and below: 'Every catholic preacher acquires eternal health (*sanitas*) for himself and his hearers', and 'the catholic doctor sets free souls when he faithfully, i.e. rightly, preaches the testimonies of the Scriptures';

'the reward of the righteous is the vision of Christ, and he that undertakes the cure of souls for the Lord's sake is wise.'

The purpose of Bede's own work in its various aspects is in his own view the laying of sound foundations of knowledge; and it is for that very reason that the quest for originality seems to him of quite secondary importance. He is indeed in this respect one of the most modest and humble-minded of scholars, and hence it is easy to under-estimate the magnitude of what he achieved. After all there had been accumulated in past ages a great store of sacred learning which might with manifold profit be taken and distributed to the less learned, and in doing this Bede was standing in a great succession. The fame of his works may be regarded as some evidence that they were found useful, and this fact is the more noteworthy because of his constant insistence on sacred theology and the dangers of heresy in days when heresy was seriously regarded. But there is a sanity and equanimity about his work which is extraordinarily attractive. The student who turns for example in the *De temporum ratione* to the chapters on the phases of the moon and its influence may think himself involved in a curious mesh of authorities as he reads what the blessed Augustine teaches in his exposition of Psalm x, a bit of calculation by Pythagoras, *vir sagacis animi*, a quotation from Plinius Secundus *in libro pulcherrimo naturalis historiae*, a reference to the *sagacitas* of Hipparchus followed by the remark: 'But lest we should seem to sum up the chapter only with the words of a *gentilis vir*, let us inquire what the *doctores ecclesiae* have thought about this', to be illustrated by a quotation from the blessed Jerome, as in the next chapter by *beatus antistes Ambrosius* and *Basilius Caesareae Cappadociae reverendissimus antistes*. But he is a poor observer who does not see that Bede is keeping his head in the use that he makes of authorities, and whether he is discussing assertions as to the alleged effect of the moon on the weather or the relation of the moon and the tides, or comparing an assertion of Jerome's disciple Philip in his commentary on the Book of Job with 'what we know who inhabit the *diversum littus* of the Britannic sea', it is with a view to conveying to his readers what he feels himself, the sense that the *magnalia Dei* are a proper subject of reverent observation and discussion, and that in this estimation true religion and sound learning go hand in hand. Certainly any scientist who reads the earlier chapters of the same treatise is less likely to complain that science is being treated as the handmaid of religion than to wish that all theologians showed equal intelligence. It is because Bede sees that the system of weights and measures is *non ignobilis inventio*, with many useful applications for the exegete, that he is careful to explain it and in doing so to lighten the difficulties of the unlearned. Nor is it any grudging tribute of admiration that is due to one who lays down, not in a twentieth-century Institute of Education but in an English monastery twelve hundred years ago, that the text-book is no substitute for the teacher, when he says that there are things that can be better taught and learnt by word of mouth than by any written exposition (*verbo melius colloquentis quam scribentis stilo*). (See p. 200.)

II

Pius labor sed periculosa praesumptio: the words which St. Jerome applies to the task imposed upon him by Pope Damasus in framing a new version of the Scriptures might serve to restrain the temerity of one who seeks to form an estimate of Bede as exegete and theologian. In any case his task is full of difficulty if he seeks to accomplish it in a manner which shall be more than perfunctory. The observation of Dr. Stubbs that a critical edition of the works of Bede can hardly be looked for at the present day remains, except for the *Historia Ecclesiastica*, still unhappily true after nearly sixty years. Yet the importance of Bede's evidence for textual purposes will be evident to the most casual student of Tischendorf's Greek Testament or of Wordsworth and White's monumental edition of the New Testament in Latin. Again he will find himself needing to be continually on his guard lest in annotating his author he should be attributing to him opinions and interpretations which are in fact taken from earlier authorities. In a well-known and much quoted passage from the epistle to Acca, bishop of Hexham, prefixed to the commentary on St. Luke, Bede, after recalling the innumerable preoccupations of the monastic profession and the fact that he has to do everything himself (*ipse mihi dictator simul notarius et librarius*), goes on to say that he has been at the utmost pains to ascertain what has been said about St. Luke's words by Ambrose and Augustine, by Gregory the Apostle of our people whose watchful care befits his name, by Jerome, *sacrae interpres historiae*, and

'all the other Fathers', and has given what they say either in
their words or, for the sake of brevity, in his own. He has indicated the sources by initials in the margin in order that he
might not be supposed to be stealing the utterances of those
who have gone before him and passing them off as his own; and
he most solemnly adjures readers who may deem any of his
works worthy of transcription to take care to reproduce these
notes. As evidence of his own labour he has also added some
things which the Author of Light has revealed to himself. That
Bede's request was not, as Dr. Plummer supposed, totally
ignored appears from the results of an extensive examination of
manuscripts summarized by Professor Laistner in the *Journal
of Theological Studies* (October 1933) which show that even if
sometimes misunderstood by copyists, and almost entirely
neglected by editors, a sufficient number of these marginal
indications do survive to make a critical edition even more
desirable. But a curious fact suggests itself for notice. In the
letter to which Bede is replying Acca, who addresses him in
terms of deep respect as *tua sanctitas* and *tua sancta fraternitas*,
had mentioned the disturbance caused to some minds by the
fact that in his exposition of the Apocalypse he had by a 'new
interpretation' identified the Lion with Matthew and the Man
with Mark. Bede replies that this is no new interpretation, but
the traditional explanation of the Fathers, and that he had called
attention to Augustine's view. It is tempting to suppose that
this misconception may have led him to give special care to the
indication of sources; but the method of procedure adopted in
doing so has proved for the modern student an inadequate
safeguard against many pitfalls. There are not wanting cases
where the use of the first person, not merely the plural of literary
convention but the singular of individual expression, leads to
the supposition that here at any rate we have Bede speaking
of himself, only to find that this passage, too, is a quotation from
another. Artistically no doubt this is a blemish; but it must be
remembered that what Bede is responsible for is the composition as a whole, and that if the reader finds in his work less of
literary finish than is shown by that, for example, of St. Bernard or of Thomas à Kempis or of Bishop Andrewes, who all of
them made copious use of the labours of others, regard must
be had alike to period, to circumstances, and to purpose.

In the letter to Acca, bishop of Hexham, which serves as a

preface to the treatise on the *Hexaemeron*, Bede cites as the most
famous commentators on the Creation story with whom he is
acquainted Basil of Caesarea (as translated by Eustathius),
Ambrose of Milan, and Augustine of Hippo. He notes that
Ambrose followed Basil, but not the influence of Philo; he
notes, too, the great variety of the contributions of Augustine,
and lays stress on the fact that the number of the volumes
made them inaccessible save to the wealthy, and their profun-
dity rendered them intelligible only to the learned. The object
that he proposes to himself, therefore, at Acca's behest, is the
modest one of providing for the *rudis lector* a kind of preliminary
introduction or summary based either directly or indirectly on
their words. He has carried the task down to the ejection of
Adam from Paradise and proposes to continue it after he has
completed another work on the book in which Ezra *propheta,
sacerdos . . . historicus* under the figures of the long captivity,
the restoration of the Temple, the rebuilding of the Holy City,
the bringing back to Jerusalem of the vessels that had been
taken away, the rewriting of the Law of God which had been
burnt, the violent separation of the people from their alien wives
and their conversion with one heart and soul to the service
of God, wrote of the sacraments of Christ and the Church. We
may venture to see in the avowed desire to make some parts
of this mystical interpretation clearer to students one of the
primary clues to the appreciation of Bede's work on Scriptural
exegesis, not only in this connexion but in others. If he is to be
understood rightly, Bede must be viewed as writing not as a
critic for critics but as a student of sacred literature whose
object is the instruction and edification of devout minds. He
is neither wholly ignorant of, nor wholly indifferent to, critical
problems; but his method of approach is not that which has
become habitual to ourselves. Again it would be misleading to
regard any of his works as merely a *catena Patrum*: his mode
of handling his materials entitles him to be considered as an
original author, and it is not his fault if through our own forgetfulness or lack of knowledge we sometimes attribute to him this
or that striking phrase or form of statement or line of argument
which he had himself done his best to indicate as derived from
the work of another. And whether it is Bede himself, as is
probable, or one of his authorities who warns us that zest for
allegorical interpretations must not be allowed to do violence to

historical records, we need not doubt that the statement contains a canon of interpretation by which he himself desired to be guided.

It is in accordance with his avowed concern for the unlearned reader that Bede does not, like Ambrose, begin his *Hexaemeron* with a discussion of Plato and Aristotle and Pythagoras and atoms, but with an assertion of the Eternity and Omnipotence of the Creator, a reference to the 'heaven of heavens' which is His dwelling-place, the *socia Dei laudatio* which Lucifer despised, and an appropriate disquisition from Jerome upon the glories of the place to which the Lord God giveth light and the lamp of which is the Lamb. After quoting Basil he goes on to insist here as elsewhere upon the co-operation of the whole Trinity in the work of creation, and at the same time is careful to maintain that the narrative affords no warrant for anthropomorphism, as though God used a human voice or spoke a human language, whether Hebrew or Greek or another. In God is *purus intellectus sine strepitu et diversitate linguarum*: the imagery of the Psalmist, as Bede warns us elsewhere, must not lead us to think of a God with smiling cheeks or nostrils curling in scorn, and even the word *anima* in such a context must be interpreted with caution. The modern reader will find it by no means unprofitable to follow Bede in his use of authorities, to note how much he compresses and how much he leaves out altogether. For example, the moral reflections and illustrations from the life of his own times with which Ambrose enriched the opening of the third book of his *Hexaemeron* are not reproduced by Bede, possibly as being far removed from the experience of his own probable readers; yet he finds room for a conventional derivation of the word *terra* and an observation borrowed from Jerome that the Hebrews called all gatherings of waters 'seas' We may wish that he had gone on to include Ambrose's reference to the foaming main that surrounds 'the Britains', but it receives no more attention than the rest of the author's lavish illustration from geography. And then suddenly the eye falls upon something that we are fain to think is not Basil nor Ambrose nor Jerome nor Augustine but Bede himself. He is commenting on Gen. i. 11–13 and says: 'It is clear from these words of God that in the springtime the ordering and adornment of the world was perfected.' Whether this be original or not, it is natural to see in it the reflection of the English monk on the newborn beauty of an English spring which seems to bring back the glory of Creation itself. There is no need to reproduce Ambrose's diversified rhetoric in reference to the things that mar the *elegantia vitae*: for Bede it is enough to reflect that man, too, for whom all things were made, once enjoyed the same youthful perfection.

' "And God said Let us make man after our image and likeness" (Gen. i. 26). In "Let us make" is shown the one operation of Three Persons; in the "after our image and likeness" . . . is indicated the one and equal substance of the same Holy Trinity.' So says Bede, where a modern student might speak of the plural of Majesty or discourse learnedly in terms of Comparative Religion; and it is to be remembered that no one without gross anachronism could expect Bede to say anything else, for he is but putting an additional link to a long catena of the Fathers and is himself to find innumerable successors down to the time at any rate of many who are still living. It is equally natural that he should add that man was created after the image of God not in respect of his body but of his reason. Yet the body, too, has a special attribute or *proprietas* which indicates the dignity of man in the erectness which distinguishes him from the beasts, 'as is most beautifully and truly expressed by one of the poets who says:

> Pronaque cum spectent animalia caetera terram,
> Os homini sublime dedit caelumque videre
> Iussit et erectos ad sidera tollere vultus.'[1]

Even as *quidam poetarum*, Ovid need not disdain so felicitous a use of his lines, though we may regard a *rôle* usually reserved for Vergil as a curious metamorphosis for himself.

With the creation of man Bede finds himself confronted by a new set of problems, some of which he can deal with readily, while others demand more abstruse investigation. Why, for example, was man given dominion over living creatures if in his innocency he lived on herbs and fruit? The answer is that perhaps God, foreseeing man's sin, gave them to him for consolation or food or clothing or other service. Inquiry why man

---

[1] Ovid, *Metamorph.* i. 84–7.

> Thus while the mute creation downward bend
> Their sight, and to their earthly mother tend,
> Man looks aloft; and with erected eyes
> Beholds his own hereditary skies.
> Dryden, *First Book of Ovid's Metam.*, 1693, ll. 107–10.

no longer possesses this complete dominion Bede deems superfluous, since man's unwillingness to be subject to his own Creator
has entailed loss of dominion over those whom the Creator
subjected to his authority; but attention is called to stories of
the submission of birds and beasts and the harmlessness of
serpents in the case of holy men who serve God in humility.
Bede does not claim to have witnessed such incidents, but only
to have heard of them: their occurrence is, however, a testimony
of the original creation. Of course he holds that before man's
sin the earth produced nothing hurtful, and that even birds and
beasts did not make others their prey: like man all other living
creatures ate herbs and fruits. But why, if man's flesh were
immortal, did he need to eat anything at all? The answer is
that he was created needing such things until he should come to
such an age as pleased God, when after a great progeny had been
created like himself he should at God's bidding take also of the
Tree of Life and, having thereby been made perfectly immortal,
should no longer need the sustenance of bodily food. By contrast the flesh which we ourselves shall receive in the resurrection through Christ will differ from that of Adam in his first
state in that it will have no such need; and with this, it is said,
in no wise conflicts the eating of angels with the patriarchs as a
mark of condescension, nor of our Lord with the disciples after
the Resurrection as demonstration that He had taken again
true flesh after death.

III

There is one aspect of Bede's theological and exegetical work
which some modern readers will find so strange and even
bewildering that they will perhaps be tempted to describe it
as absurd. The most ardent medievalist would hardly claim
permanent value for all the disquisitions upon numbers and
their mystical significance which he finds in his authorities; but
he would be justified in saying that to leave them out of the
account or to treat them with contempt is to show a singular
lack of capacity for understanding human nature. 'The boy
playing on the seashore and diverting' himself 'in now and then
finding a smoother pebble or a prettier shell than ordinary,
whilst the great ocean of truth lay undiscovered before' him,
is the self-estimate of the Newton, not only of the *Principia* but
of *Observations upon the Prophecies of Daniel and the Apocalypse.*

We may acclaim the one and disregard the other for this or that purpose, but neither is irrelevant to an understanding of the author of both. In the case of Bede, to omit this side of his mental processes is to sacrifice what seemed to himself at any rate a most important clue both to the interpretation of history and of life—its 'sacramental' value.

Bizarre as some of the interpretations may seem, it must be remembered that the method is one which Bede inherited: he did not invent it. The first observer of the fact that $6 = 1+2+3$ probably regarded it as interesting, but not as tempting to moral and religious reflections on the perfection of the *senarius numerus*. The numbers 3 and 7 have associations which make them attractive to some minds; but those minds need not be so constituted as instinctively to be directed by their occurrence to inquiry if in the case of the former the context allows or suggests a possible reference to the Trinity, in the case of the latter the conception of universality or completeness. And even though—to take a kindred form of symbolism, viz. that derivable from the number-value of letters—it may be doubtful whether arguments based on Gematria can be traced back behind Philo, there can be no doubt that when the supposed clue had once been suggested the surprising results achieved by the use of it in some directions would cause sometimes forgetfulness and sometimes illegitimate manipulation in cases which proved intractable.

The reader of Bede's treatise on Solomon's Temple is invited to find in the number of the workmen (30,000) and of the overseers (3,300) an underlying reference to the Trinity; and if it be objected that for the latter in 1 Kings v. 16 the narrative in 2 Chron. ii 2 substitutes 3,600, a lesson can be derived from that, too, as it can also from the number of the 70,000 burden-bearers and 80,000 hewers. Along the same lines the statement that the Temple is said to have been built 480 years after the Exodus leads to the consideration that $480 = 4 \times 120$; and that 4 is suited to evangelical perfection, being the number of the Evangelists, while 120 is suited to the teaching of the Law because Moses the Lawgiver lived the same number of years (Deut. xxxiv. 7) and the primitive Church received the grace of the Holy Spirit in the same number of persons (Acts i. 15; ii. 1), clearly showing that those who use the Law lawfully, i.e. recognize the grace of Christ in it, are rightly filled with the grace of His Spirit, whereby they may glow more fully in His love.

The 120, rising gradually and by increments from 1 to 15 (since 1+2+3+4 . . . +15 = 120) make the number of 15 degrees which on account of the perfection of each law is mystically contained in the Psalter, and in it the *Vas electionis* abode with Peter at Jerusalem (Gal. i. 18). For it was necessary that the 'sacrament' which the Lawgiver exhibited in years (Deut. xxxiv. 7) the preachers of the new grace should mark out by their number. Even this [on Acts 1. 15] is less curious than the argument that follows in regard to St. Peter's speech in Acts i. 16 ff.

'Peter was afraid that the Apostles should remain in the eleventh number; for every sin is an eleventh because while it acts perversely it transgresses the precepts of the Decalogue. Wherefore, because no righteousness of ours is in itself innocent, the tabernacle which contained the Ark of the Lord was covered from above with eleven curtains of goats' hair (Ex. xxvi. 7). And he completes again the number of the Apostles as 12, so that by the two parts of the number 7(= 3+4) they might preserve the grace which they preached in word with number also (3×4 = 12) and that those destined to preach the faith of the Holy Trinity to the quadriform world (as the Lord says "Go, teach all nations, baptizing them in the Name of the Father and of the Son and of the Holy Spirit") might already confirm the perfection of the work by the sacrament of number also.'

Bewildering as such ingenuity may seem to us, for Bede it leads on to a new view of Pentecost, for he adds:

'Moreover according to a loftier understanding the harm of the Church which it suffers in false brethren up to now continues for the most part uncorrected; but since at the end of the world the people of the Jews who crucified the Lord is believed meet to be reconciled to the Church, as though the fiftieth day were drawing nigh the sum of the Apostles was restored.'

We turn to the commentary on Acts ii to find that, as the forty days of the Lord with His disciples after the Resurrection designate the Church of the peregrination rising together with Christ, so the fiftieth day on which the Holy Spirit is received fittingly expresses the perfection of blessed quiet wherein the temporal labour of the Church will be rewarded with an eternal denarius (the 'penny' of the labourers in the vineyard). For the number 40 itself when computed with its equal parts adds further a denarius and makes 50; for $\frac{1}{2}$ of 40 = 20; $\frac{1}{4}$ = 10; $\frac{1}{5}$ = 8;

$\frac{1}{8}=5$; $\frac{1}{10}=4$; $\frac{1}{20}=2$; $\frac{1}{40}=1$ and $20+10+8+5+4+2+1=50$. And of this calculation the figure is very easily clear, for the present conflict as it were latently generates for us the everlasting glory of the Jubilee, as the Apostle says (2 Cor. iv. 17). Moreover, our true beatitude of body and soul is that, glorying in immortality, we should be satiated with the eternal vision of the most High and Blessed Trinity. For we are made of four most noted qualities of body, but in the inner man we are bidden to love God with our whole heart, our whole soul, our whole mind; and this is the perfect denarius of life—that we should rejoice with the present vision of divine glory. It is in the same vein that we find the comment on Acts xix. 19, where in illustration of the value of the books burnt at Ephesus (50,000 denarii) we are reminded that to the debtors also in the Gospel debts are released *sub quinquagenario numero* of denarii: I suppose, says Bede, because with the five senses of the body subsisting in this life we transgress the precepts of the Decalogue. Here, however, on account of the enormity of the crime of magic the number 1000 is added. Alternatively, the number 50 is often related to penitence and the remission of sins, whence also the fiftieth is the Psalm of Penitence and the fiftieth is the year of remission. This is hardly less astonishing than the interpretation of Acts iv. 22, in regard to the sick man 'more than 40 years of age' by saying that if the number 40 signifies the *gemina plenitudo* of the Law (for four times ten makes 40), then the transgressor of each lying sick transcends as it were the completeness of 40.

Again, while turning back to the Temple of Solomon we learn that the length of it is the *longanimitas* of Holy Church, the breadth Love (*caritas*) extending to enemies as well as to friends, and the height is hope of future reward, their measurements of 60, 20, and 30 cubits have also lessons for the devout mind. For example, the 6 denotes the perfection of the work, the 2 the twin love of God and our neighbour, the 3 the hope of the vision of God: each number is appropriately multiplied by 10, the number of the Ten Commandments, and we are promised further explanation of the *sacramenta* involved when Bede comes to deal with the total height, which is not 30 but 120 cubits. We pass on and find, as by this time we have been accustomed to expect, that the 120 has to be brought into relation with the number of the primitive Church at Jerusalem. Now we are told (cap. 8) that 15, which is 7+8, is sometimes wont to be used to signify the future life which is now being spent in the Sabbath rest of faithful souls, but will be perfected at the end of the world by the resurrection of immortal bodies. But 15 when turned into a triangle, i.e. reckoned with all its parts, makes 120 (1+2+3 . . . +15 = 120); wherefore by the number 120 is appropriately designated the great beatitude of the elect in the future life. Appropriately in this the third story of the house of the Lord is consummated, because after the present labours of the faithful, after the souls' rest received in the future, the full felicity of the whole Church will be completed in the glory of the resurrection. And, Bede adds, to this mystery may equally pertain, as we have said, the fact that the Lord, rising from the dead and ascending into heaven, to this number of men sent in fiery tongues the Spirit who by kinship of utterances caused those who had been separated from one another by diversity of tongues to have a common speech for the praise of God.

By a kindred method of calculation, the molten sea of 10 cubits from brim to brim with a height of 5 cubits and a line of 30 cubits compassing it round about (1 Kings vii. 23), the sea which was for 'the priests to wash in' (2 Chron. iv. 6), is made to yield (a) a reference to the Ten Commandments whereby in the Law 'the Lord expressed all things that we ought to do' and the pay which is the reward of benefactors—the denarius of labourers in the vineyard, (b) in the line (*resticula*) the discipline of the heavenly commandments by which we are bound from our indulgences (*voluptates*), and in its length of 30 cubits an appropriate 'sacrament' relating to this. For $6 \times 5 = 30$, and by the number 6 in which God made man when he did not exist, and remade him when he had perished, is figured our good working; and this is multiplied by 5 to make 30 when we humbly subject all the senses of our body to the divine orders. But the sea indicates baptism and its cleansing for the remission of sins, and the priests are washed in it, because in Scripture all the elect are figuratively called priests as being members of the High Priest our Lord Jesus Christ. Now $3 \times 10 = 30$, and after the Flood the human race filled the breadth of the whole world from the progeny of the three sons of Noah, the descendants of Shem populating Asia, those of Ham Africa, those of Japheth Europe and the islands of the sea. And because the mystery of baptism with the execution of good works and the hope of eternal rewards was to be ministered to all nations, appropriately a line of 30 cubits girdled the sea in which the wave of baptism was figured. Even then the symbolism is not exhausted.

An illustration of a different kind is supplied by the treatment of the well-known ending of Rev. xiii: 'Here is wisdom. He that hath understanding, let him count the number of the beast. For it is the number of a man: and the number of him is six hundred sixty-six.' We turn with some curiosity to see what Bede will make of it, and incidentally discover a feature which is a mute commentary on the somewhat large claims at times made in respect of Bede's knowledge of Greek. 'This number', he says, 'among the Greeks is said to be found in the name of the Titan, i.e. of the giant, in the following way; for T is 300, E is 5, I is 10, T is 300, A is 1, N is 50.' It is of course true that the sum arrived at is 666, but it is startling to find, apart from some explanation, the correlative for the Latin form 'Titan' being regarded as being spelt in Greek 'Teitan' by any one with a really extensive familiarity with the language. However, Bede goes on to say that Primasius adduces another name which embraces the same number: A is 1, N is 50, T is 300, E is 5, M is 40, O is 70, S is 200. The Greek name 'Antemos' we learn means 'contrary to honour', which is only less astonishing than the parallel observation that the word A (1) P (100) N (50) O (70) U (400) M (40) E (5), which yields the same number, means 'Nego'. After this we are prepared even for the added explanation that the number 6 with which the world was made indicates, as every one knows, the perfection of the work: whether alone or multiplied by 10 or 100, it shows the sixtyfold or hundredfold fruit of the same perfection. Moreover, the weight of gold that was brought to Solomon every year was 666 talents: so then what is both owed and paid to the true king as a gift (*munus*), this that seducing tyrant presumes to exact for himself. Nor does it any longer surprise us to find the 144,000 who are virgins referred to as expressing by their number the fact that they love God with all their heart, with all their soul, and with all their mind, consecrated also by virginal integrity to that body which is made up of 4 qualities. For thrice $3=9$ and $4\times4=16$; and $9\times16=144$. Here again we find simply the application of what seem to Bede certain elementary conceptions by means of appropriate combinations to yield edifying interpretations of Scriptural numbers. Even the 1,600 furlongs mentioned in regard to the blood

which came out of the press up to the horses' bridles (Rev. xiv.
20) is merely a term for the 4 quarters of the world, for 'quater-
nity is conquaternated as in the four quadriform faces and
wheels', 400 × 4 being 1,600.

> E se le fantasie nostre son basse
> A tanta altezza, non è maraviglia.[1]

After all it was the Heaven of the Sun which stood to Dante for
the symbol of Arithmetic.

When Bede comes to deal with the porch of Solomon's Temple
he tells us that it is most clearly explained by Josephus (*Ant.
Iud.* viii. 3) as being placed on the east side in order that at the
equinox the rays of the sun might completely flood the Ark of
the Covenant with light through three doors—that of the porch,
that of the Temple, and that of the Oraculum. Each of these
again has a significance of its own, and in the interpretation
places are found for the blessed protomartyr Abel, Seth, and
Enoch, for Zacharias and Elizabeth, for Simeon and Anna,
while the porch's breadth of 10 cubits signifies that, though they
had received neither the words nor the mysteries of the Gospel,
they had kept the precepts of the Decalogue.

We may wonder what Bede would have made of the *fenestrae
obliquae* if he had known (as he clearly does not) that in Hebrew
they are 'windows of fixed lattice work' (1 Kings vi. 4). What
he does say is remarkable enough. The windows of the Temple
are holy doctors and the *spirituales* in the Church who are
granted in a state of ecstasy to behold more specially than others
the arcana of heavenly mysteries; and then suddenly the course
of explanation assumes a vivid architectural interest for a
student of the eighth century A.D. These spiritual persons, while
they are spreading forth abroad to the faithful the things which
they see *in occulto*, as though after receiving the light of the sun,
are described as 'slanting windows', that is, broader within;
because of course as soon as any one has 'perceived' even for a
moment a ray of supernal contemplation he must forthwith
dilate the bosom of his heart by further chastisement and prepare by wise discipline for the obtaining of greater things.
Again, the 'storeys of the Temple' are the 'pinnacles' referred
to in the Gospel narrative of the Temptation; but Bede notes
also the reference in the fifth book of Hegesippus to James the

---

[1] Dante, *Par.* x. 46, 47.

Lord's brother being taken to one in order to address the people, adding that Scripture does not record if it was the custom for doctors sitting in these *tabulata* to discourse to those standing around on a lower level. But the meaning of the *sacramentum* is, he tells us, clear. The three stories are three grades or classes of the faithful—the married, the continent, and the virgins, distinguished by the height of their profession but all belonging to the House of God by fellowship in the same faith and truth. The highest story was 5 cubits wide, the middle 6, the lowest 7. We should expect perhaps a reference to the comparative numbers in explanation, but this is not the first idea that comes to Bede's mind. It is rather that one abode is straiter because of the way of life appropriate to those who have devoted their virginity to God; they should abstain from idle speeches, anger, strife, detraction, immodest apparel, feastings, drinking bouts, contention, emulation, in order to devote themselves to holy vigils, prayers, divine readings and psalms, teaching, almsgivings, and other fruits of the Spirit. Similarly the lowest have a wider space because they are not bidden to sell all they have and give to the poor, but not to kill, nor commit adultery, nor steal nor bear false witness (Matt. xix. 18). In other words, Bede ranks them, though he does not say so, with the young man who had great possessions. So far what has been said may seem curious, but not specially remarkable, except for the consequences that have followed from reading as Bede does in 1 Kings vi. 6 *quod super erat* for the *subter erat* of the Vulgate [cf. LXX]. But it is otherwise when he goes on to identify the intermediate class with those—*portio gloriosissima*, as he calls them—who built the primitive Church at Jerusalem, of whom St. Luke says (Acts iv. 32) that 'there was one heart and one soul of the multitude of believers' and the *History of St. Stephen* testifies that the largest part had abandoned wedded intercourse, calling the women *eadem religione pollentes* not wives but widows. It is hard to know whether the argument or the weight allowed to the authority quoted is the more surprising.

IV

A reader who has no taste for allegory had better leave Bede's commentaries alone, for he will certainly misunderstand his author and probably do real injustice to his intelligence. We may take for example a work written, so far as can be judged from

the preface, in troublous times when Bede finds consolation
in the thought of St. John at Patmos. The avowed purpose of
the 'De Templo Salomonis' is allegorical treatment of the subject. Solomon's Temple is a figure of the 'holy universal Church',
part of which is still exiled (*peregrinatur*) on earth from its Lord,
part has come through the cares of its peregrination and reigns
with Him in heaven, as the whole will some day reign when the
Last Judgement is past. Even the builders and the materials
of the earthly Temple are in Bede's view big (*gravida*) with spiritual sacraments, and there is no name which with the aid of
Jerome's notes on Hebrew names cannot be made to yield some
hidden meaning. Hiram, who in Latin, Bede learns from Jerome,
is *vivens excelse*, is a type of the believers from the Gentiles and
of the earthly rulers by whose bounty and protection the Church
has been aided and defended: the cedars of Lebanon are men of
renown cast down from the mount of pride: the artificers are
philosophers converted to the true Wisdom, men like Dionysius
the Areopagite and that *doctor suavis et fortissimus martyr*
Cyprian. The co-operation of the servants of Solomon and those
of Hiram has also its significance. Paul knew better the *sacramentum evangelii* which he had learnt by revelation, but Dionysius
could better refute the false doctrines (*dogmata*) of the Athen-
ians, whose syllogisms and arguments along with their errors he
had known from a boy. So again in mystical language Solomon's
selection of workmen from all Israel shows that choice is made
not only from the stock of Aaron the high priest but from the
whole Church. The number 30,000 is appropriate to those instructed in the faith of the Trinity, the courses of 10,000 a month
suggest the observance of the Ten Commandments of the Law,
the intervals of three months the perfection of the three
evangelical virtues—almsgiving, prayer and fasting springing
from the one root of charity. Moreover, since a month is made
up by the fullness of the course of the moon, it figures the pleni-
tude of each spiritual virtue in which the mind of the faithful
enjoys daily illumination from the Lord as the moon does from
the sun. What follows has a significance to which it is well to
draw attention in view of criticisms often made of the medieval
attitude and especially of that implied in the monastic life.
The month in which wood is being cut for the work of the Temple
is Almsgiving, i.e. the work of mercy, in which by teaching, by
rebuke, by provision of temporal goods, by showing examples

of life, we labour for the salvation of our neighbours, that by
making good progress they may attain to the unity of the
Church. The two remaining months in which the workmen
were allowed to remain in their own houses and to be at leisure
for their own needs are Prayer and Fasting, by which, besides
those things which we work for the needs of our brethren without, we take care for our own personal salvation, being turned
inwardly in our minds to the Lord. And since only those care
perfectly either for their own salvation or for that of their
brethren who submit themselves humbly to the view of divine
grace, it is rightly added: 'And Adoniram was over this levy'
(1 Kings v. 14), for Adoniram means *Dominus meus excelsus* and
whom could he better signify than the Lord the Saviour, who
tells us when we should give ourselves to the edifying of the
Church by preaching or other works of piety, when return to the
examination of our own consciences, as it were to the examination of our own house in order by prayers and fasts to make it
worthy of a visitor and inspector from on High?

We look eagerly, when we come to the significance of the
stones of which the Temple is built, to see if there will be any
allusion to the *Shepherd* of Hermas, but only to be disappointed.
Bede makes reference to the *Liber Pastoris* indeed in confirmation of the statement on Acts xii. 15 that each of us has an angel,
but we may doubt if he knew the book except at second hand.
As to the foundation of the Temple, Bede adopts the Pauline
language as a matter of course, and in regard to those who
prepare the stones he sees a parallel for the co-operation of the
cementarii of Solomon and of Hiram in the fact that from 'each
people of God', i.e. Jews and Gentiles, there have been found
those who were rightly teachers (*doctores*) of exalted teachers:
not only Jeremiah, Isaiah and the other prophets from the Cir-
cumcision, but also blessed Job and his sons from the Gentiles.
Evidence as to the colour of the stones is afforded by the statement (1 Chron. xxix. 2, Vulg. and LXX, but not we note Hebr.)
that the marble was Parian, which suggests to Bede a Vergilian
quotation (*Aen.* iii. 126–7) as to its snowy whiteness and a note
that Paros was one of the Cyclades, with a further illustrative
quotation from Josephus (*Ant. Iud.* viii. 3) which in his view,
though not perhaps in ours, confirms it. Nor, he adds, is the
sense of the mystery obscure; for it is clear to any one that
the white shining marble of which the House of the Lord is

constructed is the clean action of the elect and the conscience chastened from every blemish of corruption. The fourth year of Solomon and the second month are interpreted of the building of the Church by the Spirit, following the completion of the dispensation of the Lord's Incarnation, related in the Four Gospels, and the granting of a second Passover in the Body and Blood of our Redeemer to ourselves, who could not share in the first Passover celebrated in the body and blood of the lamb. After this it is hardly necessary to say that the building of the Temple on Mount Moriah, in the threshing-floor of Ornan the Jebusite (2 Chron. iii. 1), yields a plentiful crop of interpretations. Christ Himself is *Mons montium*: Mount Moriah is the mount of vision whereby He shows Himself to those whom He receives for the eternal vision of His brightness: the sacrifice of Isaac being a type of the Lord's Passion, the Temple is appropriately built where the sacrifice took place. The Church is the threshing-floor which the Baptist foretold that the Lord would throughly cleanse (Matt. iii. 12), and Ornan the 'illuminated' is a type of the Gentiles to be illuminated by the Lord, as Jebus, which means 'trodden down', is to become Jerusalem, the 'vision of peace'.

It may be permissible to set beside this by way of contrast and comparison in several particulars some passages from Bede's commentary on Rev. i. 11 ff. Asia, we are there told, means 'elevation' and denotes the proud loftiness of the world in which the Church is peregrinating. Seven churches are mentioned, not because the Church of Christ was only in these places, but because in the number seven all fullness 'consists'. The description that follows is glossed by the comment: 'Beautifully there is described here the *forma ecclesiae*, as it exhibits the light of divine Love in the brightness of a chaste bosom, according to the Lord's saying "Let your loins be girded and your lamps burning" (Luke xii. 35). Its perfection within and without he denotes by two parts of the number seven, for in it individuals standing (*consistentes*) with four attributes (*qualitates*) of the body love the Lord God with their whole heart, with their whole soul, and with their whole strength'—which recalls the argument based elsewhere also on the observation that $4+3 = 7$. The description of the Christ affords Bede matter of comment which seems to us a curious mixture. 'Like unto a son of man he says: since having conquered death He had ascended into heaven. For though we had known Christ after the flesh, yet now we no longer know Him' (2 Cor. v. 16). Forced as this may seem, it is less so than what follows. 'Moreover he well says "In the midst". For all, saith he, who are round about Him shall offer gifts (Ps. lxxv [lxxvi], 11).' The 'garment down to the feet' is explained by saying 'Poderis, which in Latin is called *tunica talaris*, and is a priestly garment, shows the priesthood (*sacerdotium*) of Christ by which He offered Himself on our behalf (*pro nobis*) on the altar of the Cross as a victim to His Father'. This is more important as an indication of Bede's theological views than the interpretation of the paps as the two Testaments, or the golden girdle as the choir of the saints, or the eyes of the Lord as preachers with spiritual fire giving both light to the faithful and burning to the unbelieving, or the 'feet like brass' as the Church of the last age to be tried and proved by vehement oppressions, since *orichalcum* is brass brought by much fire and doctoring (*medicamine*) to the colour of gold. This interpretation is further expanded by the statement that 'another translation which says "like brass of Libanus" signifies that in Judaea, of which Libanus is a mountain, the Church is to be persecuted, especially in the last age. For the Temple also often received the name of Libanus, to which it is said: "Open thy gates, O Libanus, and let fire consume thy cedars" (Zech. xi. 1)'.

Few books have received stranger treatment at the hands of exegetes, both Jewish and Christian, than the Song of Songs; and when Jerome regards Origen as surpassing all other commentators on other books, but on Canticles as surpassing himself, he is but affording early evidence of the attraction exercised by a method of interpretation which is so deeply rooted in tradition that no commentator can disregard it, yet yields results too fanciful to win from modern minds any general acceptance. The first of Bede's seven books of allegorical exposition of it is a polemic against the views of Julian of Eclanum on the subject of Grace contained in his treatise *De Amore* and his book on the Song of Songs. As to the latter work Bede deems it necessary to warn the reader that it must be read with caution, for in spite of its copious and alluring eloquence it is not free from dangerous doctrine which may be a pitfall to the unwary: the goodly flower has a thorn to be guarded against, and he adds the familiar Vergilian tag about the snake in the grass. Julian in his view was a most skilful rhetor and a most fierce assailant of the grace of God, second only to Pelagius himself, as may be seen from his mad writings against its most vigorous champion, the *sanctissimus et doctissimus antistes* Augustine. And he proceeds to a formal refutation by scriptural quotations and the practical experience of any intelligent man. The comments are perhaps more interesting to-day as exposition of Bede's own views than as refutation of Julian's. Bede holds that all men come to the light of day full of iniquity from the guilt of the first transgression; but, as against Julian's presentation of the views of his own opponents, he rejects with indignation the affirmation that we are born incapable of good. The heretic, that he might more cunningly deceive the weak, joined to the lie of perfidy the truth of the catholic profession: in other words, in Julian's exposition of his opinions there is the mixture of rightness and wrongness which makes him in Bede's eyes dangerous. He passes on to a further refutation of Julian's *De bono constantiae*, of which it is later said that it would greatly profit those studious of virtues if he had not mingled with it *violenta vitia* of errors, where it is clear that Bede is moved by the effectiveness of the refutation of Manichaean error while disturbed by the evidence of the writer's own mistakes. How much better would he vanquish the Manichaean if he would say that it is the grace of God which makes the mind of each of the elect to be good and kindles it to the studies of virtues whilst ever admonishing it of its own weakness and inability to do anything without grace, and, repelling from it all trust of its own virtue, persuades it to sing to God 'For thee will I keep my strength' (Ps. lviii [lix. 9, Vulg.]). Bede turns from this to a criticism of the work addressed to the virgin Demetrias *De institutione virginis*, which, he says, some of us studiously reading rashly suppose to be a work of the holy and catholic doctor Jerome, not at all perceiving that the smoothness of the eloquence which mollifies, and the perversity of the heresy that seduces, manifestly prove that this *opusculum* is not Jerome's. He admits that the instructions are admirably phrased and would make a work highly useful and wholesome if the author taught the virgin for all things to ask constantly the suffrages of divine grace and not to trust in the freedom and strength of her own mind. But errors are enumerated to inculcate caution, and in regard to Julian's contention that 'many of the philosophers had patience, chastity, modesty and other virtues from goodness of nature', Bede shows himself at once a man of his own age and beyond it when he says that it is certain that whoever of the philosophers knew not that Christ was the 'Virtue' of God and the Wisdom of God could have no true virtue nor any true wisdom. But in so far as they had some taste of any kind of wisdom or image of virtue, they received the whole of this from above, not only by the bounty of their first creation, but also by the daily grace of Him who, not even deserting His creature which deserts Himself, bestows His gifts on men as He Himself has judged, both great things to great men and small to small.

It has been noted as one of Bede's merits that he writes with his eye upon the reader, even if at times his inclusion of matters that interest himself may make us think that he exacts rather a high standard of intelligence from others. In his commentary he will follow sedulously in the steps of the Fathers, and he begs not to be considered 'superfluous' if he gives long explanations of what he has learnt in the books of the ancients as to the nature of trees or aromatic herbs. This is not, he pleads, arrogance, but out of regard for his own lack of skill and that of his people, who, 'having been born and bred far outside the world, that is in an island of the Ocean, can only know of things that go on in the first places of the world, viz. Arabia and India, Judaea and Egypt, through the writings of those who have taken part'. For him Canticles is a work in which Solomon, that wisest of kings, under the figure of a bridegroom and his bride described the mysteries of Christ and the Church, i.e. of the eternal King and His City. And we notice that he speaks of the primitive Church as drawing from the synagogue the origin of its flesh. The modern reader will be unwise if he allows himself to become impatient with a line of argument which makes of the 'breasts of Christ' the rudiments of the New Testament or the beginnings of the Christian faith, and of the 'wine of Christ' the perfection of evangelical doctrine. Bede defends himself for the imagery by the description of the Son of Man in the Apocalypse, *qui et ipse typicus liber est.* On the other hand, too much stress must not be laid on incidental contrasts such as that between the unguents with which prophets and priests were visibly anointed under the Law and those superlative unguents with which the Apostles and their successors have been invisibly anointed. We learn more of unguents from a disquisition on spikenard (interpreted as *fragrantia bonae actionis*) which naturalists (*physiologi*) speak of as the chief among ointments, the Indian being the most costly variety. This is of course borrowed, as is the elaborate description of the plant, and the reader may promise himself two or three pleasant half-hours in determining how much of what follows he may justly assign to Bede himself; for it includes not only the image of the Church ever meditating in her inmost heart the Death of her Redeemer (for who does not know that the place of the heart is between the breasts?) and a note on the grapes of Cyprus, which produces larger bunches than all lands, and on the city of Engaddi in Judaea, which has nobler vines than all others, since from them flows the liquid not of wine but of opobalsamum; for in the vineyards of Engaddi grows balsam, which in the making of chrism is wont to be mingled with the liquor of olive and consecrated by the pontifical benediction in order that all the faithful with the imposition of the sacerdotal hand, whereby the Holy Spirit is received, may be signed with this anointing: with which also the altar of the Lord when it is dedicated and all other things which must be sacrosanct are thoroughly anointed, so that by the vineyards of Engaddi are figured the divine *charismata*. Then comes an account of the appearance of the balsam shrubs cut with sharp stones or bones, since the touch of iron hurts them, and the statement that the sap flows through a cavity in the bark, whence is the name *opobalsamum*, for in Greek *opi* means a cavern. Engaddi itself, meaning 'goat's fountain', is interpreted as the laver of sacred baptism into which, as sinners worthy of a place on the left hand with the goats, we descend, to ascend, when cleansed from the foulness of our sins, worthy to be reckoned in the number of the lambs. Ingenuity could hardly go farther.

In the house, which is also the Church, the beams are holy preachers by whose word and example—the combination is one upon which Bede is again and again insistent—the structure is held together: the ceilings (*laquearia*) are the simple servants of Christ, who rather adorn the Church with their appropriate virtues than know how to defend it with words of doctrine and to fortify it against the attacks of perverse dogmas. But the ceilings hang down attached to the beams, because any who desire to shine on high in the Church resplendent with virtues must cling with their whole minds to the words and examples of the highest Fathers by which they may be suspended from the ambition of earthly things. We smile perhaps a little at the conceit, but Bede has more to say. The beams and ceilings are of cedar and cypress, because each is imperishable as well as fragrant, and cedars, as the poet (Verg. *Georg.* iii. 414, 415) tells us, frighten away snakes. This leads on to another possible interpretation of the ceilings as doctors who by virtue of the heavenly word are wont to repel the envenomed doctrines of heretics and frighten them from the seduction of simple folk. We are about to raise the question of confusion when suddenly our attention is diverted to the library to which Bede had access, as he adds: 'and the fact that its resin, which is called "cedrina", is so useful in the preservation of books that those anointed with it neither suffer from bookworms nor grow old with time, who does not see how appropriate that is to the same holy preachers by whose spiritual perception holy Scripture was made up, which can be corrupted by no astuteness of heretics, consumed by no age of passing time?' The observation that the cypress is apt for healing the passions of bodies and, since no windstorm can make it lose its leaves, is an emblem of constancy, seems tame by comparison.

Bede speaks of the version that he uses as being transfused from the *Hebraicus fons*, but any minute examination of his commentary in relation to the text on which it is based will be likely to leave on the student's mind the serious doubt if he ever made the smallest attempt at recourse to the fountain itself. Instances could easily be multiplied in which the Hebrew would have supplied him with an abundance of illustration of which, except when quoting from another, he never seems in any single instance to make use. The flower of the field (*Flos campi*) of the Vulgate and LXX in Cant. ii. 1, is in the Hebrew the Rose of Sharon, but he makes no reference to it, and the *flos campi* is made to apply to our Lord's Birth as the lily of the valleys is to the lowly estate of the parents *e quibus Deus homo nasceretur*. On the following verse we read that, as the apple-tree excels the sylvan trees in sight and smell and taste, so *homo Deus* rightly excels all holy ones who are simply men. Let all other trees of the wood furnish the miracle of their beauty, smell, and virtue: the apple-tree excels them all, for it can give food to the eater. And below on Cant. ii. 5 he says: 'by "flowers" is indicated the tender beginnings of virtues, by apples their perfection.' It is impossible not to wonder if there is not here another homely English touch; and if so we may be sure that at Jarrow and Wearmouth the monastery garden was not without God's choicest fruit.

It may be argued that this is fanciful, but it is to be observed that not only here but in passages that adjoin there are reflections which it can scarcely be called fanciful to regard as arising from personal experience. No student at any rate will fail to notice the solemn adjuration of all and each of the faithful by their own virtues which they desire to foster with a pure heart not to despise the pious studies of their brethren, lest by constantly invading they should hinder them; but that each should rejoice in the progress of his neighbour as his own, and so fear to bring losses of spiritual profit to his brethren as he fears them for himself.

V

Reference has been made to Bede's observations on the meaning of the names Stephen, Philip, Eutychus, the modifications introduced in regard to the first and the source from which he derived the last. In the Exposition of Acts, which cannot be earlier than 709, when Acca became bishop of Hexham, he says, following Jerome, that in Hebrew Stephen is interpreted 'Your norm'. Whose? The norm of course of subsequent martyrs to whom by suffering he was made a 'form' of dying for Christ. On Acts viii. 27 we are told that *Candacis* can be translated from the Hebrew 'exchanged'. It is she then to whom it is said 'Hearken, O daughter, and see and incline thine ear and forget thy people' (Ps. xlv. 10). If we ask why, the answer is that that psalm is inscribed 'For those who shall be exchanged'. If we ask where, the answer is in the LXX and Vulgate. Of the very different title of the psalm in Hebrew, Bede shows no knowledge, and it is hardly an unfair, though not of course unavoidable, inference that he had recourse neither to the Hebrew text nor to the 'Breviarium in Psalterium' in the works of Jerome, which would have given it to him in Latin together with another interpretation of the text. If on the other hand stress is to be laid on Bede's knowledge of Greek, it is strange that it never seems to occur to him to think what Philip means in that language, even when on Mark iii. 18 he is giving side by side an explanation of Andrew which connects that name with the Greek *aner*. The account of Saul's escape from Damascus in the exposition of Acts ix. 25 provides a startling example of intrepid exegesis. 'This mode of escape', we are told, 'is still preserved in the Church to-day, whenever any one surrounded by the ambushes of the old enemy or the snares of this world is saved by hope and the defence' (reading *munimine* for *minime*) 'of his faith. For the wall of Damascus, which is interpreted 'drinking blood', is the *adversitas saeculi*. King Areta, who is interpreted 'Descent', is understood as the Devil. The basket (*sporta*), which is usually made of rushes and palms, denotes the conjunction of faith and hope. For the rush signifies the greenness of faith, the palm the hope of eternal life. 'Whosoever therefore sees himself surrounded by the wall of adversity, let him hasten to climb into the basket of virtues and thereby to escape.' This may be regarded as on a par with the interpretation of Acts xviii. 3: 'Mystically, just as Peter by fishing draws us by the nets of faith out of the waves of the world (*saeculi*), so Paul by putting up umbrellas (*umbracula*) of protection defends us by word and deeds from the rain of crimes, from the heat of temptation and from the gusts of secret assaults.' It is to be hoped that this may not be regarded as too modern a version of Bede's mystical use of the *ars scenofactoria*.

As instances in the same line of allegorical exposition we may adduce the explanation of the best robe—Bede of course calls it the *stola prima*—in the parable of the Prodigal Son (Luke xv. 22), and of the incidents connected with St. Paul's preaching at Troas in Acts xx. The 'first robe', Bede says,

'is the vesture of innocence which man received having been well created, but lost, having been badly persuaded, when after the fault of transgression (*culpa praevaricationis*) he knew himself to be naked and, the glory of immortality having been lost, took a covering of skins, i.e. a mortal one. The servants who bring it forth are the preachers of reconciliation; for they bring forth the first robe when they asseverate that mortal and earthly men must be so exalted that they will not only be fellow citizens of the angels, but both heirs of God and co-heirs of Christ.'

In regard to the scene at Troas, he tells us:

'We can here say allegorically that the chamber is the height of spiritual *charismata*, the night the obscurity of the Scriptures, the abundance of lamps the exposition of more secret sayings, the Lord's Day the recollection either of the Lord's Resurrection or our own; with an admonition of the spiritual teacher (*doctor*) that, if ever he

has provoked to the heights of virtue his hearers, attracted by the
sweetness of the Resurrection and the joys of the life to come, and
by a rather prolix discussion has reached some secrets of the Scriptures, he should forthwith for the sake of weak hearers illustrate
them by the lamp of plain exposition.   Just as the Apostle, while
saying that Abraham had two sons, the one by a handmaiden and the
other by a freewoman, forthwith subjoined by way of explanation
"But these are the two covenants"'' (Gal. iv. 24).

It would be hard to criticize Bede merely for adopting in
dealing with Scripture a practice which had such eminent
apostolic authority.   But it is going rather far to expound the
alleged double meaning of the name Eutychus as we have seen
him doing with the authority of Jerome, and the resources of his
own ingenuity are not even then exhausted.   He goes on to say
that the three upper chambers in the highest of which St. Paul
was disputing are 'Faith, Hope and Charity, but the greatest of
these is Charity' (1 Cor. xiii. 13); and 'if any one through slack-
ness (*ignavia*) has deserted this and amidst the Apostle's utterances has not been afraid to slumber, he shall be reckoned as
already among the dead, for since he has offended in one, he is
made guilty of all' (James ii. 10). In any case the critic might
be'disposed to remark that the slumber preceded the fall.   However, Bede is more closely concerned to draw out the parallel-
isms and contrasts with the story of Tabitha, who was raised by
St. Peter. Tabitha had been ill and died by day: it was at midnight that Eutychus fell and died. Tabitha after death was
washed and placed in an upper chamber: Eutychus was
mourned as dead after having fallen from an upper chamber on
the third floor. Eutychus died while the master was present and
teaching, and Tabitha while he was absent. To Eutychus Paul
descended: to Tabitha Peter ascended to raise her. Tabitha, as
soon as she saw Peter, sat up: Eutychus, having died at midnight, rose again at dawn, and was brought again alive when the
Sun of Righteousness breathed upon him. We may note that
the last comment involves a strangely unexpected reading of the
story of Acts, and one which the narrative will only bear with
difficulty.   This is the more curious since from the comment on
Acts xxi. 27, where Bede is concerned to reconcile the chronology with that in St. Paul's words in Acts xxiv. 11, we note how
careful is his scrutiny of the exact language used; and the same
is true on Acts xxi 38, where he has to reconcile the statement

in Acts on the 4,000 *sicarii* with the statement of Josephus (*Bell. Iud.* vii. 9), or rather declares that no controversy need arise on the subject. But in regard to the matter of Eutychus it must be remembered that it would be natural to Bede's mind to fix a note of time if he could do so, since, as his commentary on Rev. i. 10 shows, he believed that it was the custom of Scripture to give it. After reflecting then on the congruity of the Lord's Day as a time for spiritual vision, he goes on to observe that the angels visited Abraham at noon (Gen. xviii. 1) but Sodom in the evening (Gen. xix. 1); that Adam was terrified at the voice of the Lord walking in the afternoon (Gen. iii. 8); that it was by night that wisdom was received by Solomon, who was not destined to keep it (1 Kings iii. 5). We cannot help reflecting that the call of Samuel (1 Sam. iii) might also have been cited, but that it would have been hard to adjust to the argument in the case of Solomon. In the exposition of Acts x, while Peter ascending to the upper parts of the house signifies the Church leaving earthly desires and about to have its conversation in Heaven, Peter hungering at the sixth hour in the midst of his prayers hungers, it is to be understood, for the salvation of the world which in the Sixth Age the Lord came to seek and to save—a fact which He Himself wished to indicate when at the same hour of the day He thirsted at the well of the Samaritan woman. It must be remembered that this is not to be regarded merely as a casual observation: it is a deliberate expression of Bede's mind, even if he borrowed the idea instead of originating it; and it is paralleled by the comment on Acts x, 30 that it was very fitting that he should be heard who, continuing his instancy in prayer for three hours, drew it out from the sixth hour to the ninth, at which hour the Lord Himself whom he was entreating was praying with hands stretched upon the Cross for the salvation of the whole world. But we cannot help noticing in passing that it is the acceptance of this kind of treatment as natural which, when we read the commentary on St. John iv, or the amazing arithmetical calculation in relation to the miraculous draught of 153 fishes in the same Gospel, may make the student hesitate, in spite of the arguments to be adduced on the other side, whether or not he is right in thinking that Bede had no responsibility for that commentary.

It would be absurd to pretend that Bede's use of the allegorical method is likely to recommend his commentaries on

Scripture to the majority of modern biblical students. The peculiar, indeed almost priceless, value that these works have for those who are concerned to form an estimate of the author and of the age in which he lived arises from considerations which from another point of view would be excluded as irrelevant and even pernicious. Reference is made elsewhere to the interest which Bede's notes possess for the textual critic, and, if this is especially true of the commentary on Acts and the *Liber Retractationis*, it extends also to many other works where the student finds himself speculating as to the character and history of one codex to which Bede certainly had access and which had a text with strange occasional resemblances to that which is represented by the first or second corrector of Codex Sinaiticus or perhaps just possibly of another still in Bodley's Library at Oxford (O) besides the Laudianus (E) of Acts. It is in regard to Gospel commentaries such as those on St. Luke and St. Mark that the difference of outlook is most clearly apparent at the present day. Bede as a diligent and careful investigator is necessarily aware of discrepancies of statement and divergence of presentation between the Evangelists. In that sense he can be said at least to be not wholly unaware of the existence of a Synoptic Problem and a problem of the Fourth Gospel. He is not more seriously disturbed than a modern critic would be by variations of reading, but certainly feels no obligation as a rule to decide between them, especially if each can be shown to be susceptible of an edifying interpretation, and above all if it can be supported by the authority of one of the Fathers. The use of the allegorical method, however, provides a way of escape or of reconciliation for Bede in some cases in which its use would nowadays be regarded as a mere subterfuge. We may take as an example the account of the Mission of the Twelve recorded in Matt. x, Mark vi, Luke ix. In his commentary on St. Luke, Bede says that the question is wont to be asked how it is that Matthew and Luke relate that our Lord told His disciples not even to carry a staff (*virgam*), though Mark says that He bade them not to take anything in the way save a staff only. The solution, he adds, is that the staff which according to Mark is to be carried is to be understood in one sense, the staff which according to Matthew and Luke is not to be carried is to be understood in another; and he adduces as a parallel the double use of the word 'temptation' in the text 'God tempts no man' (James i. 13) and in the text 'The Lord your God tempts you that he may know if ye love him' (Deut. xiii. 3): the one refers to leading astray, the other to proving. *Ergo* we must accept each as having been said by the Lord to His Apostles—both that they should not carry a staff and that they should carry nothing save a staff. For when according to Matthew He said to them 'Do not possess gold nor silver', &c., He forthwith added 'The labourer is worthy of his food', thereby showing quite plainly why He did not wish them to possess and carry these things. Not that they are not necessary for the sustaining of this life, but because He was sending them thus in order to show that these things were owed to them by the believers to whom they proclaimed the Gospel. Bede argues, however, that this injunction is manifestly not intended to preclude evangelists from deriving their livelihood from any other source: otherwise the Apostle who gained his food from the labours of his own hands in order not to be a burden to any one acted contrary to this precept; but the Lord gave them power whereby they might know that those things were owed to them. Moreover, when something is commanded by the Lord, there is the fault (*culpa*) of disobedience if it is not done. But when power is given, it is lawful to any one not to use it and as it were to abandon his right. *Ergo* the Lord in ordaining what the Apostle says that He ordained to those who proclaim the Gospel, that they should live of the Gospel, meant that without anxiety they should abstain from possessing or carrying the things necessary for this life either great or least. And so He put *nec virgam*, showing that His faithful ones owed all things to His ministers asking of them no superfluities. And by adding this 'The labourer is worthy of his food', He directly disclosed and illustrated the reason why He spoke of all these things. *Ergo* He signified this power by the name of *virga* when He says that they are not to carry anything in the way save a *virga* only, so that it may be understood that by the power received from the Lord which is signified by the name of *virga*, even the things which are not carried will not be wanting.

When we turn to Bede's later commentary on St. Mark vi, we find that this explanation is transcribed in full, so that like John Wesley on Justification Bede has been unable to find after the lapse of many years an explanation which seems to him more adequate. We look with some curiosity at the commentary on St.

Matt. x. 10, only to discover that *virga* is explained as *prae-sidium carnis* without further note and to draw the inference that, if the work were Bede's it could only be earlier, not later, than the other two Gospel commentaries which are included in the catalogue of his works; but this is not included in the cata-logue nor referred to by himself elsewhere; *ergo* it is not one of Bede's genuine works. It may be frankly admitted that the conclusion is one which is reached with reluctance, for there are passages in the commentary on St. Matthew which we would gladly attribute to Bede in regard to style, and others which if they could be shown to be his would supply *adnotatiunculae* of real value for the life at Jarrow and Wearmouth. But any one who compares the comments on the Lord's Prayer in the com-mentary on Luke with those on Matt. v, will find it very hard to believe that they proceed from the same mind. Nor does it tell against the conclusion unfavourable to the authenticity of the commentary on St. Matthew that in a passage where the narrative of Mark xiv and Matt. xxvi relating to the woman with the alabaster box of ointment of spikenard is being com-pared with the parallel account in John xii, not only is there in both Matthaean and Marcan commentaries a repetition of the disquisition on unguents found in the commentary on Canticles, but a long note common to both deals with the incident itself with only slight differences in phraseology, and the same is true of the observations on St. John's specific mention of Judas in contrast to the others' general statement that there were 'some' who had indignation at the waste. The explanation is the simple one that these comments are in any case not due to Bede but to other authorities who are being quoted. And it may be noted in passing that any one who takes the trouble to study the interesting but highly rhetorical commentary on St. John which passes under the name of Bede and examines what is said on John xii will find even greater difficulty than in the case of the Matthaean commentary in supposing that at any period of his life Bede could have written it.

No modern commentator would be heard to identify the friend awakened at midnight (Luke xi. 5) with God Himself, but it would be hard to blame Bede for doing so since the inter-pretation is at least as old as Tertullian's treatise on Prayer (c. v.) and the explanation of the 'three loaves' as *intelligentia Trinitatis* is in Origen, but also in line with Bede's general

principles. It is of course not the only use that he can make of
the number Three, since on Luke viii he tells us that *iuxta mora-
lem intellectum* the three dead persons whom the Saviour raised
in their bodies signify three kinds of resurrection of souls. This
is followed by a disquisition on moral theology, ending with an
observation to which the date gives a certain interest that a
public harm requires a public remedy, but light sins can be
blotted out by a lighter and secret penance (*poenitentia*). Here the
meaning can hardly be mistaken; but our thoughts perhaps go
back to the commentary on Rev. i. 7 where we read that 'those
who pierced him shall lament themselves with a belated penitence'—a note which seems to show that if *poenitentia* for Bede
sometimes means 'penance', it does not necessarily do so in all
cases where it is found. But that is only what is to be expected.

We may venture to allow ourselves space for one or two passages which show Bede wrestling with what he sees to be real
historical difficulties. The first is in relation to the statement in
St. Stephen's speech (Acts vii. 16) that Jacob and our fathers were
laid in the sepulchre that Abraham bought of the sons of Hemor
the son of Sichem. Confronted by the obvious confusion of the
narratives of Gen. xxiii and xlix on one hand and Gen. xxxiii. 19
on the other, Bede argues that the blessed Stephen *vulgo loquens,
vulgi magis in dicendo sequitur opinionem* and that, in combining
two narratives, he is concerned rather with the point of the
allusion than with the historical details. That Bede is not altogether satisfied may be judged from the comment: 'I have
given the best explanation I can without prejudice to a better
opinion, should one be ready to hand. Further, the statement
that Abraham bought "of the sons of Hemor the son of Sichem"
appears in the "Graecum exemplar" as "from the sons of
Hemor who was in Sichem", which seems to agree better with
the narrative of Genesis, though it might be the case that the
same Hemor had both a father and son named Sichem.' So far
the Exposition of Acts: when we turn to the later *Liber Retractationis* we find that no further solution has occurred to his mind.

The next difficulty also arises from a statement in a speech,
in this case that by St. Paul at Antioch in Pisidia, where, after
referring to a period of 40 years (in the wilderness) and a period
of 450 years, the Apostle is represented by St. Luke as speaking
of the rule of the Judges and of Saul, the son of Cis, 40 years
(Acts xiii. 18–21). Bede's treatment is extraordinarily interest-

ing as indicative of his attitude towards the biblical record and
the degree of exactness which he deemed it reasonable to expect
from it; and this remains true even where he may be adopting
rather than originating explanations. The argument follows in
a series of stages: (a) God told Abraham that his seed should
dwell in a land not their own 400 years (Gen. xv. 13) and that
'in Isaac shall thy seed be called' (cf. Gen. xvii. 19); (b) from the
birth of the seed to the exodus from Egypt were, as Exodus
records, 405 years (Ex. xii. 40); (c) to these add 40 years in the
wilderness and 5 in the land of Canaan after which the land
rested from wars (Jos. xi. 23) and the lot was cast, and you
will find 450 years. So far, so good. But as to his following
calculation Bede says that he supposes that, as the Book of
Kings does not openly state how many years Saul reigned, the
Apostle *vulgo loquentem*—we note the same phrase as in the
case of Stephen—intended to speak in accordance with prevalent
opinion. But, seeking diligently there, we found, as the Books
of Chronicles also attest, that Samuel and Saul ruled over
Israel 40 years. For it came to pass, the writer says, that in
the 480th year of the egress of the children of Israel from Egypt
Solomon began to build a Temple for the Lord in the fourth
year of his reign (1 Kings vi. 1; 2 Chron. iii. 2). But when to
the 396 years in which the Judges ruled, as their Book indicates,
40 are added for David and 4 of Solomon (= 440) there remain 40
of which (as Josephus is witness [*Ant. Iud.* vi. 14: cf. x. 8]) Samuel
spent 20 in ruling and Saul as many more. When in later years
Bede came to draw up the *Liber Retractationis* he recalls to mind
the above explanation of the 450 years, but adds one of those
notes indicative of further study, especially of Greek sources,
to which attention has already been called: 'But it should be
known that in Greek it is otherwise written, "and destroying
seven nations in the land of Canaan he distributed to them their
land by lot, and after this for about 450 years he gave them
Judges down to Samuel the prophet".' How, Bede adds, this
agrees with the statement (*sententia*) in the Book of Kings, that
from the exit of Israel from Egypt to the building of the Temple
were 480 years, it is not in our power to explain; unless perchance he followed *vulgarem in loquendo famam*, as the blessed
Stephen is proved to have done in the speech that he addressed
to the Jews about the burial-place of the twelve Patriarchs.
Bede turns next to the problem of Saul, and refers to his note

in the Exposition that in assigning 40 years to Saul's reign the Apostle appears *vulgi opinionem secutus*. But, he says, 'as for my former statement that Eusebius, following Josephus, assigned to the principate of Samuel and Saul 40 years equally divided between them, subsequently on a more careful examination of the histories of Josephus I found that he himself' was not responsible for the 40 years, but 'had assigned only 12 to Samuel and 20 to Saul'. This discovery sent Bede back to the Books of Chronicles, and then he saw why here and in regard to the years of Joshua Eusebius had deserted the authority of Josephus. What follows is too long to quote, but it may be noted as an admirable example of the delights which Bede's pages from time to time afford. Across 1,200 years we can still feel the thrill of excitement which the discovery brought to the man who knew more about chronology than any one in England and probably than any one in Europe at the time. With the simplicity of a great scholar Bede has set down here as elsewhere for the instruction of his readers the points which he had himself at first overlooked; but now the detective instinct is aroused, and with trained observation aided by imagination he sets himself to reconstruct what he supposes to have happened in another scholar's work-room four centuries before. We can see him with his codices around him, one of which we can still hold in our own hands, turning now to one, now to another as he proceeds to demonstrate—*ipse dictator simul notarius et librarius*—how Eusebius manipulated the figures to make the sum come right. If culinary metaphors be inappropriate to the operations of a holy bishop, the urbanity of Bede's description of the adjustment would be difficult to beat.[1] One further note must be added. Bede goes on to say that his own statement in the Exposition that the Judges ruled the people for 396 years from Moses to Samuel was made following the authority of Chronicles, when he had not yet noticed that that authority was not in agreement with the *Hebraica veritas*. If the student of Eusebius with modern texts before him hesitates to assume that Bede's is the only possible explanation of what the former did, the student of Bede will be equally on his guard

---

[1] *Liber Retractationis* in Act. Ap. xiii. 21: 'Deprehendens decem sibi annos praefiniti calculi in historia sacra iuxta editionem quam sequebatur deesse, curavit hos de suo ubi commodum et historiae sacrae minus contrarium videbatur adjicere.'

as to the necessity of caution in laying stress on the latter observation as derived from study of the Hebrew itself.

One further historical example may be added in illustration of Bede's method without staying to discuss its origin or implications. In the Exposition of Acts xv. 2, which, as he points out, has to be read with Gal. ii. 1, Bede calls attention to the significance of the visit to Jerusalem 'after 14 years' and says: 'We know (*scimus*) that the Apostles Peter and Paul suffered martyrdom in the 38th year after the Lord's Passion, i.e. in the last year of Nero, and that the blessed Peter sat on the episcopal chair at Rome for 25 years. But 25+14 = 39, not 38. It follows then that we must suppose that the blessed Peter came to Rome in the same 14th year after the Lord's Passion in which Paul addressed him at Jerusalem, i.e. in the 4th year of Claudius Caesar.' And, he adds, 'at the same time, unless I am mistaken, the blessed Paul the Apostle is proved to have come to the Faith in the same year in which the Lord suffered and rose again'.

VI

It will probably occur to patristic students that Bede's handling of theological problems is at most times somewhat conventional and recalls methods and arguments which they have constantly encountered in earlier writers. But to apply such a criticism by way of detraction is entirely to overlook the importance and significance of his work as a pioneer in the age and circumstances in which he was placed; and the influence of his writings at home and abroad may be regarded as sufficient evidence of the value attached to his work in many fields. For Bede as a Catholic teacher Orthodoxy was precious, and heresy, so far from being a pleasing mark of originality, was in all its manifold disguises an insidious delusion proceeding from the Father of Lies. If his own office was the confirmation of the Faith and the edification of the faithful, his encyclopaedic labours had in his eyes a value as elucidations of truth with theological lessons to convey. No careful reader will deny either his thirst for knowledge or his zest for research. It is a fair criticism that he sometimes allows too great weight to Authority and that the modern student will at times question his premisses or hesitate as to the cogency of his inferences. But at least he was saved from some later forms of obscurantism by the study of History and a robust confidence in Truth. In the moving address to readers and transcribers with which he concludes his commentary on the Apocalypse he bids them remember that he has laboured for them as well as for himself; and if we seek for the key-note of his lifelong devotion to sacred studies we may find it in his own comment on Rev. i. 3: 'Beati qui legunt, &c. Ideo doctores et auditores beati sunt; quia verbum Dei servantibus, tempus breve laboris gaudia sequuntur aeterna.'

CLAUDE JENKINS.

ADDITIONAL NOTE

Page 168, line 13. These words occur in the little treatise 'De Ratione Unciarum'.

VII
BEDE'S MIRACLE STORIES

IT probably comes as a shock to the reader unacquainted with medieval literature who approaches Bede's *Ecclesiastical History* for the first time, to find that a miracle occurs on almost every page. What reliance can be placed on the historian who tells us in his very first chapter that 'scrapings of leaves of books that had been brought out of Ireland being put into water have cured persons bitten by serpents',[1] who goes on to deal with the life of Alban and to describe how the river dries up to allow the holy man the more rapidly to receive his martyr's crown, while the executioner's eyes drop out at the same moment as the martyr's head drops off.[2] We read of saints who heal the blind and raise the dead, who quell storms and quench fires, who visit the lower regions and return to tell their story, who see visions of angels prophesying their death and whose bodies after their death remain uncorrupt while heavenly lights tell the faithful where they lie; and the miracles performed by the saint are even more numerous after his death than during his life.

And yet a fuller study of contemporary literature shows us that if there were none of these strange and incredible tales in Bede's History we should have had every reason for astonishment. The only cause for surprise, to the student of the ecclesiastical literature of the times, is that there are not more of them. It was as natural for Bede to relate these marvels as it is for the modern historian to avoid them. As Dill says, dealing with the same aspect in the works of Gregory of Tours, 'had he not done so, he would have done violence to his own deepest beliefs, and he would have given a maimed and misleading picture of his age'.[3] Science had not yet given men a conception of a universe ruled by unchanging laws. It was left for the eighteenth and nineteenth centuries to do that, and perhaps it is the natural reaction of the twentieth century to ask whether after all it may not be possible that there is something more in these strange stories than the earlier editors of Bede believed, and that these holy men, living lives of incredible hardships and asceticism, actually reached a state of being in which they possessed powers

---

[1] *H.E.* i. 1.   [2] *Ibid.* i. 7.
[3] Dill, *Roman Society in Gaul in the Merovingian Age*, 1926, p. 395.

—hypnotism, clairvoyance, telepathy—call them what you choose
—which are not perhaps miraculous in the strict sense of the
term but would certainly be considered so in the early middle
ages. The age of Bede was primitive in its outlook; it was
naturally credulous, and the nature of evidence was but vaguely
understood. All around them men saw inexplicable phenomena,
and the most marvellous explanation was always the easiest and
the most readily accepted; the pious and the simple-minded
were naturally ready to explain a phenomenon as the direct
interposition of God on their behalf or on behalf of those who
were especially dear to Him, such as the saints and martyrs.
The immediate forefathers of Bede and his contemporaries had
imagined themselves to be surrounded by multitudes of unseen
powers: every bush held its demon and every grove its god.
There was in their minds an elasticity about the order of nature
which made it seem probable to them that certain chosen people,
magicians and medicine-men, should be able to alter events.
When the Western lands accepted Christianity these popular
beliefs were too deeply rooted to be lost all in a minute. Gregory
the Great recognized this in his letter to Mellitus which Bede
himself quotes: Gregory recommends that the people who had
until recently slaughtered oxen and built themselves huts of the
boughs of trees about their heathen temples, shall now celebrate
the nativities of the holy martyrs and other feasts with like
ceremonies—so that whilst some outward and visible joys are
permitted them, they may more easily learn to appreciate inward and spiritual joys. 'For undoubtedly it is impossible to
efface everything at once from their obdurate hearts, because
he who seeks to climb the highest peak ascends step by step and
not by leaps.'[1] Bede himself provides us with other evidence
that the change from paganism to Christianity was a slow and
often painful process. There is, for instance, an illuminating story
in the Life of Cuthbert.[2] A party of monks from the monastery
near the mouth of the Tyne were fetching home some wood on
rafts, when the wind changed and drove them out to sea. A
crowd of people watched them from the shore, jeering at their
plight. When the youthful Cuthbert who stood among them,
rebuked them for their brutality, they answered, 'May God have
no mercy on any one of those who have robbed men of their old
ways of worship; and how the new worship is to be conducted,

---

[1] *H.E.* i. 30. [2] *Vit. Cuth.* iii.

nobody knows.' And again in the same work[1] we read that when Cuthbert was at Melrose, he used to take journeys into the neighbourhood, teaching the common people, who, in times of plague, 'forgetting the sacrament of the Gospel which they had received, took to the delusive cures of idolatry, as though, by incantations or amulets or any other mysteries of devilish art, they could ward off a stroke sent by God their maker'. Another curious instance related by Bede is the story of Redwald, king of the East Saxons, who in the same temple had an altar to Christ and another one on which to offer sacrifices to devils.[2] But perhaps one of the most striking proofs of the mixture of paganism and Christianity is to be found, not in any literary work, but in an artistic production of the period. The famous Franks casket which is usually attributed to this period has, on the same panel, carvings representing on one half the horrible heathen tale of Wayland the Smith and his vengeance on King Nithhad, and, on the other half, one of the most beautiful of the Gospel stories, the Adoration of the Magi.[3] We need only refer to the penitential literature or to the charms and leechdoms of the Anglo-Saxon period to show how long the earlier pagan faith continued to hold sway in this country. And what is true of England is equally true of the whole of western Europe.

It is clear then that the peoples of western Europe who accepted Christianity, very often under compulsion, would expect of their new Master and His saints powers no less than they had previously associated with their gods and heroes. A naïve illustration of this is found in the story of the conversion of Iceland in the year A.D. 1000. Thrangbrand the Saxon priest in his missionary journey through that island was opposed by an old woman who made a long speech on behalf of the heathen faith. 'Have you heard', she said, 'how Thor challenged Christ to single combat and how He was afraid to fight with Thor?' 'I have heard', answered Thrangbrand, 'that Thor would have been only dust and ashes, if God had not permitted him to live.'[4] The miracle stories of the Bible partly provided them with the satisfaction they sought and miraculous stories very soon came to be told of the saints as well. At first indeed the Fathers of

[1] *Ibid.* ix. [2] *H.E.* ii. 15.
[3] See *B.M. Guide to Anglo-Saxon Antiquities*, 1923, Pl. VIII.
[4] *Saga of the Burnt Njal*, xcviii.

the Church were inclined to answer this demand for miracles in much the same terms as their Lord used to those who sought for a sign. Origen, for instance, affirms that there are wonders comparable to those of past days, but nevertheless declares that they are only the vestiges of a power that has disappeared: instead of the material interventions of past days we have now the spiritual miracles worked in the souls of men.[1] It was the lives of the founders of monasticism which gave the miraculous such an important place in the stories of the saints. These stories seem to have arisen first of all in Egypt, to be repeated in the East and very soon in the West, to satisfy the craving for tales of marvels, a craving which grew rather than diminished all through the Middle Ages. In this way it came about that the *legenda*, the histories to be read on the feast of a saint, gave to the word 'legend' its modern meaning of 'any unhistoric or unauthentic story'. But it is important to notice that these stories are, from the first, popular creations and the editor of the life is no more than the transmitter of the story: for, as we shall see, even though he claims to be an eyewitness of the events he relates, or, as is more often the case, to have received the account from dependable witnesses, his claims need not be taken too seriously.

The first Latin life to attain to any considerable popularity in the West seems to have been Evagrius' Latin translation of Athanasius' Life of St. Antony, which appeared some time before 374. Somewhere about the beginning of the fifth century appeared the Life of St. Martin by Sulpicius Severus. Both these works became models for a vast number of later lives of saints, and passages were often lifted from them bodily.[2] The whole arrangement of many of them is on the model of the Life of St. Antony; beginning with a prologue in which the editor humbly declares his lack of eloquence and his inability for the task set him by his superior, they go on to describe the youth and vocation of the saint, his virtues, his search for solitude, his asceticism, his stout defence against the attacks of the devil and his satellites, his miracles and prophecies, and finish with a fairly full account of the last exhortations of the saint to his followers, his death

---

[1] See H. Delehaye, *Saint Martin et Sulpice Sévère*, Anal. Boll. xxxviii. 73.

[2] Thus the prologue to the Anonymous Life of St. Cuthbert consists entirely of a patchwork of borrowings from Evagrius' Life of St. Antony, Sulpicius Severus' Life of St. Martin, the Life of St. Silvester, and an epistle of Victor of Aquitaine to Hilarius, the proper names being changed to suit the context.

and the miracles performed at his tomb.[1] It will be seen that Bede's Life of Cuthbert follows this model fairly closely. But we must remember that all these writers of saints' lives, including Bede, were merely the people who put into writing the floating traditions. As Delehaye points out, there are two main sources in all hagiographical literature. First of all we get the people, whose imagination perpetually creates fresh products of its fancy and attaches wonders drawn from the most diverse sources to the name of its favourite saints, and secondly we get the writer whose function it is to put these floating traditions into literary shape; he has to take the material that is given him, but his ideas and standards determine its permanent form.[2] And it is here that the earlier models such as the Life of St. Antony and the Life of St. Martin show their influence.

Let us now consider in more detail the miracles described by Bede and endeavour to see how he is influenced by the hagiographical interests of his age. In the first place we notice that his miracle stories are almost confined to the *Ecclesiastical History*, the Prose and Verse Lives of Cuthbert, and of course the *Martyrology*. It is very noticeable that the Lives of the Abbots contain no miracle whatever, but recount ordinary and everyday occurrences throughout. We know indeed from the Anonymous Lives of the Abbots, which contain a contemporary account of Ceolfrid, that miracles came to be associated with that abbot after his death.[3] Bede must have known about these stories, but he refrains from mentioning them.

In the *Ecclesiastical History* the miracles related are chiefly grouped round the accounts of Alban, Germanus, Oswald, Aidan, Chad, the nuns of Barking, Hild, Cuthbert, John of Beverley. To these must be added a somewhat special form of miracle, the visions of the other world which are associated with the names of Dryhthelm and Fursey, and two other similar visions. There are a few separate miracles associated with other saints (such as Æthelthryth), but these are the chief groups. In every group except that of Hild we either know his authority independently or he informs us himself. Thus the Alban group is borrowed from an ancient life of St. Albanus, of which only a few traces

---

[1] See B. P. Kurtz, *From St. Antony to St. Guthlac*, California, 1926, *passim*.

[2] H. Delehaye, *Les Légendes hagiographiques*, Brussels, 3rd ed., 1927, p. 11.

[3] See Plummer, 1. 403 ff. Though there are several verbal likenesses between the two accounts it does not seem to be quite clear whether Bede made use of the Anonymous Lives or vice versa.

have come down to us.[1] The miracles of St. Germanus are taken from Constantius' Life of St. Germanus; and, as a glance at Plummer's edition of the text will show,[2] he has borrowed in a wholesale way from the earlier life. The account of the miracles at Barking is borrowed, as he himself tells us twice,[3] from an earlier authority, probably a life of Æthilburg. For the miracles connected with Hild he suggests no authority and we know of none. As he mentions no names of informants, it is possible that he was depending upon some life of the saint which would almost certainly exist at Whitby and might well be known to many of his northern readers. For the miracles connected with Oswald, Aidan, Chad, and John of Beverley, he mentions the names of various authorities like Bothelm, Acca, Cynimund, Trumberht, Egbert, Berhthun, and others, nearly always insisting that their authority is unimpeachable. For the vision of Fursey, he acknowledges his source to be the 'book of his life',[4] while Dryhthelm's vision was learned from one Haemgils, a monk who was still living when Bede wrote. Of the other two visions of the beyond, one was vouched for by Pehthelm the first Anglian bishop of Whithorn, while Bede himself vouches for the other one. It is worth noting in connexion with these groups of miracles, that only one is related of Wilfrid of York. It is very clear, as Raine points out,[5] that there was little sympathy between Wilfrid and Bede, hence it is interesting to note that of all the miracles described by Eddius, the only one he relates is that with which Bede's friend Acca, bishop of Hexham, is associated. It almost looks as though Bede refrained deliberately from relating any miracles about a man who had been the bitter opponent of so many of his heroes.

Bede's account of the miracles attributed to Cuthbert is worth careful study. They occur both in the *Ecclesiastical History* and also in his Prose and Metrical Lives of the Saint. In the *History* he gives two of which he learned after the other two lives had been written.[6] His chief authority was the Life of Cuthbert written by an anonymous monk of Lindisfarne. He has given us a fairly elaborate account of his methods in the prologue to his life of the saint.

---

[1] See H. Delehaye, *Origines du culte des martyres*, 1933, p. 362.
[2] Plummer, I. 34 ff.   [3] *H.E.* iv. 10, 11.   [4] *Ibid.* iii. 19.
[5] *H.C.Y.* I. xxxiv. See also Plummer, II. 315 ff.
[6] These two miracles were usually added by the scribes to the various manuscripts of the Prose Life.

'I decided', he says, 'to remind you (Eadfrith) who know and to inform those readers who perchance do not know, that I have not presumed to write down anything concerning so great a man without the most rigorous investigation of the facts, nor to hand on what I had written, to be copied for general use, without the most scrupulous investigation of credible witnesses. Nay rather it was only after diligently investigating the beginning, the progress and the end of his glorious life and activity with the help of those who knew him, that I began to set about making notes; and I have decided occasionally to place the names of my authorities in the book itself, to shew clearly how my knowledge of the truth has been gained.'

He goes on to say further how he had shown the notes to Herefrid and others for their judgement, and when all this was done, he had sent the book to Lindisfarne to be read before the elders and teachers of the community there for a final revision, though such had been his care that no changes were made. Curiously enough he does not in this introduction mention the fact that he had all through depended very fully upon the earlier and smaller life written by the anonymous monk of Lindisfarne. In the preface to the *Ecclesiastical History*, however, he states that he had used the earlier life 'yielding simple faith to the narrative'. Of the forty miracles he records of Cuthbert in his Prose Life, only eight are not found in the Anonymous Life, and of these eight, two are mentioned by the earlier writer but passed over.[1] In every instance except one where he introduces a fresh miracle, he adds the name of his authority, such as Herefrid, Cynimund, or unnamed monks from Wearmouth and Jarrow. The two Cuthbert miracles added to the *Ecclesiastical History*[2] are vouched for by the authority of the two brethren on whom the miracles were wrought. In the metrical Life no authorities are given, but as it contains only the miracles found also in the Prose Life, we need not consider it further.

Here then is an imposing array of testimony: let us next consider what is the nature of the miracles which he so abundantly vouches for. In the first place a large proportion of them are obviously based upon scriptural precedents. One of the early miracles in the *Ecclesiastical History* describes how the river dried up to allow Alban to reach his place of martyrdom quickly.[3] A blind girl is healed by Germanus,[4] a blind man by Augustine,[5]

---

[1] See Stevenson, ii. 284. [2] *H.E.* iv. 30, 31.
[3] *Ibid.* i. 7. [4] *Ibid.* i. 18. [5] *Ibid.* ii. 2.

a dumb and scurvy youth by John of Beverley;[1] evil spirits are
cast out[2] and various other cures are performed, sometimes with
the aid of holy water[3] or oil,[4] sometimes with consecrated bread,[5]
and once with the saint's girdle.[6] In addition, there are the
stories of the calming of a storm by Lupus,[7] by Aidan,[8] and by
Æthelwald.[9] Springs of water are miraculously produced from
a hill or a rock by Alban,[10] and by Cuthbert;[11] food is miraculously
provided on four occasions for Cuthbert,[12] and on one occasion
water is turned into wine for his benefit.[13] These scriptural
miracles abound in the legends of the saints: for instance, there
are, quite literally, hundreds of saints to whom the miracle of
turning water into wine has been attributed. In fact, if one were
to take any single volume of the *Acta Sanctorum* at random, it
would be possible to find analogues of practically every one of
the miracles related above. But it is worth noting that Bede
nowhere relates the miracle of a dead person being restored to
life, an extremely common miracle in other lives of saints.[14]

These scriptural miracles found in the legends naturally became standardized and usually preserved certain features of the
biblical miracles on which they were based. Thus in the account
of the cure of the sick maiden by John of Beverley,[15] we learn
that the saint on arriving at a 'monastery of virgins' learns that
the abbess's daughter is at the point of death. After much
entreaty she persuades the apparently unwilling saint to see the
maiden. He goes in, taking his disciple Berhthun with him,
blesses her and leaves her. In due course the maiden recovers
and asks to see the disciple. 'Do you desire that I should ask
for something to drink?' she said to Berhthun. 'Yes,' he replied,
'and I am delighted that you are able to drink.' The story has
clearly preserved most of the details of the miracle of the healing
of Jairus's daughter though the main thread is different.[16] The
ruler of the synagogue becomes the abbess of a monastery; the
daughter in one case is dead, in the other, dying: it is only after
entreaty that our Lord goes to the maiden. Peter, James, and

---

[1] *H.E.* v. 2.   [2] *Vit. Cuth.* xxx.

[3] *Ibid.* xxv, xxix.   [4] *Ibid.* xxx.   [5] *Ibid.* xxxi.

[6] *Ibid.* xxiii.   [7] *H.E.* i. 17.   [8] *Ibid.* iii. 15.

[9] *Ibid.* v. 1.   [10] *Ibid.* i. 7.   [11] *Vit. Cuth.* xviii.

[12] *Ibid.* v, vii, xi, xii.   [13] *Ibid.* xxxv.

[14] It is true that he described Dryhthelm as having been restored to life,
but this was without the intervention of a saint and necessarily precedes the
account of his vision of the life beyond.

[15] *H.E.* v. 3.   [16] St. Luke viii.

John go in with him just as Berhthun goes in with John; and refreshment is duly given to the healed maiden just as to the daughter of Jairus. In precisely the same way the thane's servant who is healed by John of Beverley asks for refreshment to be brought to him. Many other instances could be brought of the standardization of the miracle stories. But perhaps the most striking illustration is the comparison between the story of the healing of the thane's wife related of John of Beverley by Berhthun,[1] and the stories of the healing of the thane's wife and the thane's servant in the Prose Life of Cuthbert.[2] In the first account we learn that when John of Beverley, as bishop of Hexham, was consecrating a church in the neighbourhood of a certain thane, the latter begged him to dine in his house after the ceremony. This the bishop refused to do, but after many entreaties, he finally consented. Now this thane had a wife who had long been ill and, before going to the house, the bishop sent some consecrated water by one of the brethren. This he commanded them to give her to drink and with it to wash the parts which were most painful. The woman recovered and served the bishop and his followers with drink till the meal was over, thus following, as Bede points out, the example of Peter's mother-in-law. In the Prose Life, Bede describes how Cuthbert while bishop of Lindisfarne was attending a meeting at Melrose. On his way home a certain thane met him and earnestly sought him to return home with him. On his arrival at the thane's house, he was told that a servant of his had long been ill. Cuthbert consecrated some water and gave it to a servant, namely, the priest Baldhelm, bidding him give it to the sick man to drink. The messenger poured the water into the mouth of the patient, who forthwith fell into a tranquil sleep and was cured by the next morning. The second story in the Life describes how Bishop Cuthbert was preaching in his diocese when he called at the dwelling of a certain thane, who eagerly welcomed him in. After a hospitable greeting he told him of his wife's grave illness and besought him to bless some water wherewith to sprinkle her. The bishop did so and gave it to a priest who sprinkled her and her bed and poured some of the water into her mouth. She was immediately cured and went in to the bishop, offering him a cup of wine, and like Peter's mother-in-law she ministered to him and to his followers. For purposes of comparison it is worth

[1] *H.E.* v. 4.   [2] *Vit. Cuth.* xxv, xxix.

while to add a similar story related of Wilfrid, bishop of York, by Eddius.[1] While Wilfrid was in prison by the command of Ecgfrith, king of Northumbria, the wife of the reeve of the town in which he lay, was suddenly overtaken with a palsy. The reeve went in to the bishop, and, falling on his knees, implored his help, for she was dying. The bishop was led forth from prison and taking some consecrated water sprinkled it drop by drop upon the woman's face. She was promptly cured and like Peter's mother-in-law she ministered to the bishop.

It is not always clear how far these miracle stories, which are apparently imitations of scriptural miracles, may not also be influenced by Jewish or classical sources. Thus the miraculous provision of food for St. Cuthbert and his followers by an eagle,[2] or by the timely arrival of the porpoises,[3] or by the angel in the monastery at Ripon[4] or by the fortunate discovery made by his horse of the bread and meat in the thatch of the shepherd's hut,[5] are most likely reminiscences of the food provided for Elijah by the ravens, of Elijah under the juniper-tree, of the miraculous draught of fishes, or of the angels ministering to our Lord in the desert, but we must not forget classical stories of miraculous feeding such as the nourishment provided by Dionysus for the Maenads, described by Euripides,[6] or Hebrew stories such as that of the poor man who had no food to prepare for the sabbath, but whose wife used to heat the oven on the eve of the sabbath and put something in to make it smoke so as to hide their poverty from their neighbours. But a suspicious neighbour peered into the oven to see what was inside, and lo! a miracle—it was full of bread.[7] Or again when we read of springs of water miraculously produced by the saints, the source may be not merely such texts as Bede quotes in connexion with the spring which Cuthbert miraculously produced in his cell upon Farne:[8] 'God . . . turned the rock into a pool of water, the flint into a fountain of waters' and 'thou shalt make them to drink of the river of thy pleasures'; it may be that the stories of Hippocrene and Helicon, of Peirene and the spring behind the temple of the Acrocorinthus[9] also

[1] Eddius, xxxvii.
[2] *Vit. Cuth.* xii.
[3] *Ibid.* xi.
[4] *Ibid.* vii.
[5] *Ibid.* v.
[6] Euripides, *Bacchae*, 704–11.
[7] Quoted by H. Günter, *Die christliche Legende des Abendlandes*, Heidelberg, 1910, p. 96.
[8] *Vit. Cuth.* xviii.
[9] See Günter, *op. cit.*, p. 58.

played their part in the development of this miracle so often repeated in the legends of the saints.

Closely connected with the biblical miracles are the many visions and instances of prophetic foresight which Bede relates. Aidan foretells the storm which is going to overtake Utta on his way to fetch Eanfled, daughter of Edwin, to be the wife of King Oswiu and gives him holy oil to pour upon the troubled waters when it occurs. This he does and the storm is calmed.[1] A certain monk called Adamnan prophesies the destruction of the double monastery at Coldingham over which Æbba ruled, as a punishment for the careless life of the inmates.[2] A series of prophecies are connected with various kings and rulers. Thus Aidan predicts the death of King Oswald[3] and Cedd predicts the death of King Sigeberht of Essex.[4] A whole chapter in the Prose Life of Cuthbert is devoted to an interview between Cuthbert and Ælfflæd, the successor of Hild as abbess of Whitby. The saint and the abbess met on Coquet Island and the abbess put him through a sort of cross-examination in the course of which she elicited the facts that her brother Ecgfrith was to die the following year, that Aldfrith was to be his successor and that Cuthbert himself was to be made a bishop, to hold the office for two years and then was to return to his retreat in Farne.[5] A year afterwards, having become bishop, he was being taken round the walls of Carlisle; as he reached a certain fountain, a relic of Roman times, he suddenly stopped and became sorrowful. His followers ascertained that at that very moment Ecgfrith had been slain in his disastrous fight against the Picts at Nechtansmere in 685.[6]

Another type of prophetic vision very commonly met with in the lives of the saints, and one of which Bede is very fond, is the vision granted to the saints or to their followers, foretelling the day on which the saint was to pass away. Sometimes the day was prophesied by the appearance of angels in a vision. An example of this is the long and charming story told of the vision of the heavenly choir which appeared to Chad, a vision which was also seen by Owini, one of the brethren of the monastery, who was working in the fields. Owini learned from Chad that

---

[1] *H.E.* iii. 15. The phrase 'to cast oil on troubled waters' can scarcely be derived from this incident as is usually asserted. The idea was widespread and goes back as far as Aristotle. See Plutarch, *Moralia* (*De primo frigido*), xiii. 5.
[2] *H.E.* iv. 23.   [3] *Ibid.* iii. 14.   [4] *Ibid.* iii. 22.
[5] *Vit. Cuth.* xxiv, and compare ch. viii.   [6] *Ibid.* xxiv.

the 'loving guest who was wont to visit our brethren'[1] had appeared to him also and had summoned him to come with him seven days afterwards. A vision of men in white was seen by Earcongota, the daughter of Earconberht, king of Kent, a nun in a double monastery in Brie; they announced to her that they were to take with them 'that golden coin which had come from Kent';[2] Sebbi, king of Essex, was also visited by three men in bright garments, one of whom informed him that he was to depart from the body after three days:[3] the only miracle Bede records of Wilfrid is the story of how when he was at Meaux, he lay four days and nights in a trance, and, on awaking, told his companion Acca, afterwards bishop of Hexham, Bede's close friend, that Michael the archangel had visited him and promised him four further years of life through the intercession of the Blessed Virgin Mary.[4] Eddius[5] adds that in return he was to build a church in honour of St. Mary ever Virgin. Sometimes it was a well-known friend who came in a vision to give the warning—as in the case of Chad mentioned above. Thus one of the nuns at the monastery of Barking on her death-bed told how a certain man of God, who had died that same year, had appeared to her, to tell her she was to depart at daybreak. Another of the sisters named Torhtgyth was heard conversing with an unseen visitor. A curious conversation took place of which only Torhtgyth's part was heard and recorded. Evidently the nun was urging her unseen visitor that she might be taken from the body as soon as possible; when she had finished talking to her heavenly visitant, she told those who sat around that she had been talking to her 'beloved mother Æthilburg'. This was the abbess of the Barking monastery who had died three years before.[6] In other instances Bede infers that the saints knew of the day of their death even though we hear of no prophetic vision. Thus in the beautiful account of Boisil's death we learn how he proposed to read the Gospel of St. John, of which he had a copy, with his disciple Cuthbert. The manuscript[7] had seven gatherings, one of which was to be read every day, for Boisil declared that he had only seven days in which he could teach him. After the

---

[1] *H.E.* iv. 3. The 'loving guest' was his brother Cedd, as is explained in the latter part of the same chapter.   [2] *Ibid.* iii. 8.   [3] *Ibid.* iv. 11.
[4] *Ibid.* v. 19.   [5] Eddius, lvi.   [6] *H.E.* iv. 8, 9.
[7] The Stonyhurst Gospel was once supposed to be this very manuscript; but Baldwin Brown (vi. 8) pointed out that the Stonyhurst MS. has not seven but twelve gatherings.

seven readings were ended Boisil passed away.[1] Cuthbert, too, was warned by a divine oracle[2] that his death was approaching, though we are not definitely told that he knew the exact date. It is interesting to note that the author of the Anonymous Life knows nothing of this prophetic knowledge.

This particular form of prophecy is of course a commonplace in the lives of the saints from the Life of St. Antony onwards. It was possibly based on the story of Hezekiah who was promised fifteen more years of life by the word of the Lord through the mouth of Isaiah.[3] The idea underlying this widespread tradition was that the saint was thus granted time to prepare himself for the great change and to be fortified by receiving the Communion. The dread of sudden death was very widely spread throughout the middle ages in Christian lands, so that it was not unnatural that the saints should be granted this special grace. So far as the martyrs were concerned, the very fact of their dying for the faith was a sufficient proof of their eternal welfare. Even though a martyr were unbaptized, as was the soldier who was slain for refusing to execute Alban, he was 'cleansed by being baptized in his own blood'.[4] So they needed no divine admonition. One might even suggest that this is why the anonymous writer of Cuthbert's Life relates no such vision about his saint. For him he is a martyr because of his ascetic life and in one place he calls him such, while he frequently refers to him as confessor.[5]

Many of the visions in Bede refer to the departure of the soul of a saint. Thus a priest in Ireland saw the soul of Cedd with a company of angels, taking the soul of Chad to heaven.[6] A nun Bega, in the monastery at Hackness, thirteen miles from Whitby, heard the passing bell tolling and saw Hild's soul being carried to heaven by angels,[7] while a young novice in the remotest part of the Whitby monastery itself saw an identical vision.[8] The

[1] *Vit. Cuth.* viii.   [2] *H.E.* iv. 26.

[3] Isaiah xxxviii. The passage is actually quoted by Eddius (c. lvi) in his account of Wilfrid's vision at Meaux. Possibly Ps. xxxix. 4 and similar passages may have influenced the belief.   [4] *H.E.* i. 7.

[5] Stevenson, ii. 282, 283 (§§ 44, 45). For the whole subject of the equivalents of martyrdom cf. H. Delehaye, *Sanctus*, Brussels, 1927, pp. 109 ff.; L. Gougaud, *Devotional and Ascetic Practices*, London, 1927, pp. 205–23.

[6] *H.E.* iv. 3.   [7] *Ibid.* iv. 23.

[8] *Ibid.* Plummer (ii. 248) sees an apparent contradiction between this story and the account in the same chapter of how Hild called the nuns together to deliver her dying exhortation. But surely the explanation is that the nun who saw the vision was a novice and would therefore be separated from the others present at the death of the abbess.

brethren of the men's part of the double monastery of Brie saw a similar vision of angels when Earcongota died,[1] and Cuthbert when keeping sheep near the river Leader saw a vision of Aidan's soul being taken to heaven by angels. This vision led to his decision to take up the monastic life.[2] A similar vision came to Cuthbert one day, when he was dining with Ælfflæd, of the soul of a shepherd attached to one of Ælfflæd's lesser monasteries, being carried to heaven by angels. He had been climbing a tree to get food for his flock.[3] It will be seen that all these visions are of exactly the same type. The soul of the dying person is surrounded by a band of angels and the person to whom the vision is granted is invariably absent from the death-bed. A whole series of such visions is related in Adamnan's Life of St. Columba and in every case these two traits appear. Such visions were commonly related of the saints and these two features are almost invariably present. The vision related of Torhtgyth clearly belongs to a different type. She saw a body wrapped in a sheet being drawn up to heaven by golden cords; the body was that of Æthilburg who shortly afterwards died.[4]

One type of vision has more obviously didactic intention. It is that of the future life. Bede relates no less than four of these. One of them, at least, was more than a vision, for Dryhthelm actually died and saw the joys of the blessed and the tortures of the damned before he was restored to life.[5] Fursey's vision of the other world is the best known of all.[6] The third vision is related of a dying layman in Mercia who saw a very small and beautiful book brought to him by two beautiful youths, which contained an account of all his good deeds, and another prodigiously large book containing all his evil deeds, borne to him by a host of devils, who claimed him as their own and struck him with ploughshares.[7] The last vision is related by Bede himself of a brother whose name he will not mention, who resided in Bernicia in a 'noble monastery but himself lived ignobly'. On his death-bed he saw hell open and Satan and Caiaphas and the others who slew the Lord being consigned to everlasting perdition;[8] he also saw the place in their midst which had been appointed for himself. He died soon afterwards without receiving the viaticum and none dared to pray for him.

---

[1] *H.E.* iii. 8. [2] *Vit. Cuth.* iv. [3] *Ibid.* xxxiv; *Vit. Metr.* xxxi.
[4] *H.E.* iv. 9. [5] *Ibid.* v. 12. [6] *Ibid.* iii. 19.
[7] *Ibid.* v. 13. [8] *Ibid.* v. 14.

These visions and stories of journeys to the other world are extremely ancient and widespread. They are found in ancient Egypt and amongst the Greeks and Romans. Odysseus, Theseus, Pollux and Orpheus all visited the lower world, while Plato[1] tells the story of Er, son of Armenius, who was killed in battle, and after visiting the abodes of the dead was restored to life on his funeral pyre. Latin writers, too, notably Virgil, deal with the same theme. Saintyves has collected similar modern stories from a variety of sources from the Algonquin and Ojibway Indians, from northern Asia and Greenland, from Zululand and Oceania.[2] The literary tradition of these stories is preserved in the apocalyptic literature of the pre-Christian and early Christian period. It is found in the Book of Enoch, in the Apocalypse of Abraham and elsewhere in Jewish literature, while in the Apocalypse of Peter, a second-century work, we get the first Christian adaptation of the theme and at the end of the fourth century we get the Apocalypse of Paul which had a great influence on this branch of medieval literature. The tradition is carried on in the visions especially of the African martyrs. For our purpose it is important to notice that similar legends are told in Sulpicius Severus' Life of St. Martin[3] and in Gregory the Great's *Dialogues*. In these dialogues Gregory relates a whole series of these visions, most of which to some extent resemble the visions of Fursey and Dryhthelm. The didactic nature of these visions in Christian times is strongly marked. 'It is plain', says Gregory, after telling the vision about the priest Stephanus, 'that these punishments of hell are revealed so that they may be an encouragement to some and a testimony against others.'[4] Dryhthelm, Bede tells us, only told the story of his experiences 'to those who being either terrified by the fear of torment or delighted by the hope of everlasting joys, desired to win from his words advancement in piety'.[5]

One more vision is worth relating, because of the possible light it throws on Bede's methods. He relates in his second book of his *Ecclesiastical History*[6] the well-known story of the attempt on Edwin's life by the hand of an assassin sent by Cwichelm, king of Wessex. The king promised Paulinus that if he recovered

---

[1] *Republic*, Book 10, 614 B.
[2] P. Saintyves, *En Marge de la Légende Dorée*, Paris, 1930, ch. iv. See the whole chapter on which the above account is based. See also Plummer, ii. 294.
[3] Sulpicius Severus, *Vita Martini*, vii.   [4] Gregory, *Dialogues*, iv. 36.
[5] *H.E.* v. 12.   [6] *Ibid*. ii. 9.

from the wound he had received and succeeded in avenging himself upon the people of Wessex, he would accept Christianity. The conditions were fulfilled and Edwin renounced his heathenism, and allowed his daughter to be baptized, but refused to accept Christianity until he had had further teaching and had consulted his immediate followers. He was further encouraged by a letter from Pope Boniface. The conference with his counsellors is one of the best-known incidents in the *History*, containing the famous simile of the sparrow.[1] The king and his followers as a result of the conference were all baptized together. All this seems natural and has the appearance of strict history. But meanwhile Bede interpolates somewhat awkwardly a long account of a vision which Edwin had had when he was an exile at the court of Redwald, king of the East Angles, and in great danger. An unknown stranger had come to him and promised him safety if he would accept the teaching of one who, as a sign, was to lay his right hand on his head. The king accepted the condition. Paulinus, coming upon the king in meditation, had placed his right hand on his head, asking him if he knew the sign. The king tremblingly accepted the sign and thereupon hesitated no more. What was Bede's object in adding this story? Perhaps he felt that the conversion of his own land to Christianity was an event of such importance that it could hardly have happened without an accompanying sign from heaven: more probably it was a piece of popular tradition which was well known in Northumbria and which Bede, writing, as he acknowledges in his preface, a history that was to be 'pleasing to the inhabitants', dared not omit. Beyond all this, it was a picturesque story, and appealed to Bede's artistic sense. (See p. 229.)

A very considerable number of the miracles in Bede are associated with the bodies and relics of the saints. Bede relates how on one occasion Cuthbert's girdle healed the Abbess Ælfflæd and one of her nuns[2] just as the handkerchiefs and aprons carried from Paul's body healed the sick.[3] But from the earliest period of Christianity, the tomb, after the death of the saint, became a place of the greatest sanctity and anything which had been in contact with it acquired holiness and miraculous power. At first, in western Europe, the strict Roman laws protected the actual bodies of the saints themselves from the many translations and dismemberments which they afterwards suffered, and

[1] *H.E.* ii. 13.   [2] *Vit. Cuth.* xxiii.   [3] Acts xix. 12.

these representative relics sufficed; but by the middle of the fourth century translation of the bodies of the saints had become frequent. Later on grew up the miracles associated with the finding of the tomb of a martyr or saint and gradually there arose the habit of sending abroad bones and fragments of the body. The extent to which the rage for possession of relics grew is illustrated by the history of the bones of Bede himself and by the story of how Ælfred Westou during the eleventh century stole them from Jarrow in order to add to the collection he had already made around the incorruptible body of his patron.[1] But most of the miracles in Bede are associated with relics of the less gruesome type. Germanus, we read, had with him the limbs of saints brought together from several countries.[2] Benedict Biscop, Acca, Wilfrid, and others who travelled to Rome frequently, never failed to bring relics home to England. Occasionally a visiting prelate like Germanus brought some or else they were sent as presents from Rome. The relics of the Apostles Peter and Paul—of the holy martyrs Laurentius, John, Paul, Gregory and Pancratius were sent by Gregory the Great to St. Augustine;[3] others were sent by Pope Vitalian to King Oswiu.[4] It was customary to deposit relics in a church at its dedication, and the underground crypts at Ripon and Hexham, both of them almost the only remains left of the original churches built by Wilfrid, were intended specially for the exhibition of such relics. Pope Gregory in his letter to Mellitus bids him not destroy the temples of the idols; but, having destroyed the idols, he is to sprinkle the temples with holy water, erect altars, and place relics therein.[5] Whether these relics and the many other relics he mentions were portions of the bodies of the saints or merely some article connected with their tomb, Bede does not say.

There is sufficient testimony then to show the great reverence paid to the relics of the saints by Bede and his contemporaries, and miracles performed by these relics are very frequently related. Bede relates the story of how Germanus healed a girl of blindness by taking a reliquary from his neck and placing it on the girl's eyes. But generally the relics with which miracles were associated by Bede were those of English saints or saints connected closely with England such as Oswald, Aidan, Cuthbert, Fursey, Earconwald and Æthilburg. It may be helpful to

---

[1] See p. 37 above.   [2] *H.E.* i. 18.
[3] *Ibid.* i. 29.   [4] *Ibid.* iii. 29.   [5] *Ibid.* i. 30.

consider in detail the miracles which were associated with the body of Oswald. Oswald was slain fighting against Penda, king of the Mercians, at the battle of Maserfeld[1] in 642. The place where he had fallen in battle was discovered in the following way: a man shortly after the king's death was travelling on horseback near the site, when his horse was suddenly taken ill and began to roll about in anguish. By chance it rolled over the very place where Oswald fell, and arose cured. Shortly afterwards the rider came to an inn where the daughter of the house lay stricken with paralysis. She was placed upon a cart, put down on the exact spot which the traveller had previously noted, and was speedily cured.[2] A Briton, travelling near the same spot and noting its unusual greenness, took some of the dust of the place and put it in a linen cloth. Proceeding on his journey he came to a certain village, and entered a house where the villagers were feasting; he hung up the cloth with the dust in it on one of the wall posts. The feasting and drinking went on merrily until the huge fire in the middle of the room set the roof alight, which, being made of wattles and thatch, speedily blazed up. The whole house was burnt except for the post on which the dust was hanging.[3] As a result of the fame of these cures, earth was taken from this place and being put into water produced a healing drink for many; so famous did the place become that a hole as deep as a man's height remained there. His niece Osthryth, queen of Mercia, then decided to transfer his bones to the monastery of Bardney in the province of Lindsey. Did she take the body from the place where he fell? It would seem so, though Bede does not state clearly whence the remains were translated; but the miracles already described correspond with the usual miracles in the passions and legends associated with the invention of the body of the saint. The bones were taken on a wagon to the monastery, but the brethren did not care to receive the remains of their late enemy, and left the relics outside, spreading a tent over them. But all through the night a pillar of light, reaching to heaven and seen all over the province, stood above the wagon and convinced them.[4] The bones were washed in water and placed in a shrine. This water

[1] Usually identified with Oswestry. See Plummer, ii. 152.
[2] *H.E.* iii. 9.   [3] *Ibid.* iii. 10.
[4] The monks of Bardney never afterwards closed their doors to any stranger. Hence the Lincolnshire proverbial saying to a person who leaves the door open: 'You come from Bardney, do you?'

was thrown in a corner of the sacrarium. The earth on which it was thrown acquired the power of curing people possessed of devils.[1] Soon after this a boy was cured of fever at Oswald's tomb. At this point Bede tells us that the head, arms, and hands had been cut off the body by Penda and hung upon stakes. The head was taken to Lindisfarne[2] and the hands to Bamburgh.[3] In fact we are told in another place[4] by Bede that his right hand and arm, in accordance with a prophecy of Aidan, remained uncorrupt and were kept in a silver shrine in St. Peter's Church. A chip of the stake on which his head was placed was put in water by Willibrord when he was a priest in Ireland, and given to a man suffering from the plague. He was cured.[5] Stories are also told of how chips from the cross which he set up at the battle of Heavenfield, when put into water, healed both man and beast.

Now there is not a single detail in all these stories of Oswald's relics which is not met with time and time again in the *Acta Sanctorum*. In fact we need not go further than Bede himself to find analogues of most of them. Thus the burial-place of Peter, first abbot of the monastery of St. Peter and St. Paul at Canterbury, who had been drowned, was revealed by a heavenly light at Ambleteuse and his relics were translated to a church in Boulogne.[6] A heavenly light also revealed the place where the nuns of Barking, who died of the pestilence, were to be buried.[7] A heavenly light together with a vision revealed the whereabouts of the bodies of the martyrs Hewald the White and Hewald the Black after their bodies had been miraculously carried up stream for forty miles.[8] The post against which Aidan was leaning when he died, twice remained unharmed when the rest of the building was burnt down.[9] The water in which the body of Cuthbert was washed was poured into a pit on the south side of the church. A little of the dust from this pit, placed in water, cured a boy possessed of devils.[10] Chips from the post

[1] *H.E.* iii. 12.

[2] This head was afterwards transferred to Durham with Cuthbert's body and is probably the skull that was found within the innermost coffin when the tomb was opened up in 1827. See Raine, *St. Cuthbert*, 187.

[3] The body, however, was translated about 909 from Bardney, which had been laid waste by the Danes in 876, to St. Oswald's at Gloucester. See *Trans. Bris. and Glouc. Archaeol. Soc.* xliii. 89.

[4] *H.E.* iii. 6.

[5] *Ibid.* iii. 13.   [6] *Ibid.* i. 33.   [7] *Ibid.* iv. 7.
[8] *Ibid.* v. 10.   [9] *Ibid.* iii. 17.   [10] *Vit. Cuth.* xli.

against which Aidan died, placed in water, cured many people and their friends.[1] Chips from the horse-litter used by Earconwald were also responsible for many cures.[2] Dust from Hæddi's tomb wrought many cures and so much of the holy earth was carried away that a great hole was left.[3] Dust from Chad's sepulchre put in water cured both man and beast.[4]

Various other cures at the tombs of saints and martyrs or by their relics, are also related by Bede. Thus the wife of a certain thane was cured of blindness by the relics of the saints at Barking;[5] the linen clothes which wrapped the body of Æthelthryth cured people possessed of devils, and the wooden coffin in which she was first buried healed the eye-diseases of those who prayed with their heads touching it. A white marble coffin was miraculously found near the ruined Roman site of Grantchester;[6] it exactly fitted her and in this she was placed at her translation.[7] A somewhat similar story is told of the coffin which had been provided for Sebbi, king of the East Saxons; when they came to bury him, it proved to be too long; but after various vain efforts to make the coffin fit Sebbi, or Sebbi fit the coffin, it was found to have miraculously adapted itself to the size of the body.[8] Several cures, besides those mentioned above, were effected by the relics of Cuthbert; some of Cuthbert's hair, removed from the uncorrupt body when it was translated, cured a boy of a disease of the eye;[9] a brother called Baduthegn was healed of paralysis at his tomb;[10] Clement, bishop of Frisia, prayed at his tomb and was cured of a hopeless malady whose nature is not stated.[11] Felgeld, the anchorite who inhabited Cuthbert's cell at Farne after Cuthbert's successor Æthelwald was dead, had to reconstruct the cell which had fallen into decay; while doing so, he cut up a calf's hide which Æthelwald had placed there to protect him against the weather: pieces of this he gave to the numerous people who asked for relics of his predecessors. He placed a piece of this calf's hide in water, and washing his face with the liquid, he was cured of an inflamed swelling of the face which had long troubled him. 'But whether this ought to be ascribed to the merits of Father

---

[1] *H.E.* iii. 17.   [2] *Ibid.* iv. 6.   [3] *Ibid.* v. 18.   [4] *Ibid.* iv. 3.   [5] *Ibid.* iv. 10.
[6] The coffin was probably a Roman one. Compare the white marble sarcophagus found in Clapton and now in the Guildhall Museum: see Royal Commission on Historical Monuments, *Roman London*, p. 164 and pl. 57.
[7] *H.E.* iv. 19.   [8] *Ibid.* iv. 11.   [9] *Ibid.* iv. 30.   [10] *Ibid.* iv. 31.
[11] *Vit. Cuth.* xliv.

Cuthbert or of his successor Æthelwald . . . he alone knows who judges the heart. Nor does any reason forbid us to believe that it was wrought by the merits of both accompanied also by the faith of Felgeld.'[1] Bede gives only one example of a widespread type of relic miracle, in which, other relics having proved ineffective, the relic of the particular saint whose virtues are being extolled is successful in working the cure. This occurs in the story of the boy possessed with a devil who was cured by the dust gathered from the place where the monks had thrown water in which Cuthbert's body had been washed. He had first vainly tried those relics of the martyrs which were at Lindisfarne, but the holy martyrs of God would not grant the cure that was sought, in order that they might show what a high place Cuthbert held amongst them.[2]

We have already referred several times to the uncorrupt body of St. Cuthbert and the uncorrupt right hand and arm of Oswald. The phenomenon of the undecayed corpse is a fairly common one and has been known in all lands from the earliest times. The body of Alexander, for instance, according to Quintus Curtius, was found seven days after his death as fresh as though he were still alive.[3] Pausanias also refers to the same phenomenon[4] and there are many examples to-day of corpses preserved in a mummified form such as those still to be seen in the crypt of St. Michel at Bordeaux or in the catacomb of the Capuchins at Palermo. The preservation of the body may be due to various natural causes and sometimes just to embalming, a fact which might possibly explain the perfume so often associated with the disinterment of the uncorrupt bodies of the saints as Bede relates in connexion with the translation of the body of Earcongota.[5] The incorruptibility of the body was usually attributed, at least by the Church, to previous holiness of life. Bede tells us about Fursey's body in order that 'the sublimity of this man may be better known to my readers'.[6] He tells us of the discovery of Cuthbert's body after eleven years 'in order to show still further in what glory the holy man lived after his death'.[7] Occasionally the saints were canonized on the testimony

[1] *Vit. Cuth.* xlvi. [2] *Ibid.* xli.
[3] Quintus Curtius, x. 10. Quoted by Saintyves, *op. cit.* 284.
[4] Pausanias, v. 20.
[5] *H.E.* iii. 8. For a discussion of the natural causes which may lead to the uncorruptness of the body see Saintyves, *op. cit.* 284 ff.
[6] *H.E.* iii. 19. [7] *Vit. Cuth.* xlii.

of their undecayed remains,[1] but the Church has never made the incorruptibility of a body a certain sign of sanctity, though it is recorded of a very large number of saints and martyrs that their bodies were found uncorrupt after periods varying from a few days to hundreds of years. There are about forty examples in the first twelve volumes alone of the *Acta Sanctorum*. In popular belief, this very phenomenon was sometimes regarded with the greatest suspicion. There was a long and lingering tradition that the bodies of excommunicated people would not perish in the grave.[2] Witches and wizards too were popularly supposed to be preserved in the same way. When William of Deloraine and the monk of Melrose opened the grave of the Scottish wizard Michael Scott

> Before their eyes the wizard lay
> As if he had not been dead a day.[3]

Bede mentioned four instances of saints whose bodies were found undecayed: Æthilburg,[4] Fursey,[5] Æthelthryth,[6] and Cuthbert.[7] The tradition concerning the body of the latter lingered on until modern times. Eleven years after his burial the brethren found his body uncorrupt: 'Nay his very funeral weeds', as Hegge says in his delightful description of this event, 'were as fresh as if putrefaction had not dared to take him by the coat'.[8] Ælfred Westou, the eleventh-century sacrist at Durham, often used to open the coffin of the saint, and in 1104, when it was translated to its historic shrine in the Cathedral, the body was again found whole. In 1538 Henry VIII's commissioners visiting the monastery at Durham found the body in just the same condition. But when the tomb was opened in 1827 the mere bones were found. There are some, however, who maintain that the bones found on that occasion were not those of Cuthbert and that the incorruptible body still remains in the Cathedral in a secret spot known only to three Benedictines.

On the whole there are comparatively few examples in Bede of what one could call mere fairy-tale wonders, such as the stories of saints hanging their cloaks on sunbeams, or being miraculously protected from a shower of rain, of having their forgotten belongings, such as staves and cloaks and books, marvellously

---

[1] Saintyves, *op. cit.* 306 ff.   [2] *Ibid.* 286.
[3] Scott, *Lay of the Last Minstrel*, canto ii. 19.
[4] *H.E.* iii. 8.   [5] *Ibid.* iii. 19.   [6] *Ibid.* iv. 19.
[7] *Ibid.* iv. 30.   [8] Quoted in Raine, *St. Cuthbert*, 38.

discovered for them, often by being transported through the air to where the saint was. But there are certain miracles which perhaps may not unfairly be classed under this head. There is the story of St. Alban's executioner whose eyes dropped out as the saint's head fell to the ground.[1] There is the story of the Northumbrian captive whose fetters continually fell from him as often as they were put on him; this was due to the intercession of his brother, a priest, who, thinking he was dead, was saying masses for him.[2] There is the story of Hewald the White and Hewald the Black whose bodies were carried for forty miles against the current of the stream.[3] Apart from these, most of the more extravagant miracles are related about Cuthbert and are due to the influence of the Anonymous Life of which Bede made use. The animal and bird stories so popular in Irish hagiography are represented here and nowhere else. There is the account of how Cuthbert drove away the birds from the barley he had sown on his island, by reproving them:[4] there is the amusing and picturesque tale of the two crows who began to tear the thatch from off the roof of the guest-house he had built on Farne; these, too, he reproved and soon after one of the crows returned and alighted at his feet, spreading out its wings and uttering humble notes in token of asking forgiveness. The saint forgave the crow and gave it permission to come back with its mate. In return they brought him the half of a piece of swine's fat with which to grease his shoes.[5] Another story relates that, after he had spent the night in prayer, up to his neck in the sea, at Coldingham, seals came and dried him with their fur and warmed his feet with their breath. He blessed them and they returned to the sea.[6] Other fairy-tale stories are the provision of some building wood of exactly the right length, which was washed up by the sea on to Farne when the brethren forgot to get him the wood he had asked for;[7] the marvellous crop of barley produced out of season;[8] the story of the huge stones he carried unaided to build his cell;[9] and the interesting story of how he gave a goose to some of the brethren who came to visit him on Farne and told them to cook it; having already enough food of their own, the brethren did not do so; but a fierce storm arose and kept them in the island for

---

[1] *H.E.* i. 7. [2] *Ibid.* iv. 22. [3] *Ibid.* v. 10.
[4] *Vit. Cuth.* xix. [5] *Ibid.* xx. [6] *Ibid.* x.
[7] *Ibid.* xxi. [8] *Ibid.* xix. [9] *Ibid.* xvii.

seven days. At the end of this period the saint visited the dwelling in which they were living and saw the goose still uncooked; thereupon he reproved their disobedience very gently but told them that the sea would not become calm until the goose was eaten. This incident does not appear in the Anonymous Life, but Bede learned it 'not from any chance source but from one of those who were present, namely from Cynimund, a monk and priest of reverend life, who is still alive and well'. The story, although it may seem at first sight somewhat childish, throws light on Bede's view of the religious life and on the didactic nature of his miracle stories. The incident is, from our point of view, a simple ordinary occurence and no more than a coincidence is involved. It is a common enough happening nowadays for Farne Island to be cut off by storms for days at a time. But there could be no doubt in the mind of Bede that the two events, the eating of the goose and the calming of the sea, were intimately connected. Nor would it seem to him in any way disproportionate that the elements should rage for seven days merely because a few brethren had forgotten to eat a goose. The question of holy obedience was involved and even nature herself was at one with the saint in impressing the heinousness of their offence in disobeying even his simplest command. The story provided Bede with an opportunity of exalting the saint and of teaching a vital lesson which he was not slow to take advantage of. And his love of a picturesque incident may have played no little part in inducing him to include it: for it is abundantly clear that Bede did not fail to realize the value of miracle stories as picturesque additions to his narrative.

Such then are some of the miracles of which Bede tells us, backing them up as we have seen by appeals to numerous authorities—books which he had read or trustworthy witnesses —often eyewitnesses of the events, as in the story just related. But when we turn to the other lives of the saints we find the most extraordinary miracles related with precisely the same asseverations of truth. This feature goes back to Athanasius' Life of St. Antony, where in the preface Athanasius declares that he is writing what he himself knows and has learned from Antony himself. Then follow the stories of Antony's combats with devils, of miraculous springs, of visions of souls being carried to heaven, and of many miracles of healings. The sixth-century life of Samson of Dol is, we are told, written in a 'catholic and truthful manner' and yet we read how the saint learned to read in a day, how a dove rested upon him all through the ceremony of his ordination as deacon, how he drank poison with impunity, how a well sprang from the rock for his benefit.[1] Adamnan prefaces his Life of St. Columba with a warning that credence should be given to the stories, and very often names the witness as in the story of the pestiferous rain which the saint foresaw would destroy both men and cattle in Ireland. He sent Silnan at once to Ireland, who took some bread blessed by the saint and, putting it in water, used the infusion to heal both man and beast. 'That in all respects these things are most true, the above mentioned Silnan. . . bore witness in the presence of Seghine, the abbot, and of other aged men.' Bishop Jonas of Orleans, in the first half of the ninth century, wrote a life of St. Hubert, in the preface of which he professes to give the account as an eyewitness. But St. Hubert died in 727—Jonas in 843! It is clear then that when Bede produces his witnesses, he is acting in accordance with the hagiographical tradition of his times. This does not of course necessarily mean that he did not get the evidence as he said he did. Some of the miracles he relates, such as those connected with the life of Fursey, or of Germanus or of Cuthbert or of the nuns of Barking, are, as we have seen, based upon the lives in his possession. The stories had been written down and it is too much to expect of a historian of his age that he should have refused to give them credence. Speaking of the Anonymous Life of Cuthbert in his preface to the *Ecclesiastical History*, he tells us how he has 'yielded simple faith to the narrative'. It would almost have been an act of heresy if he had refused to believe these stories. And Bede was, as we know, particularly sensitive to any aspersion of this kind. But having the authority of tradition for finding his eyewitnesses, he would willingly accept their stories, coming as they did from the mouths of men of weight: nor need we expect that he would examine them after the manner of a modern barrister in a court of law to assure himself that the stories told by the eyewitnesses were not coloured by their imagination, or heightened in the retelling. We have learned nowadays how difficult it is to get the truth from perfectly trustworthy eyewitnesses and how often two such people, describing the same incident a few hours after its occurrence, will contradict one another flatly. How much more

---

[1] Quoted by Günter, *op. cit.* 171.

difficult was it to describe an incident which had happened years before: when the public opinion of the time demanded that a saint when alive, and his relics, when he was dead, should perform miracles: when, above all, there was the incentive to honour one's own patron saint above all other saints, and consequently to make him more glorious in his miracles! Bede has in fact done no less than he claimed to do, namely to 'labour to commit to writing with sincerity such things as we have gathered from common report, which is the true law of history'.[1]

What, we may ask ourselves, was his object in describing these miracles in his works? In the first place he has attempted to put down those things which 'were most worthy of note concerning the separate provinces or the more distinguished places, and pleasing to the inhabitants'. Popular opinion demanded that the traditions concerning the more famous saints should be duly recorded. Then the miracles of the saints were the means of testifying to the trustworthiness of the Gospel they preached. Æthilberht, for instance, was led to put his trust in the 'most pleasing promises' made by St. Augustine and his followers by the miracles they performed, as well as by the example of their lives.[2] St. Augustine healed a blind man to prove that he was a preacher of the divine truth, as opposed to the British party who were unable to cure the man.[3] Another reason was to extol the glory of the saint. For this reason he tells the story of the uncorrupt body of Fursey[4] and the miracles of Cuthbert;[5] for the same reason Gregory had collected the miracles of the saints in his *Dialogues*.[6] We have already seen that the visions of the underworld were intended to warn sinners and strengthen the faithful; so also the vision of Adamnan about Coldingham served, for a few days at any rate, to lead the inhabitants of the monastery to a better way of life.[7] We may look upon many of the miracles Bede relates in much the same light as the illustrative anecdotes with which preachers nowadays sometimes brighten their sermons; and how many of these stories, which, in all sincerity, are put forward as true, would bear a close investigation? Another, and perhaps by no means the least potent, reason was because of Bede's love for a picturesque story. His miracle stories provide some of the most famous passages in his *Ecclesiastical History*, such as the

---

[1] *H.E.* preface, *ad fin.*   [2] *Ibid.* i. 26.   [3] *Ibid.* ii. 2.
[4] *Ibid.* iii. 19.   [5] *Ibid.* iv. 30.   [6] *Ibid.* ii. 1.   [7] *Ibid.* iv. 25.

account of the death of Chad or the vision of Fursey. The Prose Life of Cuthbert is full of these picturesque narratives and although it cannot compare in historical importance with Eddius' Life of Wilfrid, it is much more readable. Few who have once read them could forget the stories about the birds on Farne Island or the vivid story of the angels who visited Ripon on a snowy day, or the account of Cuthbert's visit to the Roman ruins at Carlisle. Bede does not merely describe the incidents in threadbare language like many of the writers of legends of the saints. He so evidently takes pleasure in recounting the story with vivid details, that his pleasure transfers itself to the reader. And his skill as a literary artist makes the dry bones of many a traditional tale live again.

It has been pointed out that many of the miracles related by Bede need not necessarily be miraculous at all but merely 'coincidences brought about by perfectly natural means, though a devout mind will gladly believe that they have been divinely ordered'.[1] Such is the miracle which Bede describes as having happened to himself, when, singing the praises of Cuthbert, he was healed of an affection of the tongue,[2] or again the occasion when the young Cuthbert was cured of a swelling of the knee by applying a poultice according to the instruction of an angelic visitor on horseback.[3] Bede seems to feel a little compunction about this miracle, for he goes on to refute from scripture those who would doubt that an angel could appear on horseback. Poulticing is the remedy which the modern physician would prescribe for what he would probably diagnose as synovitis. Another similar miracle is the divine provision of wood from the sea for the building which Cuthbert was engaged upon on Farne.[4] And even Bede himself sometimes heightens the miraculous element in his stories as may be seen by comparing some of the incidents in Bede's Life of Cuthbert with the corresponding incidents in the Anonymous Life.[5]

There can be no doubt that Bede himself sincerely believed that the miracles he described really happened, but his views on the miraculous as set out in other parts of his writings seem to be hardly in keeping with his work as a hagiographer. He

---

[1] Cf. Plummer, i, p. lxiv.   [2] *Vit. Metr.* pref.   [3] *Vit. Cuth.* ii.
[4] *Ibid.* xxi.
[5] Cf. for instance ch. iv, v with the corresponding chapters in the Anonymous Life.

seems to have taken up much the same position as Gregory the Great whose works he knew so well. In one passage in the *Ecclesiastical History* he quotes at length a letter in which Gregory exhorts Augustine not to be puffed up by the miracles which he was performing. He was to remember the Master's answer to those who rejoiced in their power to cast out devils. 'In this rejoice not. . . . But rather rejoice because your names are written in heaven'.[1] They placed their joys in private and temporal affairs when they rejoiced in miracles, but these words recall them from private to public, from temporal to spiritual joys. For all the elect do not work miracles and yet all their names are written in heaven. And those who follow in the truth ought to have no joy except that which is common to all, a joy which knows no end.[2]

In another place Bede, borrowing from Gregory,[3] declares that miracles were necessary at the beginning of the church, just as when we put in a plant, we water it until we see that it has taken root: then we need no longer water it. And yet Gregory filled his *Dialogues* with the marvellous and Bede wrote his two Lives of Cuthbert. And further, neither Gregory nor Bede makes any references to these stories of marvels in their sermons and commentaries. It is true, Bede further declares that the cessation of miracles is largely due to man's sin and that some men by special holiness gain a power over creation which we have lost, because we neglect to serve the creator as we should.[4] But there seems to be in Bede as in most of the doctors of the Church, as Delehaye points out,[5] the voice of two men in each of them on the subject of miracles. Perhaps we ought to recognize three men in Bede, the theologian, the hagiographer, and the historian. To some extent the three were not altogether in harmony. When he was writing his homilies and commentaries, he was the theologian who accepted the general theory that the day of miracles was past, or at any rate that contemporary miracles were not altogether on the same footing as those of the days of Christ; when he wrote his Lives of Cuthbert he wrote as a hagiographer; when he was writing the Lives of the Abbots he wrote as a historian; but in the writing of the

---

[1] St. Luke x. 20.   [2] *H.E.* i. 31.
[3] Giles, x. 261; Gregory, *Hom. in Evang.* xxix, *P.L.* lxxvi. 1215.
[4] Giles, vii. 27, *Vit. Cuth.* xxi.
[5] *Analecta Bollandiana*, xxxviii. 77.

Ecclesiastical History both Bede the hagiographer and Bede the historian took part.[1] To exalt his heroes, to teach his lessons, and perhaps also for the sake of adding picturesque incident, he wrote down the miraculous stories which tradition provided and which he was not too careful to submit to close examination, and by quoting his authorities he cast the responsibility upon others. So, to some extent, the historian was satisfied. And when, as we have seen, his stories grew in the telling, it may well have been that the legend had grown even under his hands, for the saint's legend is essentially a popular growth: it is the people who make it and the hagiographer who writes it down. Bede the hagiographer was only a little in advance of his times. Bede the historian was far in advance of them. But how far the historical fact lies behind his hagiography is a difficult matter to decide.

We live in a time when the rapid advance in knowledge, both of the external world and of the human mind, has overwhelmed the self-confident materialism of the recent past, which, with its rigid principles, relegated most things for which it could not account to the realm of mere fiction. We can now afford to admit that there is a substantial basis of fact embedded in the stories we have considered. We may not regard the underlying facts in precisely the same light as did Bede and his contemporaries; but we are bound to treat with reverent sympathy the forms in which they embodied those facts and thus projected their own faith and hope upon the external world.

B. COLGRAVE.

---

[1] We have to remember, too, that Bede knew and used Eusebius' *Ecclesiastical History* and Rufinus' translation and continuation of it. So he may have been deliberately modelling his own history upon these works, in which the hagiographical element is kept in the background.

ADDITIONAL NOTE

Page 216, line 19. This incident also occurs in the Life of Gregory the Great, written by an anonymous monk of Whitby. It is just possible that Bede did not see this until after he had written his own account of Edwin's life. Hence the awkwardness of the interpolated incident. This theory might also account for Bede's remarkable omission of the miracles associated with the relics of Edwin which are related in the Whitby Life of Gregory.

VIII

THE MANUSCRIPTS OF BEDE

THE works of Bede, it is well known, are many and multifarious. The old printed editions extend to four or five folio volumes, and Migne's six octavos are a reprint of Giles's twelve. Bede himself at the end of the *History* records some forty titles, several of which comprise separate works. While even his list is not quite complete, the editions *en revanche* contain much that is not his.

Of the genuine works almost every one has had a great reputation in its day and has been preserved for us in quite numerous copies. The catalogues of monastic libraries give some indication of their popularity. Thus Christ Church, Canterbury, and St. Augustine's respectively give titles of twelve and twenty works. Bury St. Edmunds seems to have had forty tracts genuine and spurious, Durham nine volumes at least, Leicester about the same. A survey of continental catalogues would add vastly to the list, but is hardly worth undertaking. It would but emphasize the undoubted fact that works of Bede were a regular constituent of monastic libraries, perhaps especially during the twelfth century.

The majority of these works have suffered in popularity by the lapse of time. The largest class of them consists of commentaries upon the Scriptures. They are for the most part drawn from earlier writers whose works we possess; and though wherever Bede speaks for himself it is with a piety deserving of all admiration, he has not much that is new to tell, and his attachment to the allegorical method, especially for the old Testament, antiquates this whole department of his writings. To fill these pages with a list of the extant manuscripts of them, or of the equally popular Homilies, would be a waste of labour. We shall do better to concentrate upon the work that is very far from being antiquated—the *History*.

Of the fame and wide diffusion of this great book there is no doubt. Hardy in his well-known *Descriptive Catalogue of Materials* (Rolls Series, 1862) gives a list of over 130 manuscripts of it, ranging from the eighth to the fifteenth century, and scattered among forty or more libraries, British and foreign, and that list is neither accurate nor complete. It is exceeded in bulk in Hardy's book, as Plummer has remarked, by only one work purporting to be historical, viz. that of Geoffrey of Monmouth. Hardy's equally defective list of the manuscripts of that runs to over 170 numbers. Bede's truth was not quite so popular as Geoffrey's romance, but for all that its vogue was very great.

In this crowd of manuscripts of the *History* there are four which excel the rest in age, and upon them our standard text, that of Plummer (Oxford, 1896) is based. They are:

1. M. Cambridge University Library Kk. 5. 16. Its date is put at about 737 (almost in the author's lifetime) and the place of writing is conjectured to have been Epternach (or Echternach) or some such Anglo-Saxon colony on the other side of the Channel. It once belonged to a church of St. Julian, doubtless the cathedral of Le Mans. In 1697 it was owned by one J. B. Hautin in France and was bought from him with other manuscripts by John Moore, who died bishop of Ely in 1714. Moore's magnificent library was purchased *en bloc* by George I (at the suggestion, it is said, of Lord Townshend) and was presented to the University of Cambridge in 1715. It served as the primary authority for Smith's edition in 1722, and, though not absolutely faultless, has stood at the head of all copies of the *History* ever since. It is not distinguished for beauty of script—'Hiberno-Saxon minuscule' is the character of the hand—nor has it any but the simplest ornament. But it is one of the most important, and, like its author, venerable, books in the country.

2. B. British Museum. Cotton Tiberius A. xiv. This is pronounced by Plummer to be a sister book to M. It is of the eighth century, but we know nothing of its history or its owners before it came into the hands of Sir Robert Cotton. We might have known more but for the fact that the book was dreadfully damaged in the fire of 1731 which wrought great havoc in the Cottonian collection.

3. C. British Museum. Cotton Tiberius. C. ii. Also of the eighth century: only slightly damaged by the fire. That this is a Durham book seems to be demonstrated by the readings it contains; but no library-mark has survived, nor do the ancient Durham catalogues admit of its being identified.

4. N. Namur, Bibliothèque de la ville no. 2. Again of the eighth century. It was written abroad and copied from a

manuscript in 'insular' hand by a number of scribes. It once belonged to the abbey of St. Hubert in the Ardennes. Its text is markedly inferior to those of M, B, C.

It is not very easy to select from among later manuscripts the most important, but Plummer has to a great extent cleared the way by discriminating between the descendants of the ancient copies, particularly M, B, C. N has no perceptible descendants.

Of those which descend from M one, Brit. Mus. Harley 4978, a French book of the tenth century, is a direct copy. Indeed the scribe of it has actually made some few additions to M. But only seven copies are classed as descendants of M. One, Brit. Mus. Add. 18150, is of the eleventh century and comes from St. Georgenberg in the Tyrol. The manuscripts descended from C fall into two groups, one connected with Durham (C itself is a Durham book), another with Winchester.

The Durham group is headed by the manuscript B ii. 35, in the Durham Chapter Library. It is of the twelfth century with additions of the fourteenth, and furnishes a good text of Bede's Lives of the Abbots, as well as a text of 'Nennius' M; altogether a valuable book. A direct descendant of this is Brit. Mus. Burney 310, of the year 1381. Other manuscripts of the group traceable to this source are Brit. Mus. Harley 4124 from Worksop, of cent. XII, and Pembroke College, Cambridge, 82, also of cent. XII from Tynemouth Priory. Both these have the Lives of the Abbots.

The first of the Winchester group is a tenth-century copy in the Chapter Library at Winchester (no. 3) which is thought to come from Glastonbury. The scribe's name was Ædelelmus; and he has written a colophon, perhaps copied from an older manuscript, in 'very poor Irish'. A portion of this volume seems to have strayed into the Cotton MS. Tiberius D. iv. Only one clear descendant of W is known, viz. Balliol College 176 of cent. XII, given to the College with many other manuscripts by William Gray, bishop of Ely (d. 1478). Its provenance is uncertain.

A few more manuscripts may be picked out which seem to deserve attention from age or origin. Bodl. Hatton 43 of cent. XI is perhaps from Glastonbury; Bodl. 712 of cent. XIV was written for Robert Wyvill, bishop of Salisbury 1330–75; Brit. Mus. Royal 13. c. v of cent. X–XI is from Gloucester Abbey; Bodl. Douce 368 (cent. XII) from Winchcombe; Bodl. Laud.

Misc. 243 (cent. XII) belonged to Archbishop Ussher; Bodl. 163 of cent. XI–XII is from Peterborough and contains an early list of the books there; Bodl. Fairfax 12 (cent. XII) is from Selby; Brit. Mus. Add. 14250 (cent. XIII) from Plympton; Bodl. Digby 211 (cent. XII) from Waltham Abbey; Brit. Mus. Harley 3680 (cent XII–XIII) is from Rochester. All these have texts of the C type more or less.

It was never the fashion to make the *History* into a picture-book; indeed only two copies that I have seen are really remarkable for their ornamentation, viz. Trinity College, Cambridge, R. 7. 3 (no. 741) of cent. XIV, which has a bordered page recalling the best work in the East Anglian Psalters of that date, and Emmanuel College, no. 3, of 1481, written for Dean Gunthorpe of Wells, and embellished with his arms and with other decoration of a sumptuous kind.

Perhaps it will be best at this point to say something of the manuscripts of the Anglo-Saxon version of the *History*. There are but five, used and described by Thomas Miller for the Early English Text Society's edition. They are:

1. Bodl. Tanner 10, of late tenth-century date. Miller considers that it cannot have been produced at a large monastery; yet there is evidence in it (not noted by him) that it did belong to Thorney Abbey.

2. Brit. Mus. Cotton Otho B. xi, of similar date. Only 38 leaves or fragments of the *History* have survived the fire. The book originally contained a copy of the Anglo-Saxon Chronicle, lists of bishops, and laws. It belonged to Southwick Priory in Hampshire which owned other precious Anglo-Saxon books, perhaps even the unique copy of *Beowulf*.

3. Corpus Christi College, Cambridge, 41, of cent. XI. This was one of the books given by Leofric to his cathedral of Exeter, and has his inscription of donation. On the margins of its leaves a great deal of interesting matter has been written; prayers and charms and part of the dialogue known as *Salomon and Saturn*.

4. Corpus Christi College, Oxford, 279. of cent XI, written by a number of scribes. It shares with the next manuscript the peculiarity of omitting without notice a considerable piece of the text, where the archetype had lost two or more leaves. With it is bound up a fourteenth-century copy of the Latin text of Bede. I have a suspicion that it was the property of the celebrated Dr. John Dee, many of whose manuscripts are in the

same library and were given to it by the donor of this one, viz. Brian Twine. Dee also owned the Lauderdale manuscript of Alfred's Orosius, now at Helmingham.

5. Cambridge University Library Kk. 3. 18, of cent. XI.   In this there is some writing in a 'tremulous' hand which occurs in certain Worcester manuscripts. The book is therefore noted by Wolfgang Keller as coming from Worcester; and the link just described between it and no. 4 makes a Worcester origin likely for that also.

Bede's other historical tracts can be more shortly dealt with. Of the Lives of the Abbots, written after 716, there are eight manuscripts. The oldest is Brit. Mus. Harley 3020, of cent. X. It may come from Winchester, for the transcript of it in Bodl. Digby 112 (cent. XII) has much Winchester matter in it. Another twelfth-century copy, Brit. Mus. Cotton Tiberius D. iii once belonged to Savile of Banke, and may be from Ramsey. The rest of the group are all closely connected with Durham B. ii, 35, viz. Pembroke College, Cambridge, 82, Harley 4124, Burney 310, and Bodl. Fairfax 6.

The historical and chronological tracts, *De Temporibus* (703), *De Temporum Ratione* (725), etc., had a great vogue. Bede's masterly innovation of reckoning years from the Incarnation was deservedly popular, and we need not be surprised to find that many of the oldest manuscripts are in continental libraries. Paris Lat. 7530 and Cologne 103 may be of the eighth century: five more old ones are at Paris, three at St. Gall, two at Monte Cassino, and so on.

The two Lives of St. Cuthbert, in verse and prose, were early works, the metrical one before 705. The oldest appears to be Brit. Mus. Harley 526 of cent. IX, but the finest I reckon to be that at Corpus Christi College, Cambridge (183), given about the year 931 to the see of St. Cuthbert, then at Chester-le Street, by King Æthelstan. It is exquisitely written, and has a frontispiece showing the king presenting the book to St. Cuthbert. This is almost the only work of Bede which attracted illustrators. We have two finely pictured copies: Brit. Mus. Add. 39943, made at Durham and entered in the old Catalogues, and University College, Oxford, 165, not so certainly from Durham. A third, Trinity College, Cambridge, O. 1. 64 (no. 1088), which belonged to Coventry Cathedral, was meant to be illustrated, but was never finished.

As has been said, a vast mass of Bede's work has to be passed over: but a word is due to the Retractations on the Acts, in which he supplements his commentary on that book. It is particularly interesting as showing that he could use a Greek book, and yet more so because we happen to possess the actual manuscript which lay before him. It is not to be doubted that this was the uncial Graeco-Latin manuscript of the Acts of the seventh century, now Bodl. Laud. Gr. 35. In the interim between its sojourn at Jarrow (to which it may have been brought by Benedict Biscop or Hadrian from Italy) and its arrival at Oxford it had travelled to Germany.

I do not think that manuscripts of the Retractations are common; but I should like to note that one of cent. XII, acquired not long ago by the Royal Library at Copenhagen (Ny. Kgl. S 1854), seems to me to have come from Peterborough Abbey.

Perhaps the last topic which can conveniently be treated here is the question of the autographs of Bede. In the medieval catalogues of the Durham library certain items are marked as being 'de manu Bede'. The Catalogues in question were edited for the Surtees Society in 1838 by 'B.B.', i.e. Beriah Botfield. The volume is usually quoted as *Catalogi Veteres*. The entries in question are as follows: (1) pp. 16, 92. *D. Quatuor Evangelia, de manu Bede*: 2 fo. baptizatus. This is now A. ii. 16 in the library, of cent. VII–VIII. It is *Δ* in Wordsworth and White's N.T. and was lent to Bentley. It is in beautiful uncials of a rather Italian character. A small slip from it was presented in 1700 by the Dean and Chapter to Samuel Pepys, and is now no. 18 in his 'Calligraphical Collection', no. 2981 in the Pepysian Library in Magdalene College, Cambridge. A similar cutting from manuscript A. ii. 17 is no. 19 in the same album. (2, 3) pp. 18, 93. *K. Epistole Pauli glosate de manu Bede*: 2 fo. Paulus. On p. 93 is added 'nihil valent'. *L. Epistole Pauli glosate de manu Bede*: 2 fo. Et post. Page 93 again adds 'nihil valent'. The manuscript here marked K is not known to exist. That marked L is at Trinity College, Cambridge, B. 10. 5. (no. 216); that is to say 67 leaves of it are there. Four others are in the Cottonian collection in the volume Vitellius C. viii. These bear the old label of the fourteenth century. *L. Epistole Pauli de manu Bede*. The hand is far more irregular than that of A ii. 16. The disparaging note in the old catalogue, 'nihil valent', resembles some in the old Glastonbury catalogue, and may be taken to mean that the later monks found the hand hard to read. (4) To these must be added the book entered on pp. 13, 88: *E. Cassiodorus super psalterium*: 2 fo. modulaciones. Though not marked here as Bede's, the book, still at Durham (B. ii. 33), has an old note of the fourteenth century 'Cassiodorus super psalterium de manu Bede'. A small facsimile of it is in *Cat. Vet.* p. 213, and shows it to be in an insular hand, not very unlike that of no. 3, but more comely.

That Bede was a diligent scribe as well as author is certain, but that he studied use rather than beauty is most likely. If any of the alleged autographs are really his, nos. 3 and 4 of the above list are better claimants than no. 1; but I do not know what evidence other than that of the catalogues (which is late but must have fairly long tradition behind it) could be adduced in their favour.[1]   MONTAGUE R. JAMES.

[1] It must not be assumed that the above pages contain a complete census of the early manuscripts even of the *History*. Some of those in continental libraries are as yet imperfectly known: for instance, one at Cassel, from the abbey of Fulda, is assigned to the eighth century, and has not been used by editors, while others may emerge. My own survey has been limited almost wholly to English translations and to printed editions.

IX

THE LIBRARY OF THE VENERABLE BEDE

EVERY student interested in the intellectual history of the
Early Middle Ages must regret that, in contrast to the
substantial information available for the continent of western
Europe, so little is known of the state of English libraries during
the same period. Early catalogues of the collections at Fulda,
Würzburg, Reichenau, St. Gallen, Fleury, not to mention many
smaller religious houses, still survive ; and, even when they have
been preserved only in part, they throw an invaluable light on
the state of learning in France and Germany during the late
eighth and the ninth centuries. No such book-lists exist of the
monastic and cathedral libraries in contemporary England.
The concluding section of Alcuin's poem on the see and bishops
of York is but a poor substitute for an official inventory of what
was regarded in his day as an unusually rich collection of books,
sacred and profane. Alcuin's list is marred by two serious
defects, both inseparable from the metrical form in which the
information is imparted to the reader. The poet names only the
authors and not their writings, so that, unless one is prepared
to maintain the entirely untenable thesis that all the works of
so prolific a scholar as Augustine were to be found at York, the
occurrence of Augustine's name is not very helpful. Again, it is
certain that exigencies of metre compelled Alcuin to omit the
names of writers who were certainly represented to some extent
in the library, for example, Isidore of Seville. Thus, in order to
reconstruct as far as possible a catalogue of the books to which
Bede had access more than half a century before, one must have
recourse to his own statements and to a comparison of his works
with earlier commentators. The task is made more difficult by
the fact that a careful examination of Bede's authorities has
been carried out for very few of his writings. Plummer has
tracked down the sources of the *Ecclesiastical History* and
Mommsen has done the same for the *Chronicle*. Father Sutcliffe
has listed the borrowings from the Four Doctors of the Latin
Church in the commentary on Mark, in so far as they are indicated
by marginal letters in the two manuscripts that he used. But the
list is incomplete even for those four authors and takes no

account of the other authorities. The present attempt to determine the contents of Bede's working library does not claim
to be final. Completeness will not be attainable until the entire
corpus of Bede's works can be read in editions answering to the
demands of modern scholarship.

It would be unjustifiable to assume that all the books consulted by Bede throughout a long life devoted to scholarship
were actually to be found in his day in the libraries of Wearmouth and Jarrow. Just as friends and admirers in different
parts of the country supplied him with biographical *data* or
local traditions which he utilized in the composition of the
Ecclesiastical History, so it may be supposed that books not to
be found in the twin monasteries were occasionally borrowed
from centres like Lindisfarne or Canterbury for consultation
or copying. Indeed, when one observes that both Aldhelm and
Bede show familiarity with some relatively rare work or one by
a little known author, for instance, Cyprianus Gallus' epic on
the Pentateuch, Evagrius' translation of Athanasius' Life of
St. Antony, or even the pseudo-Clementine *Recognitiones*,
although they had a wider appeal, it is a reasonable deduction
that single examples of such works existed in the south of
England, presumably at Canterbury, before Bede's time and in
due course were borrowed by him. If time and circumstance
allowed, the copy might be duplicated by him or under his
direction. Unhappily Bede, although he has much to tell about
the early years of the two monasteries with which his name is
inseparably linked and about their first abbots, makes only very
general statements when he alludes to the libraries. Benedict
Biscop brought back many treasures to Northumbria after his
several journeys to the Continent, and amongst them were many
manuscripts. The language used by the historian makes it
clear that there was a preponderance of theological works.[1]
How large 'the most noble and abundant library' may have
been on Benedict's death it is impossible to estimate. Besides,
Bede's phraseology is a little rhetorical, since he uses almost the
identical words to describe the library collected by Bishop
Acca at Hexham.[2] Ceolfrid during his abbacy enlarged the

---

[1] The books brought back by Benedict Biscop from his fourth and sixth
journeys were theological (*H.A.* 4, 9). From his fifth journey to Rome he
returned with a more diversified selection, *innumerabilem librorum omnis
generis copiam* (*ibid.* 6).

[2] Cf. *H.A.* 11 and *H.E.* v. 20.

library of Wearmouth-Jarrow still further; indeed, if Bede's account is to be taken literally, he doubled its resources.[1] Amongst these additional books were three copies of the Vulgate. One of them, which Ceolfrid later set out to take to Rome as a gift to Gregory II, still survives, the so-called *Codex Amiatinus* in the Laurentian library at Florence.

But if Bede is vague about the twin libraries to which he had access, he fortunately was so modest about his own remarkable erudition that he was impelled to inform his readers in many places of the authorities on which his own works were based. In the introduction to his edition of the *Ecclesiastical History* the late Charles Plummer drew up a list of writers named in Bede.[2] Plummer himself was well aware that his catalogue of some 130 authors was only tentative. If it has to be pointed out here that the list needs correction in three ways, no adverse criticism is implied of that scholar. The more students of Bede use Plummer's introduction and commentary, the more they will be impressed by his profound knowledge both of Bede's life and work and of the times in which he lived. In the first place, many of the quotations from authors listed by Plummer were obtained by Bede at second hand, and consequently they cannot be used as evidence for his direct acquaintance with those writers. This, as will be seen, is especially the case with citations from classical Latin authors. For this reason some thirty names can be eliminated from Plummer's catalogue. Again, the same editor has included a good many 'phantom' authorities, for instance, Jovinianus and Helvidius, although the allusion implied by Bede is to Jerome's treatises against these two advocates of heterodoxy; or Ignatius and Polycarp, about whom Bede merely relates some biographical item.[3] Finally there are a few authors whom Bede never mentions by name; yet he can be shown to have consulted, or even copied from, their writings, for example, Victorinus of Pettau and Salonius.

In his theological treatises Bede points out over and over again that he is but following the footsteps of the Fathers.[4] Not

[1] *H.A.* 15, *bibliothecam utriusque monasterii . . . ipse non minori geminavit industria.* The author of *H.A. An.* (xx) more cautiously writes, *nobiliter ampliavit.*   [2] Plummer, i, pp. l-li.
[3] The story about Ignatius (*P.L.* xciii. 187 B) is derived from Jerome, *De viris illustribus,* that about Polycarp (*P.L.* xciii. 122 B) from Rufinus' translation of Eusebius.
[4] e.g. *P.L.* xci. 758 A, *sequens magnorum vestigia tractatorum; ibid.* 1077 B,

infrequently he adds valuable particulars, as in his preface to the commentary on Genesis where he groups together as his main authorities the *Hexaemeron* of Basil and of Ambrose and several treatises by Augustine. Or again, in the introduction to his exposition of Ezra and Nehemiah he informs his readers that he has consulted Jerome's commentaries on those prophets of the Old Testament who had foretold the events narrated in the two historical books.[1] In the commentaries themselves Bede's practice varied and he appears to follow no consistent usage. Often he merely gives an earlier writer's name as authority for a certain statement or interpretation. Less frequently the reference is more precise and indicates not only the author but the treatise cited. But far more commonly there is nothing in Bede's text to show that he has borrowed from a predecessor. His debt, for example, to Gregory the Great can be traced in all his commentaries; yet the occasions on which he names that pope are a very small percentage of the places where he cites him at greater or shorter length. In justice to Bede, however, it must be pointed out that in the prefaces to his commentaries on Luke and on Mark he expressly states that he had indicated his indebtedness to others by signs in the margins of his manuscript. Father Sutcliffe was the first to draw attention to two extant *codices* of the commentary on Mark now in the Vatican Library in which these source-marks for material taken from the Four Doctors of the Church are still preserved. More recently the present writer has been able to add other manuscripts of this work in which similar *marginalia* survive wholly or in part, and, in addition, to list some surviving *codices* of the commentary on Luke in which a similar procedure was followed.[2] Quite probably Bede adopted the same device to show what he had borrowed in his other expository works, but he does not allude to it save in the two passages named. Consequently his copyists appear to have reproduced the source-marks only in the two commentaries for which he left explicit directions and to have ignored them in others.[3] In any case the commentaries

seduli patrum vestigia sequentes; *P.L.* xcii. 134 A, *maxime quae in patrum venerabilium exemplis invenimus, hinc inde collecta ponere curabimus.* Cf. also *H.E.* 5, 24; *P.L.* xcii. 304 D.

[1] Cf. *P.L.* xci. 9 A–11 A, 808 B.

[2] E. J. Sutcliffe in *Biblica*, vii (1926), 428–39; M. L. W. Laistner in *Journ. Theol. Stud.* xxxiv (1933), 350–5.

[3] The two passages will be found in *P.L.* xcii, 134 A and 304 D. The judgement that I have ventured to express above is, of course, provisional; for the

on Luke and on Mark are very closely linked. Karl Werner long ago pointed out that the commentary on Mark, which is considerably later in date than the other, reproduces many passages from the earlier work.[1] But his brief statement hardly gives a complete picture of the facts; for a careful comparison of the two treatises shows that nearly one-third of the commentary on Mark is copied word for word from the commentary on Luke. As much of this duplicated material is borrowed, any future editor of the commentary on Luke will derive great help from studying the sources identified by Father Sutcliffe for the Mark commentary.

Such evidence as can be gleaned to demonstrate Bede's acquaintance with pagan Latin writers is to found mainly in the three school-treatises, De arte metrica, De schematibus et tropis, De orthographia. Although only the first can be approximately dated—it was composed while Bede was still a deacon, that is, before 703—it is likely that all three were early works, just as their contents suggest that they were all put together by Bede for the use of his own pupils. The De schematibus et tropis, moreover, is not so much a separate work as an appendix to the De arte metrica. This last-named work and the De orthographia are compiled from grammarians of the later Roman imperial age. It is surprising how many of these were available in England at the end of the seventh century, namely: Donatus, Charisius, Diomedes, Pompeius, Sergius, Audax, Victorinus, Mallius Theodorus, Servius, Agroecius, Caper, and possibly Dositheus. The framework of the De schematibus et tropis is derived from two chapters of Isidore's Etymologies (1, 36–7); for not only is the order in which the terms are defined almost identical, but many of the definitions are the same, or nearly so. In one respect, however, Bede diverges from his predecessors. All the illustratory quotations in the De schematibus et tropis are taken from the Bible with one exception, and that comes from the Christian poet Sedulius. In the De arte metrica and De orthographia more examples are drawn from the Bible and Christian writers than from pagan sources. But the citations from poets and prose writers of the classical period nearly all occur in the grammarians used by Bede or in the Etymologies of Isidore.

fifty odd manuscripts of various Bede commentaries, other than those on Luke and Mark, that I have seen, are but a fraction of what survives.

[1] K. Werner, Beda der Ehrwürdige, 195.

They cannot therefore be used as proof of direct acquaintance with these ancient authors.[1] In his later works quotations from pagan literature other than Virgil are exceedingly rare. A tag from Sallust in the commentary on Mark—*concordia parvae res crescunt*—is taken with the rest of the passage in which it occurs from Jerome.[2] The fable of the crow who tried to masquerade as a peacock in Bede's version differs from that in Phaedrus.[3] A line from Horace is not enough to prove that Bede had read the *Epistles*.[4] Virgil, however, Bede seems to have known at first hand; for he reproduces enough verses from the poet to warrant this assumption. Virgil was, moreover, a favourite with the Irish and the existence of his works in England before Bede's time is made certain by Aldhelm's intimate familiarity with the poems. In his later years Bede, when he introduced citations, appears to have relied on what he had learnt of the poet in his youth; for in no less than three instances he misquotes the poet, once so badly that he introduces false quantities.[5]

If Bede's knowledge of classical authors was slight and mostly acquired through intermediate sources, he had read widely in the Christian poets. Besides taking many illustrations from them for his early school-treatises, he inserted suitable passages from time to time in his later works.[6] Thus the range of his reading included Ambrose, Juvencus, Prudentius,

[1] For further particulars see *T.R.H.S.* 72–4.

[2] *P.L.* xcii. 163 c from *P.L.* xxvi. 79 c.

[3] Bede (*P.L.* xci. 489 B) calls the bird *cornix* and says that the irate peacocks robbed him of his false plumage and his life. The *graculus* in Phaedrus (i. 3), though stripped of his finery, does not die. Jerome in a letter (*Epist.* cviii. 15) with which Bede was familiar alludes to the fable in a general way.

[4] Horace, *Epist.* I. ii. 69–70 in *P.L.* xci. 1002 D. The Horace citations in Bede's school-treatises are all found in the grammarians.

[5] The examples are: *Ecl.* ii. 22 in *P.L.* xci. 1019 c (cf. *T.R.H.S.* 74); *P.L.* xci. 1101 A, where he makes three errors in two lines from the *Georgics* (iii. 414–15); and *P.L.* xci. 1189 c, where, in citing *Aen.* i. 723–4, he begins the second line in such a way as to scan *crateras* as an anapaest. It is barely possible that the printed editions, based as they are on late manuscripts, misrepresent what Bede actually wrote. But it is improbable; for the last of three lines of Arator cited by Bede in his commentary on Acts (*P.L.* xcii. 945 B) is misquoted, so that it will not scan, in nine manuscripts that I have collated. Two of these were written at the end of the eighth century, the other seven in the ninth. Another example of misquotation by Bede will be found below, p. 245, n. 2.

[6] e.g. Sedulius is cited in *P.L.* xci. 733 D; xcii. 615 D; xcii. 480 B; Paulinus in xcii. 398 D; Fortunatus in xciii. 138 and *H.E.* i. 7; Prosper in *H.E.* i. 10; Arator frequently in the commentary on Acts and also in *P.L.* xciii. 200 A.

Paulinus of Nola, whose versified *Life of Felix* Bede also turned into prose, Sedulius, Prosper, Fortunatus, Arator, and Cyprianus Gallus. Cyprianus' epic on the Pentateuch, though far less known than the other Christian poems, also figured in Aldhelm's library. A few reminiscences in the *Life of St. Cuthbert* and in certain shorter poems attributed to Bede suggest that perhaps Petrus Petricoriensis, Dracontius, and Alcimus Avitus may be added to the list, although the evidence is not strong.[1]

Bede's interest in scientific subjects, and especially in questions of chronology, persisted throughout his life. Earliest in date of the works to which he turned for guidance was the *Natural History* of Pliny. He used Book ii extensively in his three scientific treatises and also in the *Ecclesiastical History*. Occasional quotations demonstrate his use of Books iv, v, vi, xiii, and xvi. In his commentary on the Song of Songs he offers an apology for introducing disquisitions on trees and aromatic shrubs derived from 'the books of the ancients'; for he, and others born and bred in a northern island, could not learn anything about the *flora* of Arabia, India, Judaea, and Egypt save from authors familiar with those regions.[2] The ancient source proves to be Book xii of the *Natural History* from which he inserts excerpts of considerable length into his commentary.[3] With the possible exception of Book xxxvii, the later part of Pliny's encyclopaedia appears to have remained unknown to Bede. Book xviii, for example, would have been invaluable to him when he wrote his *De temporum ratione*, and the absence of all citations from it is convincing proof that it was not in Bede's library. Besides, extant manuscripts of Pliny, though very numerous, are rarely complete, and none of those belonging to the earlier group contains more than a small portion of the work. As for Book xxxvii, Bede, in commenting on the twenty-first chapter of Revelation, discourses at some length on the various gems there mentioned. Although his main guide was Isidore and, in one case, Cassiodorus, his phraseology makes it

---

[1] Cf. M. Manitius in *Sitzungsberichte*, Vienna Academy, philol.-hist. Klasse, cxii (1886), 616 ff. I have omitted Symphosius from the list in the text, as the work from which Manitius (*op. cit.* 614–17) takes his examples is probably not by Bede himself.　　　　[2] *P.L.* xci. 1077 B.

[3] e.g. *P.L.* xci. 1098 A *Arbores balsami* to 1098 B *minima ligno*, abbreviated from Pliny, *N.H.* xii. 112–18. 1143 D *Arbor est* to 1144 A *nuncupamus*, abbreviated from *N.H.* xii. 58–62. 1144 A *Regio* to 1144 B *nitrosis*, from *N.H.* xii. 52–3. 1146 A *Cyprus*, cf. *N.H.* xii. 109. 1148 A *Est autem myrrha* to *accepit myrrha*, from *N.H.* xii. 67.

likely that he knew that book of Pliny. The assumption that there was a manuscript of Book xxxvii in England is greatly strengthened by the fact that Aldhelm also makes some brief citations from it.[1] Bede in the *De temporibus* and *De natura rerum* inserted much from Isidore's *Etymologies* and *De natura rerum*. His use of Macrobius' *Saturnalia* in the *De temporibus* and *De temporum ratione* is also beyond dispute. A close examination of the last-named treatise, the maturest fruit of Bede's scientific studies, reveals remarkably wide reading in the specialized literature bearing on chronology and the Paschal question. When one remembers how bitter were the disagreements between the adherents of the Irish and the Roman usage in the matter of the Easter celebration, one can well understand why Benedict Biscop, Ceolfrid, and perhaps some others should have taken special pains to acquire as complete a collection of relevant books as possible. Thus Bede was able to peruse, besides patristic works in which these topics were touched upon incidentally, several tracts by Dionysius Exiguus, Victor of Capua, Victorius of Aquitaine, Polemius Silvius, a Latin version of Theophilus' letter to Theodosius I, the so-called Irish forgeries, and perhaps some other treatises or letters.[2]

Bede's historical library has engaged the attention of Mommsen and of Plummer. With the exception of Josephus, his authorities belong to the later Roman imperial or the early medieval period. Jerome's translation of Eusebius' *Chronicle* and Rufinus' version of Eusebius' *Ecclesiastical History* were of basic importance. More occasional use was made of Solinus, Orosius, Eutropius' *Breviarium*, Cassiodorus' *Tripartite History*; the *Chronicles* of Prosper, Marcellinus, Marius of Avenches, and Isidore of Seville; Jerome's *De viris illustribus* with Gennadius' continuation, the *Liber Pontificalis* and Gildas; also three noteworthy biographies, to wit, Paulinus' *Life of Ambrose*, Possidius' biography of Augustine, and the *Life of Germanus of Auxerre* by Constantius. The little tract, *De locis sanctis*, contains extracts from the *De situ Iudaeae* which bears the

---

[1] Cf. the index of authors in Ehwald's edition (*MGH. Auct. Antiq.* xv). His evidence that Aldhelm knew *N.H.* xxxii is quite unconvincing.

[2] No attempt has been made here to consider the source of Bede's scientific writings in detail. I have derived great help from the dissertation of C. W. Jones (cf. *T.R.H.S.* 76, note 1), who is preparing a critical text and detailed commentary of the *De temporum ratione*. Cf. also his article in *Speculum*, ix (1934), 50–6, on Bede and Polemius Silvius.

name of Eucherius of Lyons but is probably not by him. However, proof of Bede's acquaintance with these various compositions does not rest merely on the evidence of the *Chronicle* and *Ecclesiastical History*. Often valuable confirmation of his thorough familiarity with these historical authorities is found in his exegetical works. Thus, a long description of the Caspian Sea is repeated verbally from Orosius. Marcellinus is the source from which Bede transcribes the discovery of John the Baptist's head and the translation of the precious relic to Edessa. Another tradition regarding John's burial and later exhumation appears to be based on the *Tripartite History* of Cassiodorus.[1] Many biographical details about the apostles, evangelists, and other notable persons in the early centuries of the Christian era are taken from Rufinus' translation of Eusebius or from Jerome's *De viris illustribus*. In discussing the vice of slander or backbiting Bede, without naming his source, reinforces his point by repeating a tale from Possidius' Life of Augustine. According to this Augustine's dining-table bore an inscription bidding slanderers begone:[2]

> Quisquis amat dictis absentum rodere vitam
> Hanc mensam indignam noverit esse sibi.

To the list of historians already given two additions must be made, Gregory of Tours and Vegetius. In his *Retractations on Acts* Bede, in the course of commenting on the sickness of Publius (Acts xxviii. 8), transcribes part of Gregory's description of the epidemic which wrought great havoc in Gaul in A.D. 580.[3] That towards the end of his life he obtained or borrowed a copy of Vegetius' *Epitoma rei militaris* has been demonstrated by C. W. Jones.[4]

Bede's use of Josephus is a matter of some interest and not without complexity because he does not seem to adhere to any uniform practice. There are passages where the context shows clearly that he is citing Josephus from an intermediate source, for instance, Rufinus or Jerome. In one or two places he indicates this method himself, as when he introduces a quotation

---

[1] Orosius I, 2, 48–50 in *P.L.* xci. 868 D; Marcellinus (*MGH. Auct. Ant.* xi. 84–5) in *P.L.* xcii. 192 D–193 A; Cassiod. *Hist. Trip.* vi. 15 and ix. 27–8 used for *P.L.* xcii. 190 D.

[2] Possidius, 22. Bede quotes the lines (*P.L.* xci. 1010 A–B) inaccurately.

[3] *P.L.* xcii. 1032 B from Greg. Tur. *Hist. Franc.* v. 26 (34).

[4] See *Class. Rev.* xlvi (1932), 248–9. Sir George Macdonald published a slight correction in the same journal, xlvii (1933), 124.

with the words, *quia Eusebius Iosephum secutus,* or, *Hieronymus ex Iosepho scribit.*[1] Elsewhere the subject-matter is derived from the Jewish historian but the actual words are Bede's own. In the third place, Bede sometimes transcribes shorter or longer excerpts word for word from the old Latin version of Josephus which had been made at Vivarium at the instance of Cassiodorus. In Bede's commentary on Acts, five out of six citations attributed to Josephus are taken, as the context shows, from Rufinus' translation of Eusebius. The sixth refers to an episode in the Old Testament and therefore the original source was the *Jewish Antiquities* of Josephus, not the *Jewish Wars.* A passage from the treatise against Apion is introduced by Bede into his *Epistle to Plegwin,* but the phraseology of the extract does not correspond to the Cassiodorian version. It is in his commentaries on the Old Testament that Bede most often appeals to the authority of Josephus, especially in his *De tabernaculo,* an exposition of Exodus xxiv–xxx, and in the *De templo Salomonis,* a commentary on I Kings v. In these two works the longest excerpts from the Cassiodorian version of Josephus occur.[2] From Bede's *De locis sanctis* it is clear that he had at his disposal a copy of Hegesippus' abbreviated Latin version of Josephus' *Jewish Wars.* Thus, to sum up the somewhat confusing evidence, it would seem that Bede had the Cassiodorian version of the *Antiquities* only. For the *Jewish Wars* he appears to have depended primarily on intermediate sources like Rufinus and Jerome; he does not apparently quote verbally from Hegesippus in any of his commentaries on the New Testament. Unfortunately there is nothing to show whether, in addition, he had access to, or used, a text of Josephus in the original Greek. There are many passages where he appeals to the authority of the *Antiquities,* and yet comparison of the two authors shows

[1] *P.L.* xcii. 1022 c and *P.L.* xci. 482 c.

[2] For example, *P.L.* xci. 413 B–C, 440 D–441 A from *Antiq.* iii. 7; 481 B–D from *Antiq.* iii. 8; 746 A, 774 D–775 A from *Antiq.* viii. 3. The quotation in xci. 413 c was also used by Bede in his commentary on *Samuel* (*P.L.* xci. 653 A) and in part in the commentary on Luke (*P.L.* xcii. 394 A). The Cassiodorian version of the *Antiquities,* pending its publication in *C.S.E.L.,* is not easily procured, as the Latin translations published since the first half of the seventeenth century are all modern (cf. E. Schürer in Herzog-Hauck, *Realency-klopädie für protestantische Theologie und Kirche,* ix. 385). I have used an incunabulum in the Cornell University Library (Hain, *Repertorium Bibliographicum,* no. 9449). My remarks in *T.R.H.S.* 78 need correction in the light of the additional evidence given above.

no close verbal resemblance.[1] He would be a bold man who would decide whether Bede in these cases paraphrased the Cassiodorian translation or the Greek original.

Without doubt the most considerable portion of Bede's library was composed of theological works, especially those of an exegetical character. When referring in general terms, as he so frequently did, to the authority of the Fathers, he was thinking primarily of the four greatest, Ambrose, Jerome, Augustine, and Gregory I. It is therefore convenient to consider first his debt to them, rather than to follow a strictly chronological order. Of the four, Ambrose was the least well represented at Wearmouth-Jarrow and possibly in the other English libraries during Bede's lifetime. The *Hexaemeron* and the *Commentary on Luke* were certainly at Bede's elbow when he composed his own treatises on Genesis and the Third Gospel.[2] The treatise *De Noe et arca* was used in the *De temporum ratione*, a citation from the *De paradiso* occurs in Bede's exposition of Genesis, *De fide* is used in the commentary on Mark, and the *De Spiritu Sancto* is quoted more than once in his commentary on Acts. There is an allusion to the *De virginitate* in the *Epistle to Ecgberct* (5). To these Ambrosian works may probably be added the *De Abraham* and the *De poenitentia*. The explanation in the former treatise of the number 318 (T I H) corresponds to that in Bede.[3] In another place he quotes Ambrose's sentiment in the *De poenitentia* on the sinfulness of mankind: *omnes homines sub peccato nascimur quorum ipse ortus in vitio est.*[4] It cannot, however, be denied that this is the kind of epigrammatic utterance which Bede might have found cited in an intermediate source. One tract by Ambrose one can feel certain that he had not read, the *De Isaac vel anima*; for this, as Cassiodorus well knew (*Instit.* i. 6), contains an allegorical exposition of certain passages in the Song of Songs, which Bede would assuredly have studied eagerly, if he could, before composing his own lengthy commentary on that book of the Old Testament.

---

[1] e.g. *P.L.* xci. 46 A (*Antiq.* i. 6), 72 B and 76 B (*Antiq.* i. 3), 178 C–D (*Antiq.* i. 11), 427 C (*Antiq.* iii. 6), 775 D (*Antiq.* viii. 3).

[2] There is also a substantial quotation from the *Hexaemeron* (*C.S.E.L.* xxxii. 1, 92, 7–11) in *P.L.* xci. 1218 B.

[3] With *P.L.* xci. 149 B–C compare *C.E.S.L.* xxxii. 1, 513, 10–15; it should also be noted that Bede's explanation is not found in Jerome's *Quaestiones Hebraicae* which Bede used extensively elsewhere.

[4] *P.L.* xciii. 119 C; Ambr. *De poen.* (*P.L.* xvi. 470 c).

Bede's profound admiration for Gregory I is shown by his constant indebtedness to the pope's writings and by an eloquent appraisal of his life and work in the *Ecclesiastical History* (ii. 1). His library was stocked with all Gregory's genuine works except the *Letters*. There are innumerable quotations in Bede from the *Moralia*, the *Homilies* on Ezekiel and on the Gospels, and the *Regula pastoralis*; and the seventh book of Bede's commentary on the Song of Songs is nothing more than a *florilegium* from Gregory. The *Dialogues* are cited in the *De orthographia* and in the historical works. A few of the pope's letters, which had a direct bearing on the conversion of the English and were valuable contemporary documents, were treasured in England in Bede's time and inserted by him in the *Ecclesiastical History*. But, although Gregory had himself taken steps to have a collected edition of his voluminous correspondence made, this seems to have disappeared early. The largest of the existing collections was not assembled till Carolingian times and two smaller collections are only a little older.[1] Again, there is not the least doubt that the great majority of Jerome's writings were accessible to Bede. In the first place he includes in the list of his own works the following compilation: 'in Isaiam, Danihelem, duodecim prophetas, et partem Hieremiae, distinctiones capitulorum ex tractatu beati Hieronimi excerptas';[2] second, there is the evidence of actual citations from Jerome—and they are very numerous—in Bede's extant commentaries.[3] In fact, the only exegetical works that appear to be ignored by, or unknown to, Bede are the commentaries on Ephesians and on Philemon. Of other Hieronymic writings he was familiar with the treatises against Helvidius and against Jovinian, with the *Apology against Rufinus*, and possibly with the *Dialogus adversus Pelagianos*. He certainly knew of the existence of this late and scathing pamphlet from Jerome's pen, but there is nothing to show that he had seen or read it.[4] The treatise on Hebrew names and the

---

[1] The present state of the problem involved in the transmission of Gregory's *Registrum* is admirably summarized by O. Bardenhewer, *Geschichte der altkirchlichen Literatur*, v (1932), 288–90.   [2] *H.E.* v. 24.

[3] It is impossible here to list all the passages that the present writer has noted, but the commentaries of Jerome on the following books of the Old and New Testament are represented: Genesis (*Quaestiones Hebraicae*), Ecclesiastes, Isaiah, Ezekiel, Daniel, Amos, Jonah, Micah, Habakkuk, Zephaniah, Haggai, Zechariah, Malachi, Matthew, Galatians, and Titus; also the rare *commentarioli in Psalmos* first edited by Dom Morin (*Anecdota Maredsolana*, iii. 1).

[4] He calls it by its sub-title, *dialogus Attici et Critobuli* (*P.L.* xci. 1073 c).

De situ et nominibus were his main authority for Palestinian geography and the allegorical interpretation of proper names in the Scriptures. He alludes twice to the *Martyrology* but is aware of the doubts surrounding its authorship.[1] He also quotes from *Epistles* liii, lxxi, cvii, cviii, and cxii and from Jerome's translation of the *De Spiritu Sancto* by Didymus the Blind. Bede may, of course, have had other letters by Jerome; but the evidence of the earlier extant manuscripts of Jerome's correspondence, none of which contain more than a small part of the whole collection, makes it exceedingly improbable that more than a fraction of the letters had reached England by the eighth century.[2]

Next to Gregory the Great, Bede's deepest veneration was reserved for Augustine. A noteworthy instance of his attitude of mind is to be seen in Bede's discussion of the four beasts in Revelation iv. 6–9.[3] He reproduces Augustine's interpretation according to which the lion represents Matthew and the beast 'which had a face as a man' is Mark; and, though he knew Jerome's commentary on Matthew intimately, he suppresses all reference to its preface where Jerome discussed the passage in the Apocalypse. According to Jerome the lion is equivalent to Mark and the beast with human features to Matthew.[4] This was in fact the more usual interpretation and the one that ultimately prevailed. Bede's loyalty to Augustine in this instance aroused protests to which Bishop Acca drew his attention. Thereupon Bede defended himself against his critics by quoting at great length from Augustine, *De consensu evangelistarum*.[5]

Although Bede frequently mentions the African Father by name, he does not often specify the particular treatise of which he is thinking or from which he is borrowing at the time. In view of Augustine's enormous literary output it is at present impossible to speak with finality of Bede's debt to his great predecessor in exegesis; and consequently only a tentative list of Augustinian works at Wearmouth-Jarrow can be drawn up. Only when Bede's theological writings have been newly edited,

---

[1] See *T.R.H.S.* 89, note 4.

[2] Aldhelm appears to have known *Letters* xxii and lxiv, also the short *Lives of Hilarion, Malchus, and Paul.*

[3] *P.L.* xciii. 144 A, based on Aug. *Tract. in Ioann. Evang.* xxxvi (*P.L.* xxxv. 1666).   [4] *P.L.* xxvi. 19 B.

[5] *P.L.* xcii. 305–6, reproducing *C.S.E.L.* xliii. 4, ll. 4–5; 6, ll. 3–73; 9, ll. 3–10, 14.

and borrowed material in them traced to their source, will that important section in Bede's library be fully known. But even the provisional list here offered, which is based, as usual, on the quotations from Augustine that it has been possible to track down, is impressive in scope. In the earlier part of Bede's commentary on Genesis will be found nearly thirty passages transcribed from Augustine's *De Genesi ad litteram*. Some of these excerpts extend to more than a page in the Vienna edition of Augustine. The same book is also quoted more than once in the commentary on Acts. In addition, there are in the Genesis commentary of Bede citations from *De Genesi contra Manichaeos*, the treatise against Faustus, and the briefer tract, *Contra adversarium legis et prophetarum*.[1] Passages from the *Quaestiones in Heptateuchum* occur in several of Bede's commentaries. In his expositions of books of the New Testament he had recourse to the *Enarrationes in Psalmos*, *Quaestiones Evangeliorum*, the *Tractates* on the fourth Gospel and on the First Epistle of John, the *De consensu Evangelistarum*, and several sermons. The end of Book iii of the *De doctrina Christiana* is transcribed by Bede in a somewhat abbreviated form in the long introduction to his commentary on the Apocalypse. Furthermore, he knew the *Confessions*, and quotes or paraphrases passages from Books xv, xvi, and xx of the *De civitate Dei*. Of the shorter Augustinian works we find the *De sancta virginitate*, the *Enchiridion*, and the *De mendacio* represented in Bede's library,[2] and he quotes substantial passages from Epistles cxlvii, clxvii, and ccv. It should, however, be observed that each of these so-called letters is in reality a treatise on some doctrinal question. The first of the three was described by Augustine himself as *Liber de videndo Deo*.[3] The four oldest extant manuscripts of it contain no other Augustinian letters. Epistle clxvii, addressed to Jerome, discusses a passage in the General Epistle of James. The correspondence between the two great contemporaries, as early *codices* show, was regarded as a special work, distinct from their other letters, and may have been in England

---

[1] Through inadvertence Bede's reference to the *Contra adversarium legis et prophetarum* was wrongly interpreted by me (*T.R.H.S.* 88) as an allusion to the *Contra Faustum*. Bede knew both works and used the latter also in the *De temporum ratione*.

[2] I would take this opportunity of correcting a further error in *T.R.H.S.* 88. Bede's allusion in *P.L.* xci. 650 B is to *De mendacio*, xiv. 25 (*C.S.E.L.* xli. 444–5).   [3] *Retractationes*, ii. 41.

by the eighth century. *Epistle* ccv, written for Consentius, is a disquisition *de corpore Domini post resurrectionem*. The oldest manuscript containing it has only nine Augustinian letters in all. It is a ninth-century *codex*, now at Bologna, written in Anglo-Saxon script.[1] It is not, then, legitimate to assume from the presence of these three *Epistles* in Bede's library that he had access to the whole, or even the bulk, of Augustine's correspondence. Finally, the manner in which Bede refers to Augustine's *Retractations* rather suggests that he knew the book only by hearsay, although he adopted the title for his own revision of his Acts commentary.[2]

The list of theological works consulted by Bede, other than those written by the Four Doctors of the Church, is not specially long, but contains some unusual items.   Amongst the more widely known treatises were the tractate on the second Psalm by Hilary of Poitiers, Cyprian's *Liber Testimoniorum, De habitu virginum, De zelo et livore*, and perhaps *De lapsis* ; a commentary on Job attributed to Philippus ; Fulgentius' anti-Arian dissertation addressed to King Thrasamund and some other treatise or letter by the same author now no longer extant ;[3] and Cassiodorus' vast commentary on the Psalter. The authority of the pseudo-Clementine *Recognitiones* is invoked several times and Bede appears to have regarded them as the genuine work of Clement of Rome.[4] How intimate Bede's acquaintance with John Cassian may have been, it is difficult to determine. He never names him, but there is one unequivocal allusion to *Collatio* xvii.[5] Moreover, this author's writings, in spite of his semi-Pelagian taint, enjoyed a wide popularity in the middle ages ; and, in view of Benedict Biscop's connexions with the monasteries of southern France, they are likely to have been included amongst the books which he brought back from one or other of his continental journeys. Bede's familiarity with Benedict's Rule might have been tacitly assumed, but confirmatory evidence is not lacking ; for, besides several general

---

[1] For this *codex Bononiensis*, cf. A. Goldbacher in *C.S.E.L.* lviii. xxxv.

[2] *P.L.* xcii. 995 B.

[3] *P.L.* xciii. 54 A. Commenting on 1 Peter ii, 18, Bede remarks: *Fulgentius in opusculis suis sic ponit: servientes cum timore non tantum bonis et modestis sed etiam difficilioribus.*   I have failed to trace this citation in Fulgentius.

[4] See *P.L.* xci. 19 D–20 A ; xcii. 1011 C.   C. W. Jones included the *Recognitiones* among the sources of the *De temporum ratione*.

[5] *P.L.* xci. 961 C.   Aldhelm knew both the *Institutiones* and *Collationes* of Cassian.

allusions, he refers his readers specifically to chapter vii in that book.[1] The first book of Bede's commentary on the Song of Songs is an attempted refutation of the Pelagian Julian of Eclanum, in which he cites verbal extracts from that heresiarch's book *De amore*, and mentions another of his treatises, *De bono constantiae*. The contention of Bruckner, in his interesting study of this champion of Pelagianism, that the *De amore* was in reality the introductory part of Julian's commentary on the Song of Songs, carries conviction.[2] Another heretical work named by Bede in the same commentary is Pelagius' *Epistola ad Demetriadem de institutione virginis*. Neither Bede nor Aldhelm was aware of Pelagius' authorship. Aldhelm, not directly but by implication, attributed the letter to Jerome.[3] This view Bede expressly repudiates, and one is tempted to see in his use of the word *nostri* a covert allusion to the abbot of Malmesbury.[4] But he himself errs in attributing the epistle to Julian of Eclanum. In two places Bede quoted from Aponius' exposition of the Song of Songs, but as a whole this piece of exegesis does not seem to have found favour in his eyes; for his own allegorical interpretation diverges from that of the older commentator. Aponius' work was, however, a rarity. A century after Bede's time it was studied by Angelomus of Luxeuil.[5] It would be interesting to know whether the manuscript used by him was a copy of that existing in England in the eighth century.

What is probably the earliest of Bede's theological works presents some curious features to the student of his sources. The commentary on the Apocalypse probably contains far less of Bede's own ideas than do some of his later works. Moreover, in expounding the last book of the New Testament canon, which lent itself so particularly to allegorical interpretation, he had had many predecessors. Three of these were certainly by his side when he wrote his own treatise. Primasius is actually

---

[1] *P.L.* xci. 892 B, a passage that Plummer seems to have overlooked. The general allusions to the Rule will be found in *H.A.* i, vii, xi, xvi.

[2] A. Bruckner, *Julian von Eclanum*, 9, note 5, and 72, note 5. Bede's quotations from Julian have been collected by Bruckner on pp. 74–5.

[3] Cf. *MGH.*, *Auct. Ant.* xv. 303, 15, with Ehwald's note 3.

[4] *P.L.* xci. 1073 C.

[5] On the use of Aponius by Bede and Angelomus see J. Witte, *Der Kommentar des Aponius zum Hohenliede* (Dissert. Erlangen, 1903). The two citations in Bede occur in *P.L.* xci. 1112 A (= Aponius, ed. Bottino and Martini, 80) and 1162 C–D (= *ibid.* 155).

named but once; yet a very large number of Bede's comments are copied word for word from him. Tyconius, on the other hand, is mentioned no less than ten times by name, so that one is inclined to suppose that Bede acknowledged every one of his borrowings from that commentary, which unfortunately is no longer extant, because Tyconius was more than a little tinged with heresy. In the third place, Bede appears to have procured the short commentary of Victorinus of Pettau as rehandled and enlarged by Jerome. This book was also used by Primasius, and there are some eight excerpts which Bede took not directly from Victorinus but from Primasius. Two examples will illustrate this:

Victorinus	*Primasius and Bede*
(*C.S.E.L.* xlix. 8–10)	(*P.L.* lxviii. 801 B, and *P.L.* xciii. 136 B)
Et in capillis albis albatorum est multitudo lanae similis propter oves, similis nivi propter innumerabilem turbam candidatorum de caelo datorum.	. . . propter oves ad dexteram futuras, instar lanae, et propter dealbatorum innumerabilem turbam et electorum a coelo datorum, instar nivis effulgent.
(*Ibid.* 19, 13–15)	(*P.L.* lxviii. 798 D and *P.L.* xciii. 135 A)
Qui primo in suscepto homine venit occultus, post paululum in maiestate et gloria veniet ad iudicandum manifestus.	Qui iudicandus primo venit occultus, tunc iudicaturus veniet manifestus.

But there are two passages where Bede follows Victorinus and Primasius does not. The similarities of the following comments on Apocalypse 15, 1 are too close to be accidental:

Victorinus	*Bede*
(*C.S.E.L.* xlix. 137, 6–8)	(*P.L.* xciii. 177 c)
Semper enim ira Dei percutit populum contumacem septem plagis—id est perfecte ut in Levitico dicit—quae in ultimo futurae sunt, cum ecclesia de medio exierit.	Quia semper ira Dei populum percutit contumacem septem plagis, id est perfectis, sicut frequenter in Levitico: 'et percutiam', inquit, 'vos septem plagis'. Quae novissimae futurae sunt, cum ecclesia de medio eius exierit.

The second passage is one where Bede deals rather fully with the number 666.[1] He begins with the word, *Teitan*, whose letters with their numerical values in the Greek alphabet add up to the mystic number. He then passes on to Primasius' similar

[1] See p. 178 above.

calculation of the word, *Antemos*, and it is on this occasion that he refers to Primasius by name. Now the calculation of *Antemos* was taken over by Primasius from Victorinus-Jerome, but *Teitan* and its numerical computation are found only in the two later redactions of the Victorinus-Jerome commentary, to which the most recent editor, Haussleiter, has assigned the symbols Φ and S.[1] Incidentally Bede's comment on the passage shows that his library contained one or other of these versions and not the pure Victorinus-Jerome text.

Two relatively little known commentators of the fifth century who figure among Bede's authorities are Arnobius the Younger and Salonius. There is a direct citation from Arnobius' brief exposition of the Psalms in the *De temporum ratione*.[2] Dom Morin, who does not refer to this passage, has, however, pointed out an allusion to Arnobius in Bede's *explanatio* to Psalm lxxxiii, prefixed to a later commentary which he attributes to Manegold of Lauterbach.[3] A third piece of evidence is provided by a glossary that is made up chiefly of citations from Cassiodorus' commentary on the Psalms, but also contains two extracts from Arnobius. Though not by Bede himself, the glossary was in all likelihood compiled from Bede's works and not from the earlier writers; for the combination of authors used in the glossary would be hard to explain on any other hypothesis, seeing how rare two out of the three were in the Middle Ages. The gloss on *sela* is, in fact, taken from Jerome's *Commentarioli in Psalmos*, a treatise from which Bede reproduces four or five excerpts in his commentary on Acts.[4]

Salonius, bishop of Geneva and son of Eucherius of Lyons, was a prelate highly esteemed by his contemporaries. To him Salvian dedicated his treatise, *On the governance of God*. But his importance as an author seems to have been slight. The only certain work from his hand now extant is an allegorical interpretation, of no great length and cast in dialogue form, of Proverbs and Ecclesiastes. Its success or influence seems to have been negligible, so that it is all the more remarkable that

---

[1] See Haussleiter's Introduction in *C.S.E.L.* xlix.

[2] *P.L.* xc. 525 C–526 A; *P.L.* liii. 481 A–B.

[3] G. Morin, *Anecdota Maredsolana*, 2e sér. i (1913), 73 and 349.

[4] For the glossary see my note in *Speculum*, v (1930), 217–21. The gloss, *sela*, is copied exactly from Jerome's *Commentarioli* (*Anecdota Maredsolana*, iii. 1, 11, 10–18). This reference replaces those given in my article for that gloss.

the book found its way into Bede's hands.[1] Bede ignored the dialogue form, but, for the rest, constantly borrowed from it throughout his own fuller commentary on Proverbs, yet without mentioning his source by name. Although he often recasts Salonius' sentences and adds material of his own, his dependence on him is not open to question. Bede's method may be illustrated by examples taken from the opening, middle, and end of his commentary:

Salonius	*Bede*
(*P.L.* liii. 970 A)	(*P.L.* xci. 942 D)
Per caput designantur principes Iudaeorum. In capite turbarum clamitabat, quia principibus Iudaeorum, homicidium quod in eum patraverant, palam per apostolos ad memoriam reducebat et eosdem ad poenitentiae remedium vocabat.	In capite turbarum clamitabat, quia etiam principibus qui sibi ei praevaluisse, ut crucifigeretur, videbantur, reatum homicidii, quod perpetrarant, palam reducebat ad memoriam eosque ad poenitentia remedium vocabat.

975 D–976 A	972 D–973 A
Quomodo circulum aureum si infixeris in naribus suis, id est, in naribus porci, ille dum pergit terram vertere ac fodere naso, immergit circulum aureum in volutabrum luti, et tunc perdit circulus aureus decorem quem habuit. Similiter mulier fatua, si habet pulchritudinem vultus, vel si accipiat ornamenta inaurium, monilium, simul et vestimentorum, sordidat pulchritudinem suam et amittit decorem, si se coeno libidinis coinquinare diligit et adulteriis corrumpit.	Circulum aureum si in naribus suis infixeris, nihilominus illa terram vertere naso, et volutabro luti properat immergi; ita mulier fatua, si pulchritudinem vultus vel habitus acceperit, suam tamen faciem ad infima declinare, suam speciositatem ad evertendos ubique castitatis flosculos circumferre, seque coeno voluptatis inquinare diligit.

992 A–B	1039 C–1040 A
Istae filiae quas divitias congregaverunt? Orationes, ieiunia, eleemosynas, afflictionem et castimoniam carnis, linguae refrenationem, meditationem Scripturarum, et ceterorum bonorum	Quae congregaverunt divitias, videlicet bonorum operum operationes, ieiunia, eleemosynas, afflictionem et castimoniam carnis, continentiam linguae, meditationem Scripturarum, et cetera

[1] J. A. Endres, *Honorius von Augustodunum,* 74, has shown that Honorius' commentary on Proverbs is merely an abbreviated version of Salonius. He would attribute to Salonius also two nameless commentaries on John and Matthew which are found in the same manuscript and are written in dialogue form.

operum divitias: quae verae divitiae sunt, si spirituali fiant intentione, videlicet propter regni coelestis retributionem: aliter nihil prosunt agentibus. Unde filiae, videlicet haereticorum aut malorum catholicorum turbae, frustra congregaverunt sibi divitias; quia vel in fide erraverunt, vel certe huiusmodi bona opera non spirituali fecerunt intentione, de quibus in evangelio Dominus:

huiusmodi. Quae verae sunt divitiae spiritus, ubi pura mentis sinceritate geruntur; ubi autem sine fide quae per dilectionem operatur fiunt, nihil agentibus prosunt. Sed et illae filiae frustra congregaverunt divitias, de quibus Dominus ait:

Here both commentators quote Matthew vii. 22–3.

Sancta vero ecclesia catholica supergressa est: hoc est, transcendit omnes illas, quia quidquid agit, in fide tantum recta et spirituali operatur intentione.

Sed omnis istiusmodi filias ecclesia catholica supergreditur, quae fide casta, et opere perfecta Redemptoris sui vestigia sectatur.

It is in the highest degree probable that some at least of Isidore's theological works were in Bede's collection. But it is a curious fact, noted by more than one critic but still unexplained, that Bede, whose sense of literary property was in general so unusually high, especially during an age when plagiarism ordinarily was not felt to be improper, treats Isidore with more freedom or less respect than his other authorities. He names him only three times in all, in each case only to controvert him.[1] Yet the *Etymologies* was the handy encyclopedia to which he regularly turned for enlightenment on miscellaneous topics. As often as not, when he does derive his information from that source, he reproduces it, wholly or in part, in his own words. If, as has already been shown, he occasionally treats Josephus in the same way, that is less surprising; for Josephus, though highly valued, had not been a leading figure in the Catholic Church. Bede's usual, though not invariable, practice of citing verbally from his theological forerunners makes the tracking down of his sources feasible, if laborious. Again, indebtedness to Isidore's *Etymologies*, even if the information is given in Bede's own words, is, owing to the nature of that work, not as a rule difficult to establish. But with Isidore's theological writings the case is different; for, whereas many of the sources

[1] The three passages are *P.L.* xcii. 997 c and 1031 c; *De temporum ratione*, xxxv. In the first of these Bede's criticism is not confined to Isidore.

used in the compilation of the *Etymologies* were not accessible
in Bede's time, the authorities consulted by Isidore when he
composed his exegetical or homiletic works were all or mostly
in Bede's library also. Mere similarity in thought between Bede
and Isidore is therefore not enough to prove borrowing of the
one from the other, seeing that many of Bede's ideas will have
been formed or influenced by direct study of the same Fathers
whom Isidore followed. While, then, one may agree with Karl
Werner that Bede was acquainted with the bishop of Seville's
Quaestiones in Vetus Testamentum—and, it might be added,
probably with other theological works by the same author—
the general similarities between the two writers on which the
German scholar laid so much stress really do not prove his case.[1]

Bede's Greek sources were not numerous and can be disposed
of more briefly. In addition to the *Vulgate* and one or more
versions of the *Vetus Latina* he had at his disposal a Greek text
of Acts. This manuscript still survives, for the identity of *codex
Laudianus Graecus* 35 in the Bodleian Library, which contains
the Greek and Latin text of Acts side by side with the copy
collated by Bede for his earlier commentary, and especially for
the *Retractations*, is now generally accepted.[2] The chief argument for the identification of the manuscripts is the large
number of biblical readings—over seventy—in which the two
concur. Even this considerable number may prove to be an
under-estimate. Statistics made from the printed text of Bede
are unreliable because it is based on the authority of late manuscripts and early printed editions. But in some of the earlier
codices of Bede's commentary on Acts are found additional cases
where the citations from Acts coincide with *E*.[3] If Bede's use of
a Greek copy of Acts is beyond dispute, the question whether
there were in Wearmouth-Jarrow other parts of the New Testament in Greek, and, further, a copy of the Septuagint, is more
problematic. In his other commentaries on the New Testament
Bede, in strong contrast to his practice in the commentary on

---

[1] K. Werner, *op. cit.*, 167 ff.

[2] Cf. Plummer, i, p. liv, and particularly the article by E. A. Lowe in *Speculum*,
iii (1928), 1–15, with the references there given. The manuscript in question
is known to biblical scholars as *E*.

[3] Two examples may be given: in Acts. ii, 13 MS. Bibl. Nat. lat. 12283
(saec. IX) and 12284, which was probably copied from it a little later in the same
century, read with *E*, *quia musto repleti sunt*. In Acts xix, 29 *M(urbacensis)*,
now Geneva, MS. lat. 21 (saec. VIII ex.) and *Sangallensis*, 259 (saec. VIII–IX),
called *A* in my forthcoming edition, read with *E*, *unanimo*, for *uno animo*.

Acts and the *Retractations*, rarely touches on questions of textual criticism. The occasions on which he refers to, or quotes, the original are few, yet in most of these passages he does not appear to be relying on his authorities.[1] As for the Septuagint, the balance of probability that he at times used it directly is even stronger. He pays far more attention to textual variations in his commentary on Genesis than in any of his other works on the Old Testament. Many of the citations from LXX, like all those from the Hebrew original, were taken over from Jerome or occasionally from Augustine.[2] But the residue of passages where Bede appears to owe nothing to his predecessors is appreciable; and, as some of them at least contain a phrase or even a sentence, not only a single word, from LXX, the mere use of a biblical glossary is ruled out.

Of the Greek theologians, Origen is criticized several times as a heretical writer, or else a biographical detail about him is given. Bede appears to have used his second homily on Genesis, probably in Rufinus' Latin version.[3] Basil's *Hexaemeron* in Eustathius' translation is mentioned in a general way and also quoted verbally or paraphrased on several occasions. There are several references to John Chrysostom, whom Bede usually calls John of Constantinople, and his tract on the topic, *quod nemo laeditur nisi a se ipso*, is recommended for study. Bede also consulted Chrysostom's homily on the Nativity when he wrote the first chapter of his commentary on Luke. Some of the Greek Father's works reached the West early in Latin dress, and it is in this form rather than in the original text that we may suppose them to have come into Bede's hands.[4] Of eight allusions to Clement of Alexandria in Bede one is a biographical item; five others are derived from Rufinus, so that the remaining two may also be assumed to have been taken by Bede from an inter-

---

[1] e.g. *P.L.* xcii. 322 B, 369 A; *P.L.* xciii. 33 C, 40 D, 47 A, 100 A–B. *P.L.* xcii. 213 D, on the other hand, is repeated verbally from Jerome, *in Matth.* (*P.L.* xxvi. 119 B).

[2] e.g. *P.L.* xci. 79 C from Aug., *Quaest. in Heptat.* (*C.S.E.L.* xxviii. ii, 4, 25–7); 116 D–117 A from Jerome, *Quaest. Hebr.* (*P.L.* xxiii. 952 A–952 B–953 A) and *Comm. in Ezech.* (*P.L.* xxv. 259 D); 161 B and 163 D from Jerome, *Quaest. Hebr.* (*P.L.* xxiii. 963 B and 964 B).

[3] *P.L.* xci. 91 A–C; cf. *P.G.* xxx. 887 B–C. On the other hand, the reference to Origen's views in the next column (*P.L.* xci. 92 A–B) was reproduced by Bede from Aug. *Quaest. in Heptat.* (*C.S.E.L.* xxviii. ii, 5, 25–6, 4).

[4] On the Latin versions of Chrysostom cf. P. Bauer in *Revue d'histoire ecclésiastique*, viii (1907), 249–65.

mediate source.[1] Besides two allusions of a general nature to Athanasius, Bede quotes or paraphrases him when discussing I Peter iii. 18.[2] Rufinus' translation of sundry orations by Gregory of Nazianzus completes the list of Greek theologians. Bede transcribed a whole paragraph from the oration on Pentecost without acknowledgement in his commentary on Acts. Years later, in the *Retractations*, he informed his readers of the source from which he had taken over his views on the miracle of tongues, thereby hoping to silence the adverse criticisms called forth by that interpretation.[3]

The *De transitu Beatae Virginis*, wrongly attributed, as Bede himself was aware, to Melito of Sardes, and Latin translations of the *Shepherd* of Hermas, of Athanasius' Life of St. Antony, and of Lucian of Caphar Gamala are also found among Bede's sources, and prove, if proof were necessary, the width or catholicity of his reading.[4] We know from Bede himself that the Acts of the Lateran Council held in 649 under Pope Martin I were brought to England by John the Arch-chanter, and that they were copied by order of Benedict Biscop. Moreover, reference to that Council was made at the Synod of Hatfield in 680. Definite proof that Bede had familiarized himself with this document is not wanting, but the fact has hitherto been overlooked.[5] In commenting on Mark vi. 49—the miracle of Christ walking on the sea—Bede reproduced the heretical opinions of the Monothelite bishop Theodore of Pharan in Arabia and a sentence from the treatise on the Divine names by the pseudo-Dionysius. The entire passage is copied almost word for word from the Latin version of the Acts of the Lateran Council.[6]

[1] Cf. *T.R.H.S.* 91. To the references there given may be added *P.L.* xciii. 138 D–139 A on the heretic Nicolaus, a passage based on Rufinus (ed. Mommsen), 261, 6 ff.

[2] *P.L.* xciii. 58 B–C. Cf. also *T.R.H.S.* 91. I have been unable to trace the passage in Athanasius or in Vigilius of Thapsus.

[3] *P.L.* xcii. 947 B–D = *C.S.E.L.* xlvi. 160, 17–161, 11; *P.L.* xcii. 999 D.

[4] Cf. for further particulars *T.R.H.S.* 83 and 85.

[5] Cf. *H.E.* iv. 17 and 18, with Plummer's notes *ad loc.*

[6] *P.L.* xcii. 197 B = Mansi, *Concilia*, x. 967 A–B. Plummer, as is evident from his note on *H.E.* iv. 18 (ii. 234), was unaware that Bede had transcribed this passage. Hence he included Theodore and the pseudo-Dionysius in his list of authors (i, pp. li–lii). The other reference to the pseudo-Dionysius is *P.L.* xcii. 981 A. The biographical part in this passage might be derived from either Jerome or Rufinus. But the statement that Dionysius *ingenii sui volumina reliquit* can hardly mean the pastoral letters of Dionysius of Corinth listed by Rufinus. Thus Bede like every one else in his day seems to have accepted the identity of Dionysius with the author of the so-called pseudo-Dionysian

No one will deny that the catalogue of books demonstrably known to Bede is impressive in length and for his age unique. Yet there are some surprising omissions, so that one wonders with what other writings he may have been familiar, although their influence or use cannot be proved from his surviving commentaries. There are, however, certain general considerations that have an important bearing on this question. The bulk of Bede's works were exegetical or homiletic; but very much of the earlier Latin literature of the Church was apologetic or directed against contemporary heresies. Bede, whose strict orthodoxy is obvious wherever he discusses any matter of doctrine or ecclesiastical use, was, it is true, familiar with the general tenets of many heretical sects. But in the main his knowledge of them is derived from the ecclesiastical histories or one of the four doctors.[1] Was he acquainted with the numerous polemical tracts of Augustine, other than certain anti-Manichaean treatises which, as we saw, were used in the commentary on Genesis? There is no cogent reason for supposing that the anti-Donatist writings of the African Father were known in England in Bede's day; for the Donatist controversy had been localized in a way that Arianism or Pelagianism were not, and it had exerted no obvious influence on western European thought. Bede alludes several times to the sect or to its founder as men who destroyed the unity of the Christian Church; once he makes a passing allusion to their heterodox views on the doctrine of Grace. Again, the teaching of Arius, although it had called forth an immense literature in the fourth century and even later, was hardly a living issue in England in the eighth. And, while Bede makes many allusions to the madness of Arius—*vesania Arrii*—they are, when not repeated verbally from one of his usual sources, not of the kind to make it probable that he had made a real study of the earlier literature on the subject.[2] Pelagian-

works. But there is nothing to show that he had ever seen any of them; and indeed all the available evidence points to the fact that they did not reach the West till Carolingian times.

[1] e.g. *P.L.* xcii. 144 C–D, with allusions to Photinus, Arius, and the Manichaeans, is from Ambrose, *in Luc.* (*C.S.E.L.* xxxii, iv, 181, 1–10); 275 C–D, on Valentinus, Marcion, and the Manichaeans, from Ambrose, *De fide* (*P.L.* xvi. 591 A–B). Cf. also the next note.

[2] e.g. *P.L.* xcii. 944 C, a reference to Arius' ghastly end, comes from Rufinus, x. 14. *P.L.* xcii. 251 A and 950 B, with allusions to the Arian doctrine, are copied respectively from Jerome, *in Matth.* (*P.L.* xxvi. 157 C) and *Comment. in psalmos* (ed. Morin), 80, 10–16.

ism, on the other hand, was a different matter. Its founder came
from the British Isles. It was essentially a Western heresy which
had left its mark on both Gaul and Britain, and a century after
Bede's death was again to become a vital question on the continent of western Europe. Although it has not been possible to
identify any extracts in Bede's works as excerpts from Augustine's anti-Pelagian pamphlets, it is by no means improbable
that he had read some of them.

Some authors, noted in their own time, made little or no
impression on later generations. The elder Arnobius is a case
in point. His book, *Adversus nationes*, was forgotten soon after
his death and now survives in only a single manuscript. Tertullian's eclipse, at least after Augustine's time, was to a great
extent due to the unorthodoxy of his later teaching. It is evident
from the manuscript tradition of his writings that he was little
known in the early Middle Ages. A single ninth-century *codex*
contains only a portion of his works; for the rest, his modern
editors depend on two manuscripts of the eleventh and several
of the fifteenth century. Bede nowhere mentions him by name,
and evidence is lacking that he had read any Tertullianic
treatise.[1] More remarkable is the omission of Lactantius from
the authors named by Bede. In Alcuin's day there was a *codex*
of this writer at York; which of his works it contained is unfortunately not known. Nor is there anything to show that
this, or some other manuscript from which Alcuin's was copied,
had reached England in Bede's time or before. But amongst the
many extant *codices* of the *Divinae Institutiones* are two of very
early date (saec. vi–vii) and two of the ninth century. A
sentence from the shorter tract, *De opificio*, is quoted by Aldhelm, who names Lactantius as the author. It can hardly be
a pure coincidence that nearly all the theological works shown
by Ehwald in his monumental edition to have been consulted
by Aldhelm were also to be found in Bede's working library.
Hence, even without corroborative evidence from his works,
one is inclined to assume that Bede was acquainted with the
De opificio, if not with Lactantius' longest work.

Books by authors of the fifth century which may have been

---

[1] Plummer (i. 13) derives the opening sentence in *H.E.* i. 2 from Tertullian,
Adv. Iudaeos. But are the italicized words, *Brittania Romanis inaccessa*,
sufficient to warrant the attribution? In the opinion of the present writer
they are emphatically not.

in the library of Wearmouth-Jarrow, or in some other collection accessible to Bede, are the *Instructiones* by Eucherius and the *Commonitorium* of Vincent of Lérins. The latter seems to have left no trace in Bede's works nor is its author ever mentioned by him. Yet, in view of its fame and of Benedict Biscop's sojourn at Lérins, one would expect that keen lover of books to have brought back a copy to his native land. If the evidence for Bede's acquaintance with Eucherius is slight, it is perhaps sufficient to warrant the inclusion of the bishop of Lyons's name here.[1]

It remains to name an author of the sixth century whose last work is justly ranked amongst the masterpieces of the world's literature. The name of Boethius occurs neither in Aldhelm nor in Bede; nor does the internal evidence of their writings lend any support to the belief that either the *Consolation of Philosophy* or any of Boethius' other works had reached England in their day. The study and elucidation of Boethius became very active in the Carolingian age; and as early as the end of the eighth century some of his treatises were in York. Alcuin's list of books includes the names of Boethius and Aristotle. The former may refer to the *Consolatio* or the theological tractates, or both, while Aristotle is equivalent to Boethius' Latin version of the *De interpretatione* and *Categories*. But even though Bede may never have set eyes on the *Consolatio*, his life and works exemplify to the full the closing words uttered by the 'last of the Romans':[2]

Neither do we in vain put our hope in God or pray to him; for if we do this well and as we ought, we shall not lose our labour or be without effect. Wherefore fly vices, embrace virtues, possess your minds with worthy hopes, offer up humble prayers to your highest Prince. There is, if you will not dissemble, a great necessity of doing well imposed upon you, since you live in the sight of your Judge, who beholdeth all things.

M. L .W. Laistner.

---

[1] C. W. Jones includes the *Instructiones* among the possible sources of the *De temporum ratione*. Bede's language in the commentary on Genesis (*P.L.* xci. 56 B) is reminiscent of *Instr.* i. 13 (*C.S.E.L.* xxxi. 70, 20–2). The explanations of *Hebraica* in *P.L.* xci. 52 A and 72 B, though they might be from Eucherius, probably come direct from Jerome.

[2] These concluding words of the *Consolatio* are quoted in the translation of I.T., revised by Stewart and Rand (*Loeb Classical Library*).

CATALOGUE OF AUTHORS AND WORKS IN BEDE'S LIBRARY[1]

(A mark of interrogation against an author or work signifies that the evidence for inclusion in this list is not conclusive.)

Agroecius
Alcimus Avitus?
Ambrosius: De Abraham?
   De fide
   De Noe et arca
   De paradiso
   De poenitentia?
   De Spiritu Sancto
   De virginitate
   Expositio evang. sec. Lucam
   Hexaemeron
   Hymni
Aponius
Arator
Arnobius junior: Commentarii in psalmos
Athanasius: Vita S. Antonii ab Evagrio traducta
   Opus incertum
Audax
Augustinus: Confessiones
   Contra adversarium legis et prophetarum
   Contra Faustum
   De civitate Dei
   De consensu evangelistarum
   De doctrina Christiana
   De Genesi ad litteram
   De Genesi contra Manichaeos
   De mendacio
   De sancta virginitate
   Enarrationes in psalmos
   Enchiridion
   Epistolae cxlvii, clxvii, ccv
   Quaestiones in evangelia
   Quaestiones in Heptateuchum
   Sermones aliqui
   Tractatus in Ioann. epist. I
   Tractatus in Ioann. evang.
Basilius: Hexaemeron ab Eustathio traductum

---

[1] The term 'Bede's Library' is used for the sake of convenience. It does not imply that all the works here listed were necessarily in the library of Wearmouth and Jarrow.

Biblia: Versio Graeca actuum apostolorum
        Versio Graeca Novi Testamenti?
        Versio Graeca Veteris Testamenti quae LXX vocatur?
        Versio Hieronymiana
        Versio vetus Latina
Caper
Cassianus: Collationes
Cassiodorus: Commenta psalterii
            Historia tripartita
Charisius
Chrysostomus: Homilia in Nativitatem
              Quod nemo laeditur nisi a se ipso
Constantius: Vita S. Germani
Cyprianus: De habitu virginum
           De lapsis?
           De zelo et livore
           Liber testimoniorum
Cyprianus Gallus
Didymus: De spiritu Sancto liber ab Hieronymo translatus
Diomedes
Dionysius Exiguus
Donatus
Dositheus?
Dracontius?
Eucherius: Instructiones?
Eusebius: *vide* Hieronymum *et* Rufinum
Eutropius: Breviarium
Fortunatus
Fulgentius: Ad Thrasamundum libri III
            Opus incertum
Gennadius: De viris illustribus
Gildas
Gregorius I: Dialogi
             Epistolae nonnullae ad conversionem Anglorum per-
             tinentes.
             Homiliae in Ezech. et in Evang.
             Moralia
             Regula pastoralis
Gregorius Nazianzenus: Oratio in Pentecosten a Rufino translata
Gregorius Turonensis: Historia Francorum
Hegesippus: *vide* Iosephum
Hermas: Libri Pastoris versio Latina
Hieronymus: Adversus Helvidium
            Adversus Iovinianum

Hieronymus: Apologia adversus libros Rufini
Commentarii in Ecclesiasten et in omnes prophetas
Commentarii in Matth. Evang., in epist. ad Gal. et in
epist. ad Titum
Commentarioli in psalmos
De nominibus Hebraicis
De situ et nominibus
De viris illustribus
Dialogi contra Pelagianos?
Epistulae liii, lxxi, cvii, cviii, cxii
Eusebii Caesariensis Chronicon
Quaestiones Hebraicae
Hilarius Pictaviensis: Tractatus in psalmum secundum
Iosephus: Antiquitatum versio Latina
Traductio belli Iudaici ab Hegesippo confecta
Versio Graeca?
Isidorus: Chronicon
De natura rerum
Etymologiae
Quaestiones in Vetus Testamentum?
Iulianus Eclanensis: Comment. in Canticum Canticorum
De bono constantiae
Iuvencus
Lactantius: De opificio?
Divinae Institutiones?
Lateranense Concilium: Acta
Liber Pontificalis
Lucianus e Caphar Gamala
Macrobius: Saturnalia
Mallius Theodorus
Marcellinus Comes
Marius Aventicus
Origenes: Homilia secunda in Genesim a Rufino translata
Orosius
Pascha: Opuscula quattuor quae *Irish Forgeries* vocantur
Paulinus: Vita S. Ambrosii
Paulinus Nolae episcopus
Pelagius: Epistola ad Demetriadem
Petrus Petricoriensis?
Philippus: Commentarius in Iob
Plinius: Historiae naturalis libri ii, iv, v, vi, xii, xiii, xvi, xxxvii
Polemius Silvius
Pompeius
Possidius: Vita S. Augustini

Primasius: Expositio Apocalypseos
Prosper: Chronicon
         Epigrammata
Prudentius
Pseudo-Clemens: Recognitiones
Pseudo-Eucherius: De situ Iudaeae
Pseudo-Melito: De transitu beatae Virginis
Rufinus: Historia ecclesiastica Eusebii a Rufino translata
         Vide etiam Gregorium Nazianzenum *et* Originem
Salonius
Sedulius
Servius
Solinus
Theophilus: Epistolae ad Theodosianum I versio Latina
Tyconius: Expositio Apocalypseos
Vegetius
Victor Capuae episcopus
Victorinus grammaticus
Victorinus Poetovii episcopus
Victorius Aquitanus
Vincentius Lerinensis?
Virgilius

INDEX